PRAISE FOR *ELOQUENT JAVASCRIPT, 3RD EDITION*

"*Eloquent JavaScript, 3rd Edition* is a worthy and much-needed update to the popular programming book. The fact that the book covers ES6 is worth a re-read, but the new edition goes above and beyond with new illustrations, a new exercise, and tighter writing. The third edition of the book is substantially improved from its predecessors and worthy of the hype."

—BOOKS ON CODE

"It's a smart, lean JavaScript tutorial that exists as an in-print book from No Starch Press, and a free, nicely formatted web version . . . easily the most enjoyable read in this list. And there are so many useful insights that you won't be bored."

—MATTHEW MACDONALD, MEDIUM'S YOUNG CODER

"This is all the JavaScript knowledge you'll need to hit the ground running in a JavaScript project . . . it's a book I will be frequently revisiting as it has put JavaScript back on my radar."

—GEEKTECHSTUFF

"This book would make a great addition to any developer's reference books . . . I really like the author's style of writing and clarity of explanations. The sample code and exercises also work, which can be a rare feature in tech-related books."

—GARY WOODFINE, SOFTWARE DEVELOPER

"If you're at all interested in learning JavaScript, making this your first guide could mean the difference between getting discouraged and giving up and really getting into programming as a lifelong venture."

—JOSHUA JOHNSON, DESIGN SHACK

"Marijn Haverbeke is a software philosopher and all-round genius. He also has a terrific sense of humor and writes both prose and code in a friendly and unintimidating fashion. In common with the very best teachers he dispenses his wisdom with disarming simplicity. I became a better architect, author, mentor and developer because of this book. It deserves to share shelf space with Flanagan and Crockford."

—ANGUS CROLL, JAVASCRIPT WE BLOG

ELOQUENT JAVASCRIPT

3rd Edition

A Modern Introduction to Programming

by Marijn Haverbeke

no starch press

San Francisco

ELOQUENT JAVASCRIPT, 3RD EDITION. Copyright © 2019 by Marijn Haverbeke.

Printed in USA
Ninth printing

26 25 24 23 22   9 10 11 12 13

ISBN-10: 1-59327-950-7
ISBN-13: 978-1-59327-950-9

Publisher: William Pollock
Production Editor: Riley Hoffman
Cover Illustration: Madalina Tantareanu
Interior Design: Octopod Studios
Developmental Editor: Corbin Collins
Technical Reviewer: Angus Croll
Copyeditor: Kim Wimpsett
Compositor: Riley Hoffman
Proofreader: James M. Fraleigh

Chapter illustrations by Madalina Tantareanu. Pixel art in Chapters 7 and 16 by Antonio Perdomo Pastor. Regular expression diagrams in Chapter 9 generated with Regexper by Jeff Avallone (*http://regexper.com/*). Village photograph in Chapter 11 by Fabrice Creuzot. Game concept for Chapter 15 by Thomas Palef (*http://lessmilk.com/*).

For information on distribution, translations, or bulk sales, please contact No Starch Press, Inc. directly:

No Starch Press, Inc.
245 8th Street, San Francisco, CA 94103
phone: 1.415.863.9900; info@nostarch.com
www.nostarch.com

The Library of Congress has catalogued the first edition as follows:

```
Haverbeke, Marijn.
 Eloquent JavaScript: a modern introduction to programming / by Marijn Haverbeke.
     p. cm.
 Includes index.
 ISBN-13: 978-1-59327-282-1
 ISBN-10: 1-59327-282-0
 1.  JavaScript (Computer program language)  I. Title.
 QA76.73.J39H38 2009
 005.13'3--dc22
                                        2010032246
```

BRIEF CONTENTS

CONTENTS IN DETAIL

PART I: LANGUAGE

1
VALUES, TYPES, AND OPERATORS   11

2
PROGRAM STRUCTURE   23

3
FUNCTIONS
41

4
DATA STRUCTURES: OBJECTS AND ARRAYS
59

5
HIGHER-ORDER FUNCTIONS
83

6
THE SECRET LIFE OF OBJECTS
97

7
PROJECT: A ROBOT   117

8
BUGS AND ERRORS   129

9
REGULAR EXPRESSIONS   145

10
MODULES

11
ASYNCHRONOUS PROGRAMMING

12
PROJECT: A PROGRAMMING LANGUAGE 203

PART II: BROWSER

13
JAVASCRIPT AND THE BROWSER 219

14
THE DOCUMENT OBJECT MODEL

227

15
HANDLING EVENTS

247

19
PROJECT: A PIXEL ART EDITOR   333

PART III: NODE

20
NODE.JS   353

21
PROJECT: SKILL-SHARING WEBSITE 371

22
JAVASCRIPT AND PERFORMANCE 391

EXERCISE HINTS 407

For Lotte and Jan

"We think we are creating the system for our own purposes. We believe we are making it in our own image . . . But the computer is not really like us. It is a projection of a very slim part of ourselves: that portion devoted to logic, order, rule, and clarity."

—Ellen Ullman, *Close to the Machine: Technophilia and its Discontents*

INTRODUCTION

This is a book about instructing computers. Computers are about as common as screwdrivers today, but they are quite a bit more complex, and making them do what you want them to do isn't always easy.

If the task you have for your computer is a common, well-understood one, such as showing you your email or acting like a calculator, you can open the appropriate application and get to work. But for unique or open-ended tasks, there probably is no application.

That is where programming may come in. *Programming* is the act of constructing a *program*—a set of precise instructions telling a computer what to do. Because computers are dumb, pedantic beasts, programming is fundamentally tedious and frustrating.

Fortunately, if you can get over that fact, and maybe even enjoy the rigor of thinking in terms that dumb machines can deal with, programming can be rewarding. It allows you to do things in seconds that would take *forever* by hand. It is a way to make your computer tool do things that it couldn't do before. And it provides a wonderful exercise in abstract thinking.

Most programming is done with programming languages. A *programming language* is an artificially constructed language used to instruct computers. It is interesting that the most effective way we've found to communicate with a computer borrows so heavily from the way we communicate with each other.

Like human languages, computer languages allow words and phrases to be combined in new ways, making it possible to express ever new concepts.

At one point language-based interfaces, such as the BASIC and DOS prompts of the 1980s and 1990s, were the main method of interacting with computers. They have largely been replaced with visual interfaces, which are easier to learn but offer less freedom. Computer languages are still there, if you know where to look. One such language, JavaScript, is built into every modern web browser and is thus available on almost every device.

This book will try to make you familiar enough with this language to do useful and amusing things with it.

On Programming

Besides explaining JavaScript, I will introduce the basic principles of programming. Programming, it turns out, is hard. The fundamental rules are simple and clear, but programs built on top of these rules tend to become complex enough to introduce their own rules and complexity. You're building your own maze, in a way, and you might just get lost in it.

There will be times when reading this book feels terribly frustrating. If you are new to programming, there will be a lot of new material to digest. Much of this material will then be *combined* in ways that require you to make additional connections.

It is up to you to make the necessary effort. When you are struggling to follow the book, do not jump to any conclusions about your own capabilities. You are fine—you just need to keep at it. Take a break, reread some material, and make sure you read and understand the example programs and exercises. Learning is hard work, but everything you learn is yours and will make subsequent learning easier.

> When action grows unprofitable, gather information;
> when information grows unprofitable, sleep.
> —Ursula K. Le Guin, *The Left Hand of Darkness*

A program is many things. It is a piece of text typed by a programmer, it is the directing force that makes the computer do what it does, it is data in the computer's memory, yet it controls the actions performed on this same memory. Analogies that try to compare programs to objects we are familiar with tend to fall short. A superficially fitting one is that of a machine—lots of separate parts tend to be involved, and to make the whole thing tick, we have to consider the ways in which these parts interconnect and contribute to the operation of the whole.

A computer is a physical machine that acts as a host for these immaterial machines. Computers themselves can do only stupidly straightforward things. The reason they are so useful is that they do these things at an incredibly high speed. A program can ingeniously combine an enormous number of these simple actions to do very complicated things.

A program is a building of thought. It is costless to build, it is weightless, and it grows easily under our typing hands.

But without care, a program's size and complexity will grow out of control, confusing even the person who created it. Keeping programs under control is the main problem of programming. When a program works, it is beautiful. The art of programming is the skill of controlling complexity. The great program is subdued—made simple in its complexity.

Some programmers believe that this complexity is best managed by using only a small set of well-understood techniques in their programs. They have composed strict rules ("best practices") prescribing the form programs should have and carefully stay within their safe little zone.

This is not only boring, it is ineffective. New problems often require new solutions. The field of programming is young and still developing rapidly, and it is varied enough to have room for wildly different approaches. There are many terrible mistakes to make in program design, and you should go ahead and make them so that you understand them. A sense of what a good program looks like is developed in practice, not learned from a list of rules.

Why Language Matters

In the beginning, at the birth of computing, there were no programming languages. Programs looked something like this:

```
00110001 00000000 00000000
00110001 00000001 00000001
00110011 00000001 00000010
01010001 00001011 00000010
00100010 00000010 00001000
01000011 00000001 00000000
01000001 00000001 00000001
00010000 00000010 00000000
01100010 00000000 00000000
```

That is a program to add the numbers from 1 to 10 together and print out the result: 1 + 2 + ... + 10 = 55. It could run on a simple, hypothetical machine. To program early computers, it was necessary to set large arrays of switches in the right position or punch holes in strips of cardboard and feed them to the computer. You can probably imagine how tedious and error-prone this procedure was. Even writing simple programs required much cleverness and discipline. Complex ones were nearly inconceivable.

Of course, manually entering these arcane patterns of bits (the ones and zeros) did give the programmer a profound sense of being a mighty wizard. And that has to be worth something in terms of job satisfaction.

Each line of the previous program contains a single instruction. It could be written in English like this:

1. Store the number 0 in memory location 0.

2. Store the number 1 in memory location 1.

3. Store the value of memory location 1 in memory location 2.

4. Subtract the number 11 from the value in memory location 2.

5. If the value in memory location 2 is the number 0, continue with instruction 9.

6. Add the value of memory location 1 to memory location 0.

7. Add the number 1 to the value of memory location 1.

8. Continue with instruction 3.

9. Output the value of memory location 0.

Although that is already more readable than the soup of bits, it is still rather obscure. Using names instead of numbers for the instructions and memory locations helps.

```
Set "total" to 0.
Set "count" to 1.
[loop]
Set "compare" to "count".
Subtract 11 from "compare".
If "compare" is zero, continue at [end].
Add "count" to "total".
Add 1 to "count".
Continue at [loop].
[end]
Output "total".
```

Can you see how the program works at this point? The first two lines give two memory locations their starting values: total will be used to build up the result of the computation, and count will keep track of the number that we are currently looking at. The lines using compare are probably the weirdest ones. The program wants to see whether count is equal to 11 to decide whether it can stop running. Because our hypothetical machine is rather primitive, it can only test whether a number is zero and make a decision based on that. So it uses the memory location labeled compare to compute the value of count - 11 and makes a decision based on that value. The next two lines add the value of count to the result and increment count by 1 every time the program has decided that count is not 11 yet.

Here is the same program in JavaScript:

```
let total = 0, count = 1;
while (count <= 10) {
  total += count;
  count += 1;
}
console.log(total);
// → 55
```

This version gives us a few more improvements. Most important, there is no need to specify the way we want the program to jump back and forth anymore. The while construct takes care of that. It continues executing the block (wrapped in braces) below it as long as the condition it was given holds. That condition is count <= 10, which means "*count* is less than or equal to 10". We no longer have to create a temporary value and compare that to zero, which was just an uninteresting detail. Part of the power of programming languages is that they can take care of uninteresting details for us.

At the end of the program, after the while construct has finished, the console.log operation is used to write out the result.

Finally, here is what the program could look like if we happened to have the convenient operations range and sum available, which respectively create a collection of numbers within a range and compute the sum of a collection of numbers:

```
console.log(sum(range(1, 10)));
// → 55
```

The moral of this story is that the same program can be expressed in both long and short, unreadable and readable ways. The first version of the program was extremely obscure, whereas this last one is almost English: log the sum of the range of numbers from 1 to 10. (We will see in later chapters how to define operations like sum and range.)

A good programming language helps the programmer by allowing them to talk about the actions that the computer has to perform on a higher level. It helps omit details, provides convenient building blocks (such as while and console.log), allows you to define your own building blocks (such as sum and range), and makes those blocks easy to compose.

What Is JavaScript?

JavaScript was introduced in 1995 as a way to add programs to web pages in the Netscape Navigator browser. The language has since been adopted by all other major graphical web browsers. It has made modern web applications possible—applications with which you can interact directly without doing a page reload for every action. JavaScript is also used in more traditional websites to provide various forms of interactivity and cleverness.

It is important to note that JavaScript has almost nothing to do with the programming language named Java. The similar name was inspired by marketing considerations rather than good judgment. When JavaScript was being introduced, the Java language was being heavily marketed and was gaining popularity. Someone thought it was a good idea to try to ride along on this success. Now we are stuck with the name.

After its adoption outside of Netscape, a standard document was written to describe the way the JavaScript language should work so that the various pieces of software that claimed to support JavaScript were actually talking about the same language. This is called the ECMAScript standard, after the

Ecma International organization that did the standardization. In practice, the terms ECMAScript and JavaScript can be used interchangeably—they are two names for the same language.

There are those who will say *terrible* things about JavaScript. Many of these things are true. When I was required to write something in JavaScript for the first time, I quickly came to despise it. It would accept almost anything I typed but interpret it in a way that was completely different from what I meant. This had a lot to do with the fact that I did not have a clue what I was doing, of course, but there is a real issue here: JavaScript is ridiculously liberal in what it allows. The idea behind this design was that it would make programming in JavaScript easier for beginners. In actuality, it mostly makes finding problems in your programs harder because the system will not point them out to you.

This flexibility also has its advantages, though. It leaves space for a lot of techniques that are impossible in more rigid languages, and as you will see (for example in Chapter 10), it can be used to overcome some of JavaScript's shortcomings. After learning the language properly and working with it for a while, I have learned to actually *like* JavaScript.

There have been several versions of JavaScript. ECMAScript version 3 was the widely supported version in the time of JavaScript's ascent to dominance, roughly between 2000 and 2010. During this time, work was underway on an ambitious version 4, which planned a number of radical improvements and extensions to the language. Changing a living, widely used language in such a radical way turned out to be politically difficult, and work on version 4 was abandoned in 2008, leading to a much less ambitious version 5. Released in 2009, version 5 made only some uncontroversial improvements. Then in 2015 version 6 came out, a major update that included some of the ideas planned for version 4. Since then we've had new, small updates every year.

The fact that the language is evolving means that browsers have to constantly keep up, and if you're using an older browser, it may not support every feature. The language designers are careful to not make any changes that could break existing programs, so new browsers can still run old programs. In this book, I'm using the 2017 version of JavaScript.

Web browsers are not the only platforms on which JavaScript is used. Some databases, such as MongoDB and CouchDB, use JavaScript as their scripting and query language. Several platforms for desktop and server programming, most notably the Node.js project (the subject of Chapter 20), provide an environment for programming JavaScript outside of the browser.

Code, and What to Do with It

Code is the text that makes up programs. Most chapters in this book contain quite a lot of code. I believe reading code and writing code are indispensable parts of learning to program. Try to not just glance over the examples—read them attentively and understand them. This may be slow and confusing at first, but I promise that you'll quickly get the hang of it.

The same goes for the exercises. Don't assume you understand them until you've actually written a working solution.

I recommend you try your solutions to exercises in an actual JavaScript interpreter. That way, you'll get immediate feedback on whether what you are doing is working, and, I hope, you'll be tempted to experiment and go beyond the exercises.

The easiest way to run the example code in the book, and to experiment with it, is to look it up in the online version of the book at *https://eloquentjavascript.net*. There, you can click any code example to edit and run it and to see the output it produces. To work on the exercises, go to *https://eloquentjavascript.net/code*, which provides starting code for each coding exercise and allows you to look at the solutions.

If you want to run the programs defined in this book outside of the book's website, some care will be required. Many examples stand on their own and should work in any JavaScript environment. But code in later chapters is often written for a specific environment (the browser or Node.js) and can run only there. In addition, many chapters define bigger programs, and the pieces of code that appear in them depend on each other or on external files. The sandbox on the website provides links to Zip files containing all the scripts and data files necessary to run the code for a given chapter.

Overview of This Book

This book contains three parts. The first 12 chapters discuss the JavaScript language. The next seven chapters are about web browsers and the way JavaScript is used to program them. Finally, two chapters are devoted to Node.js, another environment to program JavaScript in.

Throughout the book, there are five *project chapters*, which describe larger example programs to give you a taste of actual programming. In order of appearance, we will work through building a delivery robot, a programming language, a platform game, a pixel paint program, and a dynamic website.

The language part of the book starts with four chapters that introduce the basic structure of the JavaScript language. They introduce control structures (such as the while word you saw in this introduction), functions (writing your own building blocks), and data structures. After these, you will be able to write basic programs. Next, Chapters 5 and 6 introduce techniques to use functions and objects to write more *abstract* code and keep complexity under control.

After a first project chapter, the language part of the book continues with chapters on error handling and bug fixing, regular expressions (an important tool for working with text), modularity (another defense against complexity), and asynchronous programming (dealing with events that take time). The second project chapter concludes the first part of the book.

The second part, Chapters 13 to 19, describes the tools that browser JavaScript has access to. You'll learn to display things on the screen (Chapters 14 and 17), respond to user input (Chapter 15), and communicate over the network (Chapter 18). There are again two project chapters in this part.

After that, Chapter 20 describes Node.js, and Chapter 21 builds a small website using that tool.

Finally, Chapter 22 describes some of the considerations that come up when optimizing JavaScript programs for speed.

Typographic Conventions

In this book, text written in a `monospaced` font will represent elements of programs—sometimes they are self-sufficient fragments, and sometimes they just refer to part of a nearby program. Programs (of which you have already seen a few) are written as follows:

```
function factorial(n) {
  if (n == 0) {
    return 1;
  } else {
    return factorial(n - 1) * n;
  }
}
```

Sometimes, to show the output that a program produces, the expected output is written after it, with two slashes and an arrow in front.

```
console.log(factorial(8));
// → 40320
```

Good luck!

PART I

LANGUAGE

"Below the surface of the machine, the program moves. Without effort, it expands and contracts. In great harmony, electrons scatter and regroup. The forms on the monitor are but ripples on the water. The essence stays invisibly below."

—Master Yuan-Ma, *The Book of Programming*

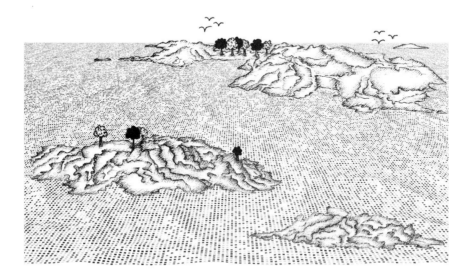

1

VALUES, TYPES, AND OPERATORS

Inside the computer's world, there is only data. You can read data, modify data, create new data—but that which isn't data cannot be mentioned. All this data is stored as long sequences of bits and is thus fundamentally alike.

Bits are any kind of two-valued things, usually described as zeros and ones. Inside the computer, they take forms such as a high or low electrical charge, a strong or weak signal, or a shiny or dull spot on the surface of a CD. Any piece of discrete information can be reduced to a sequence of zeros and ones and thus represented in bits.

For example, we can express the number 13 in bits. It works the same way as a decimal number, but instead of 10 different digits, you have only 2, and the weight of each increases by a factor of 2 from right to left. Here are the bits that make up the number 13, with the weights of the digits shown below them:

0	0	0	0	1	1	0	1
128	64	32	16	8	4	2	1

So that's the binary number 00001101. Its nonzero digits stand for 8, 4, and 1, and add up to 13.

Values

Imagine a sea of bits—an ocean of them. A typical modern computer has more than 30 billion bits in its volatile data storage (working memory). Non-volatile storage (the hard disk or equivalent) tends to have yet a few orders of magnitude more.

To be able to work with such quantities of bits without getting lost, we must separate them into chunks that represent pieces of information. In a JavaScript environment, those chunks are called *values*. Though all values are made of bits, they play different roles. Every value has a type that determines its role. Some values are numbers, some values are pieces of text, some values are functions, and so on.

To create a value, you must merely invoke its name. This is convenient. You don't have to gather building material for your values or pay for them. You just call for one, and *whoosh*, you have it. They are not really created from thin air, of course. Every value has to be stored somewhere, and if you want to use a gigantic amount of them at the same time, you might run out of memory. Fortunately, this is a problem only if you need them all simultaneously. As soon as you no longer use a value, it will dissipate, leaving behind its bits to be recycled as building material for the next generation of values.

This chapter introduces the atomic elements of JavaScript programs, that is, the simple value types and the operators that can act on such values.

Numbers

Values of the *number* type are, unsurprisingly, numeric values. In a JavaScript program, they are written as follows:

```
13
```

Use that in a program, and it will cause the bit pattern for the number 13 to come into existence inside the computer's memory.

JavaScript uses a fixed number of bits, 64 of them, to store a single number value. There are only so many patterns you can make with 64 bits, which means that the number of different numbers that can be represented is limited. With N decimal digits, you can represent 10^N numbers. Similarly, given 64 binary digits, you can represent 2^{64} different numbers, which is about 18 quintillion (an 18 with 18 zeros after it). That's a lot.

Computer memory used to be much smaller, and people tended to use groups of 8 or 16 bits to represent their numbers. It was easy to accidentally *overflow* such small numbers—to end up with a number that did not fit into the given number of bits. Today, even computers that fit in your pocket have plenty of memory, so you are free to use 64-bit chunks, and you need to worry about overflow only when dealing with truly astronomical numbers.

Not all whole numbers less than 18 quintillion fit in a JavaScript number, though. Those bits also store negative numbers, so one bit indicates the sign of the number. A bigger issue is that nonwhole numbers must also be represented. To do this, some of the bits are used to store the position of the decimal point. The actual maximum whole number that can be stored is more in the range of 9 quadrillion (15 zeros)—which is still pleasantly huge.

Fractional numbers are written by using a dot.

```
9.81
```

For very big or very small numbers, you may also use scientific notation by adding an *e* (for *exponent*), followed by the exponent of the number.

```
2.998e8
```

That is $2.998 \times 10^8 = 299{,}800{,}000$.

Calculations with whole numbers (also called *integers*) smaller than the aforementioned 9 quadrillion are guaranteed to always be precise. Unfortunately, calculations with fractional numbers are generally not. Just as π (pi) cannot be precisely expressed by a finite number of decimal digits, many numbers lose some precision when only 64 bits are available to store them. This is a shame, but it causes practical problems only in specific situations. The important thing is to be aware of it and treat fractional digital numbers as approximations, not as precise values.

Arithmetic

The main thing to do with numbers is arithmetic. Arithmetic operations such as addition or multiplication take two number values and produce a new number from them. Here is what they look like in JavaScript:

```
100 + 4 * 11
```

The + and * symbols are called *operators*. The first stands for addition, and the second stands for multiplication. Putting an operator between two values will apply it to those values and produce a new value.

But does the example mean "add 4 and 100, and multiply the result by 11," or is the multiplication done before the adding? As you might have guessed, the multiplication happens first. But as in mathematics, you can change this by wrapping the addition in parentheses.

```
(100 + 4) * 11
```

For subtraction, there is the - operator, and division can be done with the / operator.

When operators appear together without parentheses, the order in which they are applied is determined by the *precedence* of the operators. The example shows that multiplication comes before addition. The / operator has the same precedence as *. Likewise for + and -. When multiple operators with the same precedence appear next to each other, as in 1 - 2 + 1, they are applied left to right: (1 - 2) + 1.

These rules of precedence are not something you should worry about. When in doubt, just add parentheses.

There is one more arithmetic operator, which you might not immediately recognize. The % symbol is used to represent the *remainder* operation. X % Y is the remainder of dividing X by Y. For example, 314 % 100 produces 14, and 144 % 12 gives 0. The remainder operator's precedence is the same as that of multiplication and division. You'll also often see this operator referred to as *modulo*.

Special Numbers

There are three special values in JavaScript that are considered numbers but don't behave like normal numbers.

The first two are Infinity and -Infinity, which represent the positive and negative infinities. Infinity - 1 is still Infinity, and so on. Don't put too much trust in infinity-based computation, though. It isn't mathematically sound, and it will quickly lead to the next special number: NaN.

NaN stands for "not a number," even though it *is* a value of the number type. You'll get this result when you, for example, try to calculate 0 / 0 (zero divided by zero), Infinity - Infinity, or any number of other numeric operations that don't yield a meaningful result.

Strings

The next basic data type is the *string*. Strings are used to represent text. They are written by enclosing their content in quotes.

```
`Down on the sea`
"Lie on the ocean"
'Float on the ocean'
```

You can use single quotes, double quotes, or backticks to mark strings, as long as the quotes at the start and the end of the string match.

Almost anything can be put between quotes, and JavaScript will make a string value out of it. But a few characters are more difficult. You can imagine how putting quotes between quotes might be hard. *Newlines* (the characters you get when you press ENTER) can be included without escaping only when the string is quoted with backticks (`` ` ``).

To make it possible to include such characters in a string, the following notation is used: whenever a backslash (\) is found inside quoted text, it indicates that the character after it has a special meaning. This is called *escaping* the character. A quote that is preceded by a backslash will not end the string but be part of it. When an n character occurs after a backslash, it is interpreted as a newline. Similarly, a t after a backslash means a tab character. Take the following string:

```
"This is the first line\nAnd this is the second"
```

The actual text contained is this:

```
This is the first line
And this is the second
```

There are, of course, situations where you want a backslash in a string to be just a backslash, not a special code. If two backslashes follow each other, they will collapse together, and only one will be left in the resulting string value. This is how the string `"A newline character is written like "\n"."` can be expressed:

```
"A newline character is written like \"\\n\"."
```

Strings, too, have to be modeled as a series of bits to be able to exist inside the computer. The way JavaScript does this is based on the *Unicode* standard. This standard assigns a number to virtually every character you would ever need, including characters from Greek, Arabic, Japanese, Armenian, and so on. If we have a number for every character, a string can be described by a sequence of numbers.

And that's what JavaScript does. But there's a complication: JavaScript's representation uses 16 bits per string element, which can describe up to 2^{16} different characters. But Unicode defines more characters than that—about twice as many, at this point. So some characters, such as many emoji, take up two "character positions" in JavaScript strings. We'll come back to this in "Strings and Character Codes" on page 92.

Strings cannot be divided, multiplied, or subtracted, but the + operator *can* be used on them. It does not add, but it *concatenates*—it glues two strings together. The following line will produce the string `"concatenate"`:

```
"con" + "cat" + "e" + "nate"
```

String values have a number of associated functions (*methods*) that can be used to perform other operations on them. I'll say more about these in "Methods" on page 62.

Strings written with single or double quotes behave very much the same—the only difference is in which type of quote you need to escape inside of them. Backtick-quoted strings, usually called *template literals*, can do a few more tricks. Apart from being able to span lines, they can also embed other values.

```
`half of 100 is ${100 / 2}`
```

When you write something inside ${} in a template literal, its result will be computed, converted to a string, and included at that position. The example produces half of 100 is 50.

Unary Operators

Not all operators are symbols. Some are written as words. One example is the `typeof` operator, which produces a string value naming the type of the value you give it.

```
console.log(typeof 4.5)
// → number
console.log(typeof "x")
// → string
```

We will use `console.log` in example code to indicate that we want to see the result of evaluating something. More about that in the next chapter.

The other operators shown all operated on two values, but `typeof` takes only one. Operators that use two values are called *binary* operators, while those that take one are called *unary* operators. The minus operator can be used both as a binary operator and as a unary operator.

```
console.log(- (10 - 2))
// → -8
```

Boolean Values

It is often useful to have a value that distinguishes between only two possibilities, like "yes" and "no" or "on" and "off." For this purpose, JavaScript has a *Boolean* type, which has just two values, true and false, which are written as those words.

Comparison

Here is one way to produce Boolean values:

```
console.log(3 > 2)
// → true
console.log(3 < 2)
// → false
```

The > and < signs are the traditional symbols for "is greater than" and "is less than," respectively. They are binary operators. Applying them results in a Boolean value that indicates whether they hold true in this case.

Strings can be compared in the same way.

```
console.log("Aardvark" < "Zoroaster")
// → true
```

The way strings are ordered is roughly alphabetic but not really what you'd expect to see in a dictionary: uppercase letters are always "less" than lowercase ones, so "Z" < "a", and nonalphabetic characters (!, -, and so on) are also included in the ordering. When comparing strings, JavaScript goes over the characters from left to right, comparing the Unicode codes one by one.

Other similar operators are >= (greater than or equal to), <= (less than or equal to), == (equal to), and != (not equal to).

```
console.log("Itchy" != "Scratchy")
// → true
console.log("Apple" == "Orange")
// → false
```

There is only one value in JavaScript that is not equal to itself, and that is NaN ("not a number").

```
console.log(NaN == NaN)
// → false
```

NaN is supposed to denote the result of a nonsensical computation, and as such, it isn't equal to the result of any *other* nonsensical computations.

Logical Operators

There are also some operations that can be applied to Boolean values themselves. JavaScript supports three logical operators: *and*, *or*, and *not*. These can be used to "reason" about Booleans.

The && operator represents logical *and*. It is a binary operator, and its result is true only if both the values given to it are true.

```
console.log(true && false)
// → false
console.log(true && true)
// → true
```

The || operator denotes logical *or*. It produces true if either of the values given to it is true.

```
console.log(false || true)
// → true
console.log(false || false)
// → false
```

Not is written as an exclamation mark (!). It is a unary operator that flips the value given to it—!true produces false, and !false gives true.

When mixing these Boolean operators with arithmetic and other operators, it is not always obvious when parentheses are needed. In practice, you can usually get by with knowing that of the operators we have seen so far, || has the lowest precedence, then comes &&, then the comparison operators (>, ==, and so on), and then the rest. This order has been chosen such that, in typical expressions like the following one, as few parentheses as possible are necessary:

```
1 + 1 == 2 && 10 * 10 > 50
```

The last logical operator I will discuss is not unary, not binary, but *ternary*, operating on three values. It is written with a question mark and a colon, like this:

```
console.log(true ? 1 : 2);
// → 1
console.log(false ? 1 : 2);
// → 2
```

This one is called the *conditional* operator (or sometimes just the *ternary* operator since it is the only such operator in the language). The value on the left of the question mark "picks" which of the other two values will come out. When it is true, it chooses the middle value, and when it is false, it chooses the value on the right.

Empty Values

There are two special values, written null and undefined, that are used to denote the absence of a *meaningful* value. They are themselves values, but they carry no information.

Many operations in the language that don't produce a meaningful value (you'll see some later) yield undefined simply because they have to yield *some* value.

The difference in meaning between undefined and null is an accident of JavaScript's design, and it doesn't matter most of the time. In cases where you actually have to concern yourself with these values, I recommend treating them as mostly interchangeable.

Automatic Type Conversion

In the Introduction, I mentioned that JavaScript goes out of its way to accept almost any program you give it, even programs that do odd things. This is nicely demonstrated by the following expressions:

```
console.log(8 * null)
// → 0
console.log("5" - 1)
// → 4
console.log("5" + 1)
// → 51
console.log("five" * 2)
// → NaN
```

```
console.log(false == 0)
// → true
```

When an operator is applied to the "wrong" type of value, JavaScript will quietly convert that value to the type it needs, using a set of rules that often aren't what you want or expect. This is called *type coercion*. The null in the first expression becomes 0, and the "5" in the second expression becomes 5 (from string to number). Yet in the third expression, + tries string concatenation before numeric addition, so the 1 is converted to "1" (from number to string).

When something that doesn't map to a number in an obvious way (such as "five" or undefined) is converted to a number, you get the value NaN. Further arithmetic operations on NaN keep producing NaN, so if you find yourself getting one of those in an unexpected place, look for accidental type conversions.

When comparing values of the same type using ==, the outcome is easy to predict: you should get true when both values are the same, except in the case of NaN. But when the types differ, JavaScript uses a complicated and confusing set of rules to determine what to do. In most cases, it just tries to convert one of the values to the other value's type. However, when null or undefined occurs on either side of the operator, it produces true only if both sides are one of null or undefined.

```
console.log(null == undefined);
// → true
console.log(null == 0);
// → false
```

That behavior is often useful. When you want to test whether a value has a real value instead of null or undefined, you can compare it to null with the == (or !=) operator.

But what if you want to test whether something refers to the precise value false? Expressions like 0 == false and "" == false are true. When you do *not* want any automatic type conversions to happen, there are two additional operators: === and !==. The first tests whether a value is *precisely* equal to the other, and the second tests whether it is not precisely equal. So "" === false is false as expected.

I recommend using the three-character comparison operators defensively to prevent unexpected type conversions from tripping you up. But when you're certain the types on both sides will be the same, there is no problem with using the shorter operators.

Short-Circuiting of Logical Operators

The logical operators && and || handle values of different types in a peculiar way. They will convert the value on their left side to Boolean type in order to decide what to do, but depending on the operator and the result of that conversion, they will return either the *original* left-hand value or the right-hand value.

The || operator, for example, will return the value to its left when that can be converted to true and will return the value on its right otherwise. This has the expected effect when the values are Boolean and does something analogous for values of other types.

```
console.log(null || "user")
// → user
console.log("Agnes" || "user")
// → Agnes
```

We can use this functionality as a way to fall back on a default value. If you have a value that might be empty, you can put || after it with a replacement value. If the initial value can be converted to false, you'll get the replacement instead. The rules for converting strings and numbers to Boolean values state that 0, NaN, and the empty string ("") count as false, while all the other values count as true. So 0 || -1 produces -1, and "" || "!?" yields "!?".

The && operator works similarly but the other way around. When the value to its left is something that converts to false, it returns that value, and otherwise it returns the value on its right.

Another important property of these two operators is that the part to their right is evaluated only when necessary. In the case of true || X, no matter what X is—even if it's a piece of program that does something *terrible*—the result will be true, and X is never evaluated. The same goes for false && X, which is false and will ignore X. This is called *short-circuit evaluation*.

The conditional operator works in a similar way. Of the second and third values, only the one that is selected is evaluated.

Summary

We looked at four types of JavaScript values in this chapter: numbers, strings, Booleans, and undefined values.

Such values are created by typing in their name (true, null) or value (13, "abc"). You can combine and transform values with operators. We saw binary operators for arithmetic (+, -, *, /, and %), string concatenation (+), comparison (==, !=, ===, !==, <, >, <=, >=), and logic (&&, ||), as well as several unary operators (- to negate a number, ! to negate logically, and typeof to find a value's type) and a ternary operator (?:) to pick one of two values based on a third value.

This gives you enough information to use JavaScript as a pocket calculator but not much more. The next chapter will start tying these expressions together into basic programs.

"And my heart glows bright red under my filmy, translucent skin and they have to administer 10cc of JavaScript to get me to come back. (I respond well to toxins in the blood.) Man, that stuff will kick the peaches right out your gills!"

— _why, *Why's (Poignant) Guide to Ruby*

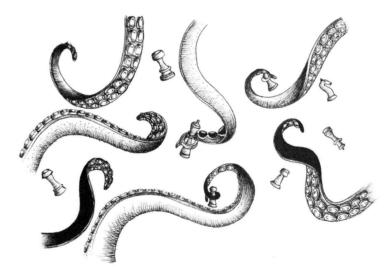

PROGRAM STRUCTURE

In this chapter, we will start to do things that can actually be called *programming*. We will expand our command of the JavaScript language beyond the nouns and sentence fragments we've seen so far, to the point where we can express meaningful prose.

Expressions and Statements

In Chapter 1, we made values and applied operators to them to get new values. Creating values like this is the main substance of any JavaScript program. But that substance has to be framed in a larger structure to be useful. So that's what we'll cover next.

A fragment of code that produces a value is called an *expression*. Every value that is written literally (such as 22 or "psychoanalysis") is an expression. An expression between parentheses is also an expression, as is a binary operator applied to two expressions or a unary operator applied to one.

This shows part of the beauty of a language-based interface. Expressions can contain other expressions in a way similar to how subsentences in human languages are nested—a subsentence can contain its own subsentences, and so on. This allows us to build expressions that describe arbitrarily complex computations.

If an expression corresponds to a sentence fragment, a JavaScript *statement* corresponds to a full sentence. A program is a list of statements.

The simplest kind of statement is an expression with a semicolon after it. This is a program:

```
1;
!false;
```

It is a useless program, though. An expression can be content to just produce a value, which can then be used by the enclosing code. A statement stands on its own, so it amounts to something only if it affects the world. It could display something on the screen—that counts as changing the world—or it could change the internal state of the machine in a way that will affect the statements that come after it. These changes are called *side effects*. The statements in the previous example just produce the values 1 and true and then immediately throw them away. This leaves no impression on the world at all. When you run this program, nothing observable happens.

In some cases, JavaScript allows you to omit the semicolon at the end of a statement. In other cases, it has to be there, or the next line will be treated as part of the same statement. The rules for when it can be safely omitted are somewhat complex and error-prone. So in this book, every statement that needs a semicolon will always get one. I recommend you do the same, at least until you've learned more about the subtleties of missing semicolons.

Bindings

How does a program keep an internal state? How does it remember things? We have seen how to produce new values from old values, but this does not change the old values, and the new value has to be immediately used or it will dissipate again. To catch and hold values, JavaScript provides a thing called a *binding*, or *variable*:

```
let caught = 5 * 5;
```

That's a second kind of statement. The special word (*keyword*) let indicates that this sentence is going to define a binding. It is followed by the name of the binding and, if we want to immediately give it a value, by an = operator and an expression.

The previous statement creates a binding called caught and uses it to grab hold of the number that is produced by multiplying 5 by 5.

After a binding has been defined, its name can be used as an expression. The value of such an expression is the value the binding currently holds. Here's an example:

```
let ten = 10;
console.log(ten * ten);
// → 100
```

When a binding points at a value, that does not mean it is tied to that value forever. The = operator can be used at any time on existing bindings to disconnect them from their current value and have them point to a new one.

```
let mood = "light";
console.log(mood);
// → light
mood = "dark";
console.log(mood);
// → dark
```

You should imagine bindings as tentacles, rather than boxes. They do not *contain* values; they *grasp* them—two bindings can refer to the same value. A program can access only the values that it still has a reference to. When you need to remember something, you grow a tentacle to hold on to it or you reattach one of your existing tentacles to it.

Let's look at another example. To remember the number of dollars that Luigi still owes you, you create a binding. And then when he pays back $35, you give this binding a new value.

```
let luigisDebt = 140;
luigisDebt = luigisDebt - 35;
console.log(luigisDebt);
// → 105
```

When you define a binding without giving it a value, the tentacle has nothing to grasp, so it ends in thin air. If you ask for the value of an empty binding, you'll get the value undefined.

A single let statement may define multiple bindings. The definitions must be separated by commas.

```
let one = 1, two = 2;
console.log(one + two);
// → 3
```

The words var and const can also be used to create bindings, in a way similar to let.

```
var name = "Ayda";
const greeting = "Hello ";
console.log(greeting + name);
// → Hello Ayda
```

The first, var (short for "variable"), is the way bindings were declared in pre-2015 JavaScript. I'll get back to the precise way it differs from let in the next chapter. For now, remember that it mostly does the same thing, but we'll rarely use it in this book because it has some confusing properties.

The word const stands for *constant*. It defines a constant binding, which points at the same value for as long as it lives. This is useful for bindings that give a name to a value so that you can easily refer to it later.

Binding Names

Binding names can be any word. Digits can be part of binding names—catch22 is a valid name, for example—but the name must not start with a digit. A binding name may include dollar signs ($) or underscores (_) but no other punctuation or special characters.

Words with a special meaning, such as let, are *keywords*, and they may not be used as binding names. There are also a number of words that are "reserved for use" in future versions of JavaScript, which also can't be used as binding names. The full list of keywords and reserved words is rather long.

```
break case catch class const continue debugger default
delete do else enum export extends false finally for
function if implements import interface in instanceof let
new package private protected public return static super
switch this throw true try typeof var void while with yield
```

Don't worry about memorizing this list. When creating a binding produces an unexpected syntax error, see whether you're trying to define a reserved word.

The Environment

The collection of bindings and their values that exist at a given time is called the *environment*. When a program starts up, this environment is not empty. It always contains bindings that are part of the language standard, and most of the time, it also has bindings that provide ways to interact with the surrounding system. For example, in a browser, there are functions to interact with the currently loaded website and to read mouse and keyboard input.

Functions

A lot of the values provided in the default environment have the type *function*. A function is a piece of program wrapped in a value. Such values can be *applied* in order to run the wrapped program. For example, in a browser environment, the binding prompt holds a function that shows a little dialog box asking for user input. It is used like this:

```
prompt("Enter passcode");
```

Executing a function is called *invoking, calling,* or *applying* it. You can call a function by putting parentheses after an expression that produces a function value. Usually you'll directly use the name of the binding that holds the function. The values between the parentheses are given to the program inside the function. In the example, the prompt function uses the string that we give it as the text to show in the dialog box. Values given to functions are called *arguments*. Different functions might need a different number or different types of arguments.

The prompt function isn't used much in modern web programming, mostly because you have no control over the way the resulting dialog looks, but it can be helpful in toy programs and experiments.

The console.log Function

In the examples, I used console.log to output values. Most JavaScript systems (including all modern web browsers and Node.js) provide a console.log function that writes out its arguments to *some* text output device. In browsers, the output lands in the JavaScript console. This part of the browser interface is hidden by default, but most browsers open it when you press F12 or, on a Mac, COMMAND-OPTION-I. If that does not work, search through the menus for an item named Developer Tools or similar.

Though binding names cannot contain period characters, console.log does have one. This is because console.log isn't a simple binding. It is actually an expression that retrieves the log property from the value held by the console binding. We'll find out exactly what this means in "Properties" on page 61.

Return Values

Showing a dialog box or writing text to the screen is a *side effect*. A lot of functions are useful because of the side effects they produce. Functions may also produce values, in which case they don't need to have a side effect to be useful. For example, the function Math.max takes any amount of number arguments and gives back the greatest.

```
console.log(Math.max(2, 4));
// → 4
```

When a function produces a value, it is said to *return* that value. Anything that produces a value is an expression in JavaScript, which means function calls can be used within larger expressions. Here a call to Math.min, which is the opposite of Math.max, is used as part of a plus expression:

```
console.log(Math.min(2, 4) + 100);
// → 102
```

The next chapter explains how to write your own functions.

Control Flow

When your program contains more than one statement, the statements are executed as if they are a story, from top to bottom. This example program has two statements. The first one asks the user for a number, and the second, which is executed after the first, shows the square of that number.

```
let theNumber = Number(prompt("Pick a number"));
console.log("Your number is the square root of " +
            theNumber * theNumber);
```

The function Number converts a value to a number. We need that conversion because the result of prompt is a string value, and we want a number. There are similar functions called String and Boolean that convert values to those types.

Here is the rather trivial schematic representation of straight-line control flow:

Conditional Execution

Not all programs are straight roads. We may, for example, want to create a branching road, where the program takes the proper branch based on the situation at hand. This is called *conditional execution.*

Conditional execution is created with the if keyword in JavaScript. In the simple case, we want some code to be executed if, and only if, a certain condition holds. We might, for example, want to show the square of the input only if the input is actually a number.

```
let theNumber = Number(prompt("Pick a number"));
if (!Number.isNaN(theNumber)) {
  console.log("Your number is the square root of " +
            theNumber * theNumber);
}
```

With this modification, if you enter "parrot," no output is shown.

The `if` keyword executes or skips a statement depending on the value of a Boolean expression. The deciding expression is written after the keyword, between parentheses, followed by the statement to execute.

The `Number.isNaN` function is a standard JavaScript function that returns true only if the argument it is given is `NaN`. The `Number` function happens to return `NaN` when you give it a string that doesn't represent a valid number. Thus, the condition translates to "unless `theNumber` is not-a-number, do this."

The statement after the `if` is wrapped in braces (`{` and `}`) in this example. The braces can be used to group any number of statements into a single statement, called a *block*. You could also have omitted them in this case, since they hold only a single statement, but to avoid having to think about whether they are needed, most JavaScript programmers use them in every wrapped statement like this. We'll mostly follow that convention in this book, except for the occasional one-liner.

```
if (1 + 1 == 2) console.log("It's true");
// → It's true
```

You often won't just have code that executes when a condition holds true, but also code that handles the other case. This alternate path is represented by the second arrow in the diagram. You can use the `else` keyword, together with `if`, to create two separate, alternative execution paths.

```
let theNumber = Number(prompt("Pick a number"));
if (!Number.isNaN(theNumber)) {
  console.log("Your number is the square root of " +
              theNumber * theNumber);
} else {
  console.log("Hey. Why didn't you give me a number?");
}
```

If you have more than two paths to choose from, you can "chain" multiple if/else pairs together. Here's an example:

```
let num = Number(prompt("Pick a number"));

if (num < 10) {
  console.log("Small");
} else if (num < 100) {
  console.log("Medium");
} else {
  console.log("Large");
}
```

The program will first check whether `num` is less than 10. If it is, it chooses that branch, shows "Small", and is done. If it isn't, it takes the else branch, which itself contains a second `if`. If the second condition (`< 100`) holds, that means the number is between 10 and 100, and `"Medium"` is shown. If it doesn't, the second and last `else` branch is chosen.

The schema for this program looks something like this:

while and do Loops

Consider a program that outputs all even numbers from 0 to 12. One way to write this is as follows:

```
console.log(0);
console.log(2);
console.log(4);
console.log(6);
console.log(8);
console.log(10);
console.log(12);
```

That works, but the idea of writing a program is to make something *less* work, not more. If we needed all even numbers less than 1,000, this approach would be unworkable. What we need is a way to run a piece of code multiple times. This form of control flow is called a *loop*.

Looping control flow allows us to go back to some point in the program where we were before and repeat it with our current program state. If we combine this with a binding that counts, we can do something like this:

```
let number = 0;
while (number <= 12) {
  console.log(number);
  number = number + 2;
}
// → 0
// → 2
//    ... etcetera
```

A statement starting with the keyword while creates a loop. The word while is followed by an expression in parentheses and then a statement, much like if. The loop keeps entering that statement as long as the expression produces a value that gives true when converted to Boolean.

The number binding demonstrates the way a binding can track the progress of a program. Every time the loop repeats, number gets a value that is 2 more than its previous value. At the beginning of every repetition, it is compared with the number 12 to decide whether the program's work is finished.

As an example that actually does something useful, we can now write a program that calculates and shows the value of 2^{10} (2 to the 10th power). We use two bindings: one to keep track of our result and one to count how often we have multiplied this result by 2. The loop tests whether the second binding has reached 10 yet and, if not, updates both bindings.

```
let result = 1;
let counter = 0;
while (counter < 10) {
  result = result * 2;
  counter = counter + 1;
}
console.log(result);
// → 1024
```

The counter could also have started at 1 and checked for <= 10, but for reasons that will become apparent in Chapter 4, it is a good idea to get used to counting from 0.

A do loop is a control structure similar to a while loop. It differs only on one point: a do loop always executes its body at least once, and it starts testing whether it should stop only after that first execution. To reflect this, the test appears after the body of the loop.

```
let yourName;
do {
  yourName = prompt("Who are you?");
} while (!yourName);
console.log(yourName);
```

This program will force you to enter a name. It will ask again and again until it gets something that is not an empty string. Applying the ! operator will convert a value to Boolean type before negating it, and all strings except "" convert to true. This means the loop continues going round until you provide a non-empty name.

Indenting Code

In the examples, I've been adding spaces in front of statements that are part of some larger statement. These spaces are not required—the computer will accept the program just fine without them. In fact, even the line breaks in programs are optional. You could write a program as a single long line if you felt like it.

The role of this indentation inside blocks is to make the structure of the code stand out. In code where new blocks are opened inside other blocks, it can become hard to see where one block ends and another begins. With proper indentation, the visual shape of a program corresponds to the shape of the blocks inside it. I like to use two spaces for every open block, but tastes differ—some people use four spaces, and some people use tab characters. The important thing is that each new block adds the same amount of space.

```
if (false != true) {
  console.log("That makes sense.");
  if (1 < 2) {
    console.log("No surprise there.");
  }
}
```

Most code editor programs will help by automatically indenting new lines the proper amount.

for Loops

Many loops follow the pattern shown in the while examples. First a "counter" binding is created to track the progress of the loop. Then comes a while loop, usually with a test expression that checks whether the counter has reached its end value. At the end of the loop body, the counter is updated to track progress.

Because this pattern is so common, JavaScript and similar languages provide a slightly shorter and more comprehensive form, the for loop.

```
for (let number = 0; number <= 12; number = number + 2) {
  console.log(number);
}
// → 0
// → 2
//   ... etcetera
```

This program is exactly equivalent to the earlier even-number-printing example (page 30). The only change is that all the statements that are related to the "state" of the loop are grouped together after for.

The parentheses after a for keyword must contain two semicolons. The part before the first semicolon *initializes* the loop, usually by defining a binding. The second part is the expression that *checks* whether the loop must continue. The final part *updates* the state of the loop after every iteration. In most cases, this is shorter and clearer than a while construct.

This is the code that computes 2^{10} using for instead of while:

```
let result = 1;
for (let counter = 0; counter < 10; counter = counter + 1) {
  result = result * 2;
}
console.log(result);
// → 1024
```

Breaking Out of a Loop

Having the looping condition produce false is not the only way a loop can finish. There is a special statement called break that has the effect of immediately jumping out of the enclosing loop.

This program illustrates the break statement. It finds the first number that is both greater than or equal to 20 and divisible by 7.

```
for (let current = 20; ; current = current + 1) {
  if (current % 7 == 0) {
    console.log(current);
    break;
  }
}
// → 21
```

Using the remainder (%) operator is an easy way to test whether a number is divisible by another number. If it is, the remainder of their division is zero.

The for construct in the example does not have a part that checks for the end of the loop. This means that the loop will never stop unless the break statement inside is executed.

If you were to remove that break statement or you accidentally write an end condition that always produces true, your program would get stuck in an *infinite loop*. A program stuck in an infinite loop will never finish running, which is usually a bad thing.

The continue keyword is similar to break, in that it influences the progress of a loop. When continue is encountered in a loop body, control jumps out of the body and continues with the loop's next iteration.

Updating Bindings Succinctly

Especially when looping, a program often needs to "update" a binding to hold a value based on that binding's previous value.

```
counter = counter + 1;
```

JavaScript provides a shortcut for this.

```
counter += 1;
```

Similar shortcuts work for many other operators, such as result *= 2 to double result or counter -= 1 to count downward.

This allows us to shorten our counting example a little more.

```
for (let number = 0; number <= 12; number += 2) {
  console.log(number);
}
```

For counter += 1 and counter -= 1, there are even shorter equivalents: counter++ and counter--.

Dispatching on a Value with switch

It is not uncommon for code to look like this:

```
if (x == "value1") action1();
else if (x == "value2") action2();
else if (x == "value3") action3();
else defaultAction();
```

There is a construct called switch that is intended to express such a "dispatch" in a more direct way. Unfortunately, the syntax JavaScript uses for this (which it inherited from the C/Java line of programming languages) is somewhat awkward—a chain of if statements may look better. Here is an example:

```
switch (prompt("What is the weather like?")) {
  case "rainy":
    console.log("Remember to bring an umbrella.");
    break;
  case "sunny":
    console.log("Dress lightly.");
  case "cloudy":
    console.log("Go outside.");
    break;
```

```
default:
  console.log("Unknown weather type!");
  break;
}
```

You may put any number of case labels inside the block opened by switch. The program will start executing at the label that corresponds to the value that switch was given, or at default if no matching value is found. It will continue executing, even across other labels, until it reaches a break statement. In some cases, such as the "sunny" case in the example, this can be used to share some code between cases (it recommends going outside for both sunny and cloudy weather). But be careful—it is easy to forget such a break, which will cause the program to execute code you do not want executed.

Capitalization

Binding names may not contain spaces, yet it is often helpful to use multiple words to clearly describe what the binding represents. These are pretty much your choices for writing a binding name with several words in it:

```
fuzzylittleturtle
fuzzy_little_turtle
FuzzyLittleTurtle
fuzzyLittleTurtle
```

The first style can be hard to read. I rather like the look of the underscores, though that style is a little painful to type. The standard JavaScript functions, and most JavaScript programmers, follow the bottom style—they capitalize every word except the first. It is not hard to get used to little things like that, and code with mixed naming styles can be jarring to read, so we follow this convention.

In a few cases, such as the Number function, the first letter of a binding is also capitalized. This was done to mark this function as a constructor. What a constructor is will become clear in Chapter 6. For now, the important thing is not to be bothered by this apparent lack of consistency.

Comments

Often, raw code does not convey all the information you want a program to convey to human readers, or it conveys it in such a cryptic way that people might not understand it. At other times, you might just want to include some related thoughts as part of your program. This is what *comments* are for.

A comment is a piece of text that is part of a program but is completely ignored by the computer. JavaScript has two ways of writing comments. To write a single-line comment, you can use two slash characters (//) and then the comment text after it.

```
let accountBalance = calculateBalance(account);
// It's a green hollow where a river sings
accountBalance.adjust();
// Madly catching white tatters in the grass.
let report = new Report();
// Where the sun on the proud mountain rings:
addToReport(accountBalance, report);
// It's a little valley, foaming like light in a glass.
```

A // comment goes only to the end of the line. A section of text between /* and */ will be ignored in its entirety, regardless of whether it contains line breaks. This is useful for adding blocks of information about a file or a chunk of program.

```
/*
  I first found this number scrawled on the back of
  an old notebook. Since then, it has often dropped by,
  showing up in phone numbers and the serial numbers of
  products that I've bought. It obviously likes me, so I've
  decided to keep it.
*/
const myNumber = 11213;
```

Summary

You now know that a program is built out of statements, which themselves sometimes contain more statements. Statements tend to contain expressions, which themselves can be built out of smaller expressions.

Putting statements after one another gives you a program that is executed from top to bottom. You can introduce disturbances in the flow of control by using conditional (if, else, and switch) and looping (while, do, and for) statements.

Bindings can be used to file pieces of data under a name, and they are useful for tracking state in your program. The environment is the set of bindings that are defined. JavaScript systems always put a number of useful standard bindings into your environment.

Functions are special values that encapsulate a piece of program. You can invoke them by writing functionName(argument1, argument2). Such a function call is an expression and may produce a value.

Exercises

If you are unsure how to test your solutions to the exercises, refer to the Introduction.

Each exercise starts with a problem description. Read this description and try to solve the exercise. If you run into problems, consider reading the hints at the end of the book. Full solutions to the exercises are not included in this book, but you can find them online at *https://eloquentjavascript.net/ code*. If you want to learn something from the exercises, I recommend looking at the solutions only after you've solved the exercise, or at least after you've attacked it long and hard enough to have a slight headache.

Looping a Triangle

Write a loop that makes seven calls to `console.log` to output the following triangle:

```
#
##
###
####
#####
######
#######
```

It may be useful to know that you can find the length of a string by writing `.length` after it.

```
let abc = "abc";
console.log(abc.length);
// → 3
```

FizzBuzz

Write a program that uses `console.log` to print all the numbers from 1 to 100, with two exceptions. For numbers divisible by 3, print "Fizz" instead of the number, and for numbers divisible by 5 (and not 3), print "Buzz" instead.

When you have that working, modify your program to print "FizzBuzz" for numbers that are divisible by both 3 and 5 (and still print "Fizz" or "Buzz" for numbers divisible by only one of those).

(This is actually an interview question that has been claimed to weed out a significant percentage of programmer candidates. So if you solved it, your labor market value just went up.)

Chessboard

Write a program that creates a string that represents an 8×8 grid, using new-line characters to separate lines. At each position of the grid there is either a space or a # character. The characters should form a chessboard.

Passing this string to `console.log` should show something like this:

```
 # # # #
# # # #
 # # # #
# # # #
 # # # #
# # # #
 # # # #
# # # #
```

When you have a program that generates this pattern, define a binding size = 8 and change the program so that it works for any size, outputting a grid of the given width and height.

"People think that computer science is the art of geniuses but the actual reality is the opposite, just many people doing things that build on each other, like a wall of mini stones."

—Donald Knuth

3

FUNCTIONS

Functions are the bread and butter of JavaScript programming. The concept of wrapping a piece of program in a value has many uses. It gives us a way to structure larger programs, to reduce repetition, to associate names with subprograms, and to isolate these subprograms from each other.

The most obvious application of functions is defining new vocabulary. Creating new words in prose is usually bad style. But in programming, it is indispensable.

Typical adult English speakers have some 20,000 words in their vocabulary. Few programming languages come with 20,000 commands built in. And the vocabulary that *is* available tends to be more precisely defined, and thus less flexible, than in human language. Therefore, we usually *have* to introduce new concepts to avoid repeating ourselves too much.

Defining a Function

A function definition is a regular binding where the value of the binding is a function. For example, the following code defines square to refer to a function that produces the square of a given number.

```
const square = function(x) {
  return x * x;
};

console.log(square(12));
// → 144
```

A function is created with an expression that starts with the keyword function. Functions have a set of *parameters* (in this case, only x) and a *body*, which contains the statements that are to be executed when the function is called. The function body of a function created this way must always be wrapped in braces, even when it consists of only a single statement.

A function can have multiple parameters or no parameters at all. In the following example, makeNoise does not list any parameter names, whereas power lists two:

```
const makeNoise = function() {
  console.log("Pling!");
};

makeNoise();
// → Pling!

const power = function(base, exponent) {
  let result = 1;
  for (let count = 0; count < exponent; count++) {
    result *= base;
  }
  return result;
};

console.log(power(2, 10));
// → 1024
```

Some functions produce a value, such as power and square, and some don't, such as makeNoise, whose only result is a side effect. A return statement determines the value the function returns. When control comes across such a statement, it immediately jumps out of the current function and gives the returned value to the code that called the function. A return keyword without an expression after it will cause the function to return undefined. Functions that don't have a return statement at all, such as makeNoise, similarly return undefined.

Parameters to a function behave like regular bindings, but their initial values are given by the *caller* of the function, not the code in the function itself.

Bindings and Scopes

Each binding has a *scope*, which is the part of the program in which the binding is visible. For bindings defined outside of any function or block, the scope is the whole program—you can refer to such bindings wherever you want. These are called *global*.

But bindings created for function parameters or declared inside a function can be referenced only in that function, so they are known as *local* bindings. Every time the function is called, new instances of these bindings are created. This provides some isolation between functions—each function call acts in its own little world (its local environment) and can often be understood without knowing a lot about what's going on in the global environment.

Bindings declared with let and const are in fact local to the *block* that they are declared in, so if you create one of those inside of a loop, the code before and after the loop cannot "see" it. In pre-2015 JavaScript, only functions created new scopes, so old-style bindings, created with the var keyword, are visible throughout the whole function that they appear in—or throughout the global scope, if they are not in a function.

```
let x = 10;
if (true) {
  let y = 20;
  var z = 30;
  console.log(x + y + z);
  // → 60
}
// y is not visible here
console.log(x + z);
// → 40
```

Each scope can "look out" into the scope around it, so x is visible inside the block in the example. The exception is when multiple bindings have the same name—in that case, code can see only the innermost one. For example, when the code inside the halve function refers to n, it is seeing its *own* n, not the global n.

```
const halve = function(n) {
  return n / 2;
};

let n = 10;
console.log(halve(100));
// → 50
console.log(n);
// → 10
```

Nested Scope

JavaScript distinguishes not just *global* and *local* bindings. Blocks and functions can be created inside other blocks and functions, producing multiple degrees of locality.

For example, this function—which outputs the ingredients needed to make a batch of hummus—has another function inside it:

```javascript
const hummus = function(factor) {
  const ingredient = function(amount, unit, name) {
    let ingredientAmount = amount * factor;
    if (ingredientAmount > 1) {
      unit += "s";
    }
    console.log(`${ingredientAmount} ${unit} ${name}`);
  };
  ingredient(1, "can", "chickpeas");
  ingredient(0.25, "cup", "tahini");
  ingredient(0.25, "cup", "lemon juice");
  ingredient(1, "clove", "garlic");
  ingredient(2, "tablespoon", "olive oil");
  ingredient(0.5, "teaspoon", "cumin");
};
```

The code inside the ingredient function can see the factor binding from the outer function. But its local bindings, such as unit or ingredientAmount, are not visible in the outer function.

The set of bindings visible inside a block is determined by the place of that block in the program text. Each local scope can also see all the local scopes that contain it, and all scopes can see the global scope. This approach to binding visibility is called *lexical scoping*.

Functions as Values

A function binding usually just acts as a name for a specific piece of the program. Such a binding is defined once and never changed. This makes it easy to confuse the function and its name.

But the two are different. A function value can do all the things that other values can do—you can use it in arbitrary expressions, not just call it. It is possible to store a function value in a new binding, pass it as an argument to a function, and so on. Similarly, a binding that holds a function is still just a regular binding and can, if not constant, be assigned a new value, like so:

```javascript
let launchMissiles = function() {
  missileSystem.launch("now");
};
if (safeMode) {
```

```
  launchMissiles = function() {/* do nothing */};
}
```

In Chapter 5, we will discuss the interesting things that can be done by passing around function values to other functions.

Declaration Notation

There is a slightly shorter way to create a function binding. When the function keyword is used at the start of a statement, it works differently.

```
function square(x) {
  return x * x;
}
```

This is a function *declaration*. The statement defines the binding square and points it at the given function. It is slightly easier to write and doesn't require a semicolon after the function.

There is one subtlety with this form of function definition.

```
console.log("The future says:", future());

function future() {
  return "You'll never have flying cars";
}
```

The preceding code works, even though the function is defined *below* the code that uses it. Function declarations are not part of the regular top-to-bottom flow of control. They are conceptually moved to the top of their scope and can be used by all the code in that scope. This is sometimes useful because it offers the freedom to order code in a way that seems meaningful, without worrying about having to define all functions before they are used.

Arrow Functions

There's a third notation for functions, which looks very different from the others. Instead of the function keyword, it uses an arrow (=>) made up of an equal sign and a greater-than character (not to be confused with the greater-than-or-equal operator, which is written >=).

```
const power = (base, exponent) => {
  let result = 1;
  for (let count = 0; count < exponent; count++) {
    result *= base;
  }
  return result;
};
```

The arrow comes *after* the list of parameters and is followed by the function's body. It expresses something like "this input (the parameters) produces this result (the body)."

When there is only one parameter name, you can omit the parentheses around the parameter list. If the body is a single expression, rather than a block in braces, that expression will be returned from the function. So, these two definitions of square do the same thing:

```
const square1 = (x) => { return x * x; };
const square2 = x => x * x;
```

When an arrow function has no parameters at all, its parameter list is just an empty set of parentheses.

```
const horn = () => {
  console.log("Toot");
};
```

There's no deep reason to have both arrow functions and `function` expressions in the language. Apart from a minor detail, which we'll discuss in Chapter 6, they do the same thing. Arrow functions were added in 2015, mostly to make it possible to write small function expressions in a less verbose way. We'll be using them a lot in Chapter 5.

The Call Stack

The way control flows through functions is somewhat involved. Let's take a closer look at it. Here is a simple program that makes a few function calls:

```
function greet(who) {
  console.log("Hello " + who);
}
greet("Harry");
console.log("Bye");
```

A run through this program goes roughly like this: the call to greet causes control to jump to the start of that function (line 2). The function calls console.log, which takes control, does its job, and then returns control to line 2. There it reaches the end of the greet function, so it returns to the place that called it, which is line 4. The line after that calls console.log again. After that returns, the program reaches its end.

We could show the flow of control schematically like this:

```
not in function
  in greet
      in console.log
  in greet
not in function
```

```
in console.log
not in function
```

Because a function has to jump back to the place that called it when it returns, the computer must remember the context from which the call happened. In one case, `console.log` has to return to the greet function when it is done. In the other case, it returns to the end of the program.

The place where the computer stores this context is the *call stack*. Every time a function is called, the current context is stored on top of this stack. When a function returns, it removes the top context from the stack and uses that context to continue execution.

Storing this stack requires space in the computer's memory. When the stack grows too big, the computer will fail with a message like "out of stack space" or "too much recursion." The following code illustrates this by asking the computer a really hard question that causes an infinite back-and-forth between two functions. Rather, it *would* be infinite, if the computer had an infinite stack. As it is, we will run out of space, or "blow the stack."

```
function chicken() {
  return egg();
}
function egg() {
  return chicken();
}
console.log(chicken() + " came first.");
// → ??
```

Optional Arguments

The following code is allowed and executes without any problem:

```
function square(x) { return x * x; }
console.log(square(4, true, "hedgehog"));
// → 16
```

We defined square with only one parameter. Yet when we call it with three, the language doesn't complain. It ignores the extra arguments and computes the square of the first one.

JavaScript is extremely broad-minded about the number of arguments you pass to a function. If you pass too many, the extra ones are ignored. If you pass too few, the missing parameters get assigned the value undefined.

The downside of this is that it is possible—likely, even—that you'll accidentally pass the wrong number of arguments to functions. And no one will tell you about it.

The upside is that this behavior can be used to allow a function to be called with different numbers of arguments. For example, the following minus function tries to imitate the - operator by acting on either one or two arguments:

```
function minus(a, b) {
  if (b === undefined) return -a;
  else return a - b;
}

console.log(minus(10));
// → -10
console.log(minus(10, 5));
// → 5
```

If you write an = operator after a parameter, followed by an expression, the value of that expression will replace the argument when it is not given.

For example, this version of power makes its second argument optional. If you don't provide it or pass the value undefined, it will default to two, and the function will behave like square.

```
function power(base, exponent = 2) {
  let result = 1;
  for (let count = 0; count < exponent; count++) {
    result *= base;
  }
  return result;
}

console.log(power(4));
// → 16
console.log(power(2, 6));
// → 64
```

In the next chapter, we will see a way in which a function body can get at the whole list of arguments it was passed (see "Rest Parameters" on page 74). This is helpful because it makes it possible for a function to accept any number of arguments. For example, console.log does this—it outputs all of the values it is given.

```
console.log("C", "O", 2);
// → C O 2
```

Closure

The ability to treat functions as values, combined with the fact that local bindings are re-created every time a function is called, brings up an interesting question. What happens to local bindings when the function call that created them is no longer active?

The following code shows an example of this. It defines a function, `wrapValue`, that creates a local binding. It then returns a function that accesses and returns this local binding.

```
function wrapValue(n) {
  let local = n;
  return () => local;
}

let wrap1 = wrapValue(1);
let wrap2 = wrapValue(2);
console.log(wrap1());
// → 1
console.log(wrap2());
// → 2
```

This is allowed and works as you'd hope—both instances of the binding can still be accessed. This situation is a good demonstration of the fact that local bindings are created anew for every call, and different calls can't trample on one another's local bindings.

This feature—being able to reference a specific instance of a local binding in an enclosing scope—is called *closure*. A function that references bindings from local scopes around it is called *a* closure. This behavior not only frees you from having to worry about lifetimes of bindings but also makes it possible to use function values in some creative ways.

With a slight change, we can turn the previous example into a way to create functions that multiply by an arbitrary amount.

```
function multiplier(factor) {
  return number => number * factor;
}

let twice = multiplier(2);
console.log(twice(5));
// → 10
```

The explicit `local` binding from the `wrapValue` example isn't really needed since a parameter is itself a local binding.

Thinking about programs like this takes some practice. A good mental model is to think of function values as containing both the code in their body and the environment in which they are created. When called, the function body sees the environment in which it was created, not the environment in which it is called.

In the example, `multiplier` is called and creates an environment in which its factor parameter is bound to 2. The function value it returns, which is stored in `twice`, remembers this environment. So when that is called, it multiplies its argument by 2.

Recursion

It is perfectly okay for a function to call itself, as long as it doesn't do it so often that it overflows the stack. A function that calls itself is called *recursive*. Recursion allows some functions to be written in a different style. Take, for example, this alternative implementation of power:

```
function power(base, exponent) {
  if (exponent == 0) {
    return 1;
  } else {
    return base * power(base, exponent - 1);
  }
}

console.log(power(2, 3));
// → 8
```

This is rather close to the way mathematicians define exponentiation and arguably describes the concept more clearly than the looping variant. The function calls itself multiple times with ever smaller exponents to achieve the repeated multiplication.

But this implementation has one problem: in typical JavaScript implementations, it's about three times slower than the looping version. Running through a simple loop is generally cheaper than calling a function multiple times.

The dilemma of speed versus elegance is an interesting one. You can see it as a kind of continuum between human-friendliness and machine-friendliness. Almost any program can be made faster by making it bigger and more convoluted. The programmer has to decide on an appropriate balance.

In the case of the power function, the inelegant (looping) version is still fairly simple and easy to read. It doesn't make much sense to replace it with the recursive version. Often, though, a program deals with such complex concepts that giving up some efficiency in order to make the program more straightforward is helpful.

Worrying about efficiency can be a distraction. It's yet another factor that complicates program design, and when you're doing something that's already difficult, that extra thing to worry about can be paralyzing.

Therefore, always start by writing something that's correct and easy to understand. If you're worried that it's too slow—which it usually isn't since most code simply isn't executed often enough to take any significant amount of time—you can measure afterward and improve it if necessary.

Recursion is not always just an inefficient alternative to looping. Some problems really are easier to solve with recursion than with loops. Most often these are problems that require exploring or processing several "branches," each of which might branch out again into even more branches.

Consider this puzzle: by starting from the number 1 and repeatedly either adding 5 or multiplying by 3, an infinite set of numbers can be produced. How would you write a function that, given a number, tries to find a sequence of such additions and multiplications that produces that number?

For example, the number 13 could be reached by first multiplying by 3 and then adding 5 twice, whereas the number 15 cannot be reached at all.

Here is a recursive solution:

```
function findSolution(target) {
  function find(current, history) {
    if (current == target) {
      return history;
    } else if (current > target) {
      return null;
    } else {
      return find(current + 5, `(${history} + 5)`) ||
             find(current * 3, `(${history} * 3)`);
    }
  }
  return find(1, "1");
}

console.log(findSolution(24));
// → (((1 * 3) + 5) * 3)
```

Note that this program doesn't necessarily find the *shortest* sequence of operations. It is satisfied when it finds any sequence at all.

It is okay if you don't see how it works right away. Let's work through it, since it makes for a great exercise in recursive thinking.

The inner function find does the actual recursing. It takes two arguments: the current number and a string that records how we reached this number. If it finds a solution, it returns a string that shows how to get to the target. If no solution can be found starting from this number, it returns null.

To do this, the function performs one of three actions. If the current number is the target number, the current history is a way to reach that target, so it is returned. If the current number is greater than the target, there's no sense in further exploring this branch because both adding and multiplying will only make the number bigger, so it returns null. Finally, if we're still below the target number, the function tries both possible paths that start from the current number by calling itself twice, once for addition and once for multiplication. If the first call returns something that is not null, it is returned. Otherwise, the second call is returned, regardless of whether it produces a string or null.

To better understand how this function produces the effect we're looking for, let's look at all the calls to find that are made when searching for a solution for the number 13.

```
find(1, "1")
  find(6, "(1 + 5)")
    find(11, "((1 + 5) + 5)")
      find(16, "(((1 + 5) + 5) + 5)")
        too big
      find(33, "(((1 + 5) + 5) * 3)")
        too big
    find(18, "((1 + 5) * 3)")
      too big
  find(3, "(1 * 3)")
    find(8, "((1 * 3) + 5)")
      find(13, "(((1 * 3) + 5) + 5)")
        found!
```

The indentation indicates the depth of the call stack. The first time find is called, it starts by calling itself to explore the solution that starts with (1 + 5). That call will further recurse to explore *every* continued solution that yields a number less than or equal to the target number. Since it doesn't find one that hits the target, it returns null back to the first call. There the || operator causes the call that explores (1 * 3) to happen. This search has more luck—its first recursive call, through yet *another* recursive call, hits upon the target number. That innermost call returns a string, and each of the || operators in the intermediate calls passes that string along, ultimately returning the solution.

Growing Functions

There are two more or less natural ways for functions to be introduced into programs.

The first is that you find yourself writing similar code multiple times. You'd prefer not to do that. Having more code means more space for mistakes to hide and more material to read for people trying to understand the program. So you take the repeated functionality, find a good name for it, and put it into a function.

The second way is that you find you need some functionality that you haven't written yet and that sounds like it deserves its own function. You'll start by naming the function, and then you'll write its body. You might even start writing code that uses the function before you actually define the function itself.

How difficult it is to find a good name for a function is a good indication of how clear a concept it is that you're trying to wrap. Let's go through an example.

We want to write a program that prints two numbers: the numbers of cows and chickens on a farm, with the words Cows and Chickens after them and zeros padded before both numbers so that they are always three digits long.

```
007 Cows
011 Chickens
```

This asks for a function of two arguments—the number of cows and the number of chickens. Let's get coding.

```javascript
function printFarmInventory(cows, chickens) {
  let cowString = String(cows);
  while (cowString.length < 3) {
    cowString = "0" + cowString;
  }
  console.log(`${cowString} Cows`);
  let chickenString = String(chickens);
  while (chickenString.length < 3) {
    chickenString = "0" + chickenString;
  }
  console.log(`${chickenString} Chickens`);
}
printFarmInventory(7, 11);
```

Writing .length after a string expression will give us the length of that string. Thus, the while loops keep adding zeros in front of the number strings until they are at least three characters long.

Mission accomplished! But just as we are about to send the farmer the code (along with a hefty invoice), she calls and tells us she's also started keeping pigs, and couldn't we please extend the software to also print pigs?

We sure can. But just as we're in the process of copying and pasting those four lines one more time, we stop and reconsider. There has to be a better way. Here's a first attempt:

```javascript
function printZeroPaddedWithLabel(number, label) {
  let numberString = String(number);
  while (numberString.length < 3) {
    numberString = "0" + numberString;
  }
  console.log(`${numberString} ${label}`);
}

function printFarmInventory(cows, chickens, pigs) {
  printZeroPaddedWithLabel(cows, "Cows");
  printZeroPaddedWithLabel(chickens, "Chickens");
  printZeroPaddedWithLabel(pigs, "Pigs");
}

printFarmInventory(7, 11, 3);
```

It works! But that name, `printZeroPaddedWithLabel`, is a little awkward. It conflates three things—printing, zero-padding, and adding a label—into a single function.

Instead of lifting out the repeated part of our program wholesale, let's try to pick out a single *concept*.

```
function zeroPad(number, width) {
  let string = String(number);
  while (string.length < width) {
    string = "0" + string;
  }
  return string;
}

function printFarmInventory(cows, chickens, pigs) {
  console.log(`${zeroPad(cows, 3)} Cows`);
  console.log(`${zeroPad(chickens, 3)} Chickens`);
  console.log(`${zeroPad(pigs, 3)} Pigs`);
}

printFarmInventory(7, 16, 3);
```

A function with a nice, obvious name like `zeroPad` makes it easier for someone who reads the code to figure out what it does. And such a function is useful in more situations than just this specific program. For example, you could use it to help print nicely aligned tables of numbers.

How smart and versatile *should* our function be? We could write anything, from a terribly simple function that can only pad a number to be three characters wide to a complicated generalized number-formatting system that handles fractional numbers, negative numbers, alignment of decimal dots, padding with different characters, and so on.

A useful principle is to not add cleverness unless you are absolutely sure you're going to need it. It can be tempting to write general "frameworks" for every bit of functionality you come across. Resist that urge. You won't get any real work done—you'll just be writing code that you never use.

Functions and Side Effects

Functions can be roughly divided into those that are called for their side effects and those that are called for their return value. (Though it is definitely also possible to both have side effects and return a value.)

The first helper function in the farm example, `printZeroPaddedWithLabel`, is called for its side effect: it prints a line. The second version, `zeroPad`, is called for its return value. It is no coincidence that the second is useful in more situations than the first. Functions that create values are easier to combine in new ways than functions that directly perform side effects.

A *pure* function is a specific kind of value-producing function that not only has no side effects but also doesn't rely on side effects from other code—for example, it doesn't read global bindings whose value might change. A pure function has the pleasant property that, when called with the same arguments, it always produces the same value (and doesn't do anything else). A call to such a function can be substituted by its return value without changing the meaning of the code. When you are not sure that a pure function is working correctly, you can test it by simply calling it and know that if it works in that context, it will work in any context. Nonpure functions tend to require more scaffolding to test.

Still, there's no need to feel bad when writing functions that are not pure or to wage a holy war to purge them from your code. Side effects are often useful. There'd be no way to write a pure version of console.log, for example, and console.log is good to have. Some operations are also easier to express in an efficient way when we use side effects, so computing speed can be a reason to avoid purity.

Summary

This chapter taught you how to write your own functions. The function keyword, when used as an expression, can create a function value. When used as a statement, it can be used to declare a binding and give it a function as its value. Arrow functions are yet another way to create functions.

```
// Define f to hold a function value
const f = function(a) {
  console.log(a + 2);
};

// Declare g to be a function
function g(a, b) {
  return a * b * 3.5;
}

// A less verbose function value
let h = a => a % 3;
```

A key aspect in understanding functions is understanding scopes. Each block creates a new scope. Parameters and bindings declared in a given scope are local and not visible from the outside. Bindings declared with var behave differently—they end up in the nearest function scope or the global scope.

Separating the tasks your program performs into different functions is helpful. You won't have to repeat yourself as much, and functions can help organize a program by grouping code into pieces that do specific things.

Exercises

Minimum

Chapter 2 introduced the standard function Math.min, which returns its smallest argument (see "Return Values" on page 27). We can build something like that now. Write a function min that takes two arguments and returns their minimum.

Recursion

We've seen that % (the remainder operator) can be used to test whether a number is even or odd by using % 2 to see whether it's divisible by two. Here's another way to define whether a positive whole number is even or odd:

- Zero is even.
- One is odd.
- For any other number N, its evenness is the same as $N - 2$.

Define a recursive function isEven corresponding to this description. The function should accept a single parameter (a positive, whole number) and return a Boolean.

Test it on 50 and 75. See how it behaves on −1. Why? Can you think of a way to fix this?

Bean Counting

You can get the Nth character, or letter, from a string by writing "string"[N]. The returned value will be a string containing only one character (for example, "b"). The first character has position 0, which causes the last one to be found at position string.length - 1. In other words, a two-character string has length 2, and its characters have positions 0 and 1.

Write a function countBs that takes a string as its only argument and returns a number that indicates how many uppercase "B" characters there are in the string.

Next, write a function called countChar that behaves like countBs, except it takes a second argument that indicates the character that is to be counted (rather than counting only uppercase "B" characters). Rewrite countBs to make use of this new function.

"On two occasions I have been asked, 'Pray, Mr. Babbage, if you put into the machine wrong figures, will the right answers come out?' . . . I am not able rightly to apprehend the kind of confusion of ideas that could provoke such a question."

—Charles Babbage,
Passages from the Life of a Philosopher (1864)

4

DATA STRUCTURES: OBJECTS AND ARRAYS

Numbers, Booleans, and strings are the atoms that data structures are built from. Many types of information require more than one atom, though. *Objects* allow us to group values—including other objects—to build more complex structures.

The programs we have built so far have been limited by the fact that they were operating only on simple data types. This chapter will introduce basic data structures. By the end of it, you'll know enough to start writing useful programs.

The chapter will work through a more or less realistic programming example, introducing concepts as they apply to the problem at hand. The example code will often build on functions and bindings that were introduced earlier in the text.

The online coding sandbox for the book (*https://eloquentjavascript.net/code*) provides a way to run code in the context of a specific chapter. If you decide to work through the examples in another environment, be sure to first download the full code for this chapter from the sandbox page.

The Weresquirrel

Every now and then, usually between 8 PM and 10 PM, Jacques finds himself transforming into a small furry rodent with a bushy tail.

On one hand, Jacques is quite glad that he doesn't have classic lycanthropy. Turning into a squirrel does cause fewer problems than turning into a wolf. Instead of having to worry about accidentally eating the neighbor (*that* would be awkward), he worries about being eaten by the neighbor's cat. After two occasions where he woke up on a precariously thin branch in the crown of an oak, naked and disoriented, he has taken to locking the doors and windows of his room at night and putting a few walnuts on the floor to keep himself busy.

That takes care of the cat and tree problems. But Jacques would prefer to get rid of his condition entirely. The irregular occurrences of the transformation make him suspect that they might be triggered by something. For a while, he believed that it happened only on days when he had been near oak trees. But avoiding oak trees did not stop the problem.

Switching to a more scientific approach, Jacques has started keeping a daily log of everything he does on a given day and whether he changed form. With this data he hopes to narrow down the conditions that trigger the transformations.

The first thing he needs is a data structure to store this information.

Data Sets

To work with a chunk of digital data, we'll first have to find a way to represent it in our machine's memory. Say, for example, that we want to represent a collection of the numbers 2, 3, 5, 7, and 11.

We could get creative with strings—after all, strings can have any length, so we can put a lot of data into them—and use "2 3 5 7 11" as our representation. But this is awkward. You'd have to somehow extract the digits and convert them back to numbers to access them.

Fortunately, JavaScript provides a data type specifically for storing sequences of values. It is called an *array* and is written as a list of values between square brackets, separated by commas.

```
let listOfNumbers = [2, 3, 5, 7, 11];
console.log(listOfNumbers[2]);
// → 5
console.log(listOfNumbers[0]);
// → 2
console.log(listOfNumbers[2 - 1]);
// → 3
```

The notation for getting at the elements inside an array also uses square brackets. A pair of square brackets immediately after an expression, with another expression inside of them, will look up the element in the left-hand expression that corresponds to the *index* given by the expression in the brackets.

The first index of an array is zero, not one. So the first element is retrieved with `listOfNumbers[0]`. Zero-based counting has a long tradition in technology and in certain ways makes a lot of sense, but it takes some getting used to. Think of the index as the amount of items to skip, counting from the start of the array.

Properties

We've seen a few suspicious-looking expressions like `myString.length` (to get the length of a string) and `Math.max` (the maximum function) in past chapters. These are expressions that access a *property* of some value. In the first case, we access the `length` property of the value in `myString`. In the second, we access the property named `max` in the `Math` object (which is a collection of mathematics-related constants and functions).

Almost all JavaScript values have properties. The exceptions are `null` and `undefined`. If you try to access a property on one of these nonvalues, you get an error.

```
null.length;
// → TypeError: null has no properties
```

The two main ways to access properties in JavaScript are with a dot and with square brackets. Both `value.x` and `value[x]` access a property on value—but not necessarily the same property. The difference is in how x is interpreted. When using a dot, the word after the dot is the literal name of the property. When using square brackets, the expression between the brackets is *evaluated* to get the property name. Whereas `value.x` fetches the property of value named "x," `value[x]` tries to evaluate the expression x and uses the result, converted to a string, as the property name.

So if you know that the property you are interested in is called *color*, you say `value.color`. If you want to extract the property named by the value held in the binding i, you say `value[i]`. Property names are strings. They can be any string, but the dot notation works only with names that look like valid binding names. So if you want to access a property named *2* or *John Doe*, you must use square brackets: `value[2]` or `value["John Doe"]`.

The elements in an array are stored as the array's properties, using numbers as property names. Because you can't use the dot notation with numbers and usually want to use a binding that holds the index anyway, you have to use the bracket notation to get at them.

The `length` property of an array tells us how many elements it has. This property name is a valid binding name, and we know its name in advance, so to find the length of an array, you typically write `array.length` because that's easier to write than `array["length"]`.

Methods

Both string and array objects contain, in addition to the length property, a number of properties that hold function values.

```
let doh = "Doh";
console.log(typeof doh.toUpperCase);
// → function
console.log(doh.toUpperCase());
// → DOH
```

Every string has a toUpperCase property. When called, it will return a copy of the string in which all letters have been converted to uppercase. There is also toLowerCase, going the other way.

Interestingly, even though the call to toUpperCase does not pass any arguments, the function somehow has access to the string "Doh", the value whose property we called. How this works is described in "Methods" on page 98.

Properties that contain functions are generally called *methods* of the value they belong to, as in "toUpperCase is a method of a string."

This example demonstrates two methods you can use to manipulate arrays:

```
let sequence = [1, 2, 3];
sequence.push(4);
sequence.push(5);
console.log(sequence);
// → [1, 2, 3, 4, 5]
console.log(sequence.pop());
// → 5
console.log(sequence);
// → [1, 2, 3, 4]
```

The push method adds values to the end of an array, and the pop method does the opposite, removing the last value in the array and returning it.

These somewhat silly names are the traditional terms for operations on a *stack*. A stack, in programming, is a data structure that allows you to push values into it and pop them out again in the opposite order so that the thing that was added last is removed first. These are common in programming—you might remember the function call stack from "The Call Stack" on page 46, which is an instance of the same idea.

Objects

Back to the weresquirrel. A set of daily log entries can be represented as an array. But the entries do not consist of just a number or a string—each entry needs to store a list of activities and a Boolean value that indicates whether Jacques turned into a squirrel or not. Ideally, we would like to group these together into a single value and then put those grouped values into an array of log entries.

Values of the type *object* are arbitrary collections of properties. One way to create an object is by using braces as an expression.

```
let day1 = {
  squirrel: false,
  events: ["work", "touched tree", "pizza", "running"]
};
console.log(day1.squirrel);
// → false
console.log(day1.wolf);
// → undefined
day1.wolf = false;
console.log(day1.wolf);
// → false
```

Inside the braces, there is a list of properties separated by commas. Each property has a name followed by a colon and a value. When an object is written over multiple lines, indenting it like in the example helps with readability. Properties whose names aren't valid binding names or valid numbers have to be quoted.

```
let descriptions = {
  work: "Went to work",
  "touched tree": "Touched a tree"
};
```

This means that braces have *two* meanings in JavaScript. At the start of a statement, they start a block of statements. In any other position, they describe an object. Fortunately, it is rarely useful to start a statement with an object in braces, so the ambiguity between these two is not much of a problem.

Reading a property that doesn't exist will give you the value undefined.

It is possible to assign a value to a property expression with the = operator. This will replace the property's value if it already existed or create a new property on the object if it didn't.

To briefly return to our tentacle model of bindings—property bindings are similar. They *grasp* values, but other bindings and properties might be holding onto those same values. You may think of objects as octopuses with any number of tentacles, each of which has a name tattooed on it.

The delete operator cuts off a tentacle from such an octopus. It is a unary operator that, when applied to an object property, will remove the named property from the object. This is not a common thing to do, but it is possible.

```
let anObject = {left: 1, right: 2};
console.log(anObject.left);
```

```
// → 1
delete anObject.left;
console.log(anObject.left);
// → undefined
console.log("left" in anObject);
// → false
console.log("right" in anObject);
// → true
```

The binary in operator, when applied to a string and an object, tells you whether that object has a property with that name. The difference between setting a property to undefined and actually deleting it is that, in the first case, the object still *has* the property (it just doesn't have a very interesting value), whereas in the second case the property is no longer present and in will return false.

To find out what properties an object has, you can use the Object.keys function. You give it an object, and it returns an array of strings—the object's property names.

```
console.log(Object.keys({x: 0, y: 0, z: 2}));
// → ["x", "y", "z"]
```

There's an Object.assign function that copies all properties from one object into another.

```
let objectA = {a: 1, b: 2};
Object.assign(objectA, {b: 3, c: 4});
console.log(objectA);
// → {a: 1, b: 3, c: 4}
```

Arrays, then, are just a kind of object specialized for storing sequences of things. If you evaluate typeof [], it produces "object". You can see them as long, flat octopuses with all their tentacles in a neat row, labeled with numbers.

We will represent the journal that Jacques keeps as an array of objects.

```
let journal = [
  {events: ["work", "touched tree", "pizza",
            "running", "television"],
   squirrel: false},
  {events: ["work", "ice cream", "cauliflower",
            "lasagna", "touched tree", "brushed teeth"],
   squirrel: false},
  {events: ["weekend", "cycling", "break", "peanuts",
            "beer"],
   squirrel: true},
  /* and so on... */
];
```

Mutability

We will get to actual programming *real* soon now. First there's one more piece of theory to understand.

We saw that object values can be modified. The types of values discussed in earlier chapters, such as numbers, strings, and Booleans, are all *immutable*—it is impossible to change values of those types. You can combine them and derive new values from them, but when you take a specific string value, that value will always remain the same. The text inside it cannot be changed. If you have a string that contains "cat", it is not possible for other code to change a character in your string to make it spell "rat".

Objects work differently. You *can* change their properties, causing a single object value to have different content at different times.

When we have two numbers, 120 and 120, we can consider them precisely the same number, whether or not they refer to the same physical bits. With objects, there is a difference between having two references to the same object and having two different objects that contain the same properties. Consider the following code:

```
let object1 = {value: 10};
let object2 = object1;
let object3 = {value: 10};

console.log(object1 == object2);
// → true
console.log(object1 == object3);
// → false

object1.value = 15;
console.log(object2.value);
// → 15
console.log(object3.value);
// → 10
```

The object1 and object2 bindings grasp the *same* object, which is why changing object1 also changes the value of object2. They are said to have the same *identity*. The binding object3 points to a different object, which initially contains the same properties as object1 but lives a separate life.

Bindings can also be changeable or constant, but this is separate from the way their values behave. Even though number values don't change, you can use a let binding to keep track of a changing number by changing the value the binding points at. Similarly, though a const binding to an object can itself not be changed and will continue to point at the same object, the *contents* of that object might change.

```
const score = {visitors: 0, home: 0};
// This is okay
score.visitors = 1;
```

```
// This isn't allowed
score = {visitors: 1, home: 1};
```

When you compare objects with JavaScript's == operator, it compares by identity: it will produce true only if both objects are precisely the same value. Comparing different objects will return false, even if they have identical properties. There is no "deep" comparison operation built into JavaScript, which compares objects by contents, but it is possible to write it yourself (which is one of the exercises at the end of this chapter).

The Lycanthrope's Log

So, Jacques starts up his JavaScript interpreter and sets up the environment he needs to keep his journal.

```
let journal = [];

function addEntry(events, squirrel) {
  journal.push({events, squirrel});
}
```

Note that the object added to the journal looks a little odd. Instead of declaring properties like events: events, it just gives a property name. This is shorthand that means the same thing—if a property name in brace notation isn't followed by a value, its value is taken from the binding with the same name.

So then, every evening at 10 PM—or sometimes the next morning, after climbing down from the top shelf of his bookcase—Jacques records the day.

```
addEntry(["work", "touched tree", "pizza", "running",
          "television"], false);
addEntry(["work", "ice cream", "cauliflower", "lasagna",
          "touched tree", "brushed teeth"], false);
addEntry(["weekend", "cycling", "break", "peanuts",
          "beer"], true);
```

Once he has enough data points, he intends to use statistics to find out which of these events may be related to the squirrelifications.

Correlation is a measure of dependence between statistical variables. A statistical variable is not quite the same as a programming variable. In statistics you typically have a set of *measurements*, and each variable is measured for every measurement. Correlation between variables is usually expressed as a value that ranges from −1 to 1. Zero correlation means the variables are not related. A correlation of 1 indicates that the two are perfectly related—if you know one, you also know the other. A correlation of −1 also means that the variables are perfectly related but that they are opposites—when one is true, the other is false.

To compute the measure of correlation between two Boolean variables, we can use the *phi coefficient* (ϕ). This is a formula whose input is a frequency table containing the number of times the different combinations of the variables were observed. The output of the formula is a number between -1 and 1 that describes the correlation.

We could take the event of eating pizza and put that in a frequency table like this, where each number indicates the amount of times that combination occurred in our measurements:

If we call that table n, we can compute ϕ using the following formula:

$$\phi = \frac{n_{11}n_{00} - n_{10}n_{01}}{\sqrt{n_{1\bullet}n_{0\bullet}n_{\bullet1}n_{\bullet0}}} \tag{4.1}$$

(If at this point you're putting the book down to focus on a terrible flashback to 10th-grade math class—hold on! I do not intend to torture you with endless pages of cryptic notation—it's just this one formula for now. And even with this one, all we do is turn it into JavaScript.)

The notation n_{01} indicates the number of measurements where the first variable (squirrelness) is false (0) and the second variable (pizza) is true (1). In the pizza table, n_{01} is 9.

The value $n_{1\bullet}$ refers to the sum of all measurements where the first variable is true, which is 5 in the example table. Likewise, $n_{\bullet0}$ refers to the sum of the measurements where the second variable is false.

So for the pizza table, the part above the division line (the dividend) would be $1 \times 76 - 4 \times 9 = 40$, and the part below it (the divisor) would be the square root of $5 \times 85 \times 10 \times 80$, or $\sqrt{340000}$. This comes out to $\phi \approx 0.069$, which is tiny. Eating pizza does not appear to have influence on the transformations.

Computing Correlation

We can represent a two-by-two table in JavaScript with a four-element array (`[76, 9, 4, 1]`). We could also use other representations, such as an array containing two two-element arrays (`[[76, 9], [4, 1]]`) or an object with property names like `"11"` and `"01"`, but the flat array is simple and makes the expressions that access the table pleasantly short. We'll interpret the indices to the array as two-bit binary numbers, where the leftmost (most significant) digit refers to the squirrel variable and the rightmost (least significant) digit refers to the event variable. For example, the binary number 10 refers to the case where Jacques did turn into a squirrel, but the event (say, "pizza") didn't occur. This happened four times. And since binary 10 is 2 in decimal notation, we will store this number at index 2 of the array.

This is the function that computes the ϕ coefficient from such an array:

```
function phi(table) {
  return (table[3] * table[0] - table[2] * table[1]) /
    Math.sqrt((table[2] + table[3]) *
              (table[0] + table[1]) *
              (table[1] + table[3]) *
              (table[0] + table[2]));
}

console.log(phi([76, 9, 4, 1]));
// → 0.068599434
```

This is a direct translation of the ϕ formula into JavaScript. Math.sqrt is the square root function, as provided by the Math object in a standard JavaScript environment. We have to add two fields from the table to get fields like $n_{1\bullet}$ because the sums of rows or columns are not stored directly in our data structure.

Jacques kept his journal for three months. The resulting data set is available in the coding sandbox for this chapter (*https://eloquentjavascript.net/code#4*), where it is stored in the JOURNAL binding and in a downloadable file.

To extract a two-by-two table for a specific event from the journal, we must loop over all the entries and tally how many times the event occurs in relation to squirrel transformations.

```
function tableFor(event, journal) {
  let table = [0, 0, 0, 0];
  for (let i = 0; i < journal.length; i++) {
    let entry = journal[i], index = 0;
    if (entry.events.includes(event)) index += 1;
    if (entry.squirrel) index += 2;
    table[index] += 1;
  }
  return table;
}

console.log(tableFor("pizza", JOURNAL));
// → [76, 9, 4, 1]
```

Arrays have an includes method that checks whether a given value exists in the array. The function uses that to determine whether the event name it is interested in is part of the event list for a given day.

The body of the loop in tableFor figures out which box in the table each journal entry falls into by checking whether the entry contains the specific event it's interested in and whether the event happens alongside a squirrel incident. The loop then adds one to the correct box in the table.

We now have the tools we need to compute individual correlations. The only step remaining is to find a correlation for every type of event that was recorded and see whether anything stands out.

Array Loops

In the tableFor function, there's a loop like this:

```
for (let i = 0; i < JOURNAL.length; i++) {
  let entry = JOURNAL[i];
  // Do something with entry
}
```

This kind of loop is common in classical JavaScript—going over arrays one element at a time is something that comes up a lot, and to do that you'd run a counter over the length of the array and pick out each element in turn.

There is a simpler way to write such loops in modern JavaScript.

```
for (let entry of JOURNAL) {
  console.log(`${entry.events.length} events.`);
}
```

When a for loop looks like this, with the word of after a variable definition, it will loop over the elements of the value given after of. This works not only for arrays but also for strings and some other data structures. We'll discuss *how* it works in Chapter 6.

The Final Analysis

We need to compute a correlation for every type of event that occurs in the data set. To do that, we first need to *find* every type of event.

```
function journalEvents(journal) {
  let events = [];
  for (let entry of journal) {
    for (let event of entry.events) {
      if (!events.includes(event)) {
        events.push(event);
      }
    }
  }
  return events;
```

```
}

console.log(journalEvents(JOURNAL));
// → ["carrot", "exercise", "weekend", "bread", ...]
```

By going over all the events and adding those that aren't already in there to the events array, the function collects every type of event.

Using that, we can see all the correlations.

```
for (let event of journalEvents(JOURNAL)) {
  console.log(event + ":", phi(tableFor(event, JOURNAL)));
}
// → carrot:   0.0140970969
// → exercise: 0.0685994341
// → weekend:  0.1371988681
// → bread:    -0.0757554019
// → pudding:  -0.0648203724
// and so on...
```

Most correlations seem to lie close to zero. Eating carrots, bread, or pudding apparently does not trigger squirrel-lycanthropy. It *does* seem to occur somewhat more often on weekends. Let's filter the results to show only correlations greater than 0.1 or less than −0.1.

```
for (let event of journalEvents(JOURNAL)) {
  let correlation = phi(tableFor(event, JOURNAL));
  if (correlation > 0.1 || correlation < -0.1) {
    console.log(event + ":", correlation);
  }
}
// → weekend:        0.1371988681
// → brushed teeth: -0.3805211953
// → candy:          0.1296407447
// → work:          -0.1371988681
// → spaghetti:      0.2425356250
// → reading:        0.1106828054
// → peanuts:        0.5902679812
```

Aha! There are two factors with a correlation that's clearly stronger than the others. Eating peanuts has a strong positive effect on the chance of turning into a squirrel, whereas brushing his teeth has a significant negative effect.

Interesting. Let's try something.

```
for (let entry of JOURNAL) {
  if (entry.events.includes("peanuts") &&
      !entry.events.includes("brushed teeth")) {
    entry.events.push("peanut teeth");
```

```
  }
}
console.log(phi(tableFor("peanut teeth", JOURNAL)));
// → 1
```

That's a strong result. The phenomenon occurs precisely when Jacques eats peanuts and fails to brush his teeth. If only he weren't such a slob about dental hygiene, he'd have never even noticed his affliction.

Knowing this, Jacques stops eating peanuts altogether and finds that his transformations don't come back.

For a few years, things go great for Jacques. But at some point he loses his job. Because he lives in a nasty country where having no job means having no medical services, he is forced to take employment with a circus where he performs as *The Incredible Squirrelman*, stuffing his mouth with peanut butter before every show.

One day, fed up with this pitiful existence, Jacques fails to change back into his human form, hops through a crack in the circus tent, and vanishes into the forest. He is never seen again.

Further Arrayology

Before finishing the chapter, I want to introduce you to a few more object-related concepts. I'll start by introducing some generally useful array methods.

We saw push and pop, which add and remove elements at the end of an array, in "Methods" on page 62. The corresponding methods for adding and removing things at the start of an array are called unshift and shift.

```
let todoList = [];
function remember(task) {
  todoList.push(task);
}
function getTask() {
  return todoList.shift();
}
function rememberUrgently(task) {
  todoList.unshift(task);
}
```

That program manages a queue of tasks. You add tasks to the end of the queue by calling remember("groceries"), and when you're ready to do something, you call getTask() to get (and remove) the front item from the queue. The rememberUrgently function also adds a task but adds it to the front instead of the back of the queue.

To search for a specific value, arrays provide an indexOf method. The method searches through the array from the start to the end and returns the index at which the requested value was found—or −1 if it wasn't found.

To search from the end instead of the start, there's a similar method called
lastIndexOf.

```
console.log([1, 2, 3, 2, 1].indexOf(2));
// → 1
console.log([1, 2, 3, 2, 1].lastIndexOf(2));
// → 3
```

Both indexOf and lastIndexOf take an optional second argument that indicates where to start searching.

Another fundamental array method is slice, which takes start and end indices and returns an array that has only the elements between them. The start index is inclusive, the end index exclusive.

```
console.log([0, 1, 2, 3, 4].slice(2, 4));
// → [2, 3]
console.log([0, 1, 2, 3, 4].slice(2));
// → [2, 3, 4]
```

When the end index is not given, slice will take all of the elements after the start index. You can also omit the start index to copy the entire array.

The concat method can be used to glue arrays together to create a new array, similar to what the + operator does for strings.

The following example shows both concat and slice in action. It takes an array and an index, and it returns a new array that is a copy of the original array with the element at the given index removed.

```
function remove(array, index) {
  return array.slice(0, index)
    .concat(array.slice(index + 1));
}
console.log(remove(["a", "b", "c", "d", "e"], 2));
// → ["a", "b", "d", "e"]
```

If you pass concat an argument that is not an array, that value will be added to the new array as if it were a one-element array.

Strings and Their Properties

We can read properties like length and toUpperCase from string values. But if you try to add a new property, it doesn't stick.

```
let kim = "Kim";
kim.age = 88;
console.log(kim.age);
// → undefined
```

Values of type string, number, and Boolean are not objects, and though the language doesn't complain if you try to set new properties on them, it doesn't actually store those properties. As mentioned earlier, such values are immutable and cannot be changed.

But these types do have built-in properties. Every string value has a number of methods. Some very useful ones are slice and indexOf, which resemble the array methods of the same name.

```
console.log("coconuts".slice(4, 7));
// → nut
console.log("coconut".indexOf("u"));
// → 5
```

One difference is that a string's indexOf can search for a string containing more than one character, whereas the corresponding array method looks only for a single element.

```
console.log("one two three".indexOf("ee"));
// → 11
```

The trim method removes whitespace (spaces, newlines, tabs, and similar characters) from the start and end of a string.

```
console.log("  okay \n ".trim());
// → okay
```

The zeroPad function from the previous chapter also exists as a method. It is called padStart and takes the desired length and padding character as arguments.

```
console.log(String(6).padStart(3, "0"));
// → 006
```

You can split a string on every occurrence of another string with split and join it again with join.

```
let sentence = "Secretarybirds specialize in stomping";
let words = sentence.split(" ");
console.log(words);
// → ["Secretarybirds", "specialize", "in", "stomping"]
console.log(words.join(". "));
// → Secretarybirds. specialize. in. stomping
```

A string can be repeated with the repeat method, which creates a new string containing multiple copies of the original string, glued together.

```
console.log("LA".repeat(3));
// → LALALA
```

We have already seen the string type's `length` property. Accessing the individual characters in a string looks like accessing array elements (with a caveat that we'll discuss in "Strings and Character Codes" on page 92).

```
let string = "abc";
console.log(string.length);
// → 3
console.log(string[1]);
// → b
```

Rest Parameters

It can be useful for a function to accept any number of arguments. For example, `Math.max` computes the maximum of *all* the arguments it is given.

To write such a function, you put three dots before the function's last parameter, like this:

```
function max(...numbers) {
  let result = -Infinity;
  for (let number of numbers) {
    if (number > result) result = number;
  }
  return result;
}
console.log(max(4, 1, 9, -2));
// → 9
```

When such a function is called, the *rest parameter* is bound to an array containing all further arguments. If there are other parameters before it, their values aren't part of that array. When, as in `max`, it is the only parameter, it will hold all arguments.

You can use a similar three-dot notation to *call* a function with an array of arguments.

```
let numbers = [5, 1, 7];
console.log(max(...numbers));
// → 7
```

This "spreads" out the array into the function call, passing its elements as separate arguments. It is possible to include an array like that along with other arguments, as in `max(9, ...numbers, 2)`.

Square bracket array notation similarly allows the triple-dot operator to spread another array into the new array.

```
let words = ["never", "fully"];
console.log(["will", ...words, "understand"]);
// → ["will", "never", "fully", "understand"]
```

The Math Object

As we've seen, Math is a grab bag of number-related utility functions, such as Math.max (maximum), Math.min (minimum), and Math.sqrt (square root).

The Math object is used as a container to group a bunch of related functionality. There is only one Math object, and it is almost never useful as a value. Rather, it provides a *namespace* so that all these functions and values do not have to be global bindings.

Having too many global bindings "pollutes" the namespace. The more names have been taken, the more likely you are to accidentally overwrite the value of some existing binding. For example, it's not unlikely to want to name something max in one of your programs. Since JavaScript's built-in max function is tucked safely inside the Math object, we don't have to worry about overwriting it.

Many languages will stop you, or at least warn you, when you are defining a binding with a name that is already taken. JavaScript does this for bindings you declared with let or const but—perversely—not for standard bindings nor for bindings declared with var or function.

Back to the Math object. If you need to do trigonometry, Math can help. It contains cos (cosine), sin (sine), and tan (tangent), as well as their inverse functions, acos, asin, and atan, respectively. The number π (pi)—or at least the closest approximation that fits in a JavaScript number—is available as Math.PI. There is an old programming tradition of writing the names of constant values in all caps.

```
function randomPointOnCircle(radius) {
  let angle = Math.random() * 2 * Math.PI;
  return {x: radius * Math.cos(angle),
          y: radius * Math.sin(angle)};
}
console.log(randomPointOnCircle(2));
// → {x: 0.3667, y: 1.966}
```

If sines and cosines are not something you are familiar with, don't worry. When they are used in this book, in Chapter 14, I'll explain them.

The previous example used Math.random. This is a function that returns a new pseudorandom number between zero (inclusive) and one (exclusive) every time you call it.

```
console.log(Math.random());
// → 0.36993729369714856
console.log(Math.random());
// → 0.727367032552138
console.log(Math.random());
// → 0.40180766698904335
```

Though computers are deterministic machines—they always react the same way if given the same input—it is possible to have them produce numbers that appear random. To do that, the machine keeps some hidden value, and whenever you ask for a new random number, it performs complicated computations on this hidden value to create a new value. It stores a new value and returns some number derived from it. That way, it can produce ever new, hard-to-predict numbers in a way that *seems* random.

If we want a whole random number instead of a fractional one, we can use Math.floor (which rounds down to the nearest whole number) on the result of Math.random.

```
console.log(Math.floor(Math.random() * 10));
// → 2
```

Multiplying the random number by 10 gives us a number greater than or equal to 0 and below 10. Since Math.floor rounds down, this expression will produce, with equal chance, any number from 0 through 9.

There are also the functions Math.ceil (for "ceiling," which rounds up to a whole number), Math.round (to the nearest whole number), and Math.abs, which takes the absolute value of a number, meaning it negates negative values but leaves positive ones as they are.

Destructuring

Let's go back to the phi function for a moment.

```
function phi(table) {
  return (table[3] * table[0] - table[2] * table[1]) /
    Math.sqrt((table[2] + table[3]) *
              (table[0] + table[1]) *
              (table[1] + table[3]) *
              (table[0] + table[2]));
}
```

One of the reasons this function is awkward to read is that we have a binding pointing at our array, but we'd much prefer to have bindings for the *elements* of the array, that is, let n00 = table[0] and so on. Fortunately, there is a succinct way to do this in JavaScript.

```
function phi([n00, n01, n10, n11]) {
  return (n11 * n00 - n10 * n01) /
    Math.sqrt((n10 + n11) * (n00 + n01) *
              (n01 + n11) * (n00 + n10));
}
```

This also works for bindings created with let, var, or const. If you know the value you are binding is an array, you can use square brackets to "look inside" of the value, binding its contents.

A similar trick works for objects, using braces instead of square brackets.

```
let {name} = {name: "Faraji", age: 23};
console.log(name);
// → Faraji
```

Note that if you try to destructure null or undefined, you get an error, much as you would if you directly try to access a property of those values.

JSON

Because properties only grasp their value, rather than contain it, objects and arrays are stored in the computer's memory as sequences of bits holding the *addresses*—the place in memory—of their contents. So an array with another array inside of it consists of (at least) one memory region for the inner array, and another for the outer array, containing (among other things) a binary number that represents the position of the inner array.

If you want to save data in a file for later or send it to another computer over the network, you have to somehow convert these tangles of memory addresses to a description that can be stored or sent. You *could* send over your entire computer memory along with the address of the value you're interested in, I suppose, but that doesn't seem like the best approach.

What we can do is *serialize* the data. That means it is converted into a flat description. A popular serialization format is called *JSON* (pronounced "Jason"), which stands for JavaScript Object Notation. It is widely used as a data storage and communication format on the web, even in languages other than JavaScript.

JSON looks similar to JavaScript's way of writing arrays and objects, with a few restrictions. All property names have to be surrounded by double quotes, and only simple data expressions are allowed—no function calls, bindings, or anything that involves actual computation. Comments are not allowed in JSON.

A journal entry might look like this when represented as JSON data:

```
{
  "squirrel": false,
  "events": ["work", "touched tree", "pizza", "running"]
}
```

JavaScript gives us the functions JSON.stringify and JSON.parse to convert data to and from this format. The first takes a JavaScript value and returns a JSON-encoded string. The second takes such a string and converts it to the value it encodes.

```
let string = JSON.stringify({squirrel: false,
                             events: ["weekend"]});
console.log(string);
// → {"squirrel":false,"events":["weekend"]}
```

```
console.log(JSON.parse(string).events);
// → ["weekend"]
```

Summary

Objects and arrays (which are a specific kind of object) provide ways to group several values into a single value. Conceptually, this allows us to put a bunch of related things in a bag and run around with the bag, instead of wrapping our arms around all of the individual things and trying to hold on to them separately.

Most values in JavaScript have properties, the exceptions being null and undefined. Properties are accessed using value.prop or value["prop"]. Objects tend to use names for their properties and store more or less a fixed set of them. Arrays, on the other hand, usually contain varying amounts of conceptually identical values and use numbers (starting from 0) as the names of their properties.

There *are* some named properties in arrays, such as length and a number of methods. Methods are functions that live in properties and (usually) act on the value they are a property of.

You can iterate over arrays using a special kind of for loop—for (let element of array).

Exercises

The Sum of a Range

The introduction of this book alluded to the following as a nice way to compute the sum of a range of numbers:

```
console.log(sum(range(1, 10)));
```

Write a range function that takes two arguments, start and end, and returns an array containing all the numbers from start up to (and including) end.

Next, write a sum function that takes an array of numbers and returns the sum of these numbers. Run the example program and see whether it does indeed return 55.

As a bonus assignment, modify your range function to take an optional third argument that indicates the "step" value used when building the array. If no step is given, the elements go up by increments of one, corresponding to the old behavior. The function call range(1, 10, 2) should return [1, 3, 5, 7, 9]. Make sure it also works with negative step values so that range(5, 2, -1) produces [5, 4, 3, 2].

Reversing an Array

Arrays have a reverse method that changes the array by inverting the order in which its elements appear. For this exercise, write two functions, reverseArray and reverseArrayInPlace. The first, reverseArray, takes an array as argument and produces a *new* array that has the same elements in the inverse order. The second, reverseArrayInPlace, does what the reverse method does: it *modifies* the array given as argument by reversing its elements. Neither may use the standard reverse method.

Thinking back to the notes about side effects and pure functions in "Functions and Side Effects" on page 54, which variant do you expect to be useful in more situations? Which one runs faster?

A List

Objects, as generic blobs of values, can be used to build all sorts of data structures. A common data structure is the *list* (not to be confused with array). A list is a nested set of objects, with the first object holding a reference to the second, the second to the third, and so on.

```
let list = {
  value: 1,
  rest: {
    value: 2,
    rest: {
      value: 3,
      rest: null
    }
  }
};
```

The resulting objects form a chain, like this:

A nice thing about lists is that they can share parts of their structure. For example, if I create two new values {value: 0, rest: list} and {value: -1, rest: list} (with list referring to the binding defined earlier), they are both independent lists, but they share the structure that makes up their last three elements. The original list is also still a valid three-element list.

Write a function arrayToList that builds up a list structure like the one shown when given [1, 2, 3] as argument. Also write a listToArray function that produces an array from a list. Then add a helper function prepend, which takes an element and a list and creates a new list that adds the element to the front of the input list, and nth, which takes a list and a number and returns the element at the given position in the list (with zero referring to the first element) or undefined when there is no such element.

If you haven't already, also write a recursive version of nth.

Deep Comparison

The == operator compares objects by identity. But sometimes you'd prefer to compare the values of their actual properties.

Write a function deepEqual that takes two values and returns true only if they are the same value or are objects with the same properties, where the values of the properties are equal when compared with a recursive call to deepEqual.

To find out whether values should be compared directly (use the === operator for that) or have their properties compared, you can use the typeof operator. If it produces "object" for both values, you should do a deep comparison. But you have to take one silly exception into account: because of a historical accident, typeof null also produces "object".

The Object.keys function will be useful when you need to go over the properties of objects to compare them.

"There are two ways of constructing a software design: One way is to make it so simple that there are obviously no deficiencies, and the other way is to make it so complicated that there are no obvious deficiencies."

—C.A.R. Hoare,
1980 ACM Turing Award Lecture

HIGHER-ORDER FUNCTIONS

A large program is a costly program, and not just because of the time it takes to build. Size almost always involves complexity, and complexity confuses programmers. Confused programmers, in turn, introduce mistakes (*bugs*) into programs. A large program then provides a lot of space for these bugs to hide, making them hard to find.

Let's briefly go back to the final two example programs in the introduction. The first is self-contained and six lines long.

```
let total = 0, count = 1;
while (count <= 10) {
  total += count;
  count += 1;
}
console.log(total);
```

The second relies on two external functions and is one line long.

```
console.log(sum(range(1, 10)));
```

Which one is more likely to contain a bug?

If we count the size of the definitions of sum and range, the second program is also big—even bigger than the first. But still, I'd argue that it is more likely to be correct.

It is more likely to be correct because the solution is expressed in a vocabulary that corresponds to the problem being solved. Summing a range of numbers isn't about loops and counters. It is about ranges and sums.

The definitions of this vocabulary (the functions sum and range) will still involve loops, counters, and other incidental details. But because they are expressing simpler concepts than the program as a whole, they are easier to get right.

Abstraction

In the context of programming, these kinds of vocabularies are usually called *abstractions*. Abstractions hide details and give us the ability to talk about problems at a higher (or more abstract) level.

As an analogy, compare these two recipes for pea soup. The first one goes like this:

> Put 1 cup of dried peas per person into a container. Add water until the peas are well covered. Leave the peas in water for at least 12 hours. Take the peas out of the water and put them in a cooking pan. Add 4 cups of water per person. Cover the pan and keep the peas simmering for two hours. Take half an onion per person. Cut it into pieces with a knife. Add it to the peas. Take a stalk of celery per person. Cut it into pieces with a knife. Add it to the peas. Take a carrot per person. Cut it into pieces. With a knife! Add it to the peas. Cook for 10 more minutes.

And this is the second recipe:

> Per person: 1 cup dried split peas, half a chopped onion, a stalk of celery, and a carrot.
>
> Soak peas for 12 hours. Simmer for 2 hours in 4 cups of water (per person). Chop and add vegetables. Cook for 10 more minutes.

The second is shorter and easier to interpret. But you do need to understand a few more cooking-related words, such as *soak, simmer, chop,* and, I guess, *vegetable.*

When programming, we can't rely on all the words we need to be waiting for us in the dictionary. Thus, we might fall into the pattern of the first recipe—work out the precise steps the computer has to perform, one by one, blind to the higher-level concepts that they express.

It is a useful skill, in programming, to notice when you are working at too low a level of abstraction.

Abstracting Repetition

Plain functions, as we've seen them so far, are a good way to build abstractions. But sometimes they fall short.

It is common for a program to do something a given number of times. You can write a for loop for that, like this:

```
for (let i = 0; i < 10; i++) {
  console.log(i);
}
```

Can we abstract "doing something *N* times" as a function? Well, it's easy to write a function that calls console.log *N* times.

```
function repeatLog(n) {
  for (let i = 0; i < n; i++) {
    console.log(i);
  }
}
```

But what if we want to do something other than logging the numbers? Since "doing something" can be represented as a function and functions are just values, we can pass our action as a function value.

```
function repeat(n, action) {
  for (let i = 0; i < n; i++) {
    action(i);
  }
}

repeat(3, console.log);
// → 0
// → 1
// → 2
```

We don't have to pass a predefined function to repeat. Often, it is easier to create a function value on the spot instead.

```
let labels = [];
repeat(5, i => {
  labels.push(`Unit ${i + 1}`);
});
console.log(labels);
// → ["Unit 1", "Unit 2", "Unit 3", "Unit 4", "Unit 5"]
```

This is structured a little like a for loop—it first describes the kind of loop and then provides a body. However, the body is now written as a function value, which is wrapped in the parentheses of the call to repeat. This is why it has to be closed with the closing brace *and* closing parenthesis. In cases like this example, where the body is a single small expression, you could also omit the braces and write the loop on a single line.

Higher-Order Functions

Functions that operate on other functions, either by taking them as arguments or by returning them, are called *higher-order functions*. Since we have already seen that functions are regular values, there is nothing particularly remarkable about the fact that such functions exist. The term comes from mathematics, where the distinction between functions and other values is taken more seriously.

Higher-order functions allow us to abstract over *actions*, not just values. They come in several forms. For example, we can have functions that create new functions.

```
function greaterThan(n) {
  return m => m > n;
}
let greaterThan10 = greaterThan(10);
console.log(greaterThan10(11));
// → true
```

And we can have functions that change other functions.

```
function noisy(f) {
  return (...args) => {
    console.log("calling with", args);
    let result = f(...args);
    console.log("called with", args, ", returned", result);
    return result;
  };
}
noisy(Math.min)(3, 2, 1);
// → calling with [3, 2, 1]
// → called with [3, 2, 1] , returned 1
```

We can even write functions that provide new types of control flow.

```
function unless(test, then) {
  if (!test) then();
}

repeat(3, n => {
  unless(n % 2 == 1, () => {
    console.log(n, "is even");
  });
});
```

```
// → 0 is even
// → 2 is even
```

There is a built-in array method, forEach, that provides something like a for/of loop as a higher-order function.

```
["A", "B"].forEach(l => console.log(l));
// → A
// → B
```

Script Data Set

One area where higher-order functions shine is data processing. To process data, we'll need some actual data. This chapter will use a data set about scripts—writing systems such as Latin, Cyrillic, or Arabic.

Remember Unicode from Chapter 1, the system that assigns a number to each character in written language? Most of these characters are associated with a specific script. The standard contains 140 different scripts—81 are still in use today, and 59 are historic.

Though I can fluently read only Latin characters, I appreciate the fact that people are writing texts in at least 80 other writing systems, many of which I wouldn't even recognize. For example, here's a sample of Tamil handwriting:

இன்னா செய்தாரை ஒறுத்தல் அவர்நாண
நன்னயம் செய்து விடல்.

The example data set contains some pieces of information about the 140 scripts defined in Unicode. It is available in the coding sandbox for this chapter (*https://eloquentjavascript.net/code#5*) as the SCRIPTS binding. The binding contains an array of objects, each of which describes a script.

```
{
  name: "Coptic",
  ranges: [[994, 1008], [11392, 11508], [11513, 11520]],
  direction: "ltr",
  year: -200,
  living: false,
  link: "https://en.wikipedia.org/wiki/Coptic_alphabet"
}
```

Such an object tells us the name of the script, the Unicode ranges assigned to it, the direction in which it is written, the (approximate) origin time, whether it is still in use, and a link to more information. The direction may be "ltr" for left to right, "rtl" for right to left (the way Arabic and

Hebrew text are written), or "ttb" for top to bottom (as with Mongolian writing).

The ranges property contains an array of Unicode character ranges, each of which is a two-element array containing a lower bound and an upper bound. Any character codes within these ranges are assigned to the script. The lower bound is inclusive (code 994 is a Coptic character), and the upper bound is non-inclusive (code 1008 isn't).

Filtering Arrays

To find the scripts in the data set that are still in use, the following function might be helpful. It filters out the elements in an array that don't pass a test.

```
function filter(array, test) {
  let passed = [];
  for (let element of array) {
    if (test(element)) {
      passed.push(element);
    }
  }
  return passed;
}

console.log(filter(SCRIPTS, script => script.living));
// → [{name: "Adlam", ...}, ...]
```

The function uses the argument named test, a function value, to fill a "gap" in the computation—the process of deciding which elements to collect.

Note how the filter function, rather than deleting elements from the existing array, builds up a new array with only the elements that pass the test. This function is *pure*. It does not modify the array it is given.

Like forEach, filter is a standard array method. The example defined the function only to show what it does internally. From now on, we'll use it like this instead:

```
console.log(SCRIPTS.filter(s => s.direction == "ttb"));
// → [{name: "Mongolian", ...}, ...]
```

Transforming with map

Say we have an array of objects representing scripts, produced by filtering the SCRIPTS array somehow. But we want an array of names, which is easier to inspect.

The map method transforms an array by applying a function to all of its elements and building a new array from the returned values. The new array will have the same length as the input array, but its content will have been *mapped* to a new form by the function.

```
function map(array, transform) {
  let mapped = [];
  for (let element of array) {
    mapped.push(transform(element));
  }
  return mapped;
}

let rtlScripts = SCRIPTS.filter(s => s.direction == "rtl");
console.log(map(rtlScripts, s => s.name));
// → ["Adlam", "Arabic", "Imperial Aramaic", ...]
```

Like forEach and filter, map is a standard array method.

Summarizing with reduce

Another common thing to do with arrays is to compute a single value from them. Our recurring example, summing a collection of numbers, is an instance of this. Another example is finding the script with the most characters.

The higher-order operation that represents this pattern is called *reduce* (sometimes also called *fold*). It builds a value by repeatedly taking a single element from the array and combining it with the current value. When summing numbers, you'd start with the number zero and, for each element, add that to the sum.

The parameters to reduce are, apart from the array, a combining function and a start value. This function is a little less straightforward than filter and map, so take a close look at it:

```
function reduce(array, combine, start) {
  let current = start;
  for (let element of array) {
    current = combine(current, element);
  }
  return current;
}

console.log(reduce([1, 2, 3, 4], (a, b) => a + b, 0));
// → 10
```

The standard array method reduce, which of course corresponds to this function, has an added convenience. If your array contains at least one element, you are allowed to leave off the start argument. The method will take the first element of the array as its start value and start reducing at the second element.

```
console.log([1, 2, 3, 4].reduce((a, b) => a + b));
// → 10
```

To use reduce (twice) to find the script with the most characters, we can write something like this:

```
function characterCount(script) {
  return script.ranges.reduce((count, [from, to]) => {
    return count + (to - from);
  }, 0);
}

console.log(SCRIPTS.reduce((a, b) => {
  return characterCount(a) < characterCount(b) ? b : a;
}));
// → {name: "Han", ...}
```

The characterCount function reduces the ranges assigned to a script by summing their sizes. Note the use of destructuring in the parameter list of the reducer function. The second call to reduce then uses this to find the largest script by repeatedly comparing two scripts and returning the larger one.

The Han script has more than 89,000 characters assigned to it in the Unicode standard, making it by far the biggest writing system in the data set. Han is a script (sometimes) used for Chinese, Japanese, and Korean text. Those languages share a lot of characters, though they tend to write them differently. The (US-based) Unicode Consortium decided to treat them as a single writing system to save character codes. This is called *Han unification* and still makes some people very angry.

Composability

Consider how we would have written the previous example (finding the biggest script) without higher-order functions. The code is not that much worse.

```
let biggest = null;
for (let script of SCRIPTS) {
  if (biggest == null ||
      characterCount(biggest) < characterCount(script)) {
    biggest = script;
  }
}
console.log(biggest);
// → {name: "Han", ...}
```

There are a few more bindings, and the program is four lines longer. But it is still very readable.

Higher-order functions start to shine when you need to *compose* operations. As an example, let's write code that finds the average year of origin for living and dead scripts in the data set.

```
function average(array) {
  return array.reduce((a, b) => a + b) / array.length;
}

console.log(Math.round(average(
  SCRIPTS.filter(s => s.living).map(s => s.year))));
// → 1165
console.log(Math.round(average(
  SCRIPTS.filter(s => !s.living).map(s => s.year))));
// → 204
```

So the dead scripts in Unicode are, on average, older than the living ones. This is not a terribly meaningful or surprising statistic. But I hope you'll agree that the code used to compute it isn't hard to read. You can see it as a pipeline: we start with all scripts, filter out the living (or dead) ones, take the years from those, average them, and round the result.

You could definitely also write this computation as one big loop.

```
let total = 0, count = 0;
for (let script of SCRIPTS) {
  if (script.living) {
    total += script.year;
    count += 1;
  }
}
console.log(Math.round(total / count));
// → 1165
```

But it is harder to see what was being computed and how. And because intermediate results aren't represented as coherent values, it'd be a lot more work to extract something like average into a separate function.

In terms of what the computer is actually doing, these two approaches are also quite different. The first will build up new arrays when running filter and map, whereas the second computes only some numbers, doing less work. You can usually afford the readable approach, but if you're processing huge arrays, and doing so many times, the less abstract style might be worth the extra speed.

Strings and Character Codes

One use of the data set would be figuring out what script a piece of text is using. Let's go through a program that does this.

Remember that each script has an array of character code ranges associated with it. So given a character code, we could use a function like this to find the corresponding script (if any):

```
function characterScript(code) {
  for (let script of SCRIPTS) {
    if (script.ranges.some(([from, to]) => {
      return code >= from && code < to;
    })) {
      return script;
    }
  }
  return null;
}

console.log(characterScript(121));
// → {name: "Latin", ...}
```

The some method is another higher-order function. It takes a test function and tells you whether that function returns true for any of the elements in the array.

But how do we get the character codes in a string?

In Chapter 1 I mentioned that JavaScript strings are encoded as a sequence of 16-bit numbers. These are called *code units*. A Unicode character code was initially supposed to fit within such a unit (which gives you a little over 65,000 characters). When it became clear that wasn't going to be enough, many people balked at the need to use more memory per character. To address these concerns, UTF-16, the format used by JavaScript strings, was invented. It describes most common characters using a single 16-bit code unit but uses a pair of two such units for others.

UTF-16 is generally considered a bad idea today. It seems almost intentionally designed to invite mistakes. It's easy to write programs that pretend code units and characters are the same thing. And if your language doesn't use two-unit characters, that will appear to work just fine. But as soon as someone tries to use such a program with some less common Chinese characters, it breaks. Fortunately, with the advent of emoji, everybody has started using two-unit characters, and the burden of dealing with such problems is more fairly distributed.

Unfortunately, obvious operations on JavaScript strings, such as getting their length through the length property and accessing their content using square brackets, deal only with code units.

```
// Two emoji characters, horse and shoe
let horseShoe = "🐎👟";
console.log(horseShoe.length);
// → 4
console.log(horseShoe[0]);
// → (Invalid half-character)
console.log(horseShoe.charCodeAt(0));
// → 55357 (Code of the half-character)
console.log(horseShoe.codePointAt(0));
// → 128052 (Actual code for horse emoji)
```

JavaScript's charCodeAt method gives you a code unit, not a full character code. The codePointAt method, added later, does give a full Unicode character. So we could use that to get characters from a string. But the argument passed to codePointAt is still an index into the sequence of code units. So to run over all characters in a string, we'd still need to deal with the question of whether a character takes up one or two code units.

In "Array Loops" on page 69, I mentioned that a for/of loop can also be used on strings. Like codePointAt, this type of loop was introduced at a time where people were acutely aware of the problems with UTF-16. When you use it to loop over a string, it gives you real characters, not code units.

```
let roseDragon = "🌹🐉";
for (let char of roseDragon) {
  console.log(char);
}
// → 🌹
// → 🐉
```

If you have a character (which will be a string of one or two code units), you can use codePointAt(0) to get its code.

Recognizing Text

We have a characterScript function and a way to correctly loop over characters. The next step is to count the characters that belong to each script. The following counting abstraction will be useful there:

```
function countBy(items, groupName) {
  let counts = [];
  for (let item of items) {
    let name = groupName(item);
    let known = counts.findIndex(c => c.name == name);
    if (known == -1) {
      counts.push({name, count: 1});
    } else {
      counts[known].count++;
    }
  }
```

```
    return counts;
}

console.log(countBy([1, 2, 3, 4, 5], n => n > 2));
// → [{name: false, count: 2}, {name: true, count: 3}]
```

The countBy function expects a collection (anything that we can loop over with for/of) and a function that computes a group name for a given element. It returns an array of objects, each of which names a group and tells you the number of elements that were found in that group.

It uses another array method—findIndex. This method is somewhat like indexOf, but instead of looking for a specific value, it finds the first value for which the given function returns true. Like indexOf, it returns −1 when no such element is found.

Using countBy, we can write the function that tells us which scripts are used in a piece of text.

```
function textScripts(text) {
  let scripts = countBy(text, char => {
    let script = characterScript(char.codePointAt(0));
    return script ? script.name : "none";
  }).filter(({name}) => name != "none");

  let total = scripts.reduce((n, {count}) => n + count, 0);
  if (total == 0) return "No scripts found";

  return scripts.map(({name, count}) => {
    return `${Math.round(count * 100 / total)}% ${name}`;
  }).join(", ");
}

console.log(textScripts('英国的狗说"woof", 俄罗斯的狗说"тяв"'));
// → 61% Han, 22% Latin, 17% Cyrillic
```

The function first counts the characters by name, using characterScript to assign them a name and falling back to the string "none" for characters that aren't part of any script. The filter call drops the entry for "none" from the resulting array since we aren't interested in those characters.

To be able to compute percentages, we first need the total number of characters that belong to a script, which we can compute with reduce. If no such characters are found, the function returns a specific string. Otherwise, it transforms the counting entries into readable strings with map and then combines them with join.

Summary

Being able to pass function values to other functions is a deeply useful aspect of JavaScript. It allows us to write functions that model computations with "gaps" in them. The code that calls these functions can fill in the gaps by providing function values.

Arrays provide a number of useful higher-order methods. You can use forEach to loop over the elements in an array. The filter method returns a new array containing only the elements that pass the predicate function. Transforming an array by putting each element through a function is done with map. You can use reduce to combine all the elements in an array into a single value. The some method tests whether any element matches a given predicate function. And findIndex finds the position of the first element that matches a predicate.

Exercises

Flattening

Use the reduce method in combination with the concat method to "flatten" an array of arrays into a single array that has all the elements of the original arrays.

Your Own Loop

Write a higher-order function loop that provides something like a for loop statement. It takes a value, a test function, an update function, and a body function. Each iteration, it first runs the test function on the current loop value and stops if that returns false. Then it calls the body function, giving it the current value. Finally, it calls the update function to create a new value and starts from the beginning.

When defining the function, you can use a regular loop to do the actual looping.

Everything

Analogous to the some method, arrays also have an every method. This one returns true when the given function returns true for *every* element in the array. In a way, some is a version of the || operator that acts on arrays, and every is like the && operator.

Implement every as a function that takes an array and a predicate function as parameters. Write two versions, one using a loop and one using the some method.

Dominant Writing Direction

Write a function that computes the dominant writing direction in a string of text. Remember that each script object has a direction property that can be "ltr" (left to right), "rtl" (right to left), or "ttb" (top to bottom).

The dominant direction is the direction of a majority of the characters that have a script associated with them. The characterScript and countBy functions defined earlier in the chapter are probably useful here.

"An abstract data type is realized by writing a special kind of program . . . which defines the type in terms of the operations which can be performed on it."
—Barbara Liskov,
Programming with Abstract Data Types

THE SECRET LIFE OF OBJECTS

Chapter 4 introduced JavaScript's objects. In programming culture, we have a thing called *object-oriented programming*, a set of techniques that use objects (and related concepts) as the central principle of program organization.

Though no one really agrees on its precise definition, object-oriented programming has shaped the design of many programming languages, including JavaScript. This chapter will describe the way these ideas can be applied in JavaScript.

Encapsulation

The core idea in object-oriented programming is to divide programs into smaller pieces and make each piece responsible for managing its own state. This way, some knowledge about the way a piece of the program works can be kept *local* to that piece. Someone working on the rest of the program does not have to remember or even be aware of that knowledge. Whenever these local details change, only the code directly around it needs to be updated.

Different pieces of such a program interact with each other through *interfaces*, limited sets of functions or bindings that provide useful functionality at a more abstract level, hiding their precise implementation.

Such program pieces are modeled using objects. Their interface consists of a specific set of methods and properties. Properties that are part of the interface are called *public*. The others, which outside code should not be touching, are called *private*.

Many languages provide a way to distinguish public and private properties and prevent outside code from accessing the private ones altogether. JavaScript, once again taking the minimalist approach, does not—not yet at least. There is work underway to add this to the language.

Even though the language doesn't have this distinction built in, JavaScript programmers *are* successfully using this idea. Typically, the available interface is described in documentation or comments. It is also common to put an underscore character (_) at the beginning of property names to indicate that those properties are private.

Separating interface from implementation is a great idea. It is usually called *encapsulation*.

Methods

Methods are nothing more than properties that hold function values. This is a simple method:

```
let rabbit = {};
rabbit.speak = function(line) {
  console.log(`The rabbit says '${line}'`);
};

rabbit.speak("I'm alive.");
// → The rabbit says 'I'm alive.'
```

Usually a method needs to do something with the object it was called on. When a function is called as a method—looked up as a property and immediately called, as in `object.method()`—the binding called this in its body automatically points at the object that it was called on.

```
function speak(line) {
  console.log(`The ${this.type} rabbit says '${line}'`);
}
let whiteRabbit = {type: "white", speak};
let hungryRabbit = {type: "hungry", speak};

whiteRabbit.speak("Oh my ears and whiskers, " +
                  "how late it's getting!");
// → The white rabbit says 'Oh my ears and whiskers, how
//   late it's getting!'
```

```
hungryRabbit.speak("I could use a carrot right now.");
// → The hungry rabbit says 'I could use a carrot right now.'
```

You can think of this as an extra parameter that is passed in a different way. If you want to pass it explicitly, you can use a function's call method, which takes the this value as its first argument and treats further arguments as normal parameters.

```
speak.call(hungryRabbit, "Burp!");
// → The hungry rabbit says 'Burp!'
```

Since each function has its own this binding, whose value depends on the way it is called, you cannot refer to the this of the wrapping scope in a regular function defined with the function keyword.

Arrow functions are different—they do not bind their own this but can see the this binding of the scope around them. Thus, you can do something like the following code, which references this from inside a local function:

```
function normalize() {
  console.log(this.coords.map(n => n / this.length));
}
normalize.call({coords: [0, 2, 3], length: 5});
// → [0, 0.4, 0.6]
```

If I had written the argument to map using the function keyword, the code wouldn't work.

Prototypes

Watch closely.

```
let empty = {};
console.log(empty.toString);
// → function toString(){...}
console.log(empty.toString());
// → [object Object]
```

I pulled a property out of an empty object. Magic!

Well, not really. I have simply been withholding information about the way JavaScript objects work. In addition to their set of properties, most objects also have a *prototype*. A prototype is another object that is used as a fallback source of properties. When an object gets a request for a property that it does not have, its prototype will be searched for the property, then the prototype's prototype, and so on.

So who is the prototype of that empty object? It is the great ancestral prototype, the entity behind almost all objects, Object.prototype.

```
console.log(Object.getPrototypeOf({}) ==
          Object.prototype);
// → true
console.log(Object.getPrototypeOf(Object.prototype));
// → null
```

As you guess, `Object.getPrototypeOf` returns the prototype of an object.

The prototype relations of JavaScript objects form a tree-shaped structure, and at the root of this structure sits `Object.prototype`. It provides a few methods that show up in all objects, such as `toString`, which converts an object to a string representation.

Many objects don't directly have `Object.prototype` as their prototype but instead have another object that provides a different set of default properties. Functions derive from `Function.prototype`, and arrays derive from `Array.prototype`.

```
console.log(Object.getPrototypeOf(Math.max) ==
          Function.prototype);
// → true
console.log(Object.getPrototypeOf([]) ==
          Array.prototype);
// → true
```

Such a prototype object will itself have a prototype, often `Object .prototype`, so that it still indirectly provides methods like `toString`.

You can use `Object.create` to create an object with a specific prototype.

```
let protoRabbit = {
  speak(line) {
    console.log(`The ${this.type} rabbit says '${line}'`);
  }
};
let killerRabbit = Object.create(protoRabbit);
killerRabbit.type = "killer";
killerRabbit.speak("SKREEEE!");
// → The killer rabbit says 'SKREEEE!'
```

A property like `speak(line)` in an object expression is a shorthand way of defining a method. It creates a property called speak and gives it a function as its value.

The "proto" rabbit acts as a container for the properties that are shared by all rabbits. An individual rabbit object, like the killer rabbit, contains properties that apply only to itself—in this case its type—and derives shared properties from its prototype.

Classes

JavaScript's prototype system can be interpreted as a somewhat informal take on an object-oriented concept called *classes*. A class defines the shape of a type of object—what methods and properties it has. Such an object is called an *instance* of the class.

Prototypes are useful for defining properties for which all instances of a class share the same value, such as methods. Properties that differ per instance, such as our rabbits' type property, need to be stored directly in the objects themselves.

So to create an instance of a given class, you have to make an object that derives from the proper prototype, but you *also* have to make sure it, itself, has the properties that instances of this class are supposed to have. This is what a *constructor* function does.

```
function makeRabbit(type) {
  let rabbit = Object.create(protoRabbit);
  rabbit.type = type;
  return rabbit;
}
```

JavaScript provides a way to make defining this type of function easier. If you put the keyword new in front of a function call, the function is treated as a constructor. This means that an object with the right prototype is automatically created, bound to this in the function, and returned at the end of the function.

The prototype object used when constructing objects is found by taking the prototype property of the constructor function.

```
function Rabbit(type) {
  this.type = type;
}
Rabbit.prototype.speak = function(line) {
  console.log(`The ${this.type} rabbit says '${line}'`);
};

let weirdRabbit = new Rabbit("weird");
```

Constructors (all functions, in fact) automatically get a property named prototype, which by default holds a plain, empty object that derives from Object.prototype. You can overwrite it with a new object if you want. Or you can add properties to the existing object, as the example does.

By convention, the names of constructors are capitalized so that they can easily be distinguished from other functions.

It's important to understand the distinction between the way a prototype is associated with a constructor (through its prototype property) and the way objects *have* a prototype (which can be found with Object.getPrototypeOf). The actual prototype of a constructor is Function.prototype since constructors are functions. Its `prototype` *property* holds the prototype used for instances created through it.

```
console.log(Object.getPrototypeOf(Rabbit) ==
           Function.prototype);
// → true
console.log(Object.getPrototypeOf(weirdRabbit) ==
           Rabbit.prototype);
// → true
```

Class Notation

So JavaScript classes are constructor functions with a prototype property. That is how they work, and until 2015, that was how you had to write them. These days, we have a less awkward notation.

```
class Rabbit {
  constructor(type) {
    this.type = type;
  }
  speak(line) {
    console.log(`The ${this.type} rabbit says '${line}'`);
  }
}

let killerRabbit = new Rabbit("killer");
let blackRabbit = new Rabbit("black");
```

The class keyword starts a class declaration, which allows us to define a constructor and a set of methods all in a single place. Any number of methods may be written inside the declaration's braces. The one named constructor is treated specially. It provides the actual constructor function, which will be bound to the name `Rabbit`. The others are packaged into that constructor's prototype. Thus, the earlier class declaration is equivalent to the constructor definition from the previous section. It just looks nicer.

Class declarations currently allow only *methods*—properties that hold functions—to be added to the prototype. This can be somewhat inconvenient when you want to save a non-function value in there. The next version of the language will probably improve this. For now, you can create such properties by directly manipulating the prototype after you've defined the class.

Like `function`, `class` can be used both in statements and in expressions. When used as an expression, it doesn't define a binding but just produces the constructor as a value. You are allowed to omit the class name in a class expression.

```
let object = new class { getWord() { return "hello"; } };
console.log(object.getWord());
// → hello
```

Overriding Derived Properties

When you add a property to an object, whether it is present in the prototype or not, the property is added to the object *itself*. If there was already a property with the same name in the prototype, this property will no longer affect the object, as it is now hidden behind the object's own property.

```
Rabbit.prototype.teeth = "small";
console.log(killerRabbit.teeth);
// → small
killerRabbit.teeth = "long, sharp, and bloody";
console.log(killerRabbit.teeth);
// → long, sharp, and bloody
console.log(blackRabbit.teeth);
// → small
console.log(Rabbit.prototype.teeth);
// → small
```

The following diagram sketches the situation after this code has run. The Rabbit and Object prototypes lie behind killerRabbit as a kind of backdrop, where properties that are not found in the object itself can be looked up.

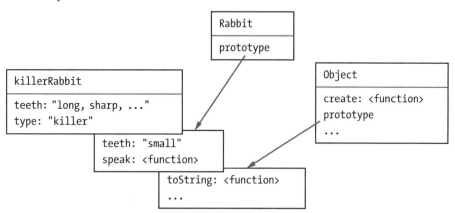

Overriding properties that exist in a prototype can be a useful thing to do. As the rabbit teeth example shows, overriding can be used to express exceptional properties in instances of a more generic class of objects, while letting the nonexceptional objects take a standard value from their prototype.

Overriding is also used to give the standard function and array prototypes a different toString method than the basic object prototype.

```
console.log(Array.prototype.toString ==
            Object.prototype.toString);
// → false
console.log([1, 2].toString());
// → 1,2
```

Calling `toString` on an array gives a result similar to calling `.join(",")` on it—it puts commas between the values in the array. Directly calling `Object.prototype.toString` with an array produces a different string. That function doesn't know about arrays, so it simply puts the word *object* and the name of the type between square brackets.

```
console.log(Object.prototype.toString.call([1, 2]));
// → [object Array]
```

Maps

We saw the word *map* used in "Transforming with Map" on page 88 for an operation that transforms a data structure by applying a function to its elements. Confusing as it is, in programming the same word is also used for a related but rather different thing.

A *map* (noun) is a data structure that associates values (the keys) with other values. For example, you might want to map names to ages. It is possible to use objects for this.

```
let ages = {
  Boris: 39,
  Liang: 22,
  Júlia: 62
};

console.log(`Júlia is ${ages["Júlia"]}`);
// → Júlia is 62
console.log("Is Jack's age known?", "Jack" in ages);
// → Is Jack's age known? false
console.log("Is toString's age known?", "toString" in ages);
// → Is toString's age known? true
```

Here, the object's property names are the people's names, and the property values are their ages. But we certainly didn't list anybody named toString in our map. Yet, because plain objects derive from `Object.prototype`, it looks like the property is there.

As such, using plain objects as maps is dangerous. There are several possible ways to avoid this problem. First, it is possible to create objects with *no* prototype. If you pass `null` to `Object.create`, the resulting object will not derive from `Object.prototype` and can safely be used as a map.

```
console.log("toString" in Object.create(null));
// → false
```

Object property names must be strings. If you need a map whose keys can't easily be converted to strings—such as objects—you cannot use an object as your map.

Fortunately, JavaScript comes with a class called Map that is written for this exact purpose. It stores a mapping and allows any type of keys.

```
let ages = new Map();
ages.set("Boris", 39);
ages.set("Liang", 22);
ages.set("Júlia", 62);

console.log(`Júlia is ${ages.get("Júlia")}`);
// → Júlia is 62
console.log("Is Jack's age known?", ages.has("Jack"));
// → Is Jack's age known? false
console.log(ages.has("toString"));
// → false
```

The methods set, get, and has are part of the interface of the Map object. Writing a data structure that can quickly update and search a large set of values isn't easy, but we don't have to worry about that. Someone else did it for us, and we can go through this simple interface to use their work.

If you do have a plain object that you need to treat as a map for some reason, it is useful to know that Object.keys returns only an object's *own* keys, not those in the prototype. As an alternative to the in operator, you can use the hasOwnProperty method, which ignores the object's prototype.

```
console.log({x: 1}.hasOwnProperty("x"));
// → true
console.log({x: 1}.hasOwnProperty("toString"));
// → false
```

Polymorphism

When you call the String function (which converts a value to a string) on an object, it will call the toString method on that object to try to create a meaningful string from it. I mentioned that some of the standard prototypes define their own version of toString so they can create a string that contains more useful information than "[object Object]". You can also do that yourself.

```
Rabbit.prototype.toString = function() {
  return `a ${this.type} rabbit`;
};
```

```
console.log(String(blackRabbit));
// → a black rabbit
```

This is a simple instance of a powerful idea. When a piece of code is written to work with objects that have a certain interface—in this case, a toString method—any kind of object that happens to support this interface can be plugged into the code, and it will just work.

This technique is called *polymorphism*. Polymorphic code can work with values of different shapes, as long as they support the interface it expects.

I noted in "Array Loops" on page 69 that a for/of loop can loop over several kinds of data structures. This is another case of polymorphism—such loops expect the data structure to expose a specific interface, which arrays and strings do. And we can also add this interface to your own objects! But before we can do that, we need to know what symbols are.

Symbols

It is possible for multiple interfaces to use the same property name for different things. For example, I could define an interface in which the toString method is supposed to convert the object into a piece of yarn. It would not be possible for an object to conform to both that interface and the standard use of toString.

That would be a bad idea, and this problem isn't that common. Most JavaScript programmers simply don't think about it. But the language designers, whose *job* it is to think about this stuff, have provided us with a solution anyway.

When I claimed that property names are strings, that wasn't entirely accurate. They usually are, but they can also be *symbols*. Symbols are values created with the Symbol function. Unlike strings, newly created symbols are unique—you cannot create the same symbol twice.

```
let sym = Symbol("name");
console.log(sym == Symbol("name"));
// → false
Rabbit.prototype[sym] = 55;
console.log(blackRabbit[sym]);
// → 55
```

The string you pass to Symbol is included when you convert it to a string and can make it easier to recognize a symbol when, for example, showing it in the console. But it has no meaning beyond that—multiple symbols may have the same name.

Being both unique and usable as property names makes symbols suitable for defining interfaces that can peacefully live alongside other properties, no matter what their names are.

```
const toStringSymbol = Symbol("toString");
Array.prototype[toStringSymbol] = function() {
  return `${this.length} cm of blue yarn`;
};

console.log([1, 2].toString());
// → 1,2
console.log([1, 2][toStringSymbol]());
// → 2 cm of blue yarn
```

It is possible to include symbol properties in object expressions and classes by using square brackets around the property name. That causes the property name to be evaluated, much like the square bracket property access notation, which allows us to refer to a binding that holds the symbol.

```
let stringObject = {
  [toStringSymbol]() { return "a jute rope"; }
};
console.log(stringObject[toStringSymbol]());
// → a jute rope
```

The Iterator Interface

The object given to a for/of loop is expected to be *iterable*. This means it has a method named with the Symbol.iterator symbol (a symbol value defined by the language, stored as a property of the Symbol function).

When called, that method should return an object that provides a second interface, *iterator*. This is the actual thing that iterates. It has a next method that returns the next result. That result should be an object with a value property that provides the next value, if there is one, and a done property, which should be true when there are no more results and false otherwise.

Note that the next, value, and done property names are plain strings, not symbols. Only Symbol.iterator, which is likely to be added to a *lot* of different objects, is an actual symbol.

We can directly use this interface ourselves.

```
let okIterator = "OK"[Symbol.iterator]();
console.log(okIterator.next());
// → {value: "O", done: false}
console.log(okIterator.next());
// → {value: "K", done: false}
console.log(okIterator.next());
// → {value: undefined, done: true}
```

Let's implement an iterable data structure. We'll build a *matrix* class, acting as a two-dimensional array.

```
class Matrix {
  constructor(width, height, element = (x, y) => undefined) {
    this.width = width;
    this.height = height;
    this.content = [];

    for (let y = 0; y < height; y++) {
      for (let x = 0; x < width; x++) {
        this.content[y * width + x] = element(x, y);
      }
    }
  }

  get(x, y) {
    return this.content[y * this.width + x];
  }
  set(x, y, value) {
    this.content[y * this.width + x] = value;
  }
}
```

The class stores its content in a single array of *width* × *height* elements. The elements are stored row by row, so, for example, the third element in the fifth row is (using zero-based indexing) stored at position 4 × *width* + 2.

The constructor function takes a width, a height, and an optional content function that will be used to fill in the initial values. There are get and set methods to retrieve and update elements in the matrix.

When looping over a matrix, you are usually interested in the position of the elements as well as the elements themselves, so we'll have our iterator produce objects with x, y, and value properties.

```
class MatrixIterator {
  constructor(matrix) {
    this.x = 0;
    this.y = 0;
    this.matrix = matrix;
  }

  next() {
    if (this.y == this.matrix.height) return {done: true};

    let value = {x: this.x,
                 y: this.y,
                 value: this.matrix.get(this.x, this.y)};
    this.x++;
```

```
    if (this.x == this.matrix.width) {
      this.x = 0;
      this.y++;
    }
    return {value, done: false};
  }
}
```

The class tracks the progress of iterating over a matrix in its x and y properties. The next method starts by checking whether the bottom of the matrix has been reached. If it hasn't, it *first* creates the object holding the current value and *then* updates its position, moving to the next row if necessary.

Let's set up the Matrix class to be iterable. Throughout this book, I'll occasionally use after-the-fact prototype manipulation to add methods to classes so that the individual pieces of code remain small and self-contained. In a regular program, where there is no need to split the code into small pieces, you'd declare these methods directly in the class instead.

```
Matrix.prototype[Symbol.iterator] = function() {
  return new MatrixIterator(this);
};
```

We can now loop over a matrix with for/of.

```
let matrix = new Matrix(2, 2, (x, y) => `value ${x},${y}`);
for (let {x, y, value} of matrix) {
  console.log(x, y, value);
}
// → 0 0 value 0,0
// → 1 0 value 1,0
// → 0 1 value 0,1
// → 1 1 value 1,1
```

Getters, Setters, and Statics

Interfaces often consist mostly of methods, but it is also okay to include properties that hold non-function values. For example, Map objects have a size property that tells you how many keys are stored in them.

It is not even necessary for such an object to compute and store such a property directly in the instance. Even properties that are accessed directly may hide a method call. Such methods are called *getters*, and they are defined by writing get in front of the method name in an object expression or class declaration.

```
let varyingSize = {
  get size() {
```

```
    return Math.floor(Math.random() * 100);
  }
};

console.log(varyingSize.size);
// → 73
console.log(varyingSize.size);
// → 49
```

Whenever someone reads from this object's size property, the associated method is called. You can do a similar thing when a property is written to, using a *setter*.

```
class Temperature {
  constructor(celsius) {
    this.celsius = celsius;
  }
  get fahrenheit() {
    return this.celsius * 1.8 + 32;
  }
  set fahrenheit(value) {
    this.celsius = (value - 32) / 1.8;
  }

  static fromFahrenheit(value) {
    return new Temperature((value - 32) / 1.8);
  }
}

let temp = new Temperature(22);
console.log(temp.fahrenheit);
// → 71.6
temp.fahrenheit = 86;
console.log(temp.celsius);
// → 30
```

The Temperature class allows you to read and write the temperature in either degrees Celsius or degrees Fahrenheit, but internally it stores only Celsius and automatically converts to and from Celsius in the fahrenheit getter and setter.

Sometimes you want to attach some properties directly to your constructor function, rather than to the prototype. Such methods won't have access to a class instance but can, for example, be used to provide additional ways to create instances.

Inside a class declaration, methods that have static written before their name are stored on the constructor. So the Temperature class allows you to write Temperature.fromFahrenheit(100) to create a temperature using degrees Fahrenheit.

Inheritance

Some matrices are known to be *symmetric*. If you mirror a symmetric matrix around its top-left-to-bottom-right diagonal, it stays the same. In other words, the value stored at *x,y* is always the same as that at *y,x*.

Imagine we need a data structure like Matrix but one that enforces the fact that the matrix is and remains symmetrical. We could write it from scratch, but that would involve repeating some code very similar to what we already wrote.

JavaScript's prototype system makes it possible to create a *new* class, much like the old class, but with new definitions for some of its properties. The prototype for the new class derives from the old prototype but adds a new definition for, say, the set method.

In object-oriented programming terms, this is called *inheritance*. The new class inherits properties and behavior from the old class.

```
class SymmetricMatrix extends Matrix {
  constructor(size, element = (x, y) => undefined) {
    super(size, size, (x, y) => {
      if (x < y) return element(y, x);
      else return element(x, y);
    });
  }

  set(x, y, value) {
    super.set(x, y, value);
    if (x != y) {
      super.set(y, x, value);
    }
  }
}

let matrix = new SymmetricMatrix(5, (x, y) => `${x},${y}`);
console.log(matrix.get(2, 3));
// → 3,2
```

The use of the word extends indicates that this class shouldn't be directly based on the default Object prototype but on some other class. This is called the *superclass*. The derived class is the *subclass*.

To initialize a SymmetricMatrix instance, the constructor calls its superclass's constructor through the super keyword. This is necessary because if this new object is to behave (roughly) like a Matrix, it is going to need the instance properties that matrices have. To ensure the matrix is symmetrical, the constructor wraps the element method to swap the coordinates for values below the diagonal.

The set method again uses super but this time not to call the constructor but to call a specific method from the superclass's set of methods. We are redefining set but do want to use the original behavior. Because this.set refers to the *new* set method, calling that wouldn't work. Inside class methods, super provides a way to call methods as they were defined in the superclass.

Inheritance allows us to build slightly different data types from existing data types with relatively little work. It is a fundamental part of the object-oriented tradition, alongside encapsulation and polymorphism. But while the latter two are now generally regarded as wonderful ideas, inheritance is more controversial.

Whereas encapsulation and polymorphism can be used to *separate* pieces of code from each other, reducing the tangledness of the overall program, inheritance fundamentally ties classes together, creating *more* tangle. When inheriting from a class, you usually have to know more about how it works than when simply using it. Inheritance can be a useful tool, and I use it now and then in my own programs, but it shouldn't be the first tool you reach for, and you probably shouldn't actively go looking for opportunities to construct class hierarchies (family trees of classes).

The instanceof Operator

It is occasionally useful to know whether an object was derived from a specific class. For this, JavaScript provides a binary operator called instanceof.

```
console.log(
  new SymmetricMatrix(2) instanceof SymmetricMatrix);
// → true
console.log(new SymmetricMatrix(2) instanceof Matrix);
// → true
console.log(new Matrix(2, 2) instanceof SymmetricMatrix);
// → false
console.log([1] instanceof Array);
// → true
```

The operator will see through inherited types, so a SymmetricMatrix is an instance of Matrix. The operator can also be applied to standard constructors like Array. Almost every object is an instance of Object.

Summary

So objects do more than just hold their own properties. They have prototypes, which are other objects. They'll act as if they have properties they don't have as long as their prototype has that property. Simple objects have Object.prototype as their prototype.

Constructors, which are functions whose names usually start with a capital letter, can be used with the new operator to create new objects. The new object's prototype will be the object found in the prototype property of the constructor. You can make good use of this by putting the properties that all values of a given type share into their prototype. There's a `class` notation that provides a clear way to define a constructor and its prototype.

You can define getters and setters to secretly call methods every time an object's property is accessed. Static methods are methods stored in a class's constructor, rather than its prototype.

The `instanceof` operator can, given an object and a constructor, tell you whether that object is an instance of that constructor.

One useful thing to do with objects is to specify an interface for them and tell everybody that they are supposed to talk to your object only through that interface. The rest of the details that make up your object are now *encapsulated*, hidden behind the interface.

More than one type may implement the same interface. Code written to use an interface automatically knows how to work with any number of different objects that provide the interface. This is called *polymorphism*.

When implementing multiple classes that differ in only some details, it can be helpful to write the new classes as *subclasses* of an existing class, *inheriting* part of its behavior.

Exercises

A Vector Type

Write a class `Vec` that represents a vector in two-dimensional space. It takes x and y parameters (numbers), which it should save to properties of the same name.

Give the `Vec` prototype two methods, `plus` and `minus`, that take another vector as a parameter and return a new vector that has the sum or difference of the two vectors' (`this` and the parameter) *x* and *y* values.

Add a getter property `length` to the prototype that computes the length of the vector—that is, the distance of the point (x, y) from the origin $(0, 0)$.

Groups

The standard JavaScript environment provides another data structure called `Set`. Like an instance of `Map`, a set holds a collection of values. Unlike `Map`, it does not associate other values with those—it just tracks which values are part of the set. A value can be part of a set only once—adding it again doesn't have any effect.

Write a class called `Group` (since `Set` is already taken). Like `Set`, it has `add`, `delete`, and `has` methods. Its constructor creates an empty group, `add` adds a value to the group (but only if it isn't already a member), `delete` removes its argument from the group (if it was a member), and `has` returns a Boolean value indicating whether its argument is a member of the group.

Use the `===` operator, or something equivalent such as `indexOf`, to determine whether two values are the same.

Give the class a static `from` method that takes an iterable object as argument and creates a group that contains all the values produced by iterating over it.

Iterable Groups

Make the Group class from the previous exercise iterable. Refer to the section about the iterator interface earlier in the chapter if you aren't clear on the exact form of the interface anymore.

If you used an array to represent the group's members, don't just return the iterator created by calling the Symbol.iterator method on the array. That would work, but it defeats the purpose of this exercise.

It is okay if your iterator behaves strangely when the group is modified during iteration.

Borrowing a Method

Earlier in the chapter I mentioned that an object's hasOwnProperty can be used as a more robust alternative to the in operator when you want to ignore the prototype's properties. But what if your map needs to include the word "hasOwnProperty"? You won't be able to call that method anymore because the object's own property hides the method value.

Can you think of a way to call hasOwnProperty on an object that has its own property by that name?

"The question of whether
Machines Can Think . . . is about as
relevant as the question of whether
Submarines Can Swim."

—Edsger Dijkstra,
The Threats to Computing Science

7

PROJECT: A ROBOT

In "project" chapters, I'll stop pummeling you with new theory for a brief moment, and instead we'll work through a program together. Theory is necessary to learn to program, but reading and understanding actual programs is just as important.

Our project in this chapter is to build an automaton, a little program that performs a task in a virtual world. Our automaton will be a mail-delivery robot picking up and dropping off parcels.

Meadowfield

The village of Meadowfield isn't very big. It consists of 11 places with 14 roads between them. It can be described with this array of roads:

```
const roads = [
  "Alice's House-Bob's House",    "Alice's House-Cabin",
  "Alice's House-Post Office",    "Bob's House-Town Hall",
  "Daria's House-Ernie's House",  "Daria's House-Town Hall",
  "Ernie's House-Grete's House",  "Grete's House-Farm",
  "Grete's House-Shop",           "Marketplace-Farm",
  "Marketplace-Post Office",      "Marketplace-Shop",
```

```
    "Marketplace-Town Hall",        "Shop-Town Hall"
];
```

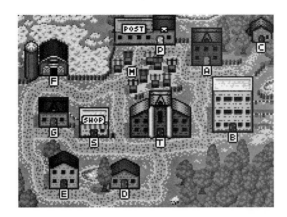

The network of roads in the village forms a *graph*. A graph is a collection of points (places in the village) with lines between them (roads). This graph will be the world that our robot moves through.

The array of strings isn't very easy to work with. What we're interested in is the destinations that we can reach from a given place. Let's convert the list of roads to a data structure that, for each place, tells us what can be reached from there.

```
function buildGraph(edges) {
  let graph = Object.create(null);
  function addEdge(from, to) {
    if (graph[from] == null) {
      graph[from] = [to];
    } else {
      graph[from].push(to);
    }
  }
  for (let [from, to] of edges.map(r => r.split("-"))) {
    addEdge(from, to);
    addEdge(to, from);
  }
  return graph;
}

const roadGraph = buildGraph(roads);
```

Given an array of edges, `buildGraph` creates a map object that, for each node, stores an array of connected nodes.

It uses the `split` method to go from the road strings, which have the form `"Start-End"`, to two-element arrays containing the start and end as separate strings.

The Task

Our robot will be moving around the village. There are parcels in various places, each addressed to some other place. The robot picks up parcels when it comes to them and delivers them when it arrives at their destinations.

The automaton must decide, at each point, where to go next. It has finished its task when all parcels have been delivered.

To be able to simulate this process, we must define a virtual world that can describe it. This model tells us where the robot is and where the parcels are. When the robot has decided to move somewhere, we need to update the model to reflect the new situation.

If you're thinking in terms of object-oriented programming, your first impulse might be to start defining objects for the various elements in the world: a class for the robot, one for a parcel, maybe one for places. These could then hold properties that describe their current state, such as the pile of parcels at a location, which we could change when updating the world.

This is wrong.

At least, it usually is. The fact that something sounds like an object does not automatically mean that it should be an object in your program. Reflexively writing classes for every concept in your application tends to leave you with a collection of interconnected objects that each have their own internal, changing state. Such programs are often hard to understand and thus easy to break.

Instead, let's condense the village's state down to the minimal set of values that define it. There's the robot's current location and the collection of undelivered parcels, each of which has a current location and a destination address. That's it.

And while we're at it, let's make it so that we don't *change* this state when the robot moves but rather compute a *new* state for the situation after the move.

```
class VillageState {
  constructor(place, parcels) {
    this.place = place;
    this.parcels = parcels;
  }

  move(destination) {
    if (!roadGraph[this.place].includes(destination)) {
      return this;
    } else {
      let parcels = this.parcels.map(p => {
        if (p.place != this.place) return p;
        return {place: destination, address: p.address};
      }).filter(p => p.place != p.address);
      return new VillageState(destination, parcels);
    }
  }
```

```
    }
  }
```

The move method is where the action happens. It first checks whether there is a road going from the current place to the destination, and if not, it returns the old state since this is not a valid move.

Then it creates a new state with the destination as the robot's new place. But it also needs to create a new set of parcels—parcels that the robot is carrying (that are at the robot's current place) need to be moved along to the new place. And parcels that are addressed to the new place need to be delivered—that is, they need to be removed from the set of undelivered parcels. The call to map takes care of the moving, and the call to filter does the delivering.

Parcel objects aren't changed when they are moved but re-created. The move method gives us a new village state but leaves the old one entirely intact.

```
let first = new VillageState(
  "Post Office",
  [{place: "Post Office", address: "Alice's House"}]
);
let next = first.move("Alice's House");

console.log(next.place);
// → Alice's House
console.log(next.parcels);
// → []
console.log(first.place);
// → Post Office
```

The move causes the parcel to be delivered, and this is reflected in the next state. But the initial state still describes the situation where the robot is at the post office and the parcel is undelivered.

Persistent Data

Data structures that don't change are called *immutable* or *persistent.* They behave a lot like strings and numbers in that they are who they are and stay that way, rather than containing different things at different times.

In JavaScript, just about everything *can* be changed, so working with values that are supposed to be persistent requires some restraint. There is a function called Object.freeze that changes an object so that writing to its properties is ignored. You could use that to make sure your objects aren't changed, if you want to be careful. Freezing does require the computer to do some extra work, and having updates ignored is just about as likely to confuse someone as having them do the wrong thing. So I usually prefer to just tell people that a given object shouldn't be messed with and hope they remember it.

```
let object = Object.freeze({value: 5});
object.value = 10;
console.log(object.value);
// → 5
```

Why am I going out of my way to not change objects when the language is obviously expecting me to?

Because it helps me understand my programs. This is about complexity management again. When the objects in my system are fixed, stable things, I can consider operations on them in isolation—moving to Alice's house from a given start state always produces the same new state. When objects change over time, that adds a whole new dimension of complexity to this kind of reasoning.

For a small system like the one we are building in this chapter, we could handle that bit of extra complexity. But the most important limit on what kind of systems we can build is how much we can understand. Anything that makes your code easier to understand makes it possible to build a more ambitious system.

Unfortunately, although understanding a system built on persistent data structures is easier, *designing* one, especially when your programming language isn't helping, can be a little harder. We'll look for opportunities to use persistent data structures in this book, but we'll also be using changeable ones.

Simulation

A delivery robot looks at the world and decides in which direction it wants to move. As such, we could say that a robot is a function that takes a VillageState object and returns the name of a nearby place.

Because we want robots to be able to remember things, so that they can make and execute plans, we also pass them their memory and allow them to return a new memory. Thus, the thing a robot returns is an object containing both the direction it wants to move in and a memory value that will be given back to it the next time it is called.

```
function runRobot(state, robot, memory) {
  for (let turn = 0;; turn++) {
    if (state.parcels.length == 0) {
      console.log(`Done in ${turn} turns`);
      break;
    }
    let action = robot(state, memory);
    state = state.move(action.direction);
    memory = action.memory;
    console.log(`Moved to ${action.direction}`);
  }
}
```

Consider what a robot has to do to "solve" a given state. It must pick up all parcels by visiting every location that has a parcel and deliver them by visiting every location that a parcel is addressed to, but only after picking up the parcel.

What is the dumbest strategy that could possibly work? The robot could just walk in a random direction every turn. That means, with great likelihood, it will eventually run into all parcels and then also at some point reach the place where they should be delivered.

Here's what that could look like:

```
function randomPick(array) {
  let choice = Math.floor(Math.random() * array.length);
  return array[choice];
}

function randomRobot(state) {
  return {direction: randomPick(roadGraph[state.place])};
}
```

Remember that Math.random() returns a number between zero and one—but always below one. Multiplying such a number by the length of an array and then applying Math.floor to it gives us a random index for the array.

Since this robot does not need to remember anything, it ignores its second argument (remember that JavaScript functions can be called with extra arguments without ill effects) and omits the memory property in its returned object.

To put this sophisticated robot to work, we'll first need a way to create a new state with some parcels. A static method (written here by directly adding a property to the constructor) is a good place to put that functionality.

```
VillageState.random = function(parcelCount = 5) {
  let parcels = [];
  for (let i = 0; i < parcelCount; i++) {
    let address = randomPick(Object.keys(roadGraph));
    let place;
    do {
      place = randomPick(Object.keys(roadGraph));
    } while (place == address);
    parcels.push({place, address});
  }
  return new VillageState("Post Office", parcels);
};
```

We don't want any parcels that are sent from the same place that they are addressed to. For this reason, the do loop keeps picking new places when it gets one that's equal to the address.

Let's start up a virtual world.

```
runRobot(VillageState.random(), randomRobot);
// → Moved to Marketplace
// → Moved to Town Hall
// → ...
// → Done in 63 turns
```

It takes the robot a lot of turns to deliver the parcels because it isn't planning ahead very well. We'll address that soon.

The Mail Truck's Route

We should be able to do a lot better than the random robot. An easy improvement would be to take a hint from the way real-world mail delivery works. If we find a route that passes all places in the village, the robot could run that route twice, at which point it is guaranteed to be done. Here is one such route (starting from the post office):

```
const mailRoute = [
  "Alice's House", "Cabin", "Alice's House", "Bob's House",
  "Town Hall", "Daria's House", "Ernie's House",
  "Grete's House", "Shop", "Grete's House", "Farm",
  "Marketplace", "Post Office"
];
```

To implement the route-following robot, we'll need to make use of robot memory. The robot keeps the rest of its route in its memory and drops the first element every turn.

```
function routeRobot(state, memory) {
  if (memory.length == 0) {
    memory = mailRoute;
  }
  return {direction: memory[0], memory: memory.slice(1)};
}
```

This robot is a lot faster already. It'll take a maximum of 26 turns (twice the 13-step route) but usually less.

Pathfinding

Still, I wouldn't really call blindly following a fixed route intelligent behavior. The robot could work more efficiently if it adjusted its behavior to the actual work that needs to be done.

To do that, it has to be able to deliberately move toward a given parcel or toward the location where a parcel has to be delivered. Doing that, even when the goal is more than one move away, will require some kind of route-finding function.

The problem of finding a route through a graph is a typical *search problem*. We can tell whether a given solution (a route) is a valid solution, but we can't directly compute the solution the way we could for 2 + 2. Instead, we have to keep creating potential solutions until we find one that works.

The number of possible routes through a graph is infinite. But when searching for a route from *A* to *B*, we are interested only in the ones that start at *A*. We also don't care about routes that visit the same place twice—those are definitely not the most efficient route anywhere. So that cuts down on the number of routes that the route finder has to consider.

In fact, we are mostly interested in the *shortest* route. So we want to make sure we look at short routes before we look at longer ones. A good approach would be to "grow" routes from the starting point, exploring every reachable place that hasn't been visited yet, until a route reaches the goal. That way, we'll only explore routes that are potentially interesting, and we'll find the shortest route (or one of the shortest routes, if there are more than one) to the goal.

Here is a function that does this:

```
function findRoute(graph, from, to) {
  let work = [{at: from, route: []}];
  for (let i = 0; i < work.length; i++) {
    let {at, route} = work[i];
    for (let place of graph[at]) {
      if (place == to) return route.concat(place);
      if (!work.some(w => w.at == place)) {
        work.push({at: place, route: route.concat(place)});
      }
    }
  }
}
```

The exploring has to be done in the right order—the places that were reached first have to be explored first. We can't immediately explore a place as soon as we reach it because that would mean places reached *from there* would also be explored immediately, and so on, even though there may be other, shorter paths that haven't yet been explored.

Therefore, the function keeps a *work list*. This is an array of places that should be explored next, along with the route that got us there. It starts with just the start position and an empty route.

The search then operates by taking the next item in the list and exploring that, which means all roads going from that place are looked at. If one of them is the goal, a finished route can be returned. Otherwise, if we haven't looked at this place before, a new item is added to the list. If we have looked at it before, since we are looking at short routes first, we've found either a longer route to that place or one precisely as long as the existing one, and we don't need to explore it.

You can visually imagine this as a web of known routes crawling out from the start location, growing evenly on all sides (but never tangling back into itself). As soon as the first thread reaches the goal location, that thread is traced back to the start, giving us our route.

Our code doesn't handle the situation where there are no more work items on the work list because we know that our graph is *connected*, meaning that every location can be reached from all other locations. We'll always be able to find a route between two points, and the search can't fail.

```javascript
function goalOrientedRobot({place, parcels}, route) {
  if (route.length == 0) {
    let parcel = parcels[0];
    if (parcel.place != place) {
      route = findRoute(roadGraph, place, parcel.place);
    } else {
      route = findRoute(roadGraph, place, parcel.address);
    }
  }
  return {direction: route[0], memory: route.slice(1)};
}
```

This robot uses its memory value as a list of directions to move in, just like the route-following robot. Whenever that list is empty, it has to figure out what to do next. It takes the first undelivered parcel in the set and, if that parcel hasn't been picked up yet, plots a route toward it. If the parcel *has* been picked up, it still needs to be delivered, so the robot creates a route toward the delivery address instead.

This robot usually finishes the task of delivering 5 parcels in about 16 turns. That's slightly better than `routeRobot` but still definitely not optimal.

Exercises

Measuring a Robot

It's hard to objectively compare robots by just letting them solve a few scenarios. Maybe one robot just happened to get easier tasks or the kind of tasks that it is good at, whereas the other didn't.

Write a function `compareRobots` that takes two robots (and their starting memory). It should generate 100 tasks and let each of the robots solve each of these tasks. When done, it should output the average number of steps each robot took per task.

For the sake of fairness, make sure you give each task to both robots, rather than generating different tasks per robot.

Robot Efficiency

Can you write a robot that finishes the task faster than `goalOrientedRobot`? If you observe that robot's behavior, what obviously stupid things does it do? How could those be improved?

If you solved the previous exercise, you might want to use your compareRobots function to verify whether you improved the robot.

Persistent Group

Most data structures provided in a standard JavaScript environment aren't very well suited for persistent use. Arrays have slice and concat methods, which allow us to easily create new arrays without damaging the old one. But Set, for example, has no methods for creating a new set with an item added or removed.

Write a new class PGroup, similar to the Group class from "Groups" on page 113, which stores a set of values. Like Group, it has add, delete, and has methods.

Its add method, however, should return a *new* PGroup instance with the given member added and leave the old one unchanged. Similarly, delete creates a new instance without a given member.

The class should work for values of any type, not just strings. It does *not* have to be efficient when used with large amounts of values.

The constructor shouldn't be part of the class's interface (though you'll definitely want to use it internally). Instead, there is an empty instance, PGroup.empty, that can be used as a starting value.

Why do you need only one PGroup.empty value, rather than having a function that creates a new, empty map every time?

"Debugging is twice as hard as writing the code in the first place. Therefore, if you write the code as cleverly as possible, you are, by definition, not smart enough to debug it."

—Brian Kernighan and P. J. Plauger,
The Elements of Programming Style

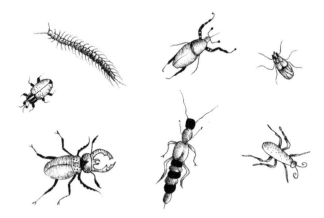

BUGS AND ERRORS

Flaws in computer programs are usually called *bugs*.
It makes programmers feel good to imagine them as
little things that just happen to crawl into our work. In
reality, of course, we put them there ourselves.

If a program is crystallized thought, you can roughly categorize bugs
into those caused by the thoughts being confused and those caused by mistakes introduced while converting a thought to code. The former type is
generally harder to diagnose and fix than the latter.

Language

Many mistakes could be pointed out to us automatically by the computer, if
it knew enough about what we're trying to do. But here JavaScript's loose-
ness is a hindrance. Its concept of bindings and properties is vague enough
that it will rarely catch typos before actually running the program. And even
then, it allows you to do some clearly nonsensical things without complaint,
such as computing true * "monkey".

There are some things that JavaScript does complain about. Writing
a program that does not follow the language's grammar will immediately
make the computer complain. Other things, such as calling something that's
not a function or looking up a property on an undefined value, will cause an
error to be reported when the program tries to perform the action.

But often, your nonsense computation will merely produce NaN (not a number) or an undefined value, while the program happily continues, convinced that it's doing something meaningful. The mistake will manifest itself only later, after the bogus value has traveled through several functions. It might not trigger an error at all but silently cause the program's output to be wrong. Finding the source of such problems can be difficult.

The process of finding mistakes—bugs—in programs is called *debugging*.

Strict Mode

JavaScript can be made a *little* stricter by enabling *strict mode*. This is done by putting the string "use strict" at the top of a file or a function body. Here's an example:

```
function canYouSpotTheProblem() {
  "use strict";
  for (counter = 0; counter < 10; counter++) {
    console.log("Happy happy");
  }
}

canYouSpotTheProblem();
// → ReferenceError: counter is not defined
```

Normally, when you forget to put let in front of your binding, as with counter in the example, JavaScript quietly creates a global binding and uses that. In strict mode, an error is reported instead. This is very helpful. It should be noted, though, that this doesn't work when the binding in question already exists as a global binding. In that case, the loop will still quietly overwrite the value of the binding.

Another change in strict mode is that the this binding holds the value undefined in functions that are not called as methods. When making such a call outside of strict mode, this refers to the global scope object, which is an object whose properties are the global bindings. So if you accidentally call a method or constructor incorrectly in strict mode, JavaScript will produce an error as soon as it tries to read something from this, rather than happily writing to the global scope.

For example, consider the following code, which calls a constructor function without the new keyword so that its this will *not* refer to a newly constructed object:

```
function Person(name) { this.name = name; }
let ferdinand = Person("Ferdinand"); // oops
console.log(name);
// → Ferdinand
```

So the bogus call to Person succeeded but returned an undefined value and created the global binding name. In strict mode, the result is different.

```
"use strict";
function Person(name) { this.name = name; }
let ferdinand = Person("Ferdinand"); // forgot new
// → TypeError: Cannot set property 'name' of undefined
```

We are immediately told that something is wrong. This is helpful.

Fortunately, constructors created with the `class` notation will always complain if they are called without `new`, making this less of a problem even in non-strict mode.

Strict mode does a few more things. It disallows giving a function multiple parameters with the same name and removes certain problematic language features entirely (such as the `with` statement, which is so wrong it is not further discussed in this book).

In short, putting `"use strict"` at the top of your program rarely hurts and might help you spot a problem.

Types

Some languages want to know the types of all your bindings and expressions before even running a program. They will tell you right away when a type is used in an inconsistent way. JavaScript considers types only when actually running the program, and even there often tries to implicitly convert values to the type it expects, so it's not much help.

Still, types provide a useful framework for talking about programs. A lot of mistakes come from being confused about the kind of value that goes into or comes out of a function. If you have that information written down, you're less likely to get confused.

You could add a comment like the following before the `goalOrientedRobot` function from the previous chapter to describe its type:

```
// (VillageState, Array) → {direction: string, memory: Array}
function goalOrientedRobot(state, memory) {
  // ...
}
```

There are a number of different conventions for annotating JavaScript programs with types.

One thing about types is that they need to introduce their own complexity to be able to describe enough code to be useful. What do you think would be the type of the `randomPick` function that returns a random element from an array? You'd need to introduce a *type variable*, T, which can stand in for any type, so that you can give `randomPick` a type like `([T]) → T` (function from an array of Ts to a T).

When the types of a program are known, it's possible for the computer to *check* them for you, pointing out mistakes before the program is run. There are several JavaScript dialects that add types to the language and check them. The most popular one is called TypeScript. If you are interested in adding more rigor to your programs, I recommend you give it a try.

In this book, we'll continue using raw, dangerous, untyped JavaScript code.

Testing

If the language is not going to do much to help us find mistakes, we'll have to find them the hard way: by running the program and seeing whether it does the right thing.

Doing this by hand, again and again, is a really bad idea. Not only is it annoying, it also tends to be ineffective since it takes too much time to exhaustively test everything every time you make a change.

Computers are good at repetitive tasks, and testing is the ideal repetitive task. Automated testing is the process of writing a program that tests another program. Writing tests is a bit more work than testing manually, but once you've done it, you gain a kind of superpower: it takes you only a few seconds to verify that your program still behaves properly in all the situations you wrote tests for. When you break something, you'll immediately notice, rather than randomly running into it at some later time.

Tests usually take the form of little labeled programs that verify some aspect of your code. For example, a set of tests for the (standard, probably already tested by someone else) toUpperCase method might look like this:

```
function test(label, body) {
  if (!body()) console.log(`Failed: ${label}`);
}

test("convert Latin text to uppercase", () => {
  return "hello".toUpperCase() == "HELLO";
});
test("convert Greek text to uppercase", () => {
  return "Χαίρετε".toUpperCase() == "ΧΑΊΡΕΤΕ";
});
test("don't convert case-less characters", () => {
  return "你好".toUpperCase() == "你好";
});
```

Writing tests like this tends to produce rather repetitive, awkward code. Fortunately, there exist pieces of software that help you build and run collections of tests (*test suites*) by providing a language (in the form of functions and methods) suited to expressing tests and by outputting informative information when a test fails. These are usually called *test runners*.

Some code is easier to test than other code. Generally, the more external objects that the code interacts with, the harder it is to set up the context in which to test it. The style of programming shown in the previous chapter, which uses self-contained persistent values rather than changing objects, tends to be easy to test.

Debugging

Once you notice there is something wrong with your program because it misbehaves or produces errors, the next step is to figure out *what* the problem is.

Sometimes it is obvious. The error message will point at a specific line of your program, and if you look at the error description and that line of code, you can often see the problem.

But not always. Sometimes the line that triggered the problem is simply the first place where a flaky value produced elsewhere gets used in an invalid way. If you have been solving the exercises in earlier chapters, you will probably have already experienced such situations.

The following example program tries to convert a whole number to a string in a given base (decimal, binary, and so on) by repeatedly picking out the last digit and then dividing the number to get rid of this digit. But the strange output that it currently produces suggests that it has a bug.

```
function numberToString(n, base = 10) {
  let result = "", sign = "";
  if (n < 0) {
    sign = "-";
    n = -n;
  }
  do {
    result = String(n % base) + result;
    n /= base;
  } while (n > 0);
  return sign + result;
}
console.log(numberToString(13, 10));
// → 1.5e-3231.3e-3221.3e-3211.3e-3201.3e-3191.3e-3181.3...
```

Even if you see the problem already, pretend for a moment that you don't. We know that our program is malfunctioning, and we want to find out why.

This is where you must resist the urge to start making random changes to the code to see whether that makes it better. Instead, *think*. Analyze what is happening and come up with a theory of why it might be happening. Then, make additional observations to test this theory—or, if you don't yet have a theory, make additional observations to help you come up with one.

Putting a few strategic console.log calls into the program is a good way to get additional information about what the program is doing. In this case, we want n to take the values 13, 1, and then 0. Let's write out its value at the start of the loop.

```
13
1.3
0.13
```

```
0.013
...
1.5e-323
```

Right. Dividing 13 by 10 does not produce a whole number. Instead of `n /= base`, what we actually want is `n = Math.floor(n / base)` so that the number is properly "shifted" to the right.

An alternative to using `console.log` to peek into the program's behavior is to use the *debugger* capabilities of your browser. Browsers come with the ability to set a *breakpoint* on a specific line of your code. When the execution of the program reaches a line with a breakpoint, it is paused, and you can inspect the values of bindings at that point. I won't go into details, as debuggers differ from browser to browser, but look in your browser's developer tools or search the web for more information.

Another way to set a breakpoint is to include a `debugger` statement (consisting of simply that keyword) in your program. If the developer tools of your browser are active, the program will pause whenever it reaches such a statement.

Error Propagation

Not all problems can be prevented by the programmer, unfortunately. If your program communicates with the outside world in any way, it is possible to get malformed input, to become overloaded with work, or to have the network fail.

If you're programming only for yourself, you can afford to just ignore such problems until they occur. But if you build something that is going to be used by anybody else, you usually want the program to do better than just crash. Sometimes the right thing to do is take the bad input in stride and continue running. In other cases, it is better to report to the user what went wrong and then give up. But in either situation, the program has to actively do something in response to the problem.

Say you have a function `promptNumber` that asks the user for a number and returns it. What should it return if the user inputs "orange?"

One option is to make it return a special value. Common choices for such values are `null`, `undefined`, or `-1`.

```
function promptNumber(question) {
  let result = Number(prompt(question));
  if (Number.isNaN(result)) return null;
  else return result;
}

console.log(promptNumber("How many trees do you see?"));
```

Now any code that calls `promptNumber` must check whether an actual number was read and, failing that, must somehow recover—maybe by asking again or by filling in a default value. Or it could again return a special value to *its* caller to indicate that it failed to do what it was asked.

In many situations, mostly when errors are common and the caller should be explicitly taking them into account, returning a special value is a good way to indicate an error. It does, however, have its downsides. First, what if the function can already return every possible kind of value? In such a function, you'll have to do something like wrap the result in an object to be able to distinguish success from failure.

```
function lastElement(array) {
  if (array.length == 0) {
    return {failed: true};
  } else {
    return {element: array[array.length - 1]};
  }
}
```

The second issue with returning special values is that it can lead to awkward code. If a piece of code calls promptNumber 10 times, it has to check 10 times whether null was returned. And if its response to finding null is to simply return null itself, callers of the function will in turn have to check for it, and so on.

Exceptions

When a function cannot proceed normally, what we would *like* to do is just stop what we are doing and immediately jump to a place that knows how to handle the problem. This is what *exception handling* does.

Exceptions are a mechanism that makes it possible for code that runs into a problem to *raise* (or *throw*) an exception. An exception can be any value. Raising one somewhat resembles a super-charged return from a function: it jumps out of not just the current function but also its callers, all the way down to the first call that started the current execution. This is called *unwinding the stack*. You may remember the stack of function calls that was mentioned in "The Call Stack" on page 46. An exception zooms down this stack, throwing away all the call contexts it encounters.

If exceptions always zoomed right down to the bottom of the stack, they would not be of much use. They'd just provide a novel way to blow up your program. Their power lies in the fact that you can set "obstacles" along the stack to *catch* the exception as it is zooming down. Once you've caught an exception, you can do something with it to address the problem and then continue to run the program.

Here's an example:

```
function promptDirection(question) {
  let result = prompt(question);
  if (result.toLowerCase() == "left") return "L";
  if (result.toLowerCase() == "right") return "R";
```

```
    throw new Error("Invalid direction: " + result);
  }

function look() {
  if (promptDirection("Which way?") == "L") {
    return "a house";
  } else {
    return "two angry bears";
  }
}

try {
  console.log("You see", look());
} catch (error) {
  console.log("Something went wrong: " + error);
}
```

The throw keyword is used to raise an exception. Catching one is done by wrapping a piece of code in a try block, followed by the keyword catch. When the code in the try block causes an exception to be raised, the catch block is evaluated, with the name in parentheses bound to the exception value. After the catch block finishes—or if the try block finishes without problems—the program proceeds beneath the entire try/catch statement.

In this case, we used the Error constructor to create our exception value. This is a standard JavaScript constructor that creates an object with a message property. In most JavaScript environments, instances of this constructor also gather information about the call stack that existed when the exception was created, a so-called *stack trace*. This information is stored in the stack property and can be helpful when trying to debug a problem: it tells us the function where the problem occurred and which functions made the failing call.

Note that the look function completely ignores the possibility that promptDirection might go wrong. This is the big advantage of exceptions: error-handling code is necessary only at the point where the error occurs and at the point where it is handled. The functions in between can forget all about it.

Well, almost . . .

Cleaning Up After Exceptions

The effect of an exception is another kind of control flow. Every action that might cause an exception, which is pretty much every function call and property access, might cause control to suddenly leave your code.

This means when code has several side effects, even if its "regular" control flow looks like they'll always all happen, an exception might prevent some of them from taking place.

Here is some really bad banking code.

```
const accounts = {
  a: 100,
  b: 0,
  c: 20
};

function getAccount() {
  let accountName = prompt("Enter an account name");
  if (!accounts.hasOwnProperty(accountName)) {
    throw new Error(`No such account: ${accountName}`);
  }
  return accountName;
}

function transfer(from, amount) {
  if (accounts[from] < amount) return;
  accounts[from] -= amount;
  accounts[getAccount()] += amount;
}
```

The transfer function transfers a sum of money from a given account to another, asking for the name of the other account in the process. If given an invalid account name, getAccount throws an exception.

But transfer *first* removes the money from the account and *then* calls getAccount before it adds it to another account. If it is broken off by an exception at that point, it'll just make the money disappear.

That code could have been written a little more intelligently, for example by calling getAccount before it starts moving money around. But often problems like this occur in more subtle ways. Even functions that don't look like they will throw an exception might do so in exceptional circumstances or when they contain a programmer mistake.

One way to address this is to use fewer side effects. Again, a programming style that computes new values instead of changing existing data helps. If a piece of code stops running in the middle of creating a new value, no one ever sees the half-finished value, and there is no problem.

But that isn't always practical. So there is another feature that try statements have. They may be followed by a finally block either instead of or in addition to a catch block. A finally block says "no matter *what* happens, run this code after trying to run the code in the try block."

```
function transfer(from, amount) {
  if (accounts[from] < amount) return;
  let progress = 0;
  try {
    accounts[from] -= amount;
    progress = 1;
```

```
    accounts[getAccount()] += amount;
    progress = 2;
  } finally {
    if (progress == 1) {
      accounts[from] += amount;
    }
  }
}
```

This version of the function tracks its progress, and if, when leaving, it notices that it was aborted at a point where it had created an inconsistent program state, it repairs the damage it did.

Note that even though the `finally` code is run when an exception is thrown in the `try` block, it does not interfere with the exception. After the `finally` block runs, the stack continues unwinding.

Writing programs that operate reliably even when exceptions pop up in unexpected places is hard. Many people simply don't bother, and because exceptions are typically reserved for exceptional circumstances, the problem may occur so rarely that it is never even noticed. Whether that is a good thing or a really bad thing depends on how much damage the software will do when it fails.

Selective Catching

When an exception makes it all the way to the bottom of the stack without being caught, it gets handled by the environment. What this means differs between environments. In browsers, a description of the error typically gets written to the JavaScript console (reachable through the browser's Tools or Developer menu). Node.js, the browserless JavaScript environment we will discuss in Chapter 20, is more careful about data corruption. It aborts the whole process when an unhandled exception occurs.

For programmer mistakes, just letting the error go through is often the best you can do. An unhandled exception is a reasonable way to signal a broken program, and the JavaScript console will, on modern browsers, provide you with some information about which function calls were on the stack when the problem occurred.

For problems that are *expected* to happen during routine use, crashing with an unhandled exception is a terrible strategy.

Invalid uses of the language, such as referencing a nonexistent binding, looking up a property on `null`, or calling something that's not a function, will also result in exceptions being raised. Such exceptions can also be caught.

When a catch body is entered, all we know is that *something* in our try body caused an exception. But we don't know *what* did or *which* exception it caused.

JavaScript (in a rather glaring omission) doesn't provide direct support for selectively catching exceptions: either you catch them all or you don't catch any. This makes it tempting to *assume* that the exception you get is the one you were thinking about when you wrote the catch block.

But it might not be. Some other assumption might be violated, or you might have introduced a bug that is causing an exception. Here is an example that *attempts* to keep on calling promptDirection until it gets a valid answer:

```
for (;;) {
  try {
    let dir = promtDirection("Where?"); // ← typo!
    console.log("You chose ", dir);
    break;
  } catch (e) {
    console.log("Not a valid direction. Try again.");
  }
}
```

The for (;;) construct is a way to intentionally create a loop that doesn't terminate on its own. We break out of the loop only when a valid direction is given. *But* we misspelled promptDirection, which will result in an "undefined variable" error. Because the catch block completely ignores its exception value (e), assuming it knows what the problem is, it wrongly treats the binding error as indicating bad input. Not only does this cause an infinite loop, it "buries" the useful error message about the misspelled binding.

As a general rule, don't blanket-catch exceptions unless it is for the purpose of "routing" them somewhere—for example, over the network to tell another system that our program crashed. And even then, think carefully about how you might be hiding information.

So we want to catch a *specific* kind of exception. We can do this by checking in the catch block whether the exception we got is the one we are interested in and rethrowing it otherwise. But how do we recognize an exception?

We could compare its message property against the error message we happen to expect. But that's a shaky way to write code—we'd be using information that's intended for human consumption (the message) to make a programmatic decision. As soon as someone changes (or translates) the message, the code will stop working.

Rather, let's define a new type of error and use instanceof to identify it.

```
class InputError extends Error {}

function promptDirection(question) {
  let result = prompt(question);
  if (result.toLowerCase() == "left") return "L";
  if (result.toLowerCase() == "right") return "R";
  throw new InputError("Invalid direction: " + result);
}
```

The new error class extends `Error`. It doesn't define its own constructor, which means that it inherits the `Error` constructor, which expects a string message as argument. In fact, it doesn't define anything at all—the class is empty. `InputError` objects behave like `Error` objects, except that they have a different class by which we can recognize them.

Now the loop can catch these more carefully.

```
for (;;) {
  try {
    let dir = promptDirection("Where?");
    console.log("You chose ", dir);
    break;
  } catch (e) {
    if (e instanceof InputError) {
      console.log("Not a valid direction. Try again.");
    } else {
      throw e;
    }
  }
}
```

This will catch only instances of `InputError` and let unrelated exceptions through. If you reintroduce the typo, the undefined binding error will be properly reported.

Assertions

Assertions are checks inside a program that verify that something is the way it is supposed to be. They are used not to handle situations that can come up in normal operation but to find programmer mistakes.

If, for example, `firstElement` is described as a function that should never be called on empty arrays, we might write it like this:

```
function firstElement(array) {
  if (array.length == 0) {
    throw new Error("firstElement called with []");
  }
  return array[0];
}
```

Now, instead of silently returning undefined (which you get when reading an array property that does not exist), this will loudly blow up your program as soon as you misuse it. This makes it less likely for such mistakes to go unnoticed and easier to find their cause when they occur.

I do not recommend trying to write assertions for every possible kind of bad input. That'd be a lot of work and would lead to very noisy code. You'll want to reserve them for mistakes that are easy to make (or that you find yourself making).

Summary

Mistakes and bad input are facts of life. An important part of programming is finding, diagnosing, and fixing bugs. Problems can become easier to notice if you have an automated test suite or add assertions to your programs.

Problems caused by factors outside the program's control should usually be handled gracefully. Sometimes, when the problem can be handled locally, special return values are a good way to track them. Otherwise, exceptions may be preferable.

Throwing an exception causes the call stack to be unwound until the next enclosing try/catch block or until the bottom of the stack. The exception value will be given to the catch block that catches it, which should verify that it is actually the expected kind of exception and then do something with it. To help address the unpredictable control flow caused by exceptions, finally blocks can be used to ensure that a piece of code *always* runs when a block finishes.

Exercises

Retry

Say you have a function primitiveMultiply that in 20 percent of cases multiplies two numbers and in the other 80 percent of cases raises an exception of type MultiplicatorUnitFailure. Write a function that wraps this clunky function and just keeps trying until a call succeeds, after which it returns the result.

Make sure you handle only the exceptions you are trying to handle.

The Locked Box

Consider the following (rather contrived) object:

```
const box = {
  locked: true,
  unlock() { this.locked = false; },
  lock() { this.locked = true;  },
  _content: [],
  get content() {
    if (this.locked) throw new Error("Locked!");
    return this._content;
  }
};
```

It is a box with a lock. There is an array in the box, but you can get at it only when the box is unlocked. Directly accessing the private _content property is forbidden.

Write a function called `withBoxUnlocked` that takes a function value as argument, unlocks the box, runs the function, and then ensures that the box is locked again before returning, regardless of whether the argument function returned normally or threw an exception.

```
const box = {
  locked: true,
  unlock() { this.locked = false; },
  lock() { this.locked = true;  },
  _content: [],
  get content() {
    if (this.locked) throw new Error("Locked!");
    return this._content;
  }
};

function withBoxUnlocked(body) {
  // Your code here.
}

withBoxUnlocked(function() {
  box.content.push("gold piece");
});

try {
  withBoxUnlocked(function() {
    throw new Error("Pirates on the horizon! Abort!");
  });
} catch (e) {
  console.log("Error raised:", e);
}
console.log(box.locked);
// → true
```

For extra points, make sure that if you call `withBoxUnlocked` when the box is already unlocked, the box stays unlocked.

"Some people, when confronted
with a problem, think 'I know,
I'll use regular expressions.'
Now they have two problems."

—Jamie Zawinski

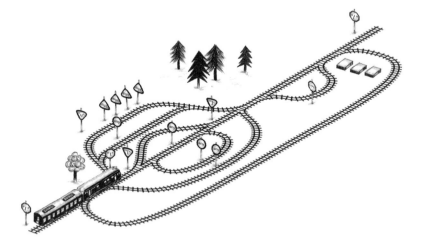

9

REGULAR EXPRESSIONS

Programming tools and techniques survive and spread in a chaotic, evolutionary way. It's not always the pretty or brilliant ones that win but rather the ones that function well enough within the right niche or that happen to be integrated with another successful piece of technology.

In this chapter, I will discuss one such tool, *regular expressions*. Regular expressions are a way to describe patterns in string data. They form a small, separate language that is part of JavaScript and many other languages and systems.

Regular expressions are both terribly awkward and extremely useful. Their syntax is cryptic, and the programming interface JavaScript provides for them is clumsy. But they are a powerful tool for inspecting and processing strings. Properly understanding regular expressions will make you a more effective programmer.

Creating a Regular Expression

A regular expression is a type of object. It can be either constructed with the RegExp constructor or written as a literal value by enclosing a pattern in forward slash (/) characters.

```
let re1 = new RegExp("abc");
let re2 = /abc/;
```

Both of those regular expression objects represent the same pattern: an *a* character followed by a *b* followed by a *c*.

When using the RegExp constructor, the pattern is written as a normal string, so the usual rules apply for backslashes.

The second notation, where the pattern appears between slash characters, treats backslashes somewhat differently. First, since a forward slash ends the pattern, we need to put a backslash before any forward slash that we want to be *part* of the pattern. In addition, backslashes that aren't part of special character codes (like \n) will be *preserved*, rather than ignored as they are in strings, and change the meaning of the pattern. Some characters, such as question marks and plus signs, have special meanings in regular expressions and must be preceded by a backslash if they are meant to represent the character itself.

```
let eighteenPlus = /eighteen\+/;
```

Testing for Matches

Regular expression objects have a number of methods. The simplest one is test. If you pass it a string, it will return a Boolean telling you whether the string contains a match of the pattern in the expression.

```
console.log(/abc/.test("abcde"));
// → true
console.log(/abc/.test("abxde"));
// → false
```

A regular expression consisting of only nonspecial characters simply represents that sequence of characters. If *abc* occurs anywhere in the string we are testing against (not just at the start), test will return true.

Sets of Characters

Finding out whether a string contains *abc* could just as well be done with a call to indexOf. Regular expressions allow us to express more complicated patterns.

Say we want to match any number. In a regular expression, putting a set of characters between square brackets makes that part of the expression match any of the characters between the brackets.

Both of the following expressions match all strings that contain a digit:

```
console.log(/[0123456789]/.test("in 1992"));
// → true
console.log(/[0-9]/.test("in 1992"));
// → true
```

Within square brackets, a hyphen (-) between two characters can be used to indicate a range of characters, where the ordering is determined by the character's Unicode number. Characters 0 to 9 sit right next to each other in this ordering (codes 48 to 57), so [0-9] covers all of them and matches any digit.

A number of common character groups have their own built-in shortcuts. Digits are one of them: \d means the same thing as [0-9].

\d	Any digit character
\w	An alphanumeric character ("word character")
\s	Any whitespace character (space, tab, newline, and similar)
\D	A character that is *not* a digit
\W	A nonalphanumeric character
\S	A nonwhitespace character
.	Any character except for newline

So you could match a date and time format like 01-30-2003 15:20 with the following expression:

```
let dateTime = /\d\d-\d\d-\d\d\d\d \d\d:\d\d/;
console.log(dateTime.test("01-30-2003 15:20"));
// → true
console.log(dateTime.test("30-jan-2003 15:20"));
// → false
```

That looks completely awful, doesn't it? Half of it is backslashes, producing a background noise that makes it hard to spot the actual pattern expressed. We'll see a slightly improved version of this expression in the next section.

These backslash codes can also be used inside square brackets. For example, [\d.] means any digit or a period character. But the period itself, between square brackets, loses its special meaning. The same goes for other special characters, such as +.

To *invert* a set of characters—that is, to express that you want to match any character *except* the ones in the set—you can write a caret (^) character after the opening square bracket.

```
let notBinary = /[^01]/;
console.log(notBinary.test("1100100010100110"));
// → false
console.log(notBinary.test("1100100010200110"));
// → true
```

Repeating Parts of a Pattern

We now know how to match a single digit. What if we want to match a whole number—a sequence of one or more digits?

When you put a plus sign (+) after something in a regular expression, it indicates that the element may be repeated more than once. Thus, /\d+/ matches one or more digit characters.

```
console.log(/'\d+'/.test("'123'"));
// → true
console.log(/'\d+'/.test("''"));
// → false
console.log(/'\d*'/.test("'123'"));
// → true
console.log(/'\d*'/.test("''"));
// → true
```

The star (*) has a similar meaning but also allows the pattern to match zero times. Something with a star after it never prevents a pattern from matching—it'll just match zero instances if it can't find any suitable text to match.

A question mark makes a part of a pattern *optional*, meaning it may occur zero times or one time. In the following example, the *u* character is allowed to occur, but the pattern also matches when it is missing.

```
let neighbor = /neighbou?r/;
console.log(neighbor.test("neighbour"));
// → true
console.log(neighbor.test("neighbor"));
// → true
```

To indicate that a pattern should occur a precise number of times, use braces. Putting {4} after an element, for example, requires it to occur exactly four times. It is also possible to specify a range this way: {2,4} means the element must occur at least twice and at most four times.

Here is another version of the date and time pattern that allows both single- and double-digit days, months, and hours. It is also slightly easier to decipher.

```
let dateTime = /\d{1,2}-\d{1,2}-\d{4} \d{1,2}:\d{2}/;
console.log(dateTime.test("1-30-2003 8:45"));
// → true
```

You can also specify open-ended ranges when using braces by omitting the number after the comma. So, {5,} means five or more times.

Grouping Subexpressions

To use an operator like * or + on more than one element at a time, you have to use parentheses. A part of a regular expression that is enclosed in parentheses counts as a single element as far as the operators following it are concerned.

```
let cartoonCrying = /boo+(hoo+)+/i;
console.log(cartoonCrying.test("Boohoooohoohooo"));
// → true
```

The first and second + characters apply only to the second *o* in *boo* and *hoo*, respectively. The third + applies to the whole group (hoo+), matching one or more sequences like that.

The i at the end of the expression in the example makes this regular expression case insensitive, allowing it to match the uppercase *B* in the input string, even though the pattern is itself all lowercase.

Matches and Groups

The test method is the absolute simplest way to match a regular expression. It tells you only whether it matched and nothing else. Regular expressions also have an exec (execute) method that will return null if no match was found and return an object with information about the match otherwise.

```
let match = /\d+/.exec("one two 100");
console.log(match);
// → ["100"]
console.log(match.index);
// → 8
```

An object returned from exec has an index property that tells us *where* in the string the successful match begins. Other than that, the object looks like (and in fact is) an array of strings, whose first element is the string that was matched. In the previous example, this is the sequence of digits that we were looking for.

String values have a match method that behaves similarly.

```
console.log("one two 100".match(/\d+/));
// → ["100"]
```

When the regular expression contains subexpressions grouped with parentheses, the text that matched those groups will also show up in the array. The whole match is always the first element. The next element is the part matched by the first group (the one whose opening parenthesis comes first in the expression), then the second group, and so on.

```
let quotedText = /'([^']*)'/;
console.log(quotedText.exec("she said 'hello'"));
// → ["'hello'", "hello"]
```

When a group does not end up being matched at all (for example,
when followed by a question mark), its position in the output array will hold
undefined. Similarly, when a group is matched multiple times, only the last
match ends up in the array.

```
console.log(/bad(ly)?/.exec("bad"));
// → ["bad", undefined]
console.log(/(\d)+/.exec("123"));
// → ["123", "3"]
```

Groups can be useful for extracting parts of a string. If we don't just
want to verify whether a string contains a date but also extract it and construct an object that represents it, we can wrap parentheses around the digit
patterns and directly pick the date out of the result of exec.

But first we'll take a brief detour, in which we discuss the built-in way to
represent date and time values in JavaScript.

The Date Class

JavaScript has a standard class for representing dates—or, rather, points in
time. It is called Date. If you simply create a date object using new, you get the
current date and time.

```
console.log(new Date());
// → Sat Sep 01 2018 15:24:32 GMT+0200 (CEST)
```

You can also create an object for a specific time.

```
console.log(new Date(2009, 11, 9));
// → Wed Dec 09 2009 00:00:00 GMT+0100 (CET)
console.log(new Date(2009, 11, 9, 12, 59, 59, 999));
// → Wed Dec 09 2009 12:59:59 GMT+0100 (CET)
```

JavaScript uses a convention where month numbers start at zero (so
December is 11), yet day numbers start at one. This is confusing and silly.
Be careful.

The last four arguments (hours, minutes, seconds, and milliseconds) are
optional and taken to be zero when not given.

Timestamps are stored as the number of milliseconds since the start of
1970, in the UTC time zone. This follows a convention set by "Unix time,"
which was invented around that time. You can use negative numbers for
times before 1970. The getTime method on a date object returns this number. It is big, as you can imagine.

```
console.log(new Date(2013, 11, 19).getTime());
// → 1387407600000
console.log(new Date(1387407600000));
// → Thu Dec 19 2013 00:00:00 GMT+0100 (CET)
```

If you give the Date constructor a single argument, that argument is treated as such a millisecond count. You can get the current millisecond count by creating a new Date object and calling getTime on it or by calling the Date.now function.

Date objects provide methods such as getFullYear, getMonth, getDate, getHours, getMinutes, and getSeconds to extract their components. Besides getFullYear there's also getYear, which gives you the year minus 1900 (98 or 119) and is mostly useless.

Putting parentheses around the parts of the expression that we are interested in, we can now create a date object from a string.

```
function getDate(string) {
  let [_, month, day, year] =
    /(\d{1,2})-(\d{1,2})-(\d{4})/.exec(string);
  return new Date(year, month - 1, day);
}
console.log(getDate("1-30-2003"));
// → Thu Jan 30 2003 00:00:00 GMT+0100 (CET)
```

The _ (underscore) binding is ignored and used only to skip the full match element in the array returned by exec.

Word and String Boundaries

Unfortunately, getDate will also happily extract the nonsensical date 00-1-3000 from the string "100-1-30000". A match may happen anywhere in the string, so in this case, it'll just start at the second character and end at the second-to-last character.

If we want to enforce that the match must span the whole string, we can add the markers ^ and $. The caret matches the start of the input string, whereas the dollar sign matches the end. So, /^\d+$/ matches a string consisting entirely of one or more digits, /^!/ matches any string that starts with an exclamation mark, and /x^/ does not match any string (there cannot be an *x* before the start of the string).

If, on the other hand, we just want to make sure the date starts and ends on a word boundary, we can use the marker \b. A word boundary can be the start or end of the string or any point in the string that has a word character (as in \w) on one side and a nonword character on the other.

```
console.log(/cat/.test("concatenate"));
// → true
```

```
console.log(/\bcat\b/.test("concatenate"));
// → false
```

Note that a boundary marker doesn't match an actual character. It just enforces that the regular expression matches only when a certain condition holds at the place where it appears in the pattern.

Choice Patterns

Say we want to know whether a piece of text contains not only a number but a number followed by one of the words *pig, cow,* or *chicken*, or any of their plural forms.

We could write three regular expressions and test them in turn, but there is a nicer way. The pipe character (|) denotes a choice between the pattern to its left and the pattern to its right. So I can say this:

```
let animalCount = /\b\d+ (pig|cow|chicken)s?\b/;
console.log(animalCount.test("15 pigs"));
// → true
console.log(animalCount.test("15 pigchickens"));
// → false
```

Parentheses can be used to limit the part of the pattern that the pipe operator applies to, and you can put multiple such operators next to each other to express a choice between more than two alternatives.

The Mechanics of Matching

Conceptually, when you use exec or test, the regular expression engine looks for a match in your string by trying to match the expression first from the start of the string, then from the second character, and so on, until it finds a match or reaches the end of the string. It'll either return the first match that can be found or fail to find any match at all.

To do the actual matching, the engine treats a regular expression something like a flow diagram. This is the diagram for the livestock expression in the previous example:

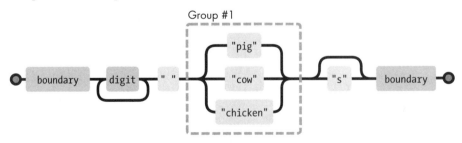

Our expression matches if we can find a path from the left side of the diagram to the right side. We keep a current position in the string, and every time we move through a box, we verify that the part of the string after our current position matches that box.

So if we try to match "the 3 pigs" from position 4, our progress through the flow chart would look like this:

- At position 4, there is a word boundary, so we can move past the first box.

- Still at position 4, we find a digit, so we can also move past the second box.

- At position 5, one path loops back to before the second (digit) box, while the other moves forward through the box that holds a single space character. There is a space here, not a digit, so we must take the second path.

- We are now at position 6 (the start of *pigs*) and at the three-way branch in the diagram. We don't see *cow* or *chicken* here, but we do see *pig*, so we take that branch.

- At position 9, after the three-way branch, one path skips the *s* box and goes straight to the final word boundary, while the other path matches an *s*. There is an *s* character here, not a word boundary, so we go through the *s* box.

- We're at position 10 (the end of the string) and can match only a word boundary. The end of a string counts as a word boundary, so we go through the last box and have successfully matched this string.

Backtracking

The regular expression /\b([01]+b|[\da-f]+h|\d+)\b/ matches either a binary number followed by a *b*, a hexadecimal number (that is, base 16, with the letters *a* to *f* standing for the digits 10 to 15) followed by an *h*, or a regular decimal number with no suffix character. This is the corresponding diagram:

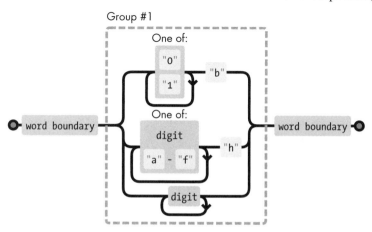

When matching this expression, it will often happen that the top (binary) branch is entered even though the input does not actually contain a binary number. When matching the string "103", for example, it becomes clear only at the 3 that we are in the wrong branch. The string *does* match the expression, just not the branch we are currently in.

So the matcher *backtracks*. When entering a branch, it remembers its current position (in this case, at the start of the string, just past the first boundary box in the diagram) so that it can go back and try another branch if the current one does not work out. For the string "103", after encountering the 3 character, it will start trying the branch for hexadecimal numbers, which fails again because there is no *h* after the number. So it tries the decimal number branch. This one fits, and a match is reported after all.

The matcher stops as soon as it finds a full match. This means that if multiple branches could potentially match a string, only the first one (ordered by where the branches appear in the regular expression) is used.

Backtracking also happens for repetition operators like + and *. If you match /^.*x/ against "abcxe", the .* part will first try to consume the whole string. The engine will then realize that it needs an *x* to match the pattern. Since there is no *x* past the end of the string, the star operator tries to match one character less. But the matcher doesn't find an *x* after abcx either, so it backtracks again, matching the star operator to just abc. *Now* it finds an *x* where it needs it and reports a successful match from positions 0 to 4.

It is possible to write regular expressions that will do a *lot* of backtracking. This problem occurs when a pattern can match a piece of input in many different ways. For example, if we get confused while writing a binary-number regular expression, we might accidentally write something like /([01]+)+b/.

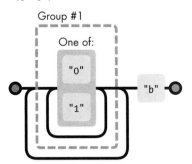

If that tries to match some long series of zeros and ones with no trailing *b* character, the matcher first goes through the inner loop until it runs out of digits. Then it notices there is no *b*, so it backtracks one position, goes through the outer loop once, and gives up again, trying to backtrack out of the inner loop once more. It will continue to try every possible route through these two loops. This means the amount of work *doubles* with each additional character. For even just a few dozen characters, the resulting match will take practically forever.

The replace Method

String values have a replace method that can be used to replace part of the string with another string.

```
console.log("papa".replace("p", "m"));
// → mapa
```

The first argument can also be a regular expression, in which case the first match of the regular expression is replaced. When a g option (for *global*) is added to the regular expression, *all* matches in the string will be replaced, not just the first.

```
console.log("Borobudur".replace(/[ou]/, "a"));
// → Barobudur
console.log("Borobudur".replace(/[ou]/g, "a"));
// → Barabadar
```

It would have been sensible if the choice between replacing one match or all matches was made through an additional argument to replace or by providing a different method, replaceAll. But for some unfortunate reason, the choice relies on a property of the regular expression instead.

The real power of using regular expressions with replace comes from the fact that we can refer to matched groups in the replacement string. For example, say we have a big string containing the names of people, one name per line, in the format Lastname, Firstname. If we want to swap these names and remove the comma to get a Firstname Lastname format, we can use the following code:

```
console.log(
  "Liskov, Barbara\nMcCarthy, John\nWadler, Philip"
    .replace(/(\w+), (\w+)/g, "$2 $1"));
// → Barbara Liskov
//   John McCarthy
//   Philip Wadler
```

The $1 and $2 in the replacement string refer to the parenthesized groups in the pattern. $1 is replaced by the text that matched against the first group, $2 by the second, and so on, up to $9. The whole match can be referred to with $&.

It is possible to pass a function—rather than a string—as the second argument to replace. For each replacement, the function will be called with the matched groups (as well as the whole match) as arguments, and its return value will be inserted into the new string.

Here's a small example:

```
let s = "the cia and fbi";
console.log(s.replace(/\b(fbi|cia)\b/g,
```

```
          str => str.toUpperCase()));
// → the CIA and FBI
```

Here's a more interesting one:

```
let stock = "1 lemon, 2 cabbages, and 101 eggs";
function minusOne(match, amount, unit) {
  amount = Number(amount) - 1;
  if (amount == 1) { // only one left, remove the 's'
    unit = unit.slice(0, unit.length - 1);
  } else if (amount == 0) {
    amount = "no";
  }
  return amount + " " + unit;
}
console.log(stock.replace(/(\d+) (\w+)/g, minusOne));
// → no lemon, 1 cabbage, and 100 eggs
```

This takes a string, finds all occurrences of a number followed by an alphanumeric word, and returns a string wherein every such occurrence is decremented by one.

The (\d+) group ends up as the amount argument to the function, and the (\w+) group gets bound to unit. The function converts amount to a number—which always works since it matched \d+—and makes some adjustments in case there is only one or zero left.

Greed

It is possible to use replace to write a function that removes all comments from a piece of JavaScript code. Here is a first attempt:

```
function stripComments(code) {
  return code.replace(/\/\/.*|\/\*[^]*\*\//g, "");
}
console.log(stripComments("1 + /* 2 */3"));
// → 1 + 3
console.log(stripComments("x = 10;// ten!"));
// → x = 10;
console.log(stripComments("1 /* a */+/* b */ 1"));
// → 1  1
```

The part before the *or* operator matches two slash characters followed by any number of non-newline characters. The part for multiline comments is more involved. We use [^] (any character that is not in the empty set of characters) as a way to match any character. We cannot just use a period here because block comments can continue on a new line, and the period character does not match newline characters.

But the output for the last line appears to have gone wrong. Why?

The [^]* part of the expression, as I described in the section on back-tracking, will first match as much as it can. If that causes the next part of the pattern to fail, the matcher moves back one character and tries again from there. In the example, the matcher first tries to match the whole rest of the string and then moves back from there. It will find an occurrence of */ after going back four characters and match that. This is not what we wanted—the intention was to match a single comment, not to go all the way to the end of the code and find the end of the last block comment.

Because of this behavior, we say the repetition operators (+, *, ?, and {}) are *greedy*, meaning they match as much as they can and backtrack from there. If you put a question mark after them (+?, *?, ??, {}?), they become nongreedy and start by matching as little as possible, matching more only when the remaining pattern does not fit the smaller match.

And that is exactly what we want in this case. By having the star match the smallest stretch of characters that brings us to a */, we consume one block comment and nothing more.

```
function stripComments(code) {
  return code.replace(/\/\/.*|\/\*[^]*?\*\//g, "");
}
console.log(stripComments("1 /* a */+/* b */ 1"));
// → 1 + 1
```

A lot of bugs in regular expression programs can be traced to unintentionally using a greedy operator where a nongreedy one would work better. When using a repetition operator, consider the nongreedy variant first.

Dynamically Creating RegExp Objects

There are cases where you might not know the exact pattern you need to match against when you are writing your code. Say you want to look for the user's name in a piece of text and enclose it in underscore characters to make it stand out. Since you will know the name only once the program is actually running, you can't use the slash-based notation.

But you can build up a string and use the RegExp constructor on that. Here's an example:

```
let name = "harry";
let text = "Harry is a suspicious character.";
let regexp = new RegExp("\\b(" + name + ")\\b", "gi");
console.log(text.replace(regexp, "_$1_"));
// → _Harry_ is a suspicious character.
```

When creating the \b boundary markers, we have to use two backslashes because we are writing them in a normal string, not a slash-enclosed regular expression. The second argument to the RegExp constructor contains the options for the regular expression—in this case, "gi" for global and case insensitive.

But what if the name is "dea+hl[]rd" because our user is a nerdy teen-ager? That would result in a nonsensical regular expression that won't actually match the user's name.

To work around this, we can add backslashes before any character that has a special meaning.

```
let name = "dea+hl[]rd";
let text = "This dea+hl[]rd guy is super annoying.";
let escaped = name.replace(/[\\[.+*?(){|^$]/g, "\\$&");
let regexp = new RegExp("\\b" + escaped + "\\b", "gi");
console.log(text.replace(regexp, "_$&_"));
// → This _dea+hl[]rd_ guy is super annoying.
```

The search Method

The indexOf method on strings cannot be called with a regular expression. But there is another method, search, that does expect a regular expression. Like indexOf, it returns the first index on which the expression was found, or −1 when it wasn't found.

```
console.log("  word".search(/\S/));
// → 2
console.log("    ".search(/\S/));
// → -1
```

Unfortunately, there is no way to indicate that the match should start at a given offset (like we can with the second argument to indexOf), which would often be useful.

The lastIndex Property

The exec method similarly does not provide a convenient way to start searching from a given position in the string. But it does provide an *in*convenient way.

Regular expression objects have properties. One such property is source, which contains the string that expression was created from. Another property is lastIndex, which controls, in some limited circumstances, where the next match will start.

Those circumstances are that the regular expression must have the global (g) or sticky (y) option enabled, and the match must happen through the exec method. Again, a less confusing solution would have been to just allow an extra argument to be passed to exec, but confusion is an essential feature of JavaScript's regular expression interface.

```
let pattern = /y/g;
pattern.lastIndex = 3;
let match = pattern.exec("xyzzy");
```

```
console.log(match.index);
// → 4
console.log(pattern.lastIndex);
// → 5
```

If the match was successful, the call to exec automatically updates the lastIndex property to point after the match. If no match was found, lastIndex is set back to zero, which is also the value it has in a newly constructed regular expression object.

The difference between the global and the sticky options is that, when sticky is enabled, the match will succeed only if it starts directly at lastIndex, whereas with global, it will search ahead for a position where a match can start.

```
let global = /abc/g;
console.log(global.exec("xyz abc"));
// → ["abc"]
let sticky = /abc/y;
console.log(sticky.exec("xyz abc"));
// → null
```

When using a shared regular expression value for multiple exec calls, these automatic updates to the lastIndex property can cause problems. Your regular expression might be accidentally starting at an index that was left over from a previous call.

```
let digit = /\d/g;
console.log(digit.exec("here it is: 1"));
// → ["1"]
console.log(digit.exec("and now: 1"));
// → null
```

Another interesting effect of the global option is that it changes the way the match method on strings works. When called with a global expression, instead of returning an array similar to that returned by exec, match will find *all* matches of the pattern in the string and return an array containing the matched strings.

```
console.log("Banana".match(/an/g));
// → ["an", "an"]
```

So be cautious with global regular expressions. The cases where they are necessary—calls to replace and places where you want to explicitly use lastIndex—are typically the only places where you want to use them.

Looping Over Matches

A common thing to do is to scan through all occurrences of a pattern in a string, in a way that gives us access to the match object in the loop body. We can do this by using lastIndex and exec.

```
let input = "A string with 3 numbers in it... 42 and 88.";
let number = /\b\d+\b/g;
let match;
while (match = number.exec(input)) {
  console.log("Found", match[0], "at", match.index);
}
// → Found 3 at 14
//   Found 42 at 33
//   Found 88 at 40
```

This makes use of the fact that the value of an assignment expression (=) is the assigned value. So by using match = number.exec(input) as the condition in the while statement, we perform the match at the start of each iteration, save its result in a binding, and stop looping when no more matches are found.

Parsing an INI File

To conclude the chapter, we'll take a look at a problem that calls for regular expressions. Imagine we are writing a program to automatically collect information about our enemies from the internet. (We will not actually write that program here, just the part that reads the configuration file. Sorry.) The configuration file looks like this:

```
searchengine=https://duckduckgo.com/?q=$1
spitefulness=9.7

; comments are preceded by a semicolon...
; each section concerns an individual enemy
[larry]
fullname=Larry Doe
type=kindergarten bully
website=http://www.geocities.com/CapeCanaveral/11451

[davaeorn]
fullname=Davaeorn
type=evil wizard
outputdir=/home/marijn/enemies/davaeorn
```

The exact rules for this format (which is a widely used format, usually called an *INI* file) are as follows:

- Blank lines and lines starting with semicolons are ignored.

- Lines wrapped in [and] start a new section.

- Lines containing an alphanumeric identifier followed by an = character add a setting to the current section.

- Anything else is invalid.

Our task is to convert a string like this into an object whose properties hold strings for settings written before the first section header and subobjects for sections, with those subobjects holding the section's settings.

Since the format has to be processed line by line, splitting up the file into separate lines is a good start. We saw the split method in "Strings and Their Properties" on page 72. Some operating systems, however, use not just a newline character to separate lines but a carriage return character followed by a newline ("\r\n"). Given that the split method also allows a regular expression as its argument, we can use a regular expression like /\r?\n/ to split in a way that allows both "\n" and "\r\n" between lines.

```
function parseINI(string) {
  // Start with an object to hold the top-level fields
  let result = {};
  let section = result;
  string.split(/\r?\n/).forEach(line => {
    let match;
    if (match = line.match(/^(\w+)=(.*)$/)) {
      section[match[1]] = match[2];
    } else if (match = line.match(/^\[(.*)\]$/)) {
      section = result[match[1]] = {};
    } else if (!/^\s*(;.*)?$/.test(line)) {
      throw new Error("Line '" + line + "' is not valid.");
    }
  });
  return result;
}

console.log(parseINI(`
name=Vasilis
[address]
city=Tessaloniki`));
// → {name: "Vasilis", address: {city: "Tessaloniki"}}
```

The code goes over the file's lines and builds up an object. Properties at the top are stored directly into that object, whereas properties found in sections are stored in a separate section object. The section binding points at the object for the current section.

There are two kinds of significant lines—section headers or property lines. When a line is a regular property, it is stored in the current section. When it is a section header, a new section object is created, and section is set to point at it.

Note the recurring use of ^ and $ to make sure the expression matches the whole line, not just part of it. Leaving these out results in code that mostly works but behaves strangely for some input, which can be a difficult bug to track down.

The pattern if (match = string.match(...)) is similar to the trick of using an assignment as the condition for while. You often aren't sure that your call to match will succeed, so you can access the resulting object only inside an if statement that tests for this. To not break the pleasant chain of else if forms, we assign the result of the match to a binding and immediately use that assignment as the test for the if statement.

If a line is not a section header or a property, the function checks whether it is a comment or an empty line using the expression /^\s*(;.*)?$/. Do you see how it works? The part between the parentheses will match comments, and the ? makes sure it also matches lines containing only whitespace. When a line doesn't match any of the expected forms, the function throws an exception.

International Characters

Because of JavaScript's initial simplistic implementation and the fact that this simplistic approach was later set in stone as standard behavior, JavaScript's regular expressions are rather dumb about characters that do not appear in the English language. For example, as far as JavaScript's regular expressions are concerned, a "word character" is only one of the 26 characters in the Latin alphabet (uppercase or lowercase), decimal digits, and, for some reason, the underscore character. Things like *é* or *β*, which most definitely are word characters, will not match \w (and *will* match uppercase \W, the nonword category).

By a strange historical accident, \s (whitespace) does not have this problem and matches all characters that the Unicode standard considers whitespace, including things like the nonbreaking space and the Mongolian vowel separator.

Another problem is that, by default, regular expressions work on code units (as discussed in "Strings and Character Codes" on page 92), not actual characters. This means characters that are composed of two code units behave strangely.

```
console.log(/🌹{3}/.test("🌹🌹🌹"));
// → false
console.log(/<.>/.test("<🌹>"));
// → false
console.log(/<.>/u.test("<🌹>"));
// → true
```

The problem is that the 🌹 in the first line is treated as two code units, and the {3} part is applied only to the second one. Similarly, the dot matches a single code unit, not the two that make up the rose emoji.

You must add a u option (for Unicode) to your regular expression to make it treat such characters properly. The wrong behavior remains the default, unfortunately, because changing that might cause problems for existing code that depends on it.

Though this was only just standardized and is, at the time of writing, not widely supported yet, it is possible to use \p in a regular expression (that must have the Unicode option enabled) to match all characters to which the Unicode standard assigns a given property.

```
console.log(/\p{Script=Greek}/u.test("α"));
// → true
console.log(/\p{Script=Arabic}/u.test("α"));
// → false
console.log(/\p{Alphabetic}/u.test("α"));
// → true
console.log(/\p{Alphabetic}/u.test("!"));
// → false
```

Unicode defines a number of useful properties, though finding the one that you need may not always be trivial. You can use the \p{Property=Value} notation to match any character that has the given value for that property. If the property name is left off, as in \p{Name}, the name is assumed to be either a binary property such as Alphabetic or a category such as Number.

Summary

Regular expressions are objects that represent patterns in strings. They use their own language to express these patterns.

/abc/	A sequence of characters
/[abc]/	Any character from a set of characters
/[^abc]/	Any character *not* in a set of characters
/[0-9]/	Any character in a range of characters
/x+/	One or more occurrences of the pattern x
/x+?/	One or more occurrences, nongreedy
/x*/	Zero or more occurrences
/x?/	Zero or one occurrence
/x{2,4}/	Two to four occurrences
/(abc)/	A group
/a|b|c/	Any one of several patterns
/\d/	Any digit character
/\w/	An alphanumeric character ("word character")
/\s/	Any whitespace character
/./	Any character except newlines
/\b/	A word boundary
/^/	Start of input
/$/	End of input

A regular expression has a method test to test whether a given string matches it. It also has a method exec that, when a match is found, returns an array containing all matched groups. Such an array has an `index` property that indicates where the match started.

Strings have a `match` method to match them against a regular expression and a `search` method to search for one, returning only the starting position of the match. Their `replace` method can replace matches of a pattern with a replacement string or function.

Regular expressions can have options, which are written after the closing slash. The `i` option makes the match case insensitive. The `g` option makes the expression *global*, which, among other things, causes the `replace` method to replace all instances instead of just the first. The `y` option makes it sticky, which means that it will not search ahead and skip part of the string when looking for a match. The `u` option turns on Unicode mode, which fixes a number of problems around the handling of characters that take up two code units.

Regular expressions are a sharp tool with an awkward handle. They simplify some tasks tremendously but can quickly become unmanageable when applied to complex problems. Part of knowing how to use them is resisting the urge to try to shoehorn things that they cannot cleanly express into them.

Exercises

It is almost unavoidable that, in the course of working on these exercises, you will get confused and frustrated by some regular expression's inexplicable behavior. Sometimes it helps to enter your expression into an online tool like *https://debuggex.com* to see whether its visualization corresponds to what you intended and to experiment with the way it responds to various input strings.

Regexp Golf

Code golf is a term used for the game of trying to express a particular program in as few characters as possible. Similarly, *regexp golf* is the practice of writing as tiny a regular expression as possible to match a given pattern, and *only* that pattern.

For each of the following items, write a regular expression to test whether any of the given substrings occur in a string. The regular expression should match only strings containing one of the substrings described. Do not worry about word boundaries unless explicitly mentioned. When your expression works, see whether you can make it any smaller.

1. *car* and *cat*
2. *pop* and *prop*
3. *ferret*, *ferry*, and *ferrari*
4. Any word ending in *ious*

5. A whitespace character followed by a period, comma, colon, or semicolon

6. A word longer than six letters

7. A word without the letter *e* (or *E*)

Refer to the table in the chapter summary for help. Test each solution with a few test strings.

Quoting Style

Imagine you have written a story and used single quotation marks throughout to mark pieces of dialogue. Now you want to replace all the dialogue quotes with double quotes, while keeping the single quotes used in contractions like *aren't*.

Think of a pattern that distinguishes these two kinds of quote usage and craft a call to the `replace` method that does the proper replacement.

Numbers Again

Write an expression that matches only JavaScript-style numbers. It must support an optional minus *or* plus sign in front of the number, the decimal dot, and exponent notation—`5e-3` or `1E10`—again with an optional sign in front of the exponent. Also note that it is not necessary for there to be digits in front of or after the dot, but the number cannot be a dot alone. That is, `.5` and `5.` are valid JavaScript numbers, but a lone dot *isn't*.

"Write code that is easy to delete,
not easy to extend."

—Tef, *Programming Is Terrible*

10

MODULES

The ideal program has a crystal-clear structure. The way it works is easy to explain, and each part plays a well-defined role.

A typical real program grows organically. New pieces of functionality are added as new needs come up. Structuring—and preserving structure—is additional work. It's work that will pay off only in the future, the *next* time someone works on the program. So it is tempting to neglect it and allow the parts of the program to become deeply entangled.

This causes two practical issues. First, understanding such a system is hard. If everything can touch everything else, it is difficult to look at any given piece in isolation. You are forced to build up a holistic understanding of the entire thing. Second, if you want to use any of the functionality from such a program in another situation, rewriting it may be easier than trying to disentangle it from its context.

The phrase "big ball of mud" is often used for such large, structureless programs. Everything sticks together, and when you try to pick out a piece, the whole thing comes apart, and your hands get dirty.

Modules as Building Blocks

Modules are an attempt to avoid these problems. A module is a piece of program that specifies which other pieces it relies on and which functionality it provides for other modules to use (its *interface*).

Module interfaces have a lot in common with object interfaces, as we saw them in "Encapsulation" on page 97. They make part of the module available to the outside world and keep the rest private. By restricting the ways in which modules interact with each other, the system becomes more like LEGO, where pieces interact through well-defined connectors, and less like mud, where everything mixes with everything.

The relations between modules are called *dependencies*. When a module needs a piece from another module, it is said to depend on that module. When this fact is clearly specified in the module itself, it can be used to figure out which other modules need to be present to be able to use a given module and to automatically load dependencies.

To separate modules in that way, each needs its own private scope.

Just putting your JavaScript code into different files does not satisfy these requirements. The files still share the same global namespace. They can, intentionally or accidentally, interfere with each other's bindings. And the dependency structure remains unclear. We can do better, as we'll see later in the chapter.

Designing a fitting module structure for a program can be difficult. In the phase where you are still exploring the problem, trying different things to see what works, you might want to not worry about it too much since it can be a big distraction. Once you have something that feels solid, that's a good time to take a step back and organize it.

Packages

One of the advantages of building a program out of separate pieces, and being actually able to run those pieces on their own, is that you might be able to apply the same piece in different programs.

But how do you set this up? Say I want to use the `parseINI` function from "Parsing an INI File" on page 160 in another program. If it is clear what the function depends on (in this case, nothing), I can just copy all the necessary code into my new project and use it. But then, if I find a mistake in that code, I'll probably fix it in whichever program I'm working with at the time and forget to also fix it in the other program.

Once you start duplicating code, you'll quickly find yourself wasting time and energy moving copies around and keeping them up to date.

That's where *packages* come in. A package is a chunk of code that can be distributed (copied and installed). It may contain one or more modules and has information about which other packages it depends on. A package also usually comes with documentation explaining what it does so that people who didn't write it might still be able to use it.

When a problem is found in a package or a new feature is added, the package is updated. Now the programs that depend on it (which may also be packages) can upgrade to the new version.

Working in this way requires infrastructure. We need a place to store and find packages and a convenient way to install and upgrade them. In the JavaScript world, this infrastructure is provided by NPM (*https://npmjs.org*).

NPM is two things: an online service where one can download (and upload) packages and a program (bundled with Node.js) that helps you install and manage them.

At the time of writing, there are more than half a million different packages available on NPM. A large portion of those are rubbish, I should mention, but almost every useful, publicly available package can be found on there. For example, an INI file parser, similar to the one we built in Chapter 9, is available under the package name ini.

Chapter 20 will show how to install such packages locally using the npm command line program.

Having quality packages available for download is extremely valuable. It means that we can often avoid reinventing a program that 100 people have written before and get a solid, well-tested implementation at the press of a few keys.

Software is cheap to copy, so once someone has written it, distributing it to other people is an efficient process. But writing it in the first place *is* work, and responding to people who have found problems in the code, or who want to propose new features, is even more work.

By default, you own the copyright to the code you write, and other people may use it only with your permission. But because some people are just nice and because publishing good software can help make you a little bit famous among programmers, many packages are published under a license that explicitly allows other people to use it.

Most code on NPM is licensed this way. Some licenses require you to also publish code that you build on top of the package under the same license. Others are less demanding, just requiring that you keep the license with the code as you distribute it. The JavaScript community mostly uses the latter type of license. When using other people's packages, make sure you are aware of their license.

Improvised Modules

Until 2015, the JavaScript language had no built-in module system. Yet people had been building large systems in JavaScript for more than a decade, and they *needed* modules.

So they designed their own module systems on top of the language. You can use JavaScript functions to create local scopes and objects to represent module interfaces.

This is a module for going between day names and numbers (as returned by Date's getDay method). Its interface consists of weekDay.name and weekDay.number, and it hides its local binding names inside the scope of a function expression that is immediately invoked.

```
const weekDay = function() {
  const names = ["Sunday", "Monday", "Tuesday", "Wednesday",
                 "Thursday", "Friday", "Saturday"];
  return {
    name(number) { return names[number]; },
    number(name) { return names.indexOf(name); }
  };
}();

console.log(weekDay.name(weekDay.number("Sunday")));
// → Sunday
```

This style of modules provides isolation, to a certain degree, but it does not declare dependencies. Instead, it just puts its interface into the global scope and expects its dependencies, if any, to do the same. For a long time this was the main approach used in web programming, but it is mostly obsolete now.

If we want to make dependency relations part of the code, we'll have to take control of loading dependencies. Doing that requires being able to execute strings as code. JavaScript can do this.

Evaluating Data as Code

There are several ways to take data (a string of code) and run it as part of the current program.

The most obvious way is the special operator eval, which will execute a string in the *current* scope. This is usually a bad idea because it breaks some of the properties that scopes normally have, such as it being easily predictable which binding a given name refers to.

```
const x = 1;
function evalAndReturnX(code) {
  eval(code);
  return x;
}

console.log(evalAndReturnX("var x = 2"));
// → 2
console.log(x);
// → 1
```

A less scary way of interpreting data as code is to use the Function constructor. It takes two arguments: a string containing a comma-separated list of argument names and a string containing the function body. It wraps the code in a function value so that it gets its own scope and won't do odd things with other scopes.

```
let plusOne = Function("n", "return n + 1;");
console.log(plusOne(4));
// → 5
```

This is precisely what we need for a module system. We can wrap the module's code in a function and use that function's scope as module scope.

CommonJS

The most widely used approach to bolted-on JavaScript modules is called *CommonJS modules.* Node.js uses it and is the system used by most packages on NPM.

The main concept in CommonJS modules is a function called require. When you call this with the module name of a dependency, it makes sure the module is loaded and returns its interface.

Because the loader wraps the module code in a function, modules automatically get their own local scope. All they have to do is call require to access their dependencies and put their interface in the object bound to exports.

This example module provides a date-formatting function. It uses two packages from NPM—ordinal to convert numbers to strings like "1st" and "2nd", and date-names to get the English names for weekdays and months. It exports a single function, formatDate, which takes a Date object and a template string.

The template string may contain codes that direct the format, such as YYYY for the full year and Do for the ordinal day of the month. You could give it a string like "MMMM Do YYYY" to get output like "November 22nd 2019."

```
const ordinal = require("ordinal");
const {days, months} = require("date-names");

exports.formatDate = function(date, format) {
  return format.replace(/YYYY|M(MMM)?|Do?|dddd/g, tag => {
    if (tag == "YYYY") return date.getFullYear();
    if (tag == "M") return date.getMonth();
    if (tag == "MMMM") return months[date.getMonth()];
    if (tag == "D") return date.getDate();
    if (tag == "Do") return ordinal(date.getDate());
    if (tag == "dddd") return days[date.getDay()];
  });
};
```

The interface of ordinal is a single function, whereas date-names exports an object containing multiple things—days and months are arrays of names.

Destructuring is very convenient when creating bindings for imported interfaces.

The module adds its interface function to exports so that modules that depend on it get access to it. We could use the module like this:

```
const {formatDate} = require("./format-date");

console.log(formatDate(new Date(2019, 8, 13),
                       "dddd the Do"));
// → Friday the 13th
```

We can define require, in its most minimal form, like this:

```
require.cache = Object.create(null);

function require(name) {
  if (!(name in require.cache)) {
    let code = readFile(name);
    let module = {exports: {}};
    require.cache[name] = module;
    let wrapper = Function("require, exports, module", code);
    wrapper(require, module.exports, module);
  }
  return require.cache[name].exports;
}
```

In this code, readFile is a made-up function that reads a file and returns its contents as a string. Standard JavaScript provides no such functionality—but different JavaScript environments, such as the browser and Node.js, provide their own ways of accessing files. The example just pretends that readFile exists.

To avoid loading the same module multiple times, require keeps a store (cache) of already loaded modules. When called, it first checks if the requested module has been loaded and, if not, loads it. This involves reading the module's code, wrapping it in a function, and calling it.

The interface of the ordinal package we saw before is not an object but a function. A quirk of the CommonJS modules is that, though the module system will create an empty interface object for you (bound to exports), you can replace that with any value by overwriting module.exports. This is done by many modules to export a single value instead of an interface object.

By defining require, exports, and module as parameters for the generated wrapper function (and passing the appropriate values when calling it), the loader makes sure that these bindings are available in the module's scope.

The way the string given to require is translated to an actual filename or web address differs in different systems. When it starts with "./" or "../", it is generally interpreted as relative to the current module's filename. So "./format-date" would be the file named format-date.js in the same directory.

When the name isn't relative, Node.js will look for an installed package by that name. In the example code in this chapter, we'll interpret such names as referring to NPM packages. We'll go into more detail on how to install and use NPM modules in Chapter 20.

Now, instead of writing our own INI file parser, we can use one from NPM.

```
const {parse} = require("ini");

console.log(parse("x = 10\ny = 20"));
// → {x: "10", y: "20"}
```

ECMAScript Modules

CommonJS modules work quite well and, in combination with NPM, have allowed the JavaScript community to start sharing code on a large scale.

But they remain a bit of a duct-tape hack. The notation is slightly awkward—the things you add to exports are not available in the local scope, for example. And because require is a normal function call taking any kind of argument, not just a string literal, it can be hard to determine the dependencies of a module without running its code.

This is why the JavaScript standard from 2015 introduces its own, different module system. It is usually called *ES modules*, where *ES* stands for ECMAScript. The main concepts of dependencies and interfaces remain the same, but the details differ. For one thing, the notation is now integrated into the language. Instead of calling a function to access a dependency, you use a special import keyword.

```
import ordinal from "ordinal";
import {days, months} from "date-names";

export function formatDate(date, format) { /* ... */ }
```

Similarly, the export keyword is used to export things. It may appear in front of a function, class, or binding definition (let, const, or var).

An ES module's interface is not a single value but a set of named bindings. The preceding module binds formatDate to a function. When you import from another module, you import the *binding*, not the value, which means an exporting module may change the value of the binding at any time, and the modules that import it will see its new value.

When there is a binding named default, it is treated as the module's main exported value. If you import a module like ordinal in the example, without braces around the binding name, you get its default binding. Such modules can still export other bindings under different names alongside their default export.

To create a default export, you write `export default` before an expression, a function declaration, or a class declaration.

```
export default ["Winter", "Spring", "Summer", "Autumn"];
```

It is possible to rename imported bindings using the word as.

```
import {days as dayNames} from "date-names";

console.log(dayNames.length);
// → 7
```

Another important difference is that ES module imports happen before a module's script starts running. That means `import` declarations may not appear inside functions or blocks, and the names of dependencies must be quoted strings, not arbitrary expressions.

At the time of writing, the JavaScript community is in the process of adopting this module style. But it has been a slow process. It took a few years, after the format was specified, for browsers and Node.js to start supporting it. And though they mostly support it now, this support still has issues, and the discussion on how such modules should be distributed through NPM is still ongoing.

Many projects are written using ES modules and then automatically converted to some other format when published. We are in a transitional period in which two different module systems are used side by side, and it is useful to be able to read and write code in either of them.

Building and Bundling

In fact, many JavaScript projects aren't even, technically, written in JavaScript. There are extensions, such as the type checking dialect mentioned in "Types" on page 131, that are widely used. People also often start using planned extensions to the language long before they have been added to the platforms that actually run JavaScript.

To make this possible, they *compile* their code, translating it from their chosen JavaScript dialect to plain old JavaScript—or even to a past version of JavaScript—so that old browsers can run it.

Including a modular program that consists of 200 different files in a web page produces its own problems. If fetching a single file over the network takes 50 milliseconds, loading the whole program takes 10 seconds, or maybe half that if you can load several files simultaneously. That's a lot of wasted time. Because fetching a single big file tends to be faster than fetching a lot of tiny ones, web programmers have started using tools that roll their programs (which they painstakingly split into modules) back into a single big file before they publish it to the web. Such tools are called *bundlers*.

And we can go further. Apart from the number of files, the *size* of the files also determines how fast they can be transferred over the network. Thus, the JavaScript community has invented *minifiers*. These are tools that take a JavaScript program and make it smaller by automatically removing comments and whitespace, renaming bindings, and replacing pieces of code with equivalent code that take up less space.

So it is not uncommon for the code that you find in an NPM package or that runs on a web page to have gone through *multiple* stages of transformation—converted from modern JavaScript to historic JavaScript, from ES module format to CommonJS, bundled, and minified. We won't go into the details of these tools in this book since they tend to be boring and change rapidly. Just be aware that the JavaScript code you run is often not the code as it was written.

Module Design

Structuring programs is one of the subtler aspects of programming. Any nontrivial piece of functionality can be modeled in various ways.

Good program design is subjective—there are trade-offs involved and matters of taste. The best way to learn the value of well-structured design is to read or work on a lot of programs and notice what works and what doesn't. Don't assume that a painful mess is "just the way it is." You can improve the structure of almost everything by putting more thought into it.

One aspect of module design is ease of use. If you are designing something that is intended to be used by multiple people—or even by yourself, in three months when you no longer remember the specifics of what you did—it is helpful if your interface is simple and predictable.

That may mean following existing conventions. A good example is the `ini` package. This module imitates the standard `JSON` object by providing `parse` and `stringify` (to write an INI file) functions, and, like `JSON`, converts between strings and plain objects. So the interface is small and familiar, and after you've worked with it once, you're likely to remember how to use it.

Even if there's no standard function or widely used package to imitate, you can keep your modules predictable by using simple data structures and doing a single, focused thing. Many of the INI-file parsing modules on NPM provide a function that directly reads such a file from the hard disk and parses it, for example. This makes it impossible to use such modules in the browser, where we don't have direct file system access, and adds complexity that would have been better addressed by *composing* the module with some file-reading function.

This points to another helpful aspect of module design—the ease with which something can be composed with other code. Focused modules that compute values are applicable in a wider range of programs than bigger modules that perform complicated actions with side effects. An INI file reader that insists on reading the file from disk is useless in a scenario where the file's content comes from some other source.

Relatedly, stateful objects are sometimes useful or even necessary, but if something can be done with a function, use a function. Several of the INI file readers on NPM provide an interface style that requires you to first create an object, then load the file into your object, and finally use specialized methods to get at the results. This type of thing is common in the object-oriented tradition, and it's terrible. Instead of making a single function call and moving on, you have to perform the ritual of moving your object through various states. And because the data is now wrapped in a specialized object type, all code that interacts with it has to know about that type, creating unnecessary interdependencies.

Often defining new data structures can't be avoided—only a few basic ones are provided by the language standard, and many types of data have to be more complex than an array or a map. But when an array suffices, use an array.

An example of a slightly more complex data structure is the graph from Chapter 7. There is no single obvious way to represent a graph in JavaScript. In that chapter, we used an object whose properties hold arrays of strings—the other nodes reachable from that node.

There are several different pathfinding packages on NPM, but none of them uses this graph format. They usually allow the graph's edges to have a weight, which is the cost or distance associated with it. That isn't possible in our representation.

For example, there's the dijkstrajs package. A well-known approach to pathfinding, quite similar to our findRoute function, is called *Dijkstra's algorithm*, after Edsger Dijkstra, who first wrote it down. The js suffix is often added to package names to indicate the fact that they are written in JavaScript. This dijkstrajs package uses a graph format similar to ours, but instead of arrays, it uses objects whose property values are numbers—the weights of the edges.

So if we wanted to use that package, we'd have to make sure that our graph was stored in the format it expects. All edges get the same weight since our simplified model treats each road as having the same cost (one turn).

```
const {find_path} = require("dijkstrajs");

let graph = {};
for (let node of Object.keys(roadGraph)) {
  let edges = graph[node] = {};
  for (let dest of roadGraph[node]) {
    edges[dest] = 1;
  }
}

console.log(find_path(graph, "Post Office", "Cabin"));
// → ["Post Office", "Alice's House", "Cabin"]
```

This can be a barrier to composition—when various packages are using different data structures to describe similar things, combining them is difficult. Therefore, if you want to design for composability, find out what data structures other people are using and, when possible, follow their example.

Summary

Modules provide structure to bigger programs by separating the code into pieces with clear interfaces and dependencies. The interface is the part of the module that's visible from other modules, and the dependencies are the other modules that it makes use of.

Because JavaScript historically did not provide a module system, the CommonJS system was built on top of it. Then at some point it *did* get a built-in system, which now coexists uneasily with the CommonJS system.

A package is a chunk of code that can be distributed on its own. NPM is a repository of JavaScript packages. You can download all kinds of useful (and useless) packages from it.

Exercises

A Modular Robot

These are the bindings that the project from Chapter 7 creates:

```
roads
buildGraph
roadGraph
VillageState
runRobot
randomPick
randomRobot
mailRoute
routeRobot
findRoute
goalOrientedRobot
```

If you were to write that project as a modular program, what modules would you create? Which module would depend on which other module, and what would their interfaces look like?

Which pieces are likely to be available prewritten on NPM? Would you prefer to use an NPM package or write them yourself?

Roads Module

Write a CommonJS module, based on the example from Chapter 7, that contains the array of roads and exports the graph data structure representing them as roadGraph. It should depend on a module ./graph, which exports a function `buildGraph` that is used to build the graph. This function expects an array of two-element arrays (the start and end points of the roads).

Circular Dependencies

A circular dependency is a situation where module A depends on B, and B also, directly or indirectly, depends on A. Many module systems simply forbid this because whichever order you choose for loading such modules, you cannot make sure that each module's dependencies have been loaded before it runs.

CommonJS modules allow a limited form of cyclic dependencies. As long as the modules do not replace their default exports object and don't access each other's interface until after they finish loading, cyclic dependencies are okay.

The `require` function given in "CommonJS" on page 171 supports this type of dependency cycle. Can you see how it handles cycles? What would go wrong when a module in a cycle *does* replace its default exports object?

"Who can wait quietly while the mud settles? Who can remain still until the moment of action?"

—Laozi, *Tao Te Ching*

11

ASYNCHRONOUS PROGRAMMING

The central part of a computer, the part that carries out the individual steps that make up our programs, is called the *processor*. The programs we have seen so far are things that will keep the processor busy until they have finished their work. The speed at which something like a loop that manipulates numbers can be executed depends pretty much entirely on the speed of the processor.

But many programs interact with things outside of the processor. For example, they may communicate over a computer network or request data from the hard disk—which is a lot slower than getting it from memory.

When such a thing is happening, it would be a shame to let the processor sit idle—there might be some other work it could do in the meantime. In part, this is handled by your operating system, which will switch the processor between multiple running programs. But that doesn't help when we want a *single* program to be able to make progress while it is waiting for a network request.

Asynchronicity

In a *synchronous* programming model, things happen one at a time. When you call a function that performs a long-running action, it returns only when the action has finished and it can return the result. This stops your program for the time the action takes.

An *asynchronous* model allows multiple things to happen at the same time. When you start an action, your program continues to run. When the action finishes, the program is informed and gets access to the result (for example, the data read from disk).

We can compare synchronous and asynchronous programming using a small example: a program that fetches two resources from the network and then combines results.

In a synchronous environment, where the request function returns only after it has done its work, the easiest way to perform this task is to make the requests one after the other. This has the drawback that the second request will be started only when the first has finished. The total time taken will be at least the sum of the two response times.

The solution to this problem, in a synchronous system, is to start additional threads of control. A *thread* is another running program whose execution may be interleaved with other programs by the operating system—since most modern computers contain multiple processors, multiple threads may even run at the same time, on different processors. A second thread could start the second request, and then both threads wait for their results to come back, after which they resynchronize to combine their results.

In the following diagram, the thick lines represent time the program spends running normally, and the thin lines represent time spent waiting for the network. In the synchronous model, the time taken by the network is *part* of the timeline for a given thread of control. In the asynchronous model, starting a network action conceptually causes a *split* in the timeline. The program that initiated the action continues running, and the action happens alongside it, notifying the program when it is finished.

synchronous, single thread of control

synchronous, two threads of control

asynchronous

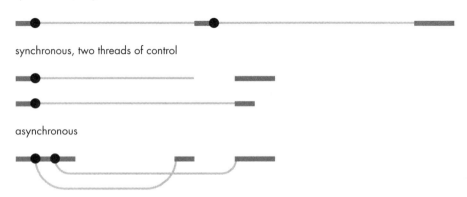

Another way to describe the difference is that waiting for actions to finish is *implicit* in the synchronous model, while it is *explicit*, under our control, in the asynchronous one.

Asynchronicity cuts both ways. It makes expressing programs that do not fit the straight-line model of control easier, but it can also make expressing programs that do follow a straight line more awkward. We'll see some ways to address this awkwardness later in the chapter.

Both of the important JavaScript programming platforms—browsers and Node.js—make operations that might take a while asynchronous, rather than relying on threads. Since programming with threads is notoriously hard (understanding what a program does is much more difficult when it's doing multiple things at once), this is generally considered a good thing.

Crow Tech

Most people are aware of the fact that crows are very smart birds. They can use tools, plan ahead, remember things, and even communicate these things among themselves.

What most people don't know is that they are capable of many things that they keep well hidden from us. I've been told by a reputable (if somewhat eccentric) expert on corvids that crow technology is not far behind human technology, and they are catching up.

For example, many crow cultures have the ability to construct computing devices. These are not electronic, as human computing devices are, but operate through the actions of tiny insects, a species closely related to the termite, which has developed a symbiotic relationship with the crows. The birds provide them with food, and in return the insects build and operate their complex colonies that, with the help of the living creatures inside them, perform computations.

Such colonies are usually located in big, long-lived nests. The birds and insects work together to build a network of bulbous clay structures, hidden between the twigs of the nest, in which the insects live and work.

To communicate with other devices, these machines use light signals. The crows embed pieces of reflective material in special communication stalks, and the insects aim these to reflect light at another nest, encoding data as a sequence of quick flashes. This means that only nests that have an unbroken visual connection can communicate.

Our friend the corvid expert has mapped the network of crow nests in the village of Hières-sur-Amby, on the banks of the river Rhône. The following map shows the nests and their connections.

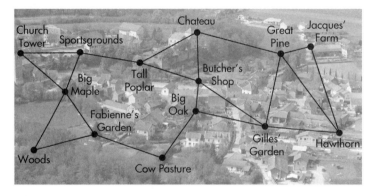

In an astounding example of convergent evolution, crow computers run JavaScript. In this chapter we'll write some basic networking functions for them.

Callbacks

One approach to asynchronous programming is to make functions that perform a slow action take an extra argument, a *callback function*. The action is started, and when it finishes, the callback function is called with the result.

As an example, the `setTimeout` function, available both in Node.js and in browsers, waits a given number of milliseconds (a second is a thousand milliseconds) and then calls a function.

```
setTimeout(() => console.log("Tick"), 500);
```

Waiting is not generally a very important type of work, but it can be useful when doing something like updating an animation or checking whether something is taking longer than a given amount of time.

Performing multiple asynchronous actions in a row using callbacks means that you have to keep passing new functions to handle the continuation of the computation after the actions.

Most crow nest computers have a long-term data storage bulb, where pieces of information are etched into twigs so that they can be retrieved later. Etching, or finding a piece of data, takes a moment, so the interface to long-term storage is asynchronous and uses callback functions.

Storage bulbs store pieces of JSON-encodable data under names. A crow might store information about the places where it's hidden food under the name `"food caches"`, which could hold an array of names that point at other pieces of data, describing the actual cache. To look up a food cache in the storage bulbs of the *Big Oak* nest, a crow could run code like this:

```
import {bigOak} from "./crow-tech";

bigOak.readStorage("food caches", caches => {
  let firstCache = caches[0];
  bigOak.readStorage(firstCache, info => {
```

```
    console.log(info);
  });
});
```

(All binding names and strings have been translated from crow language to English.)

This style of programming is workable, but the indentation level increases with each asynchronous action because you end up in another function. Doing more complicated things, such as running multiple actions at the same time, can get a little awkward.

Crow nest computers are built to communicate using request-response pairs. That means one nest sends a message to another nest, which then immediately sends a message back, confirming receipt and possibly including a reply to a question asked in the message.

Each message is tagged with a *type*, which determines how it is handled. Our code can define handlers for specific request types, and when such a request comes in, the handler is called to produce a response.

The interface exported by the "./crow-tech" module provides callback-based functions for communication. Nests have a send method that sends off a request. It expects the name of the target nest, the type of the request, and the content of the request as its first three arguments, and it expects a function to call when a response comes in as its fourth and last argument.

```
bigOak.send("Cow Pasture", "note", "Let's caw loudly at 7PM",
            () => console.log("Note delivered."));
```

But to make nests capable of receiving that request, we first have to define a request type named "note". The code that handles the requests has to run not just on this nest-computer but on all nests that can receive messages of this type. We'll just assume that a crow flies over and installs our handler code on all the nests.

```
import {defineRequestType} from "./crow-tech";

defineRequestType("note", (nest, content, source, done) => {
  console.log(`${nest.name} received note: ${content}`);
  done();
});
```

The defineRequestType function defines a new type of request. The example adds support for "note" requests, which just sends a note to a given nest. Our implementation calls console.log so that we can verify that the request arrived. Nests have a name property that holds their name.

The fourth argument given to the handler, done, is a callback function that it must call when it is done with the request. If we had used the handler's return value as the response value, that would mean that a request handler can't itself perform asynchronous actions. A function doing asynchronous work typically returns before the work is done, having arranged for a callback to be called when it completes. So we need some asynchronous mechanism—in this case, another callback function—to signal when a response is available.

In a way, asynchronicity is *contagious*. Any function that calls a function that works asynchronously must itself be asynchronous, using a callback or similar mechanism to deliver its result. Calling a callback is somewhat more involved and error-prone than simply returning a value, so needing to structure large parts of your program that way is not great.

Promises

Working with abstract concepts is often easier when those concepts can be represented by values. In the case of asynchronous actions, you could, instead of arranging for a function to be called at some point in the future, return an object that represents this future event.

This is what the standard class Promise is for. A *promise* is an asynchronous action that may complete at some point and produce a value. It is able to notify anyone who is interested when its value is available.

The easiest way to create a promise is by calling Promise.resolve. This function ensures that the value you give it is wrapped in a promise. If it's already a promise, it is simply returned—otherwise, you get a new promise that immediately finishes with your value as its result.

```
let fifteen = Promise.resolve(15);
fifteen.then(value => console.log(`Got ${value}`));
// → Got 15
```

To get the result of a promise, you can use its then method. This registers a callback function to be called when the promise resolves and produces a value. You can add multiple callbacks to a single promise, and they will be called, even if you add them after the promise has already *resolved* (finished).

But that's not all the then method does. It returns another promise, which resolves to the value that the handler function returns or, if that returns a promise, waits for that promise and then resolves to its result.

It is useful to think of promises as a device to move values into an asynchronous reality. A normal value is simply there. A promised value is a value that *might* already be there or might appear at some point in the future. Computations defined in terms of promises act on such wrapped values and are executed asynchronously as the values become available.

To create a promise, you can use Promise as a constructor. It has a somewhat odd interface—the constructor expects a function as argument, which it immediately calls, passing it a function that it can use to resolve the promise. It works this way, instead of, for example, with a resolve method, so that only the code that created the promise can resolve it.

This is how you'd create a promise-based interface for the `readStorage` function:

```
function storage(nest, name) {
  return new Promise(resolve => {
    nest.readStorage(name, result => resolve(result));
  });
}

storage(bigOak, "enemies")
  .then(value => console.log("Got", value));
```

This asynchronous function returns a meaningful value. This is the main advantage of promises—they simplify the use of asynchronous functions. Instead of having to pass around callbacks, promise-based functions look similar to regular ones: they take input as arguments and return their output. The only difference is that the output may not be available yet.

Failure

Regular JavaScript computations can fail by throwing an exception. Asynchronous computations often need something like that. A network request may fail, or some code that is part of the asynchronous computation may throw an exception.

One of the most pressing problems with the callback style of asynchronous programming is that it makes it extremely difficult to make sure failures are properly reported to the callbacks.

A widely used convention is that the first argument to the callback is used to indicate that the action failed, and the second contains the value produced by the action when it was successful. Such callback functions must always check whether they received an exception and make sure that any problems they cause, including exceptions thrown by functions they call, are caught and given to the right function.

Promises make this easier. They can be either resolved (the action finished successfully) or rejected (it failed). Resolve handlers (as registered with then) are called only when the action is successful, and rejections are automatically propagated to the new promise that is returned by then. And when a handler throws an exception, this automatically causes the promise produced by its then call to be rejected. So if any element in a chain of asynchronous actions fails, the outcome of the whole chain is marked as rejected, and no success handlers are called beyond the point where it failed.

Much like resolving a promise provides a value, rejecting one also provides one, usually called the *reason* of the rejection. When an exception in a handler function causes the rejection, the exception value is used as the reason. Similarly, when a handler returns a promise that is rejected, that rejection flows into the next promise. There's a Promise.reject function that creates a new, immediately rejected promise.

To explicitly handle such rejections, promises have a catch method that registers a handler to be called when the promise is rejected, similar to how then handlers handle normal resolution. It's also very much like then in that it returns a new promise, which resolves to the original promise's value if it resolves normally and to the result of the catch handler otherwise. If a catch handler throws an error, the new promise is also rejected.

As a shorthand, then also accepts a rejection handler as a second argument, so you can install both types of handlers in a single method call.

A function passed to the Promise constructor receives a second argument, alongside the resolve function, which it can use to reject the new promise.

The chains of promise values created by calls to then and catch can be seen as a pipeline through which asynchronous values or failures move. Since such chains are created by registering handlers, each link has a success handler or a rejection handler (or both) associated with it. Handlers that don't match the type of outcome (success or failure) are ignored. But those that do match are called, and their outcome determines what kind of value comes next—success when it returns a non-promise value, rejection when it throws an exception, and the outcome of a promise when it returns one of those.

```
new Promise((_, reject) => reject(new Error("Fail")))
  .then(value => console.log("Handler 1"))
  .catch(reason => {
    console.log("Caught failure " + reason);
    return "nothing";
  })
  .then(value => console.log("Handler 2", value));
// → Caught failure Error: Fail
// → Handler 2 nothing
```

Much like an uncaught exception is handled by the environment, JavaScript environments can detect when a promise rejection isn't handled and will report this as an error.

Networks Are Hard

Occasionally, there isn't enough light for the crows' mirror systems to transmit a signal, or something is blocking the path of the signal. It is possible for a signal to be sent but never received.

As it is, that will just cause the callback given to send to never be called, which will probably cause the program to stop without even noticing there is a problem. It would be nice if, after a given period of not getting a response, a request would *time out* and report failure.

Often, transmission failures are random accidents, like a car's headlight interfering with the light signals, and simply retrying the request may cause it to succeed. So while we're at it, let's make our request function automatically retry the sending of the request a few times before it gives up.

And, since we've established that promises are a good thing, we'll also make our request function return a promise. In terms of what they can express, callbacks and promises are equivalent. Callback-based functions can be wrapped to expose a promise-based interface, and vice versa.

Even when a request and its response are successfully delivered, the response may indicate failure—for example, if the request tries to use a request type that hasn't been defined or the handler throws an error. To support this, send and defineRequestType follow the convention mentioned before, where the first argument passed to callbacks is the failure reason, if any, and the second is the actual result.

These can be translated to promise resolution and rejection by our wrapper.

```
class Timeout extends Error {}

function request(nest, target, type, content) {
  return new Promise((resolve, reject) => {
    let done = false;
    function attempt(n) {
      nest.send(target, type, content, (failed, value) => {
        done = true;
        if (failed) reject(failed);
        else resolve(value);
      });
      setTimeout(() => {
        if (done) return;
        else if (n < 3) attempt(n + 1);
        else reject(new Timeout("Timed out"));
      }, 250);
    }
    attempt(1);
  });
}
```

Because promises can be resolved (or rejected) only once, this will work. The first time resolve or reject is called determines the outcome of the promise, and any further calls, such as the timeout arriving after the request finishes or a request coming back after another request finished, are ignored.

To build an asynchronous loop, for the retries, we need to use a recursive function—a regular loop doesn't allow us to stop and wait for an asynchronous action. The attempt function makes a single attempt to send a request. It also sets a timeout that, if no response has come back after 250 milliseconds, either starts the next attempt or, if this was the third attempt, rejects the promise with an instance of Timeout as the reason.

Retrying every quarter-second and giving up when no response has come in after three-quarter second is definitely somewhat arbitrary. It is even possible, if the request did come through but the handler is just taking a bit longer, for requests to be delivered multiple times. We'll write our handlers with that problem in mind—duplicate messages should be harmless.

In general, we will not be building a world-class, robust network today. But that's okay—crows don't have very high expectations yet when it comes to computing.

To isolate ourselves from callbacks altogether, we'll go ahead and also define a wrapper for defineRequestType that allows the handler function to return a promise or plain value and wires that up to the callback for us.

```
function requestType(name, handler) {
  defineRequestType(name, (nest, content, source,
                           callback) => {
    try {
      Promise.resolve(handler(nest, content, source))
        .then(response => callback(null, response),
              failure => callback(failure));
    } catch (exception) {
      callback(exception);
    }
  });
}
```

Promise.resolve is used to convert the value returned by handler to a promise if it isn't already.

Note that the call to handler had to be wrapped in a try block to make sure any exception it raises directly is given to the callback. This nicely illustrates the difficulty of properly handling errors with raw callbacks—it is easy to forget to properly route exceptions like that, and if you don't do it, failures won't get reported to the right callback. Promises make this mostly automatic and thus less error-prone.

Collections of Promises

Each nest computer keeps an array of other nests within transmission distance in its neighbors property. To check which of those are currently reachable, you could write a function that tries to send a "ping" request (a request that simply asks for a response) to each of them and see which ones come back.

When working with collections of promises running at the same time, the Promise.all function can be useful. It returns a promise that waits for all of the promises in the array to resolve and then resolves to an array of the values that these promises produced (in the same order as the original array). If any promise is rejected, the result of Promise.all is itself rejected.

```
requestType("ping", () => "pong");

function availableNeighbors(nest) {
  let requests = nest.neighbors.map(neighbor => {
    return request(nest, neighbor, "ping")
      .then(() => true, () => false);
  });
  return Promise.all(requests).then(result => {
    return nest.neighbors.filter((_, i) => result[i]);
  });
}
```

When a neighbor isn't available, we don't want the entire combined promise to fail since then we still wouldn't know anything. So the function that is mapped over the set of neighbors to turn them into request promises attaches handlers that make successful requests produce true and rejected ones produce false.

In the handler for the combined promise, filter is used to remove those elements from the neighbors array whose corresponding value is false. This makes use of the fact that filter passes the array index of the current element as a second argument to its filtering function (map, some, and similar higher-order array methods do the same).

Network Flooding

The fact that nests can talk only to their neighbors greatly inhibits the usefulness of this network.

For broadcasting information to the whole network, one solution is to set up a type of request that is automatically forwarded to neighbors. These neighbors then in turn forward it to their neighbors, until the whole network has received the message.

```
import {everywhere} from "./crow-tech";

everywhere(nest => {
  nest.state.gossip = [];
});

function sendGossip(nest, message, exceptFor = null) {
  nest.state.gossip.push(message);
  for (let neighbor of nest.neighbors) {
    if (neighbor == exceptFor) continue;
    request(nest, neighbor, "gossip", message);
  }
}
```

```
requestType("gossip", (nest, message, source) => {
  if (nest.state.gossip.includes(message)) return;
  console.log(`${nest.name} received gossip '${
              message}' from ${source}`);
  sendGossip(nest, message, source);
});
```

To avoid sending the same message around the network forever, each
nest keeps an array of gossip strings that it has already seen. To define this
array, we use the everywhere function—which runs code on every nest—to
add a property to the nest's state object, which is where we'll keep nest-local
state.

When a nest receives a duplicate gossip message, which is very likely to
happen with everybody blindly resending them, it ignores it. But when it
receives a new message, it excitedly tells all its neighbors except for the one
who sent it the message.

This will cause a new piece of gossip to spread through the network like
an ink stain in water. Even when some connections aren't currently working,
if there is an alternative route to a given nest, the gossip will reach it through
there.

This style of network communication is called *flooding*—it floods the
network with a piece of information until all nodes have it.

Message Routing

If a given node wants to talk to a single other node, flooding is not a very
efficient approach. Especially when the network is big, that would lead to a
lot of useless data transfers.

An alternative approach is to set up a way for messages to hop from
node to node until they reach their destination. The difficulty with that is
it requires knowledge about the layout of the network. To send a request
in the direction of a faraway nest, it is necessary to know which neighboring
nest gets it closer to its destination. Sending it in the wrong direction will
not do much good.

Since each nest knows only about its direct neighbors, it doesn't have
the information it needs to compute a route. We must somehow spread the
information about these connections to all nests, preferably in a way that
allows it to change over time, when nests are abandoned or new nests are
built.

We can use flooding again, but instead of checking whether a given
message has already been received, we now check whether the new set of
neighbors for a given nest matches the current set we have for it.

```
requestType("connections", (nest, {name, neighbors},
                            source) => {
  let connections = nest.state.connections;
  if (JSON.stringify(connections.get(name)) ==
```

```
      JSON.stringify(neighbors)) return;
    connections.set(name, neighbors);
    broadcastConnections(nest, name, source);
  });

  function broadcastConnections(nest, name, exceptFor = null) {
    for (let neighbor of nest.neighbors) {
      if (neighbor == exceptFor) continue;
      request(nest, neighbor, "connections", {
        name,
        neighbors: nest.state.connections.get(name)
      });
    }
  }
}

everywhere(nest => {
  nest.state.connections = new Map();
  nest.state.connections.set(nest.name, nest.neighbors);
  broadcastConnections(nest, nest.name);
});
```

The comparison uses JSON.stringify because ==, on objects or arrays, will return true only when the two are the exact same value, which is not what we need here. Comparing the JSON strings is a crude but effective way to compare their content.

The nodes immediately start broadcasting their connections, which should, unless some nests are completely unreachable, quickly give every nest a map of the current network graph.

A thing you can do with graphs is find routes in them, as we saw in Chapter 7. If we have a route toward a message's destination, we know which direction to send it in.

This findRoute function, which greatly resembles the findRoute function from Chapter 7, searches for a way to reach a given node in the network. But instead of returning the whole route, it just returns the next step. That next nest, using its current information about the network, will decide where *it* sends the message.

```
function findRoute(from, to, connections) {
  let work = [{at: from, via: null}];
  for (let i = 0; i < work.length; i++) {
    let {at, via} = work[i];
    for (let next of connections.get(at) || []) {
      if (next == to) return via;
      if (!work.some(w => w.at == next)) {
        work.push({at: next, via: via || next});
      }
    }
  }
}
```

```
    return null;
  }
}
```

Now we can build a function that can send long-distance messages. If the message is addressed to a direct neighbor, it is delivered as usual. If not, it is packaged in an object and sent to a neighbor that is closer to the target, using the "route" request type, which will cause that neighbor to repeat the same behavior.

```
function routeRequest(nest, target, type, content) {
  if (nest.neighbors.includes(target)) {
    return request(nest, target, type, content);
  } else {
    let via = findRoute(nest.name, target,
                        nest.state.connections);
    if (!via) throw new Error(`No route to ${target}`);
    return request(nest, via, "route",
                   {target, type, content});
  }
}

requestType("route", (nest, {target, type, content}) => {
  return routeRequest(nest, target, type, content);
});
```

We've constructed several layers of functionality on top of a primitive communication system to make it convenient to use. This is a nice (though simplified) model of how real computer networks work.

A distinguishing property of computer networks is that they aren't reliable—abstractions built on top of them can help, but you can't abstract away network failure. So network programming is typically very much about anticipating and dealing with failures.

Async Functions

To store important information, crows are known to duplicate it across nests. That way, when a hawk destroys a nest, the information isn't lost.

To retrieve a given piece of information that it doesn't have in its own storage bulb, a nest computer might consult random other nests in the network until it finds one that has it.

```
requestType("storage", (nest, name) => storage(nest, name));

function findInStorage(nest, name) {
  return storage(nest, name).then(found => {
    if (found != null) return found;
    else return findInRemoteStorage(nest, name);
```

```
    });
  }

  function network(nest) {
    return Array.from(nest.state.connections.keys());
  }

  function findInRemoteStorage(nest, name) {
    let sources = network(nest).filter(n => n != nest.name);
    function next() {
      if (sources.length == 0) {
        return Promise.reject(new Error("Not found"));
      } else {
        let source = sources[Math.floor(Math.random() *
                                        sources.length)];
        sources = sources.filter(n => n != source);
        return routeRequest(nest, source, "storage", name)
          .then(value => value != null ? value : next(),
                next);
      }
    }
    return next();
  }
```

Because connections is a Map, Object.keys doesn't work on it. It has a keys *method*, but that returns an iterator rather than an array. An iterator (or iterable value) can be converted to an array with the Array.from function.

Even with promises this is some rather awkward code. Multiple asynchronous actions are chained together in non-obvious ways. We again need a recursive function (next) to model looping through the nests.

And the thing the code actually does is completely linear—it always waits for the previous action to complete before starting the next one. In a synchronous programming model, it'd be simpler to express.

The good news is that JavaScript allows you to write pseudo-synchronous code to describe asynchronous computation. An async function is a function that implicitly returns a promise and that can, in its body, await other promises in a way that *looks* synchronous.

We can rewrite findInStorage like this:

```
async function findInStorage(nest, name) {
  let local = await storage(nest, name);
  if (local != null) return local;

  let sources = network(nest).filter(n => n != nest.name);
  while (sources.length > 0) {
    let source = sources[Math.floor(Math.random() *
                                    sources.length)];
    sources = sources.filter(n => n != source);
```

```
    try {
      let found = await routeRequest(nest, source, "storage",
                                     name);
      if (found != null) return found;
    } catch (_) {}
  }
  throw new Error("Not found");
}
```

An async function is marked by the word async before the function key-word. Methods can also be made async by writing async before their name. When such a function or method is called, it returns a promise. As soon as the body returns something, that promise is resolved. If it throws an exception, the promise is rejected.

Inside an async function, the word await can be put in front of an expression to wait for a promise to resolve and only then continue the execution of the function.

Such a function no longer, like a regular JavaScript function, runs from start to completion in one go. Instead, it can be *frozen* at any point that has an await, and can be resumed at a later time.

For nontrivial asynchronous code, this notation is usually more convenient than directly using promises. Even if you need to do something that doesn't fit the synchronous model, such as perform multiple actions at the same time, it is easy to combine await with the direct use of promises.

Generators

This ability of functions to be paused and then resumed again is not exclusive to async functions. JavaScript also has a feature called *generator* functions. These are similar, but without the promises.

When you define a function with function* (placing an asterisk after the word function), it becomes a generator. When you call a generator, it returns an iterator, which we already saw in Chapter 6.

```
function* powers(n) {
  for (let current = n;; current *= n) {
    yield current;
  }
}

for (let power of powers(3)) {
  if (power > 50) break;
  console.log(power);
}
// → 3
// → 9
// → 27
```

Initially, when you call powers, the function is frozen at its start. Every time you call next on the iterator, the function runs until it hits a yield expression, which pauses it and causes the yielded value to become the next value produced by the iterator. When the function returns (the one in the example never does), the iterator is done.

Writing iterators is often much easier when you use generator functions. The iterator for the Group class (from the exercise in "Iterable Groups" on page 114) can be written with this generator:

```
Group.prototype[Symbol.iterator] = function*() {
  for (let i = 0; i < this.members.length; i++) {
    yield this.members[i];
  }
};
```

There's no longer a need to create an object to hold the iteration state—generators automatically save their local state every time they yield.

Such yield expressions may occur only directly in the generator function itself and not in an inner function you define inside of it. The state a generator saves, when yielding, is only its *local* environment and the position where it yielded.

An async function is a special type of generator. It produces a promise when called, which is resolved when it returns (finishes) and rejected when it throws an exception. Whenever it yields (awaits) a promise, the result of that promise (value or thrown exception) is the result of the await expression.

The Event Loop

Asynchronous programs are executed piece by piece. Each piece may start some actions and schedule code to be executed when the action finishes or fails. In between these pieces, the program sits idle, waiting for the next action.

So callbacks are not directly called by the code that scheduled them. If I call setTimeout from within a function, that function will have returned by the time the callback function is called. And when the callback returns, control does not go back to the function that scheduled it.

Asynchronous behavior happens on its own empty function call stack. This is one of the reasons that, without promises, managing exceptions across asynchronous code is hard. Since each callback starts with a mostly empty stack, your catch handlers won't be on the stack when they throw an exception.

```
try {
  setTimeout(() => {
    throw new Error("Woosh");
  }, 20);
} catch (_) {
```

```
  // This will not run
  console.log("Caught!");
}
```

No matter how closely together events—such as timeouts or incoming requests—happen, a JavaScript environment will run only one program at a time. You can think of this as it running a big loop *around* your program, called the *event loop*. When there's nothing to be done, that loop is stopped. But as events come in, they are added to a queue, and their code is executed one after the other. Because no two things run at the same time, slow-running code might delay the handling of other events.

This example sets a timeout but then dallies until after the timeout's intended point of time, causing the timeout to be late.

```
let start = Date.now();
setTimeout(() => {
  console.log("Timeout ran at", Date.now() - start);
}, 20);
while (Date.now() < start + 50) {}
console.log("Wasted time until", Date.now() - start);
// → Wasted time until 50
// → Timeout ran at 55
```

Promises always resolve or reject as a new event. Even if a promise is already resolved, waiting for it will cause your callback to run after the current script finishes, rather than right away.

```
Promise.resolve("Done").then(console.log);
console.log("Me first!");
// → Me first!
// → Done
```

In later chapters we'll see various other types of events that run on the event loop.

Asynchronous Bugs

When your program runs synchronously, in a single go, there are no state changes happening except those that the program itself makes. For asynchronous programs this is different—they may have *gaps* in their execution during which other code can run.

Let's look at an example. One of the hobbies of our crows is to count the number of chicks that hatch throughout the village every year. Nests store this count in their storage bulbs. The following code tries to enumerate the counts from all the nests for a given year:

```
function anyStorage(nest, source, name) {
  if (source == nest.name) return storage(nest, name);
```

```
    else return routeRequest(nest, source, "storage", name);
}

async function chicks(nest, year) {
  let list = "";
  await Promise.all(network(nest).map(async name => {
    list += `${name}: ${
      await anyStorage(nest, name, `chicks in ${year}`)
    }\n`;
  }));
  return list;
}
```

The `async name =>` part shows that arrow functions can also be made async by putting the word async in front of them.

The code doesn't immediately look suspicious . . . it maps the `async` arrow function over the set of nests, creating an array of promises, and then uses `Promise.all` to wait for all of these before returning the list they build up.

But it is seriously broken. It'll always return only a single line of output, listing the nest that was slowest to respond.

Can you work out why?

The problem lies in the `+=` operator, which takes the *current* value of `list` at the time where the statement starts executing and then, when the `await` finishes, sets the `list` binding to be that value plus the added string.

But between the time where the statement starts executing and the time where it finishes there's an asynchronous gap. The `map` expression runs before anything has been added to the list, so each of the `+=` operators starts from an empty string and ends up, when its storage retrieval finishes, setting `list` to a single-line list—the result of adding its line to the empty string.

This could have easily been avoided by returning the lines from the mapped promises and calling `join` on the result of `Promise.all`, instead of building up the list by changing a binding. As usual, computing new values is less error-prone than changing existing values.

```
async function chicks(nest, year) {
  let lines = network(nest).map(async name => {
    return name + ": " +
      await anyStorage(nest, name, `chicks in ${year}`);
  });
  return (await Promise.all(lines)).join("\n");
}
```

Mistakes like this are easy to make, especially when using `await`, and you should be aware of where the gaps in your code occur. An advantage of JavaScript's *explicit* asynchronicity (whether through callbacks, promises, or await) is that spotting these gaps is relatively easy.

Summary

Asynchronous programming makes it possible to express waiting for long-running actions without freezing the program during these actions. JavaScript environments typically implement this style of programming using callbacks, functions that are called when the actions complete. An event loop schedules such callbacks to be called when appropriate, one after the other, so that their execution does not overlap.

Programming asynchronously is made easier by promises, objects that represent actions that might complete in the future, and async functions, which allow you to write an asynchronous program as if it were synchronous.

Exercises

Tracking the Scalpel

The village crows own an old scalpel that they occasionally use on special missions—say, to cut through screen doors or packaging. To be able to quickly track it down, every time the scalpel is moved to another nest, an entry is added to the storage of both the nest that had it and the nest that took it, under the name "scalpel", with its new location as the value.

This means that finding the scalpel is a matter of following the bread-crumb trail of storage entries, until you find a nest where that points at the nest itself.

Write an async function locateScalpel that does this, starting at the nest on which it runs. You can use the anyStorage function defined earlier to access storage in arbitrary nests. The scalpel has been going around long enough that you may assume that every nest has a "scalpel" entry in its data storage.

Next, write the same function again without using async and await.

Do request failures properly show up as rejections of the returned promise in both versions? How?

Building Promise.all

Given an array of promises, Promise.all returns a promise that waits for all of the promises in the array to finish. It then succeeds, yielding an array of result values. If a promise in the array fails, the promise returned by all fails too, with the failure reason from the failing promise.

Implement something like this yourself as a regular function called Promise_all.

Remember that after a promise has succeeded or failed, it can't succeed or fail again, and further calls to the functions that resolve it are ignored. This can simplify the way you handle failure of your promise.

"The evaluator, which determines the meaning of expressions in a programming language, is just another program."
—Hal Abelson and Gerald Sussman, *Structure and Interpretation of Computer Programs*

12

PROJECT:
A PROGRAMMING LANGUAGE

Building your own programming language is surprisingly easy (as long as you do not aim too high) and very enlightening.

The main thing I want to show in this chapter is that there is no magic involved in building your own language. I've often felt that some human inventions were so immensely clever and complicated that I'd never be able to understand them. But with a little reading and experimenting, they often turn out to be quite mundane.

We will build a programming language called Egg. It will be a tiny, simple language—but one that is powerful enough to express any computation you can think of. It will allow simple abstraction based on functions.

Parsing

The most immediately visible part of a programming language is its *syntax*, or notation. A *parser* is a program that reads a piece of text and produces a data structure that reflects the structure of the program contained in that text. If the text does not form a valid program, the parser should point out the error.

Our language will have a simple and uniform syntax. Everything in Egg is an expression. An expression can be the name of a binding, a number, a string, or an *application*. Applications are used for function calls but also for constructs such as if or while.

To keep the parser simple, strings in Egg do not support anything like backslash escapes. A string is simply a sequence of characters that are not double quotes, wrapped in double quotes. A number is a sequence of digits. Binding names can consist of any character that is not whitespace and that does not have a special meaning in the syntax.

Applications are written the way they are in JavaScript, by putting parentheses after an expression and having any number of arguments between those parentheses, separated by commas.

```
do(define(x, 10),
   if(>(x, 5),
      print("large"),
      print("small")))
```

The uniformity of the Egg language means that things that are operators in JavaScript (such as >) are normal bindings in this language, applied just like other functions. And since the syntax has no concept of a block, we need a do construct to represent doing multiple things in sequence.

The data structure that the parser will use to describe a program consists of expression objects, each of which has a type property indicating the kind of expression it is and other properties to describe its content.

Expressions of type "value" represent literal strings or numbers. Their value property contains the string or number value that they represent. Expressions of type "word" are used for identifiers (names). Such objects have a name property that holds the identifier's name as a string. Finally, "apply" expressions represent applications. They have an operator property that refers to the expression that is being applied, as well as an args property that holds an array of argument expressions.

The >(x, 5) part of the previous program would be represented like this:

```
{
  type: "apply",
  operator: {type: "word", name: ">"},
  args: [
    {type: "word", name: "x"},
    {type: "value", value: 5}
  ]
}
```

Such a data structure is called a *syntax tree*. If you imagine the objects as dots and the links between them as lines between those dots, it has a treelike shape. The fact that expressions contain other expressions, which in turn might contain more expressions, is similar to the way tree branches split and split again.

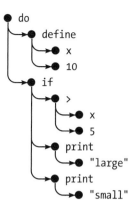

Contrast this to the parser we wrote for the configuration file format in "Parsing an INI File" on page 160, which had a simple structure: it split the input into lines and handled those lines one at a time. There were only a few simple forms that a line was allowed to have.

Here we must find a different approach. Expressions are not separated into lines, and they have a recursive structure. Application expressions *contain* other expressions.

Fortunately, this problem can be solved very well by writing a parser function that is recursive in a way that reflects the recursive nature of the language.

We define a function parseExpression, which takes a string as input and returns an object containing the data structure for the expression at the start of the string, along with the part of the string left after parsing this expression. When parsing subexpressions (the argument to an application, for example), this function can be called again, yielding the argument expression as well as the text that remains. This text may in turn contain more arguments or may be the closing parenthesis that ends the list of arguments.

This is the first part of the parser:

```
function parseExpression(program) {
  program = skipSpace(program);
  let match, expr;
  if (match = /^"([^"]*)"/.exec(program)) {
    expr = {type: "value", value: match[1]};
  } else if (match = /^\d+\b/.exec(program)) {
    expr = {type: "value", value: Number(match[0])};
  } else if (match = /^[^\s(),#"]+/.exec(program)) {
    expr = {type: "word", name: match[0]};
  } else {
    throw new SyntaxError("Unexpected syntax: " + program);
  }

  return parseApply(expr, program.slice(match[0].length));
}
```

```
function skipSpace(string) {
  let first = string.search(/\S/);
  if (first == -1) return "";
  return string.slice(first);
}
```

Because Egg, like JavaScript, allows any amount of whitespace between its elements, we have to repeatedly cut the whitespace off the start of the program string. That is what the skipSpace function helps with.

After skipping any leading space, parseExpression uses three regular expressions to spot the three atomic elements that Egg supports: strings, numbers, and words. The parser constructs a different kind of data structure depending on which one matches. If the input does not match one of these three forms, it is not a valid expression, and the parser throws an error. We use SyntaxError instead of Error as the exception constructor, which is another standard error type, because it is a little more specific—it is also the error type thrown when an attempt is made to run an invalid JavaScript program.

We then cut off the part that was matched from the program string and pass that, along with the object for the expression, to parseApply, which checks whether the expression is an application. If so, it parses a parenthesized list of arguments.

```
function parseApply(expr, program) {
  program = skipSpace(program);
  if (program[0] != "(") {
    return {expr: expr, rest: program};
  }

  program = skipSpace(program.slice(1));
  expr = {type: "apply", operator: expr, args: []};
  while (program[0] != ")") {
    let arg = parseExpression(program);
    expr.args.push(arg.expr);
    program = skipSpace(arg.rest);
    if (program[0] == ",") {
      program = skipSpace(program.slice(1));
    } else if (program[0] != ")") {
      throw new SyntaxError("Expected ',' or ')'");
    }
  }
  return parseApply(expr, program.slice(1));
}
```

If the next character in the program is not an opening parenthesis, this is not an application, and parseApply returns the expression it was given.

Otherwise, it skips the opening parenthesis and creates the syntax tree object for this application expression. It then recursively calls parseExpression to parse each argument until a closing parenthesis is found. The recursion is indirect, through parseApply and parseExpression calling each other.

Because an application expression can itself be applied (such as in multiplier(2)(1)), parseApply must, after it has parsed an application, call itself again to check whether another pair of parentheses follows.

This is all we need to parse Egg. We wrap it in a convenient parse function that verifies that it has reached the end of the input string after parsing the expression (an Egg program is a single expression), and that gives us the program's data structure.

```
function parse(program) {
  let {expr, rest} = parseExpression(program);
  if (skipSpace(rest).length > 0) {
    throw new SyntaxError("Unexpected text after program");
  }
  return expr;
}

console.log(parse("+(a, 10)"));
// → {type: "apply",
//    operator: {type: "word", name: "+"},
//    args: [{type: "word", name: "a"},
//           {type: "value", value: 10}]}
```

It works! It doesn't give us very helpful information when it fails and doesn't store the line and column on which each expression starts, which might be helpful when reporting errors later, but it's good enough for our purposes.

The Evaluator

What can we do with the syntax tree for a program? Run it, of course! And that is what the evaluator does. You give it a syntax tree and a scope object that associates names with values, and it will evaluate the expression that the tree represents and return the value that this produces.

```
const specialForms = Object.create(null);

function evaluate(expr, scope) {
  if (expr.type == "value") {
    return expr.value;
  } else if (expr.type == "word") {
    if (expr.name in scope) {
      return scope[expr.name];
    } else {
```

```
        throw new ReferenceError(
          `Undefined binding: ${expr.name}`);
      }
    } else if (expr.type == "apply") {
      let {operator, args} = expr;
      if (operator.type == "word" &&
          operator.name in specialForms) {
        return specialForms[operator.name](expr.args, scope);
      } else {
        let op = evaluate(operator, scope);
        if (typeof op == "function") {
          return op(...args.map(arg => evaluate(arg, scope)));
        } else {
          throw new TypeError("Applying a non-function.");
        }
      }
    }
  }
}
```

The evaluator has code for each of the expression types. A literal value expression produces its value. (For example, the expression 100 just evaluates to the number 100.) For a binding, we must check whether it is actually defined in the scope and, if it is, fetch the binding's value.

Applications are more involved. If they are a special form, like if, we do not evaluate anything and pass the argument expressions, along with the scope, to the function that handles this form. If it is a normal call, we evaluate the operator, verify that it is a function, and call it with the evaluated arguments.

We use plain JavaScript function values to represent Egg's function values. We will come back to this in "Functions" on page 211, when the special form called fun is defined.

The recursive structure of evaluate resembles the similar structure of the parser, and both mirror the structure of the language itself. It would also be possible to integrate the parser with the evaluator and evaluate during parsing, but splitting them up this way makes the program clearer.

This is really all that is needed to interpret Egg. It is that simple. But without defining a few special forms and adding some useful values to the environment, you can't do much with this language yet.

Special Forms

The specialForms object is used to define special syntax in Egg. It associates words with functions that evaluate such forms. It is currently empty. Let's add if.

```
specialForms.if = (args, scope) => {
  if (args.length != 3) {
```

```
      throw new SyntaxError("Wrong number of args to if");
    } else if (evaluate(args[0], scope) !== false) {
      return evaluate(args[1], scope);
    } else {
      return evaluate(args[2], scope);
    }
};
```

Egg's if construct expects exactly three arguments. It will evaluate the first, and if the result isn't the value false, it will evaluate the second. Otherwise, the third gets evaluated. This if form is more similar to JavaScript's ternary ?: operator than to JavaScript's if. It is an expression, not a statement, and it produces a value, namely, the result of the second or third argument.

Egg also differs from JavaScript in how it handles the condition value to if. It will not treat things like zero or the empty string as false, only the precise value false.

The reason we need to represent if as a special form, rather than a regular function, is that all arguments to functions are evaluated before the function is called, whereas if should evaluate only *either* its second or its third argument, depending on the value of the first.

The while form is similar.

```
specialForms.while = (args, scope) => {
  if (args.length != 2) {
    throw new SyntaxError("Wrong number of args to while");
  }
  while (evaluate(args[0], scope) !== false) {
    evaluate(args[1], scope);
  }

  // Since undefined does not exist in Egg, we return false,
  // for lack of a meaningful result.
  return false;
};
```

Another basic building block is do, which executes all its arguments from top to bottom. Its value is the value produced by the last argument.

```
specialForms.do = (args, scope) => {
  let value = false;
  for (let arg of args) {
    value = evaluate(arg, scope);
  }
  return value;
};
```

To be able to create bindings and give them new values, we also create a form called define. It expects a word as its first argument and an expression producing the value to assign to that word as its second argument. Since define, like everything, is an expression, it must return a value. We'll make it return the value that was assigned (just like JavaScript's = operator).

```
specialForms.define = (args, scope) => {
  if (args.length != 2 || args[0].type != "word") {
    throw new SyntaxError("Incorrect use of define");
  }
  let value = evaluate(args[1], scope);
  scope[args[0].name] = value;
  return value;
};
```

The Environment

The scope accepted by evaluate is an object with properties whose names correspond to binding names and whose values correspond to the values those bindings are bound to. Let's define an object to represent the global scope.

To be able to use the if construct we just defined, we must have access to Boolean values. Since there are only two Boolean values, we do not need special syntax for them. We simply bind two names to the values true and false and use them.

```
const topScope = Object.create(null);

topScope.true = true;
topScope.false = false;
```

We can now evaluate a simple expression that negates a Boolean value.

```
let prog = parse(`if(true, false, true)`);
console.log(evaluate(prog, topScope));
// → false
```

To supply basic arithmetic and comparison operators, we will also add some function values to the scope. In the interest of keeping the code short, we'll use Function to synthesize a bunch of operator functions in a loop, instead of defining them individually.

```
for (let op of ["+", "-", "*", "/", "==", "<", ">"]) {
  topScope[op] = Function("a, b", `return a ${op} b;`);
}
```

A way to output values is also useful, so we'll wrap `console.log` in a function and call it `print`.

```
topScope.print = value => {
  console.log(value);
  return value;
};
```

That gives us enough elementary tools to write simple programs. The following function provides a convenient way to parse a program and run it in a fresh scope:

```
function run(program) {
  return evaluate(parse(program), Object.create(topScope));
}
```

We'll use object prototype chains to represent nested scopes so that the program can add bindings to its local scope without changing the top-level scope.

```
run(`
do(define(total, 0),
   define(count, 1),
   while(<(count, 11),
         do(define(total, +(total, count)),
            define(count, +(count, 1)))),
   print(total))
`);
// → 55
```

This is the program we've seen several times before, which computes the sum of the numbers 1 to 10, expressed in Egg. It is clearly uglier than the equivalent JavaScript program—but not bad for a language implemented in less than 150 lines of code.

Functions

A programming language without functions is a poor programming language indeed.

Fortunately, it isn't hard to add a `fun` construct, which treats its last argument as the function's body and uses all arguments before that as the names of the function's parameters.

```
specialForms.fun = (args, scope) => {
  if (!args.length) {
    throw new SyntaxError("Functions need a body");
  }
  let body = args[args.length - 1];
```

```
    let params = args.slice(0, args.length - 1).map(expr => {
      if (expr.type != "word") {
        throw new SyntaxError("Parameter names must be words");
      }
      return expr.name;
    });

    return function() {
      if (arguments.length != params.length) {
        throw new TypeError("Wrong number of arguments");
      }
      let localScope = Object.create(scope);
      for (let i = 0; i < arguments.length; i++) {
        localScope[params[i]] = arguments[i];
      }
      return evaluate(body, localScope);
    };
};
```

Functions in Egg get their own local scope. The function produced by the fun form creates this local scope and adds the argument bindings to it. It then evaluates the function body in this scope and returns the result.

```
run(`
do(define(plusOne, fun(a, +(a, 1))),
   print(plusOne(10)))
`);
// → 11

run(`
do(define(pow, fun(base, exp,
     if(==(exp, 0),
        1,
        *(base, pow(base, -(exp, 1)))))),
   print(pow(2, 10)))
`);
// → 1024
```

Compilation

What we have built is an interpreter. During evaluation, it acts directly on the representation of the program produced by the parser.

Compilation is the process of adding another step between the parsing and the running of a program, which transforms the program into something that can be evaluated more efficiently by doing as much work as possible in advance. For example, in well-designed languages it is obvious, for each use of a binding, which binding is being referred to, without actually running the program. This can be used to avoid looking up the binding by name every time it is accessed, instead directly fetching it from some predetermined memory location.

Traditionally, compilation involves converting the program to machine code, the raw format that a computer's processor can execute. But any process that converts a program to a different representation can be thought of as compilation.

It would be possible to write an alternative evaluation strategy for Egg, one that first converts the program to a JavaScript program, uses `Function` to invoke the JavaScript compiler on it, and then runs the result. When done right, this would make Egg run very fast while still being quite simple to implement.

If you are interested in this topic and willing to spend some time on it, I encourage you to try to implement such a compiler as an exercise.

Cheating

When we defined `if` and `while`, you probably noticed that they were more or less trivial wrappers around JavaScript's own `if` and `while`. Similarly, the values in Egg are just regular old JavaScript values.

If you compare the implementation of Egg, built on top of JavaScript, with the amount of work and complexity required to build a programming language directly on the raw functionality provided by a machine, the difference is huge. Regardless, this example ideally gave you an impression of the way programming languages work.

And when it comes to getting something done, cheating is more effective than doing everything yourself. Though the toy language in this chapter doesn't do anything that couldn't be done better in JavaScript, there *are* situations where writing small languages helps get real work done.

Such a language does not have to resemble a typical programming language. If JavaScript didn't come equipped with regular expressions, for example, you could write your own parser and evaluator for regular expressions.

Or imagine you are building a giant robotic dinosaur and need to program its behavior. JavaScript might not be the most effective way to do this. You might instead opt for a language that looks like this:

```
behavior walk
  perform when
    destination ahead
  actions
    move left-foot
    move right-foot

behavior attack
  perform when
    Godzilla in-view
```

```
actions
  fire laser-eyes
  launch arm-rockets
```

This is what is usually called a *domain-specific language*, a language tailored to express a narrow domain of knowledge. Such a language can be more expressive than a general-purpose language because it is designed to describe exactly the things that need to be described in its domain, and nothing else.

Exercises

Arrays

Add support for arrays to Egg by adding the following three functions to the top scope: array(...values) to construct an array containing the argument values, length(array) to get an array's length, and element(array, n) to fetch the nth element from an array.

Closure

The way we have defined fun allows functions in Egg to reference the surrounding scope, allowing the function's body to use local values that were visible at the time the function was defined, just like JavaScript functions do.

The following program illustrates this: function f returns a function that adds its argument to f's argument, meaning that it needs access to the local scope inside f to be able to use binding a.

```
run(`
do(define(f, fun(a, fun(b, +(a, b)))),
   print(f(4)(5)))
`);
// → 9
```

Go back to the definition of the fun form and explain which mechanism causes this to work.

Comments

It would be nice if we could write comments in Egg. For example, whenever we find a hash sign (#), we could treat the rest of the line as a comment and ignore it, similar to // in JavaScript.

We do not have to make any big changes to the parser to support this. We can simply change skipSpace to skip comments as if they are whitespace so that all the points where skipSpace is called will now also skip comments. Make this change.

Fixing Scope

Currently, the only way to assign a binding a value is `define`. This construct acts as a way both to define new bindings and to give existing ones a new value.

This ambiguity causes a problem. When you try to give a nonlocal binding a new value, you will end up defining a local one with the same name instead. Some languages work like this by design, but I've always found it an awkward way to handle scope.

Add a special form `set`, similar to `define`, which gives a binding a new value, updating the binding in an outer scope if it doesn't already exist in the inner scope. If the binding is not defined at all, throw a `ReferenceError` (another standard error type).

The technique of representing scopes as simple objects, which has made things convenient so far, will get in your way a little at this point. You might want to use the `Object.getPrototypeOf` function, which returns the prototype of an object. Also remember that scopes do not derive from `Object.prototype`, so if you want to call `hasOwnProperty` on them, you have to use this clumsy expression:

```
Object.prototype.hasOwnProperty.call(scope, name);
```

PART II

BROWSER

"The dream behind the Web is of a common information space in which we communicate by sharing information. Its universality is essential: the fact that a hypertext link can point to anything, be it personal, local or global, be it draft or highly polished."
—Tim Berners-Lee,
The World Wide Web: A very short personal history

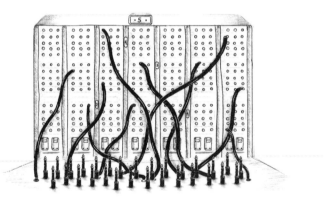

13

JAVASCRIPT AND THE BROWSER

The next chapters of this book will talk about web browsers. Without web browsers, there would be no JavaScript. Or even if there were, no one would ever have paid any attention to it.

Web technology has been decentralized from the start, not just technically but also in the way it evolved. Various browser vendors have added new functionality in ad hoc and sometimes poorly thought-out ways, which then, sometimes, ended up being adopted by others—and finally set down as standards.

This is both a blessing and a curse. On the one hand, it is empowering to not have a central party control a system but have it be improved by various parties working in loose collaboration (or occasionally open hostility). On the other hand, the haphazard way in which the web was developed means that the resulting system is not exactly a shining example of internal consistency. Some parts of it are downright confusing and poorly conceived.

Networks and the Internet

Computer networks have been around since the 1950s. If you put cables between two or more computers and allow them to send data back and forth through these cables, you can do all kinds of wonderful things.

And if connecting two machines in the same building allows us to do wonderful things, connecting machines all over the planet should be even better. The technology to start implementing this vision was developed in the 1980s, and the resulting network is called the *internet*. It has lived up to its promise.

A computer can use this network to shoot bits at another computer. For any effective communication to arise out of this bit-shooting, the computers on both ends must know what the bits are supposed to represent. The meaning of any given sequence of bits depends entirely on the kind of thing that it is trying to express and on the encoding mechanism used.

A *network protocol* describes a style of communication over a network. There are protocols for sending email, for fetching email, for sharing files, and even for controlling computers that happen to be infected by malicious software.

For example, the *Hypertext Transfer Protocol* (HTTP) is a protocol for retrieving named resources (chunks of information, such as web pages or pictures). It specifies that the side making the request should start with a line like this, naming the resource and the version of the protocol that it is trying to use:

```
GET /index.html HTTP/1.1
```

There are a lot more rules about the way the requester can include more information in the request and the way the other side, which returns the resource, packages up its content. We'll look at HTTP in a little more detail in Chapter 18.

Most protocols are built on top of other protocols. HTTP treats the network as a streamlike device into which you can put bits and have them arrive at the correct destination in the correct order. As we saw in Chapter 11, ensuring those things is already a rather difficult problem.

The *Transmission Control Protocol* (TCP) is a protocol that addresses this problem. All internet-connected devices "speak" it, and most communication on the internet is built on top of it.

A TCP connection works as follows: one computer must be waiting, or *listening*, for other computers to start talking to it. To be able to listen for different kinds of communication at the same time on a single machine, each listener has a number (called a *port*) associated with it. Most protocols specify which port should be used by default. For example, when we want to send an email using the SMTP protocol, the machine through which we send it is expected to be listening on port 25.

Another computer can then establish a connection by connecting to the target machine using the correct port number. If the target machine can be reached and is listening on that port, the connection is successfully created. The listening computer is called the *server*, and the connecting computer is called the *client*.

Such a connection acts as a two-way pipe through which bits can flow—the machines on both ends can put data into it. Once the bits are successfully transmitted, they can be read out again by the machine on the other side. This is a convenient model. You could say that TCP provides an abstraction of the network.

The Web

The *World Wide Web* (not to be confused with the internet as a whole) is a set of protocols and formats that allow us to visit web pages in a browser. The "Web" part in the name refers to the fact that such pages can easily link to each other, thus connecting into a huge mesh that users can move through.

To become part of the web, all you need to do is connect a machine to the internet and have it listen on port 80 with the HTTP protocol so that other computers can ask it for documents.

Each document on the web is named by a *Uniform Resource Locator* (URL), which looks something like this:

```
http://eloquentjavascript.net/13_browser.html
 |       |                  |          |
protocol      server              path
```

The first part tells us that this URL uses the HTTP protocol (as opposed to, for example, encrypted HTTP, which would be *https://*). Then comes the part that identifies which server we are requesting the document from. Last is a path string that identifies the specific document (or *resource*) we are interested in.

Machines connected to the internet get an *IP address*, which is a number that can be used to send messages to that machine, and looks something like `149.210.142.219` or `2001:4860:4860::8888`. But lists of more or less random numbers are hard to remember and awkward to type, so you can instead register a *domain name* for a specific address or set of addresses. I registered the domain name *eloquentjavascript.net* to point at the IP address of a machine I control and can thus use that name to serve web pages.

If you type this URL into your browser's address bar, the browser will try to retrieve and display the document at that URL. First, your browser has to find out what address *eloquentjavascript.net* refers to. Then, using the HTTP protocol, it will make a connection to the server at that address and ask for the resource */13_browser.html*. If all goes well, the server sends back a document, which your browser then displays on your screen.

HTML

HTML, which stands for *Hypertext Markup Language*, is the document format used for web pages. An HTML document contains text, as well as *tags* that give structure to the text, describing things such as links, paragraphs, and headings.

A short HTML document might look like this:

```html
<!doctype html>
<html>
  <head>
    <meta charset="utf-8">
    <title>My home page</title>
  </head>
  <body>
    <h1>My home page</h1>
    <p>Hello, I am Marijn and this is my home page.</p>
    <p>I also wrote a book! Read it
      <a href="http://eloquentjavascript.net">here</a>.</p>
  </body>
</html>
```

This is what such a document would look like in the browser:

My home page

Hello, I am Marijn and this is my home page.

I also wrote a book! Read it <u>here</u>.

The tags, wrapped in angle brackets (< and >, the symbols for *less than* and *greater than*), provide information about the structure of the document. The other text is just plain text.

The document starts with `<!doctype html>`, which tells the browser to interpret the page as *modern* HTML, as opposed to various dialects that were in use in the past.

HTML documents have a head and a body. The head contains information *about* the document, and the body contains the document itself. In this case, the head declares that the title of this document is "My home page" and that it uses the UTF-8 encoding, which is a way to encode Unicode text as binary data. The document's body contains a heading (`<h1>`, meaning "heading 1"—`<h2>` to `<h6>` produce subheadings) and two paragraphs (`<p>`).

Tags come in several forms. An element (such as the body, a paragraph, or a link) is started by an *opening tag* like `<p>` and ended by a *closing tag* like `</p>`. Some opening tags, such as the one for the link (`<a>`), contain extra information in the form of `name="value"` pairs. These are called *attributes*. In this case, the destination of the link is indicated with `href="http://eloquentjavascript.net"`, where `href` stands for "hypertext reference."

Some kinds of tags do not enclose anything and thus do not need to be closed. The metadata tag `<meta charset="utf-8">` is an example of this.

To be able to include angle brackets in the text of a document, even though they have a special meaning in HTML, yet another form of special notation has to be introduced. A plain opening angle bracket is written as

< ("less than"), and a closing bracket is written as > ("greater than"). In HTML, an ampersand (&) character followed by a name or character code and a semicolon (;) is called an *entity* and will be replaced by the character it encodes.

This is analogous to the way backslashes are used in JavaScript strings. Since this mechanism gives ampersand characters a special meaning, too, they need to be escaped as &. Inside attribute values, which are wrapped in double quotes, " can be used to insert an actual quote character.

HTML is parsed in a remarkably error-tolerant way. When tags that should be there are missing, the browser reconstructs them. The way in which this is done has been standardized, and you can rely on all modern browsers to do it in the same way.

The following document will be treated just like the one shown previously:

```
<!doctype html>

<meta charset=utf-8>
<title>My home page</title>

<h1>My home page</h1>
<p>Hello, I am Marijn and this is my home page.
<p>I also wrote a book! Read it
  <a href=http://eloquentjavascript.net>here</a>.
```

The <html>, <head>, and <body> tags are gone completely. The browser knows that <meta> and <title> belong in the head and that <h1> means the body has started. Furthermore, I am no longer explicitly closing the paragraphs since opening a new paragraph or ending the document will close them implicitly. The quotes around the attribute values are also gone.

This book will usually omit the <html>, <head>, and <body> tags from examples to keep them short and free of clutter. But I *will* close tags and include quotes around attributes.

I will also usually omit the doctype and charset declaration. This is not to be taken as an encouragement to drop these from HTML documents. Browsers will often do ridiculous things when you forget them. You should consider the doctype and the charset metadata to be implicitly present in examples, even when they are not actually shown in the text.

HTML and JavaScript

In the context of this book, the most important HTML tag is <script>. This tag allows us to include a piece of JavaScript in a document.

```
<h1>Testing alert</h1>
<script>alert("hello!");</script>
```

Such a script will run as soon as its `<script>` tag is encountered while the browser reads the HTML. This page will pop up a dialog when opened—the alert function resembles `prompt`, in that it pops up a little window, but only shows a message without asking for input.

Including large programs directly in HTML documents is often impractical. The `<script>` tag can be given an `src` attribute to fetch a script file (a text file containing a JavaScript program) from a URL.

```
<h1>Testing alert</h1>
<script src="code/hello.js"></script>
```

The *code/hello.js* file included here contains the same program—`alert("hello!")`. When an HTML page references other URLs as part of itself—for example, an image file or a script—web browsers will retrieve them immediately and include them in the page.

A script tag must always be closed with `</script>`, even if it refers to a script file and doesn't contain any code. If you forget this, the rest of the page will be interpreted as part of the script.

You can load ES modules (see "ECMAScript Modules" on page 173) in the browser by giving your script tag a `type="module"` attribute. Such modules can depend on other modules by using URLs relative to themselves as module names in `import` declarations.

Some attributes can also contain a JavaScript program. The `<button>` tag shown next (which shows up as a button) has an `onclick` attribute. The attribute's value will be run whenever the button is clicked.

```
<button onclick="alert('Boom!');">DO NOT PRESS</button>
```

Note that I had to use single quotes for the string in the `onclick` attribute because double quotes are already used to quote the whole attribute. I could also have used `&quot;`.

In the Sandbox

Running programs downloaded from the internet is potentially dangerous. You do not know much about the people behind most sites you visit, and they do not necessarily mean well. Running programs by people who do not mean well is how you get your computer infected by viruses, your data stolen, and your accounts hacked.

Yet the attraction of the web is that you can browse it without necessarily trusting all the pages you visit. This is why browsers severely limit the things a JavaScript program may do: it can't look at the files on your computer or modify anything not related to the web page it was embedded in.

Isolating a programming environment in this way is called *sandboxing*, the idea being that the program is harmlessly playing in a sandbox. But you should imagine this particular kind of sandbox as having a cage of thick steel bars over it so that the programs playing in it can't actually get out.

The hard part of sandboxing is allowing the programs enough room to be useful yet at the same time restricting them from doing anything dangerous. Lots of useful functionality, such as communicating with other servers or reading the content of the copy-paste clipboard, can also be used to do problematic, privacy-invading things.

Every now and then, someone comes up with a new way to circumvent the limitations of a browser and do something harmful, ranging from leaking minor private information to taking over the whole machine that the browser runs on. The browser developers respond by fixing the hole, and all is well again—until the next problem is discovered, and hopefully publicized, rather than secretly exploited by some government agency or mafia.

Compatibility and the Browser Wars

In the early stages of the web, a browser called Mosaic dominated the market. After a few years, the balance shifted to Netscape, which was then, in turn, largely supplanted by Microsoft's Internet Explorer. At any point where a single browser was dominant, that browser's vendor would feel entitled to unilaterally invent new features for the web. Since most users used the most popular browser, websites would simply start using those features—never mind the other browsers.

This was the dark age of compatibility, often called the *browser wars*. Web developers were left with not one unified web but two or three incompatible platforms. To make things worse, the browsers in use around 2003 were all full of bugs, and of course the bugs were different for each browser. Life was hard for people writing web pages.

Mozilla Firefox, a not-for-profit offshoot of Netscape, challenged Internet Explorer's position in the late 2000s. Because Microsoft was not particularly interested in staying competitive at the time, Firefox took a lot of market share away from it. Around the same time, Google introduced its Chrome browser, and Apple's Safari browser gained popularity, leading to a situation where there were four major players, rather than one.

The new players had a more serious attitude toward standards and better engineering practices, giving us less incompatibility and fewer bugs. Microsoft, seeing its market share crumble, came around and adopted these attitudes in its Edge browser, which replaces Internet Explorer. If you are starting to learn web development today, consider yourself lucky. The latest versions of the major browsers behave quite uniformly and have relatively few bugs.

"Too bad! Same old story! Once you've finished building your house you notice you've accidentally learned something that you really should have known—before you started."

—Friedrich Nietzsche,
Beyond Good and Evil

14

THE DOCUMENT OBJECT MODEL

When you open a web page in your browser, the browser retrieves the page's HTML text and parses it, much like the way our parser from Chapter 12 parsed programs. The browser builds up a model of the document's structure and uses this model to draw the page on the screen.

This representation of the document is one of the toys that a JavaScript program has available in its sandbox. It is a data structure that you can read or modify. It acts as a *live* data structure: when it's modified, the page on the screen is updated to reflect the changes.

Document Structure

You can imagine an HTML document as a nested set of boxes. Tags such as <body> and </body> enclose other tags, which in turn contain other tags or text. Here's the example document from the previous chapter:

```
<!doctype html>
<html>
  <head>
    <title>My home page</title>
```

```
    </head>
    <body>
      <h1>My home page</h1>
      <p>Hello, I am Marijn and this is my home page.</p>
      <p>I also wrote a book! Read it
        <a href="http://eloquentjavascript.net">here</a>.</p>
    </body>
  </html>
```

This page has the following structure:

The data structure the browser uses to represent the document follows this shape. For each box, there is an object, which we can interact with to find out things such as what HTML tag it represents and which boxes and text it contains. This representation is called the *Document Object Model*, or DOM for short.

The global binding document gives us access to these objects. Its documentElement property refers to the object representing the <html> tag. Since every HTML document has a head and a body, it also has head and body properties, pointing at those elements.

Trees

Think back for a moment to the syntax trees from "Parsing" on page 203. Their structures are strikingly similar to the structure of a browser's document. Each *node* may refer to other nodes, *children*, which in turn may have their own children. This shape is typical of nested structures where elements can contain subelements that are similar to themselves.

We call a data structure a *tree* when it has a branching structure, has no cycles (a node may not contain itself, directly or indirectly), and has a single, well-defined *root*. In the case of the DOM, `document.documentElement` serves as the root.

Trees come up a lot in computer science. In addition to representing recursive structures such as HTML documents or programs, they are often used to maintain sorted sets of data because elements can usually be found or inserted more efficiently in a tree than in a flat array.

A typical tree has different kinds of nodes. The syntax tree for the Egg language had identifiers, values, and application nodes. Application nodes may have children, whereas identifiers and values are *leaves*, or nodes without children.

The same goes for the DOM. Nodes for *elements*, which represent HTML tags, determine the structure of the document. These can have child nodes. An example of such a node is `document.body`. Some of these children can be leaf nodes, such as pieces of text or comment nodes.

Each DOM node object has a `nodeType` property, which contains a code (number) that identifies the type of node. Elements have code 1, which is also defined as the constant property `Node.ELEMENT_NODE`. Text nodes, representing a section of text in the document, get code 3 (`Node.TEXT_NODE`). Comments have code 8 (`Node.COMMENT_NODE`).

Another way to visualize our document tree is as follows:

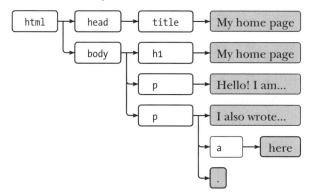

The leaves are text nodes, and the arrows indicate parent-child relationships between nodes.

The Standard

Using cryptic numeric codes to represent node types is not a very JavaScript-like thing to do. Later in this chapter, we'll see that other parts of the DOM interface also feel cumbersome and alien. The reason for this is that the DOM wasn't designed for just JavaScript. Rather, it tries to be a language-neutral interface that can be used in other systems as well—not just for

HTML but also for XML, which is a generic data format with an HTML-like syntax.

This is unfortunate. Standards are often useful. But in this case, the advantage (cross-language consistency) isn't all that compelling. Having an interface that is properly integrated with the language you are using will save you more time than having a familiar interface across languages.

As an example of this poor integration, consider the childNodes property that element nodes in the DOM have. This property holds an array-like object, with a length property and properties labeled by numbers to access the child nodes. But it is an instance of the NodeList type, not a real array, so it does not have methods such as slice and map.

Then there are issues that are simply poor design. For example, there is no way to create a new node and immediately add children or attributes to it. Instead, you have to first create it and then add the children and attributes one by one, using side effects. Code that interacts heavily with the DOM tends to get long, repetitive, and ugly.

But these flaws aren't fatal. Since JavaScript allows us to create our own abstractions, it is possible to design improved ways to express the operations you are performing. Many libraries intended for browser programming come with such tools.

Moving Through the Tree

DOM nodes contain a wealth of links to other nearby nodes. The following diagram illustrates these:

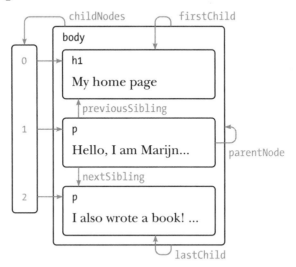

Although the diagram shows only one link of each type, every node has a parentNode property that points to the node it is part of, if any. Likewise, every element node (node type 1) has a childNodes property that points to an array-like object holding its children.

In theory, you could move anywhere in the tree using just these parent and child links. But JavaScript also gives you access to a number of additional convenience links. The firstChild and lastChild properties point to the first and last child elements or have the value null for nodes without children. Similarly, previousSibling and nextSibling point to adjacent nodes, which are nodes with the same parent that appear immediately before or after the node itself. For a first child, previousSibling will be null, and for a last child, nextSibling will be null.

There's also the children property, which is like childNodes but contains only element (type 1) children, not other types of child nodes. This can be useful when you aren't interested in text nodes.

When dealing with a nested data structure like this one, recursive functions are often useful. The following function scans a document for text nodes containing a given string and returns true when it has found one:

```
function talksAbout(node, string) {
  if (node.nodeType == Node.ELEMENT_NODE) {
    for (let child of node.childNodes) {
      if (talksAbout(child, string)) {
        return true;
      }
    }
    return false;
  } else if (node.nodeType == Node.TEXT_NODE) {
    return node.nodeValue.indexOf(string) > -1;
  }
}

console.log(talksAbout(document.body, "book"));
// → true
```

The nodeValue property of a text node holds the string of text that it represents.

Finding Elements

Navigating these links among parents, children, and siblings is often useful. But if we want to find a specific node in the document, reaching it by starting at document.body and following a fixed path of properties is a bad idea. Doing so bakes assumptions into our program about the precise structure of the document—a structure you might want to change later. Another complicating factor is that text nodes are created even for the whitespace between nodes. The example document's <body> tag does not have just three children (<h1> and two <p> elements) but actually has seven: those three, plus the spaces before, after, and between them.

So if we want to get the href attribute of the link in that document, we don't want to say something like "Get the second child of the sixth child of the document body." It'd be better if we could say "Get the first link in the document." And we can.

```
let link = document.body.getElementsByTagName("a")[0];
console.log(link.href);
```

All element nodes have a getElementsByTagName method, which collects all elements with the given tag name that are descendants (direct or indirect children) of that node and returns them as an array-like object.

To find a specific *single* node, you can give it an id attribute and use document.getElementById instead.

```
<p>My ostrich Gertrude:</p>
<p><img id="gertrude" src="img/ostrich.png"></p>

<script>
  let ostrich = document.getElementById("gertrude");
  console.log(ostrich.src);
</script>
```

A third, similar method is getElementsByClassName, which, like getElementsByTagName, searches through the contents of an element node and retrieves all elements that have the given string in their class attribute.

Changing the Document

Almost everything about the DOM data structure can be changed. The shape of the document tree can be modified by changing parent-child relationships. Nodes have a remove method to remove them from their current parent node. To add a child node to an element node, we can use appendChild, which puts it at the end of the list of children, or insertBefore, which inserts the node given as the first argument before the node given as the second argument.

```
<p>One</p>
<p>Two</p>
<p>Three</p>

<script>
  let paragraphs = document.body.getElementsByTagName("p");
  document.body.insertBefore(paragraphs[2], paragraphs[0]);
</script>
```

A node can exist in the document in only one place. Thus, inserting paragraph *Three* in front of paragraph *One* will first remove it from the end of the document and then insert it at the front, resulting in *Three/One/Two*. All operations that insert a node somewhere will, as a side effect, cause it to be removed from its current position (if it has one).

The `replaceChild` method is used to replace a child node with another one. It takes as arguments two nodes: a new node and the node to be replaced. The replaced node must be a child of the element the method is called on. Note that both `replaceChild` and `insertBefore` expect the *new* node as their first argument.

Creating Nodes

Say we want to write a script that replaces all images (`<img>` tags) in the document with the text held in their `alt` attributes, which specifies an alternative textual representation of the image.

This involves not only removing the images but adding a new text node to replace them. Text nodes are created with the `document.createTextNode` method.

```
<p>The <img src="img/cat.png" alt="Cat"> in the
  <img src="img/hat.png" alt="Hat">.</p>

<p><button onclick="replaceImages()">Replace</button></p>

<script>
  function replaceImages() {
    let images = document.body.getElementsByTagName("img");
    for (let i = images.length - 1; i >= 0; i--) {
      let image = images[i];
      if (image.alt) {
        let text = document.createTextNode(image.alt);
        image.parentNode.replaceChild(text, image);
      }
    }
  }
</script>
```

Given a string, `createTextNode` gives us a text node that we can insert into the document to make it show up on the screen.

The loop that goes over the images starts at the end of the list. This is necessary because the node list returned by `getElementsByTagName` (or a property like `childNodes`) is *live*. That is, it is updated as the document changes. If we started from the front, removing the first image would cause the list to lose its first element so that the second time the loop repeats, where `i` is 1, it would stop because the length of the collection is now also 1.

If you want a *solid* collection of nodes, as opposed to a live one, you can convert the collection to a real array by calling `Array.from`.

```
let arrayish = {0: "one", 1: "two", length: 2};
let array = Array.from(arrayish);
console.log(array.map(s => s.toUpperCase()));
// → ["ONE", "TWO"]
```

To create element nodes, you can use the `document.createElement` method. This method takes a tag name and returns a new empty node of the given type.

The following example defines a utility `elt`, which creates an element node and treats the rest of its arguments as children to that node. This function is then used to add an attribution to a quote.

```
<blockquote id="quote">
  No book can ever be finished. While working on it we learn
  just enough to find it immature the moment we turn away
  from it.
</blockquote>

<script>
  function elt(type, ...children) {
    let node = document.createElement(type);
    for (let child of children) {
      if (typeof child != "string") node.appendChild(child);
      else node.appendChild(document.createTextNode(child));
    }
    return node;
  }

  document.getElementById("quote").appendChild(
    elt("footer", "--",
        elt("strong", "Karl Popper"),
        ", preface to the second edition of ",
        elt("em", "The Open Society and Its Enemies"),
        ", 1950"));
</script>
```

This is what the resulting document looks like:

No book can ever be finished. While working on it we learn just enough to find it immature the moment we turn away from it.
—**Karl Popper**, preface to the second editon of *The Open Society and Its Enemies*, 1950

Attributes

Some element attributes, such as href for links, can be accessed through a property of the same name on the element's DOM object. This is the case for most commonly used standard attributes.

But HTML allows you to set any attribute you want on nodes. This can be useful because it allows you to store extra information in a document. If you make up your own attribute names, though, such attributes will not be present as properties on the element's node. Instead, you have to use the getAttribute and setAttribute methods to work with them.

```
<p data-classified="secret">The launch code is 00000000.</p>
<p data-classified="unclassified">I have two feet.</p>

<script>
  let paras = document.body.getElementsByTagName("p");
  for (let para of Array.from(paras)) {
    if (para.getAttribute("data-classified") == "secret") {
      para.remove();
    }
  }
</script>
```

It is recommended to prefix the names of such made-up attributes with data- to ensure they do not conflict with any other attributes. There is a commonly used attribute, class, which is a keyword in the JavaScript language. For historical reasons—some old JavaScript implementations could not handle property names that matched keywords—the property used to access this attribute is called className. You can also access it under its real name, "class", by using the getAttribute and setAttribute methods.

Layout

You may have noticed that different types of elements are laid out differently. Some, such as paragraphs (<p>) or headings (<h1>), take up the whole width of the document and are rendered on separate lines. These are called *block* elements. Others, such as links (<a>) or the <strong> element, are rendered on the same line with their surrounding text. Such elements are called *inline* elements.

For any given document, browsers are able to compute a layout, which gives each element a size and position based on its type and content. This layout is then used to actually draw the document.

The size and position of an element can be accessed from JavaScript. The offsetWidth and offsetHeight properties give you the space the element takes up in *pixels*. A pixel is the basic unit of measurement in the browser. It traditionally corresponds to the smallest dot that the screen can draw, but on modern displays, which can draw *very* small dots, that may no longer be the case, and a browser pixel may span multiple display dots.

Similarly, clientWidth and clientHeight give you the size of the space *inside* the element, ignoring border width.

```
<p style="border: 3px solid red">
  I'm boxed in
</p>

<script>
  let para = document.body.getElementsByTagName("p")[0];
  console.log("clientHeight:", para.clientHeight);
  console.log("offsetHeight:", para.offsetHeight);
</script>
```

Giving a paragraph a border causes a rectangle to be drawn around it.

I'm boxed in

The most effective way to find the precise position of an element on the screen is the getBoundingClientRect method. It returns an object with top, bottom, left, and right properties, indicating the pixel positions of the sides of the element relative to the top left of the screen. If you want them relative to the whole document, you must add the current scroll position, which you can find in the pageXOffset and pageYOffset bindings.

Laying out a document can be quite a lot of work. In the interest of speed, browser engines do not immediately re-layout a document every time you change it but wait as long as they can. When a JavaScript program that changed the document finishes running, the browser will have to compute a new layout to draw the changed document to the screen. When a program *asks* for the position or size of something by reading properties such as offsetHeight or calling getBoundingClientRect, providing correct information also requires computing a layout.

A program that repeatedly alternates between reading DOM layout information and changing the DOM forces a lot of layout computations to happen and will consequently run very slowly. The following code is an example of this. It contains two different programs that build up a line of *X* characters 2,000 pixels wide and measures the time each one takes.

```
<p><span id="one"></span></p>
<p><span id="two"></span></p>

<script>
  function time(name, action) {
    let start = Date.now(); // Current time in milliseconds
    action();
    console.log(name, "took", Date.now() - start, "ms");
  }
```

```
    time("naive", () => {
      let target = document.getElementById("one");
      while (target.offsetWidth < 2000) {
        target.appendChild(document.createTextNode("X"));
      }
    });
    // → naive took 32 ms

    time("clever", function() {
      let target = document.getElementById("two");
      target.appendChild(document.createTextNode("XXXXX"));
      let total = Math.ceil(2000 / (target.offsetWidth / 5));
      target.firstChild.nodeValue = "X".repeat(total);
    });
    // → clever took 1 ms
</script>
```

Styling

We have seen that different HTML elements are drawn differently. Some are displayed as blocks, others inline. Some add styling—<strong> makes its content bold, and <a> makes it blue and underlines it.

The way an <img> tag shows an image or an <a> tag causes a link to be followed when it is clicked is strongly tied to the element type. But we can change the styling associated with an element, such as the text color or underline. Here is an example that uses the style property:

```
<p><a href=".">Normal link</a></p>
<p><a href="." style="color: green">Green link</a></p>
```

The second link will be green instead of the default link color.

<u>Normal link</u>

<u>Green link</u>

A style attribute may contain one or more *declarations*, which are a property (such as color) followed by a colon and a value (such as green). When there is more than one declaration, they must be separated by semicolons, as in "color: red; border: none".

A lot of aspects of the document can be influenced by styling. For example, the display property controls whether an element is displayed as a block or an inline element.

```
This text is displayed <strong>inline</strong>,
<strong style="display: block">as a block</strong>, and
<strong style="display: none">not at all</strong>.
```

The block tag will end up on its own line since block elements are not displayed inline with the text around them. The last tag is not displayed at all—display: none prevents an element from showing up on the screen. This is a way to hide elements. It is often preferable to removing them from the document entirely because it makes it easy to reveal them again later.

This text is displayed **inline**,
as a block
, and .

JavaScript code can directly manipulate the style of an element through the element's style property. This property holds an object that has properties for all possible style properties. The values of these properties are strings, which we can write to in order to change a particular aspect of the element's style.

```
<p id="para" style="color: purple">
  Nice text
</p>

<script>
  let para = document.getElementById("para");
  console.log(para.style.color);
  para.style.color = "magenta";
</script>
```

There are some style property names that contain hyphens, such as font-family. Because such property names are awkward to work with in Java-Script (you'd have to say style["font-family"]), the property names in the style object for such properties have their hyphens removed and the letters after them capitalized (style.fontFamily).

Cascading Styles

The styling system for HTML is called CSS, for *Cascading Style Sheets*. A *style sheet* is a set of rules for how to style elements in a document. It can be given inside a <style> tag.

```
<style>
  strong {
    font-style: italic;
    color: gray;
  }
</style>
<p>Now <strong>strong text</strong> is italic and gray.</p>
```

The *cascading* in the name refers to the fact that multiple such rules are combined to produce the final style for an element. In the example, the default styling for <strong> tags, which gives them font-weight: bold, is overlaid by the rule in the <style> tag, which adds font-style and color.

When multiple rules define a value for the same property, the most recently read rule gets a higher precedence and wins. So if the rule in the <style> tag included font-weight: normal, contradicting the default font-weight rule, the text would be normal, *not* bold. Styles in a style attribute applied directly to the node have the highest precedence and always win.

It is possible to target things other than tag names in CSS rules. A rule for .abc applies to all elements with "abc" in their class attribute. A rule for #xyz applies to the element with an id attribute of "xyz" (which should be unique within the document).

```
.subtle {
  color: gray;
  font-size: 80%;
}
#header {
  background: blue;
  color: white;
}
/* p elements with id main and with classes a and b */
p#main.a.b {
  margin-bottom: 20px;
}
```

The precedence rule favoring the most recently defined rule applies only when the rules have the same *specificity*. A rule's specificity is a measure of how precisely it describes matching elements, determined by the number and kind (tag, class, or ID) of element aspects it requires. For example, a rule that targets p.a is more specific than rules that target p or just .a and would thus take precedence over them.

The notation p > a {...} applies the given styles to all <a> tags that are direct children of <p> tags. Similarly, p a {...} applies to all <a> tags inside <p> tags, whether they are direct or indirect children.

Query Selectors

We won't be using style sheets all that much in this book. Understanding them is helpful when programming in the browser, but they are complicated enough to warrant a separate book.

The main reason I introduced *selector* syntax—the notation used in style sheets to determine which elements a set of styles apply to—is that we can use this same mini-language as an effective way to find DOM elements.

The querySelectorAll method, which is defined both on the document object and on element nodes, takes a selector string and returns a NodeList containing all the elements that it matches.

```
<p>And if you go chasing
  <span class="animal">rabbits</span></p>
<p>And you know you're going to fall</p>
<p>Tell 'em a <span class="character">hookah smoking
  <span class="animal">caterpillar</span></span></p>
<p>Has given you the call</p>

<script>
  function count(selector) {
    return document.querySelectorAll(selector).length;
  }
  console.log(count("p"));            // All <p> elements
  // → 4
  console.log(count(".animal"));      // Class animal
  // → 2
  console.log(count("p .animal"));    // Animal inside of <p>
  // → 2
  console.log(count("p > .animal")); // Direct child of <p>
  // → 1
</script>
```

Unlike methods such as getElementsByTagName, the object returned by querySelectorAll is *not* live. It won't change when you change the document. It is still not a real array, though, so you still need to call Array.from if you want to treat it like one.

The querySelector method (without the All part) works in a similar way. This one is useful if you want a specific, single element. It will return only the first matching element or null when no element matches.

Positioning and Animating

The position style property influences layout in a powerful way. By default it has a value of static, meaning the element sits in its normal place in the document. When it is set to relative, the element still takes up space in the document, but now the top and left style properties can be used to move it relative to that normal place. When position is set to absolute, the element is removed from the normal document flow—that is, it no longer takes up space and may overlap with other elements. Also, its top and left properties can be used to absolutely position it relative to the top-left corner of the nearest enclosing element whose position property isn't static, or relative to the document if no such enclosing element exists.

We can use this to create an animation. The following document displays a picture of a cat that moves around in an ellipse:

```
<p style="text-align: center">
  <img src="img/cat.png" style="position: relative">
</p>
```

```
<script>
  let cat = document.querySelector("img");
  let angle = Math.PI / 2;
  function animate(time, lastTime) {
    if (lastTime != null) {
      angle += (time - lastTime) * 0.001;
    }
    cat.style.top = (Math.sin(angle) * 20) + "px";
    cat.style.left = (Math.cos(angle) * 200) + "px";
    requestAnimationFrame(newTime => animate(newTime, time));
  }
  requestAnimationFrame(animate);
</script>
```

The gray arrow shows the path along which the image moves.

Our picture is centered on the page and given a position of relative.
We'll repeatedly update that picture's top and left styles to move it.

The script uses requestAnimationFrame to schedule the animate function
to run whenever the browser is ready to repaint the screen. The animate
function itself again calls requestAnimationFrame to schedule the next update.
When the browser window (or tab) is active, this will cause updates to happen at a rate of about 60 per second, which tends to produce a good-looking
animation.

If we just updated the DOM in a loop, the page would freeze, and nothing would show up on the screen. Browsers do not update their display
while a JavaScript program is running, nor do they allow any interaction
with the page. This is why we need requestAnimationFrame—it lets the browser
know that we are done for now, and it can go ahead and do the things that
browsers do, such as updating the screen and responding to user actions.

The animation function is passed the current time as an argument. To
ensure that the motion of the cat per millisecond is stable, it bases the speed
at which the angle changes on the difference between the current time and
the last time the function ran. If it just moved the angle by a fixed amount
per step, the motion would stutter if, for example, another heavy task running on the same computer were to prevent the function from running for a
fraction of a second.

Moving in circles is done using the trigonometry functions Math.cos and
Math.sin. For those who aren't familiar with these, I'll briefly introduce them
since we will occasionally use them in this book.

`Math.cos` and `Math.sin` are useful for finding points that lie on a circle around point (0,0) with a radius of one. Both functions interpret their argument as the position on this circle, with zero denoting the point on the far right of the circle, going clockwise until 2π (about 6.28) has taken us around the whole circle. `Math.cos` tells you the x-coordinate of the point that corresponds to the given position, and `Math.sin` yields the y-coordinate. Positions (or angles) greater than 2π or less than 0 are valid—the rotation repeats so that $a + 2\pi$ refers to the same angle as a.

This unit for measuring angles is called radians—a full circle is 2π radians, similar to how it is 360 degrees when measuring in degrees. The constant π is available as `Math.PI` in JavaScript.

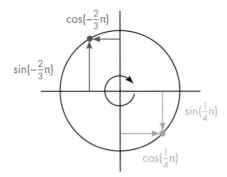

The cat animation code keeps a counter, `angle`, for the current angle of the animation and increments it every time the `animate` function is called. It can then use this angle to compute the current position of the image element. The `top` style is computed with `Math.sin` and multiplied by 20, which is the vertical radius of our ellipse. The `left` style is based on `Math.cos` and multiplied by 200 so that the ellipse is much wider than it is high.

Note that styles usually need *units*. In this case, we have to append `"px"` to the number to tell the browser that we are counting in pixels (as opposed to centimeters, "ems," or other units). This is easy to forget. Using numbers without units will result in your style being ignored—unless the number is 0, which always means the same thing, regardless of its unit.

Summary

JavaScript programs may inspect and interfere with the document that the browser is displaying through a data structure called the DOM. This data structure represents the browser's model of the document, and a JavaScript program can modify it to change the visible document.

The DOM is organized like a tree, in which elements are arranged hierarchically according to the structure of the document. The objects representing elements have properties such as `parentNode` and `childNodes`, which can be used to navigate through this tree.

The way a document is displayed can be influenced by *styling*, both by attaching styles to nodes directly and by defining rules that match certain nodes. There are many different style properties, such as `color` or `display`. JavaScript code can manipulate an element's style directly through its `style` property.

Exercises

Build a Table

An HTML table is built with the following tag structure:

```
<table>
  <tr>
    <th>name</th>
    <th>height</th>
    <th>place</th>
  </tr>
  <tr>
    <td>Kilimanjaro</td>
    <td>5895</td>
    <td>Tanzania</td>
  </tr>
</table>
```

For each *row*, the `<table>` tag contains a `<tr>` tag. Inside of these `<tr>` tags, we can put cell elements: either heading cells (`<th>`) or regular cells (`<td>`).

Given a data set of mountains, an array of objects with `name`, `height`, and `place` properties, generate the DOM structure for a table that enumerates the objects. It should have one column per key and one row per object, plus a header row with `<th>` elements at the top, listing the column names.

Write this so that the columns are automatically derived from the objects, by taking the property names of the first object in the data.

Add the resulting table to the element with an `id` attribute of `"mountains"` so that it becomes visible in the document.

Once you have this working, right-align cells that contain number values by setting their `style.textAlign` property to `"right"`.

Elements by Tag Name

The `document.getElementsByTagName` method returns all child elements with a given tag name. Implement your own version of this as a function that takes a node and a string (the tag name) as arguments and returns an array containing all descendant element nodes with the given tag name.

To find the tag name of an element, use its `nodeName` property. But note that this will return the tag name in all uppercase. Use the `toLowerCase` or `toUpperCase` string methods to compensate for this.

The Cat's Hat

Extend the cat animation defined in "Positioning and Animating" on page 240 so that both the cat and his hat (`<img src="img/hat.png">`) orbit at opposite sides of the ellipse.

Or make the hat circle around the cat. Or alter the animation in some other interesting way.

To make positioning multiple objects easier, it is probably a good idea to switch to absolute positioning. This means that top and left are counted relative to the top left of the document. To avoid using negative coordinates, which would cause the image to move outside of the visible page, you can add a fixed number of pixels to the position values.

"You have power over your mind—
not outside events. Realize this,
and you will find strength."

—Marcus Aurelius, *Meditations*

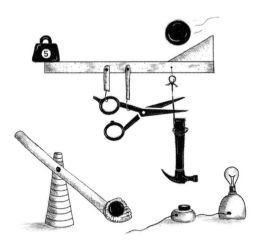

15

HANDLING EVENTS

Some programs work with direct user input, such as mouse and keyboard actions. That kind of input isn't available as a well-organized data structure—it comes in piece by piece, in real time, and the program is expected to respond to it as it happens.

Event Handlers

Imagine an interface where the only way to find out whether a key on the keyboard is being pressed is to read the current state of that key. To be able to react to keypresses, you would have to constantly read the key's state so that you'd catch it before it's released again. It would be dangerous to perform other time-intensive computations since you might miss a keypress.

Some primitive machines do handle input like that. A step up from this would be for the hardware or operating system to notice the keypress and put it in a queue. A program can then periodically check the queue for new events and react to what it finds there.

Of course, it has to remember to look at the queue, and to do it often, because any time between the key being pressed and the program noticing the event will cause the software to feel unresponsive. This approach is called *polling*. Most programmers prefer to avoid it.

A better mechanism is for the system to actively notify our code when an event occurs. Browsers do this by allowing us to register functions as *handlers* for specific events.

```
<p>Click this document to activate the handler.</p>
<script>
  window.addEventListener("click", () => {
    console.log("You knocked?");
  });
</script>
```

The `window` binding refers to a built-in object provided by the browser. It represents the browser window that contains the document. Calling its `addEventListener` method registers the second argument to be called whenever the event described by its first argument occurs.

Events and DOM Nodes

Each browser event handler is registered in a context. In the previous example we called `addEventListener` on the `window` object to register a handler for the whole window. Such a method can also be found on DOM elements and some other types of objects. Event listeners are called only when the event happens in the context of the object they are registered on.

```
<button>Click me</button>
<p>No handler here.</p>
<script>
  let button = document.querySelector("button");
  button.addEventListener("click", () => {
    console.log("Button clicked.");
  });
</script>
```

That example attaches a handler to the button node. Clicks on the button cause that handler to run, but clicks on the rest of the document do not.

Giving a node an `onclick` attribute has a similar effect. This works for most types of events—you can attach a handler through the attribute whose name is the event name with `on` in front of it.

But a node can have only one `onclick` attribute, so you can register only one handler per node that way. The `addEventListener` method allows you to add any number of handlers so that it is safe to add handlers even if there is already another handler on the element.

The `removeEventListener` method, called with arguments similar to `addEventListener`, removes a handler.

```
<button>Act-once button</button>
<script>
  let button = document.querySelector("button");
```

```
  function once() {
    console.log("Done.");
    button.removeEventListener("click", once);
  }
  button.addEventListener("click", once);
</script>
```

The function given to removeEventListener has to be the same function value that was given to addEventListener. So, to unregister a handler, you'll want to give the function a name (once, in the example) to be able to pass the same function value to both methods.

Event Objects

Though we have ignored it so far, event handler functions are passed an argument: the *event object*. This object holds additional information about the event. For example, if we want to know *which* mouse button was pressed, we can look at the event object's button property.

```
<button>Click me any way you want</button>
<script>
  let button = document.querySelector("button");
  button.addEventListener("mousedown", event => {
    if (event.button == 0) {
      console.log("Left button");
    } else if (event.button == 1) {
      console.log("Middle button");
    } else if (event.button == 2) {
      console.log("Right button");
    }
  });
</script>
```

The information stored in an event object differs per type of event. We'll discuss different types later in the chapter. The object's type property always holds a string identifying the event (such as "click" or "mousedown").

Propagation

For most event types, handlers registered on nodes with children will also receive events that happen in the children. If a button inside a paragraph is clicked, event handlers on the paragraph will also see the click event.

But if both the paragraph and the button have a handler, the more specific handler—the one on the button—gets to go first. The event is said to *propagate* outward, from the node where it happened to that node's parent node and on to the root of the document. Finally, after all handlers registered on a specific node have had their turn, handlers registered on the whole window get a chance to respond to the event.

At any point, an event handler can call the stopPropagation method on the event object to prevent handlers further up from receiving the event. This can be useful when, for example, you have a button inside another clickable element and you don't want clicks on the button to activate the outer element's click behavior.

The following example registers "mousedown" handlers on both a button and the paragraph around it. When clicked with the right mouse button, the handler for the button calls stopPropagation, which will prevent the handler on the paragraph from running. When the button is clicked with another mouse button, both handlers will run.

```
<p>A paragraph with a <button>button</button>.</p>
<script>
  let para = document.querySelector("p");
  let button = document.querySelector("button");
  para.addEventListener("mousedown", () => {
    console.log("Handler for paragraph.");
  });
  button.addEventListener("mousedown", event => {
    console.log("Handler for button.");
    if (event.button == 2) event.stopPropagation();
  });
</script>
```

Most event objects have a target property that refers to the node where they originated. You can use this property to ensure that you're not accidentally handling something that propagated up from a node you do not want to handle.

It is also possible to use the target property to cast a wide net for a specific type of event. For example, if you have a node containing a long list of buttons, it may be more convenient to register a single click handler on the outer node and have it use the target property to figure out whether a button was clicked, rather than register individual handlers on all of the buttons.

```
<button>A</button>
<button>B</button>
<button>C</button>
<script>
  document.body.addEventListener("click", event => {
    if (event.target.nodeName == "BUTTON") {
      console.log("Clicked", event.target.textContent);
    }
  });
</script>
```

Default Actions

Many events have a default action associated with them. If you click a link, you will be taken to the link's target. If you press the down arrow, the browser will scroll the page down. If you right-click, you'll get a context menu. And so on.

For most types of events, the JavaScript event handlers are called *before* the default behavior takes place. If the handler doesn't want this normal behavior to happen, typically because it has already taken care of handling the event, it can call the `preventDefault` method on the event object.

This can be used to implement your own keyboard shortcuts or context menu. It can also be used to obnoxiously interfere with the behavior that users expect. For example, here is a link that cannot be followed:

```
<a href="https://developer.mozilla.org/">MDN</a>
<script>
  let link = document.querySelector("a");
  link.addEventListener("click", event => {
    console.log("Nope.");
    event.preventDefault();
  });
</script>
```

Try not to do such things unless you have a really good reason to. It'll be unpleasant for people who use your page when expected behavior is broken.

Depending on the browser, some events can't be intercepted at all. On Chrome, for example, the keyboard shortcut to close the current tab (CTRL-W or COMMAND-W) cannot be handled by JavaScript.

Key Events

When a key on the keyboard is pressed, your browser fires a "keydown" event. When it is released, you get a "keyup" event.

```
<p>This page turns violet when you hold the V key.</p>
<script>
  window.addEventListener("keydown", event => {
    if (event.key == "v") {
      document.body.style.background = "violet";
    }
  });
  window.addEventListener("keyup", event => {
    if (event.key == "v") {
      document.body.style.background = "";
    }
  });
</script>
```

Despite its name, "keydown" fires not only when the key is physically pushed down. When a key is pressed and held, the event fires again every time the key *repeats*. Sometimes you have to be careful about this. For example, if you add a button to the DOM when a key is pressed and remove it again when the key is released, you might accidentally add hundreds of buttons when the key is held down longer.

The example looked at the key property of the event object to see which key the event is about. This property holds a string that, for most keys, corresponds to the thing that pressing that key would type. For special keys such as ENTER, it holds a string that names the key ("Enter", in this case). If you hold SHIFT while pressing a key, that might also influence the name of the key—"v" becomes "V", and "1" may become "!", if that is what pressing SHIFT-1 produces on your keyboard.

Modifier keys such as SHIFT, CTRL, ALT, and meta (COMMAND on Mac) generate key events just like normal keys. But when looking for key combinations, you can also find out whether these keys are held down by looking at the shiftKey, ctrlKey, altKey, and metaKey properties of keyboard and mouse events.

```
<p>Press Control-Space to continue.</p>
<script>
  window.addEventListener("keydown", event => {
    if (event.key == " " && event.ctrlKey) {
      console.log("Continuing!");
    }
  });
</script>
```

The DOM node where a key event originates depends on the element that has focus when the key is pressed. Most nodes cannot have focus unless you give them a tabindex attribute, but things like links, buttons, and form fields can. We'll come back to form fields in Chapter 18. When nothing in particular has focus, document.body acts as the target node of key events.

When the user is typing text, using key events to figure out what is being typed is problematic. Some platforms, most notably the virtual keyboard on Android phones, don't fire key events. But even when you have an old-fashioned keyboard, some types of text input don't match key presses in a straightforward way, such as *input method editor* (IME) software used by people whose scripts don't fit on a keyboard, where multiple key strokes are combined to create characters.

To notice when something was typed, elements that you can type into, such as the <input> and <textarea> tags, fire "input" events whenever the user changes their content. To get the actual content that was typed, it is best to directly read it from the focused field. "Form Fields" on page 317 will show how.

Pointer Events

There are currently two widely used ways to point at things on a screen: mice (including devices that act like mice, such as touchpads and trackballs) and touchscreens. These produce different kinds of events.

Mouse Clicks

Pressing a mouse button causes a number of events to fire. The `"mousedown"` and `"mouseup"` events are similar to `"keydown"` and `"keyup"` and fire when the button is pressed and released. These happen on the DOM nodes that are immediately below the mouse pointer when the event occurs.

After the `"mouseup"` event, a `"click"` event fires on the most specific node that contained both the press and the release of the button. For example, if I press down the mouse button on one paragraph and then move the pointer to another paragraph and release the button, the `"click"` event will happen on the element that contains both those paragraphs.

If two clicks happen close together, a `"dblclick"` (double-click) event also fires, after the second click event.

To get precise information about the place where a mouse event happened, you can look at its `clientX` and `clientY` properties, which contain the event's coordinates (in pixels) relative to the top-left corner of the window, or `pageX` and `pageY`, which are relative to the top-left corner of the whole document (which may be different when the window has been scrolled).

The following implements a primitive drawing program. Every time you click the document, it adds a dot under your mouse pointer. See Chapter 19 for a less primitive drawing program.

```
<style>
  body {
    height: 200px;
    background: beige;
  }
  .dot {
    height: 8px; width: 8px;
    border-radius: 4px; /* rounds corners */
    background: blue;
    position: absolute;
  }
</style>
<script>
  window.addEventListener("click", event => {
    let dot = document.createElement("div");
    dot.className = "dot";
    dot.style.left = (event.pageX - 4) + "px";
```

```
    dot.style.top = (event.pageY - 4) + "px";
    document.body.appendChild(dot);
  });
</script>
```

Mouse Motion

Every time the mouse pointer moves, a "mousemove" event is fired. This event can be used to track the position of the mouse. A common situation in which this is useful is when implementing some form of mouse-dragging functionality.

As an example, the following program displays a bar and sets up event handlers so that dragging to the left or right on this bar makes it narrower or wider:

```
<p>Drag the bar to change its width:</p>
<div style="background: orange; width: 60px; height: 20px">
</div>
<script>
  let lastX; // Tracks the last observed mouse X position
  let bar = document.querySelector("div");
  bar.addEventListener("mousedown", event => {
    if (event.button == 0) {
      lastX = event.clientX;
      window.addEventListener("mousemove", moved);
      event.preventDefault(); // Prevent selection
    }
  });

  function moved(event) {
    if (event.buttons == 0) {
      window.removeEventListener("mousemove", moved);
    } else {
      let dist = event.clientX - lastX;
      let newWidth = Math.max(10, bar.offsetWidth + dist);
      bar.style.width = newWidth + "px";
      lastX = event.clientX;
    }
  }
</script>
```

The resulting page looks like this:

Drag the bar to change its width:

Note that the "mousemove" handler is registered on the whole window. Even if the mouse goes outside of the bar during resizing, as long as the button is held we still want to update its size.

We must stop resizing the bar when the mouse button is released. For that, we can use the buttons property (note the plural), which tells us about the buttons that are currently held down. When this is zero, no buttons are down. When buttons are held, its value is the sum of the codes for those buttons—the left button has code 1, the right button 2, and the middle one 4. With the left and right buttons held, for example, the value of buttons will be 3.

Note that the order of these codes is different from the one used by button, where the middle button came before the right one. As mentioned, consistency isn't really a strong point of the browser's program-ming interface.

Touch Events

The style of graphical browser that we use was designed with mouse interfaces in mind, at a time where touchscreens were rare. To make the web "work" on early touchscreen phones, browsers for those devices pretended, to a certain extent, that touch events were mouse events. If you tap your screen, you'll get "mousedown", "mouseup", and "click" events.

But this illusion isn't very robust. A touchscreen works differently from a mouse: it doesn't have multiple buttons, you can't track the finger when it isn't on the screen (to simulate "mousemove"), and it allows multiple fingers to be on the screen at the same time.

Mouse events cover touch interaction only in straightforward cases—if you add a "click" handler to a button, touch users will still be able to use it. But something like the resizeable bar in the previous example does not work on a touchscreen.

There are specific event types fired by touch interaction. When a finger starts touching the screen, you get a "touchstart" event. When it is moved while touching, "touchmove" events fire. Finally, when it stops touching the screen, you'll see a "touchend" event.

Because many touchscreens can detect multiple fingers at the same time, these events don't have a single set of coordinates associated with them. Rather, their event objects have a touches property, which holds an array-like object of points, each of which has its own clientX, clientY, pageX, and pageY properties.

You could do something like this to show red circles around every touching finger:

```
<style>
  dot { position: absolute; display: block;
        border: 2px solid red; border-radius: 50px;
        height: 100px; width: 100px; }
</style>
<p>Touch this page</p>
```

```
<script>
  function update(event) {
    for (let dot; dot = document.querySelector("dot");) {
      dot.remove();
    }
    for (let i = 0; i < event.touches.length; i++) {
      let {pageX, pageY} = event.touches[i];
      let dot = document.createElement("dot");
      dot.style.left = (pageX - 50) + "px";
      dot.style.top = (pageY - 50) + "px";
      document.body.appendChild(dot);
    }
  }
  window.addEventListener("touchstart", update);
  window.addEventListener("touchmove", update);
  window.addEventListener("touchend", update);
</script>
```

You'll often want to call preventDefault in touch event handlers to override the browser's default behavior (which may include scrolling the page on swiping) and to prevent the mouse events from being fired, for which you may *also* have a handler.

Scroll Events

Whenever an element is scrolled, a "scroll" event is fired on it. This has various uses, such as knowing what the user is currently looking at (for disabling off-screen animations or sending spy reports to your evil headquarters) or showing some indication of progress (by highlighting part of a table of contents or showing a page number).

The following example draws a progress bar above the document and updates it to fill up as you scroll down:

```
<style>
  #progress {
    border-bottom: 2px solid blue;
    width: 0;
    position: fixed;
    top: 0; left: 0;
  }
</style>
<div id="progress"></div>
<script>
  // Create some content
  document.body.appendChild(document.createTextNode(
    "supercalifragilisticexpialidocious ".repeat(1000)));
```

```
  let bar = document.querySelector("#progress");
  window.addEventListener("scroll", () => {
    let max = document.body.scrollHeight - innerHeight;
    bar.style.width = `${(pageYOffset / max) * 100}%`;
  });
</script>
```

Giving an element a position of fixed acts much like an absolute position but also prevents it from scrolling along with the rest of the document. The effect is to make our progress bar stay at the top. Its width is changed to indicate the current progress. We use %, rather than px, as a unit when setting the width so that the element is sized relative to the page width.

The global innerHeight binding gives us the height of the window, which we have to subtract from the total scrollable height—you can't keep scrolling when you hit the bottom of the document. There is also an innerWidth for the window width. By dividing pageYOffset, the current scroll position, by the maximum scroll position and multiplying by 100, we get the percentage for the progress bar.

Calling preventDefault on a scroll event does not prevent the scrolling from happening. In fact, the event handler is called only *after* the scrolling takes place.

Focus Events

When an element gains focus, the browser fires a "focus" event on it. When it loses focus, the element gets a "blur" event.

Unlike the events discussed earlier, these two events do not propagate. A handler on a parent element is not notified when a child element gains or loses focus.

The following example displays help text for the text field that currently has focus:

```
<p>Name: <input type="text" data-help="Your full name"></p>
<p>Age: <input type="text" data-help="Age in years"></p>
<p id="help"></p>

<script>
  let help = document.querySelector("#help");
  let fields = document.querySelectorAll("input");
  for (let field of Array.from(fields)) {
    field.addEventListener("focus", event => {
      let text = event.target.getAttribute("data-help");
      help.textContent = text;
    });
```

```
    field.addEventListener("blur", event => {
      help.textContent = "";
    });
  }
</script>
```

This screenshot shows the help text for the age field.

Name: `Hieronimus`

Age: `I`

Age in years

The window object will receive "focus" and "blur" events when the user moves from or to the browser tab or window in which the document is shown.

Load Event

When a page finishes loading, the "load" event fires on the window and the document body objects. This is often used to schedule initialization actions that require the whole document to have been built. Remember that the content of <script> tags is run immediately when the tag is encountered. This may be too soon, for example when the script needs to do something with parts of the document that appear after the <script> tag.

Elements such as images and script tags that load an external file also have a "load" event that indicates the files they reference were loaded. Like the focus-related events, loading events do not propagate.

When a page is closed or navigated away from (for example, by following a link), a "beforeunload" event fires. The main use of this event is to prevent the user from accidentally losing work by closing a document. If you prevent the default behavior on this event *and* set the returnValue property on the event object to a string, the browser will show the user a dialog asking if they really want to leave the page. That dialog might include your string, but because some malicious sites try to use these dialogs to confuse people into staying on their page to look at dodgy weight-loss ads, most browsers no longer display them.

Events and the Event Loop

In the context of the event loop, as discussed in Chapter 11, browser event handlers behave like other asynchronous notifications. They are scheduled when the event occurs but must wait for other scripts that are running to finish before they get a chance to run.

The fact that events can be processed only when nothing else is running means that, if the event loop is tied up with other work, any interaction with the page (which happens through events) will be delayed until there's time to process it. So if you schedule too much work, either with long-running event handlers or with lots of short-running ones, the page will become slow and cumbersome to use.

For cases where you *really* do want to do some time-consuming thing in the background without freezing the page, browsers provide something called *web workers*. A worker is a JavaScript process that runs alongside the main script, on its own timeline.

Imagine that squaring a number is a heavy, long-running computation that we want to perform in a separate thread. We could write a file called code/squareworker.js that responds to messages by computing a square and sending a message back.

```
addEventListener("message", event => {
  postMessage(event.data * event.data);
});
```

To avoid the problems of having multiple threads touching the same data, workers do not share their global scope or any other data with the main script's environment. Instead, you have to communicate with them by sending messages back and forth.

This code spawns a worker running that script, sends it a few messages, and outputs the responses.

```
let squareWorker = new Worker("code/squareworker.js");
squareWorker.addEventListener("message", event => {
  console.log("The worker responded:", event.data);
});
squareWorker.postMessage(10);
squareWorker.postMessage(24);
```

The postMessage function sends a message, which will cause a "message" event to fire in the receiver. The script that created the worker sends and receives messages through the Worker object, whereas the worker talks to the script that created it by sending and listening directly on its global scope. Only values that can be represented as JSON can be sent as messages—the other side will receive a *copy* of them, rather than the value itself.

Timers

We saw the setTimeout function in Chapter 11. It schedules another function to be called later, after a given number of milliseconds.

Sometimes you need to cancel a function you have scheduled. This is done by storing the value returned by setTimeout and calling clearTimeout on it.

```
let bombTimer = setTimeout(() => {
  console.log("BOOM!");
}, 500);
```

```
if (Math.random() < 0.5) { // 50% chance
  console.log("Defused.");
  clearTimeout(bombTimer);
}
```

The cancelAnimationFrame function works in the same way as clearTimeout—calling it on a value returned by requestAnimationFrame will cancel that frame (assuming it hasn't already been called).

A similar set of functions, setInterval and clearInterval, are used to set timers that should *repeat* every X milliseconds.

```
let ticks = 0;
let clock = setInterval(() => {
  console.log("tick", ticks++);
  if (ticks == 10) {
    clearInterval(clock);
    console.log("stop.");
  }
}, 200);
```

Debouncing

Some types of events have the potential to fire rapidly, many times in a row (the "mousemove" and "scroll" events, for example). When handling such events, you must be careful not to do anything too time-consuming or your handler will take up so much time that interaction with the document starts to feel slow.

If you do need to do something nontrivial in such a handler, you can use setTimeout to make sure you are not doing it too often. This is usually called *debouncing* the event. There are several slightly different approaches to this.

In the first example, we want to react when the user has typed something, but we don't want to do it immediately for every input event. When they are typing quickly, we just want to wait until a pause occurs. Instead of immediately performing an action in the event handler, we set a timeout. We also clear the previous timeout (if any) so that when events occur close together (closer than our timeout delay), the timeout from the previous event will be canceled.

```
<textarea>Type something here...</textarea>
<script>
  let textarea = document.querySelector("textarea");
  let timeout;
  textarea.addEventListener("input", () => {
    clearTimeout(timeout);
    timeout = setTimeout(() => console.log("Typed!"), 500);
```

```
  });
</script>
```

Giving an undefined value to `clearTimeout` or calling it on a timeout that has already fired has no effect. Thus, we don't have to be careful about when to call it, and we simply do so for every event.

We can use a slightly different pattern if we want to space responses so that they're separated by at least a certain length of time but want to fire them *during* a series of events, not just afterward. For example, we might want to respond to "mousemove" events by showing the current coordinates of the mouse but only every 250 milliseconds.

```
<script>
  let scheduled = null;
  window.addEventListener("mousemove", event => {
    if (!scheduled) {
      setTimeout(() => {
        document.body.textContent =
          `Mouse at ${scheduled.pageX}, ${scheduled.pageY}`;
        scheduled = null;
      }, 250);
    }
    scheduled = event;
  });
</script>
```

Summary

Event handlers make it possible to detect and react to events happening in our web page. The `addEventListener` method is used to register such a handler.

Each event has a type ("keydown", "focus", and so on) that identifies it. Most events are called on a specific DOM element and then *propagate* to that element's ancestors, allowing handlers associated with those elements to handle them.

When an event handler is called, it is passed an event object with additional information about the event. This object also has methods that allow us to stop further propagation (`stopPropagation`) and prevent the browser's default handling of the event (`preventDefault`).

Pressing a key fires "keydown" and "keyup" events. Pressing a mouse button fires "mousedown", "mouseup", and "click" events. Moving the mouse fires "mousemove" events. Touchscreen interaction will result in "touchstart", "touchmove", and "touchend" events.

Scrolling can be detected with the "scroll" event, and focus changes can be detected with the "focus" and "blur" events. When the document finishes loading, a "load" event fires on the window.

Exercises

Balloon

Write a page that displays a balloon (using the balloon emoji, ◯). When you press the up arrow, it should inflate (grow) 10 percent, and when you press the down arrow, it should deflate (shrink) 10 percent.

You can control the size of text (emoji are text) by setting the `font-size` CSS property (`style.fontSize`) on its parent element. Remember to include a unit in the value—for example, pixels (`10px`).

The key names of the arrow keys are `"ArrowUp"` and `"ArrowDown"`. Make sure the keys change only the balloon, without scrolling the page.

When that works, add a feature where, if you blow up the balloon past a certain size, it explodes. In this case, exploding means that it is replaced with an 💥 emoji, and the event handler is removed (so that you can't inflate or deflate the explosion).

Mouse Trail

In JavaScript's early days, which was the high time of gaudy home pages with lots of animated images, people came up with some truly inspiring ways to use the language.

One of these was the *mouse trail*—a series of elements that would follow the mouse pointer as you moved it across the page.

In this exercise, I want you to implement a mouse trail. Use absolutely positioned `<div>` elements with a fixed size and background color (refer to the code in "Mouse Clicks" on page 253 for an example). Create a bunch of such elements and, when the mouse moves, display them in the wake of the mouse pointer.

There are various possible approaches here. You can make your solution as simple or as complex as you want. A simple solution to start with is to keep a fixed number of trail elements and cycle through them, moving the next one to the mouse's current position every time a `"mousemove"` event occurs.

Tabs

Tabbed panels are widely used in user interfaces. They allow you to select an interface panel by choosing from a number of tabs "sticking out" above an element.

In this exercise you must implement a simple tabbed interface. Write a function, `asTabs`, that takes a DOM node and creates a tabbed interface showing the child elements of that node. It should insert a list of `<button>` elements at the top of the node, one for each child element, containing text retrieved from the `data-tabname` attribute of the child. All but one of the original children should be hidden (given a `display` style of `none`). The currently visible node can be selected by clicking the buttons.

When that works, extend it to style the button for the currently selected tab differently so that it is obvious which tab is selected.

"All reality is a game."
—Iain Banks, *The Player of Games*

16

PROJECT: A PLATFORM GAME

Much of my initial fascination with computers, like that of many nerdy kids, had to do with computer games. I was drawn into the tiny simulated worlds that I could manipulate and in which stories (sort of) unfolded—more, I suppose, because of the way I projected my imagination into them than because of the possibilities they actually offered.

I don't wish a career in game programming on anyone. Much like the music industry, the discrepancy between the number of eager young people wanting to work in it and the actual demand for such people creates a rather unhealthy environment. But writing games for fun is amusing.

This chapter will walk through the implementation of a small platform game. Platform games (or "jump and run" games) are games that expect the player to move a figure through a world, which is usually two-dimensional and viewed from the side, while jumping over and onto things.

The Game

Our game will be roughly based on Dark Blue (*www.lessmilk.com/games/10*) by Thomas Palef. I chose that game because it is both entertaining and minimalist and because it can be built without too much code.

It looks like this:

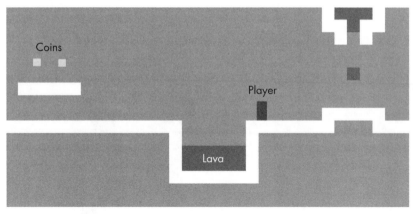

The dark box represents the player, whose task is to collect the small boxes (coins) while avoiding the lava. A level is completed when all coins have been collected.

The player can walk around with the left and right arrow keys and can jump with the up arrow. Jumping is a specialty of this game character. It can reach several times its own height and can change direction in midair. This may not be entirely realistic, but it helps give the player the feeling of being in direct control of the on-screen avatar.

The game consists of a static background, laid out like a grid, with the moving elements overlaid on that background. Each field on the grid is either empty, solid, or lava. The moving elements are the player, coins, and certain pieces of lava. The positions of these elements are not constrained to the grid—their coordinates may be fractional, allowing smooth motion.

The Technology

We will use the browser DOM to display the game, and we'll read user input by handling key events.

The screen- and keyboard-related code is only a small part of the work we need to do to build this game. Since everything looks like colored boxes, drawing is uncomplicated: we create DOM elements and use styling to give them a background color, size, and position.

We can represent the background as a table since it is an unchanging grid of squares. The free-moving elements can be overlaid using absolutely positioned elements.

In games and other programs that should animate graphics and respond to user input without noticeable delay, efficiency is important. Although the DOM was not originally designed for high-performance graphics, it is actually better at this than you would expect. (You saw some animations in Chapter 14.) On a modern machine, a simple game like this performs well, even if we don't worry about optimization very much.

In the next chapter, we will explore another browser technology, the <canvas> tag, which provides a more traditional way to draw graphics, working in terms of shapes and pixels rather than DOM elements.

Levels

We'll want a human-readable, human-editable way to specify levels. Since it is okay for everything to start out on a grid, we could use big strings in which each character represents an element—either a part of the background grid or a moving element.

The plan for a small level might look like this:

```
let simpleLevelPlan = `
......................
..#................#..
..#..............=.#..
..#.........o.o....#..
..#.@......#####...#..
..#####............#..
......#+++++++++++#..
......#############..
......................`;
```

Periods are empty space, hash marks (#) are walls, and plus signs are lava. The player's starting position is the at sign (@). Every o character is a coin, and the equal sign (=) at the top is a block of lava that moves back and forth horizontally.

We'll support two additional kinds of moving lava: the pipe character (|) creates vertically moving blobs, and v indicates *dripping* lava—vertically moving lava that doesn't bounce back and forth but only moves down, jumping back to its starting position when it hits the floor.

A whole game consists of multiple levels that the player must complete. A level is completed when all coins have been collected. If the player touches lava, the current level is restored to its starting position, and the player may try again.

Reading a Level

The following class stores a level object. Its argument should be the string that defines the level.

```
class Level {
  constructor(plan) {
    let rows = plan.trim().split("\n").map(l => [...l]);
    this.height = rows.length;
    this.width = rows[0].length;
    this.startActors = [];
```

```
    this.rows = rows.map((row, y) => {
      return row.map((ch, x) => {
        let type = levelChars[ch];
        if (typeof type == "string") return type;
        this.startActors.push(
          type.create(new Vec(x, y), ch));
        return "empty";
      });
    });
  }
}
```

The trim method is used to remove whitespace at the start and end of the plan string. This allows our example plan to start with a newline so that all the lines are directly below each other. The remaining string is split on newline characters, and each line is spread into an array, producing arrays of characters.

So rows holds an array of arrays of characters, the rows of the plan. We can derive the level's width and height from these. But we must still separate the moving elements from the background grid. We'll call moving elements *actors*. They'll be stored in an array of objects. The background will be an array of arrays of strings, holding field types such as "empty", "wall", or "lava".

To create these arrays, we map over the rows and then over their content. Remember that map passes the array index as a second argument to the mapping function, which tells us the x- and y-coordinates of a given character. Positions in the game will be stored as pairs of coordinates, with the top left being 0,0 and each background square being 1 unit high and wide.

To interpret the characters in the plan, the Level constructor uses the levelChars object, which maps background elements to strings and actor characters to classes. When type is an actor class, its static create method is used to create an object, which is added to startActors, and the mapping function returns "empty" for this background square.

The position of the actor is stored as a Vec object. This is a two-dimensional vector, an object with x and y properties, as seen in the exercises in Chapter 6.

As the game runs, actors will end up in different places or even disappear entirely (as coins do when collected). We'll use a State class to track the state of a running game.

```
class State {
  constructor(level, actors, status) {
    this.level = level;
    this.actors = actors;
    this.status = status;
  }
```

```
  static start(level) {
    return new State(level, level.startActors, "playing");
  }

  get player() {
    return this.actors.find(a => a.type == "player");
  }
}
```

The status property will switch to "lost" or "won" when the game has ended.

This is again a persistent data structure—updating the game state creates a new state and leaves the old one intact.

Actors

Actor objects represent the current position and state of a given moving element in our game. All actor objects conform to the same interface. Their pos property holds the coordinates of the element's top-left corner, and their size property holds its size.

Then they have an update method, which is used to compute their new state and position after a given time step. It simulates the thing the actor does—moving in response to the arrow keys for the player and bouncing back and forth for the lava—and returns a new, updated actor object.

A type property contains a string that identifies the type of the actor—"player", "coin", or "lava". This is useful when drawing the game—the look of the rectangle drawn for an actor is based on its type.

Actor classes have a static create method that is used by the Level constructor to create an actor from a character in the level plan. It is given the coordinates of the character and the character itself, which is needed because the Lava class handles several different characters.

This is the Vec class that we'll use for our two-dimensional values, such as the position and size of actors:

```
class Vec {
  constructor(x, y) {
    this.x = x; this.y = y;
  }
  plus(other) {
    return new Vec(this.x + other.x, this.y + other.y);
  }
  times(factor) {
    return new Vec(this.x * factor, this.y * factor);
  }
}
```

The times method scales a vector by a given number. It will be useful when we need to multiply a speed vector by a time interval to get the distance traveled during that time.

The different types of actors get their own classes since their behavior is very different. Let's define these classes. We'll get to their update methods later.

The Player class has a property speed that stores its current speed to simulate momentum and gravity.

```
class Player {
  constructor(pos, speed) {
    this.pos = pos;
    this.speed = speed;
  }

  get type() { return "player"; }

  static create(pos) {
    return new Player(pos.plus(new Vec(0, -0.5)),
                      new Vec(0, 0));
  }
}

Player.prototype.size = new Vec(0.8, 1.5);
```

Because a player is one-and-a-half squares high, its initial position is set to be half a square above the position where the @ character appeared. This way, its bottom aligns with the bottom of the square it appeared in.

The size property is the same for all instances of Player, so we store it on the prototype rather than on the instances themselves. We could have used a getter like type, but that would create and return a new Vec object every time the property is read, which would be wasteful. (Strings, being immutable, don't have to be re-created every time they are evaluated.)

When constructing a Lava actor, we need to initialize the object differently depending on the character it is based on. Dynamic lava moves along at its current speed until it hits an obstacle. At that point, if it has a reset property, it will jump back to its starting position (dripping). If it does not, it will invert its speed and continue in the other direction (bouncing).

The create method looks at the character that the Level constructor passes and creates the appropriate lava actor.

```
class Lava {
  constructor(pos, speed, reset) {
    this.pos = pos;
    this.speed = speed;
    this.reset = reset;
  }
```

```
  get type() { return "lava"; }

  static create(pos, ch) {
    if (ch == "=") {
      return new Lava(pos, new Vec(2, 0));
    } else if (ch == "|") {
      return new Lava(pos, new Vec(0, 2));
    } else if (ch == "v") {
      return new Lava(pos, new Vec(0, 3), pos);
    }
  }
}

Lava.prototype.size = new Vec(1, 1);
```

Coin actors are relatively simple. They mostly just sit in their place. But to liven up the game a little, they are given a "wobble," a slight vertical back-and-forth motion. To track this, a coin object stores a base position as well as a wobble property that tracks the phase of the bouncing motion. Together, these determine the coin's actual position (stored in the pos property).

```
class Coin {
  constructor(pos, basePos, wobble) {
    this.pos = pos;
    this.basePos = basePos;
    this.wobble = wobble;
  }

  get type() { return "coin"; }

  static create(pos) {
    let basePos = pos.plus(new Vec(0.2, 0.1));
    return new Coin(basePos, basePos,
                    Math.random() * Math.PI * 2);
  }
}

Coin.prototype.size = new Vec(0.6, 0.6);
```

In "Positioning and Animating" on page 240, we saw that Math.sin gives us the y-coordinate of a point on a circle. That coordinate goes back and forth in a smooth waveform as we move along the circle, which makes the sine function useful for modeling a wavy motion.

To avoid a situation where all coins move up and down synchronously, the starting phase of each coin is randomized. The *period* of Math.sin's wave, the width of a wave it produces, is 2π. We multiply the value returned by

`Math.random` by that number to give the coin a random starting position on the wave.

We can now define the `levelChars` object that maps plan characters to either background grid types or actor classes.

```
const levelChars = {
  ".": "empty", "#": "wall", "+": "lava",
  "@": Player, "o": Coin,
  "=": Lava, "|": Lava, "v": Lava
};
```

That gives us all the parts needed to create a `Level` instance.

```
let simpleLevel = new Level(simpleLevelPlan);
console.log(`${simpleLevel.width} by ${simpleLevel.height}`);
// → 22 by 9
```

The task ahead is to display such levels on the screen and to model time and motion inside them.

Encapsulation as a Burden

Most of the code in this chapter does not worry about encapsulation very much, for two reasons. First, encapsulation takes extra effort. It makes programs bigger and requires additional concepts and interfaces to be introduced. Since there is only so much code you can throw at a reader before their eyes glaze over, I've made an effort to keep the program small.

Second, the various elements in this game are so closely tied together that if the behavior of one of them changed, it is unlikely that any of the others would be able to stay the same. Interfaces between the elements would end up encoding a lot of assumptions about the way the game works. This makes them a lot less effective—whenever you change one part of the system, you still have to worry about the way it impacts the other parts because their interfaces wouldn't cover the new situation.

Some *cutting points* in a system lend themselves well to separation through rigorous interfaces, but others don't. Trying to encapsulate something that isn't a suitable boundary is a sure way to waste a lot of energy. When you are making this mistake, you'll usually notice that your interfaces are getting awkwardly large and detailed and that they need to be changed often as the program evolves.

There is one thing that we *will* encapsulate, and that is the drawing subsystem. The reason for this is that we'll display the same game in a different way in the next chapter. By putting the drawing behind an interface, we can load the same game program there and plug in a new display module.

Drawing

The encapsulation of the drawing code is done by defining a *display* object, which displays a given level and state. The display type we define in this chapter is called DOMDisplay because it uses DOM elements to show the level.

We'll be using a style sheet to set the actual colors and other fixed properties of the elements that make up the game. It would also be possible to directly assign these to the elements' style property when we create them, but that would produce more verbose programs.

The following helper function provides a succinct way to create an element and give it some attributes and child nodes:

```
function elt(name, attrs, ...children) {
  let dom = document.createElement(name);
  for (let attr of Object.keys(attrs)) {
    dom.setAttribute(attr, attrs[attr]);
  }
  for (let child of children) {
    dom.appendChild(child);
  }
  return dom;
}
```

A display is created by giving it a parent element to which it should append itself and a level object.

```
class DOMDisplay {
  constructor(parent, level) {
    this.dom = elt("div", {class: "game"}, drawGrid(level));
    this.actorLayer = null;
    parent.appendChild(this.dom);
  }

  clear() { this.dom.remove(); }
}
```

The level's background grid, which never changes, is drawn once. Actors are redrawn every time the display is updated with a given state. The actorLayer property will be used to track the element that holds the actors so that they can be easily removed and replaced.

Our coordinates and sizes are tracked in grid units, where a size or distance of 1 means one grid block. When setting pixel sizes, we will have to scale these coordinates up—everything in the game would be ridiculously small at a single pixel per square. The scale constant gives the number of pixels that a single unit takes up on the screen.

```
const scale = 20;

function drawGrid(level) {
  return elt("table", {
    class: "background",
    style: `width: ${level.width * scale}px`
  }, ...level.rows.map(row =>
    elt("tr", {style: `height: ${scale}px`},
        ...row.map(type => elt("td", {class: type})))
  ));
}
```

As mentioned, the background is drawn as a <table> element. This nicely corresponds to the structure of the rows property of the level—each row of the grid is turned into a table row (<tr> element). The strings in the grid are used as class names for the table cell (<td>) elements. The spread (triple dot) operator is used to pass arrays of child nodes to elt as separate arguments.

The following CSS makes the table look like the background we want:

```
.background       { background: rgb(52, 166, 251);
                    table-layout: fixed;
                    border-spacing: 0;               }
.background td { padding: 0;                          }
.lava             { background: rgb(255, 100, 100); }
.wall             { background: white;               }
```

Some of these (table-layout, border-spacing, and padding) are used to suppress unwanted default behavior. We don't want the layout of the table to depend upon the contents of its cells, and we don't want space between the table cells or padding inside them.

The background rule sets the background color. CSS allows colors to be specified both as words (white) or with a format such as rgb(R, G, B), where the red, green, and blue components of the color are separated into three numbers from 0 to 255. So, in rgb(52, 166, 251), the red component is 52, green is 166, and blue is 251. Since the blue component is the largest, the resulting color will be bluish. You can see that in the .lava rule, the first number (red) is the largest.

We draw each actor by creating a DOM element for it and setting that element's position and size based on the actor's properties. The values have to be multiplied by scale to go from game units to pixels.

```
function drawActors(actors) {
  return elt("div", {}, ...actors.map(actor => {
    let rect = elt("div", {class: `actor ${actor.type}`});
    rect.style.width = `${actor.size.x * scale}px`;
    rect.style.height = `${actor.size.y * scale}px`;
```

```
    rect.style.left = `${actor.pos.x * scale}px`;
    rect.style.top = `${actor.pos.y * scale}px`;
    return rect;
  }));
}
```

To give an element more than one class, we separate the class names by spaces. In the CSS code shown next, the actor class gives the actors their absolute position. Their type name is used as an extra class to give them a color. We don't have to define the lava class again because we're reusing the class for the lava grid squares we defined earlier.

```
.actor  { position: absolute;              }
.coin   { background: rgb(241, 229, 89); }
.player { background: rgb(64, 64, 64);   }
```

The syncState method is used to make the display show a given state. It first removes the old actor graphics, if any, and then redraws the actors in their new positions. It may be tempting to try to reuse the DOM elements for actors, but to make that work, we would need a lot of additional book-keeping to associate actors with DOM elements and to make sure we remove elements when their actors vanish. Since there will typically be only a handful of actors in the game, redrawing all of them is not expensive.

```
DOMDisplay.prototype.syncState = function(state) {
  if (this.actorLayer) this.actorLayer.remove();
  this.actorLayer = drawActors(state.actors);
  this.dom.appendChild(this.actorLayer);
  this.dom.className = `game ${state.status}`;
  this.scrollPlayerIntoView(state);
};
```

By adding the level's current status as a class name to the wrapper, we can style the player actor slightly differently when the game is won or lost by adding a CSS rule that takes effect only when the player has an ancestor element with a given class.

```
.lost .player {
  background: rgb(160, 64, 64);
}
.won .player {
  box-shadow: -4px -7px 8px white, 4px -7px 8px white;
}
```

After touching lava, the player's color turns dark red, suggesting scorching. When the last coin has been collected, we add two blurred white shadows—one to the top left and one to the top right—to create a white halo effect.

We can't assume that the level always fits in the *viewport*—the element into which we draw the game. That is why the scrollPlayerIntoView call is needed. It ensures that if the level is protruding outside the viewport, we scroll that viewport to make sure the player is near its center. The following CSS gives the game's wrapping DOM element a maximum size and ensures that anything that sticks out of the element's box is not visible. We also give it a relative position so that the actors inside it are positioned relative to the level's top-left corner.

```css
.game {
  overflow: hidden;
  max-width: 600px;
  max-height: 450px;
  position: relative;
}
```

In the scrollPlayerIntoView method, we find the player's position and update the wrapping element's scroll position. We change the scroll position by manipulating that element's scrollLeft and scrollTop properties when the player is too close to the edge.

```js
DOMDisplay.prototype.scrollPlayerIntoView = function(state) {
  let width = this.dom.clientWidth;
  let height = this.dom.clientHeight;
  let margin = width / 3;

  // The viewport
  let left = this.dom.scrollLeft, right = left + width;
  let top = this.dom.scrollTop, bottom = top + height;

  let player = state.player;
  let center = player.pos.plus(player.size.times(0.5))
                         .times(scale);

  if (center.x < left + margin) {
    this.dom.scrollLeft = center.x - margin;
  } else if (center.x > right - margin) {
    this.dom.scrollLeft = center.x + margin - width;
  }
  if (center.y < top + margin) {
    this.dom.scrollTop = center.y - margin;
  } else if (center.y > bottom - margin) {
    this.dom.scrollTop = center.y + margin - height;
  }
};
```

The way the player's center is found shows how the methods on our Vec type allow computations with objects to be written in a relatively readable way. To find the actor's center, we add its position (its top-left corner) and half its size. That is the center in level coordinates, but we need it in pixel coordinates, so we then multiply the resulting vector by our display scale.

Next, a series of checks verifies that the player position isn't outside of the allowed range. Note that sometimes this will set nonsense scroll coordinates that are below zero or beyond the element's scrollable area. This is okay—the DOM will constrain them to acceptable values. Setting scrollLeft to −10 will cause it to become 0.

It would have been slightly simpler to always try to scroll the player to the center of the viewport. But this creates a rather jarring effect. As you are jumping, the view will constantly shift up and down. It is more pleasant to have a "neutral" area in the middle of the screen where you can move around without causing any scrolling.

We are now able to display our tiny level.

```
<link rel="stylesheet" href="css/game.css">

<script>
  let simpleLevel = new Level(simpleLevelPlan);
  let display = new DOMDisplay(document.body, simpleLevel);
  display.syncState(State.start(simpleLevel));
</script>
```

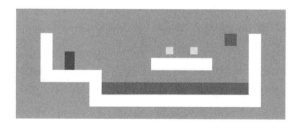

The <link> tag, when used with rel="stylesheet", is a way to load a CSS file into a page. The file game.css contains the styles necessary for our game.

Motion and Collision

Now we're at the point where we can start adding motion—the most interesting aspect of the game. The basic approach, taken by most games like this, is to split time into small steps and, for each step, move the actors by a distance corresponding to their speed multiplied by the size of the time step. We'll measure time in seconds, so speeds are expressed in units per second.

Moving things is easy. The difficult part is dealing with the interactions between the elements. When the player hits a wall or floor, they should not simply move through it. The game must notice when a given motion causes an object to hit another object and respond accordingly. For walls, the motion must be stopped. When hitting a coin, the coin must be collected. When touching lava, the game should be lost.

Solving this for the general case is a big task. You can find libraries, usually called *physics engines*, that simulate interaction between physical objects in two or three dimensions. We'll take a more modest approach in this chapter, handling only collisions between rectangular objects and handling them in a rather simplistic way.

Before moving the player or a block of lava, we test whether the motion would take it inside of a wall. If it does, we simply cancel the motion altogether. The response to such a collision depends on the type of actor—the player will stop, whereas a lava block will bounce back.

This approach requires our time steps to be rather small since it will cause motion to stop before the objects actually touch. If the time steps (and thus the motion steps) are too big, the player would end up hovering a noticeable distance above the ground. Another approach, arguably better but more complicated, would be to find the exact collision spot and move there. We will take the simple approach and hide its problems by ensuring the animation proceeds in small steps.

This method tells us whether a rectangle (specified by a position and a size) touches a grid element of the given type.

```
Level.prototype.touches = function(pos, size, type) {
  let xStart = Math.floor(pos.x);
  let xEnd = Math.ceil(pos.x + size.x);
  let yStart = Math.floor(pos.y);
  let yEnd = Math.ceil(pos.y + size.y);

  for (let y = yStart; y < yEnd; y++) {
    for (let x = xStart; x < xEnd; x++) {
      let isOutside = x < 0 || x >= this.width ||
                      y < 0 || y >= this.height;
      let here = isOutside ? "wall" : this.rows[y][x];
      if (here == type) return true;
    }
  }
  return false;
};
```

The method computes the set of grid squares that the body overlaps with by using Math.floor and Math.ceil on its coordinates. Remember that grid squares are 1 by 1 units in size. By rounding the sides of a box up and down, we get the range of background squares that the box touches.

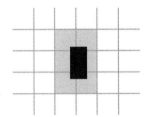

We loop over the block of grid squares found by rounding the coordinates and return true when a matching square is found. Squares outside of the level are always treated as "wall" to ensure that the player can't leave the world and that we won't accidentally try to read outside of the bounds of our rows array.

The state update method uses touches to figure out whether the player is touching lava.

```
State.prototype.update = function(time, keys) {
  let actors = this.actors
    .map(actor => actor.update(time, this, keys));
  let newState = new State(this.level, actors, this.status);

  if (newState.status != "playing") return newState;

  let player = newState.player;
  if (this.level.touches(player.pos, player.size, "lava")) {
    return new State(this.level, actors, "lost");
  }

  for (let actor of actors) {
    if (actor != player && overlap(actor, player)) {
      newState = actor.collide(newState);
    }
  }
  return newState;
};
```

The method is passed a time step and a data structure that tells it which keys are being held down. The first thing it does is call the update method on all actors, producing an array of updated actors. The actors also get the time step, the keys, and the state, so that they can base their update on those. Only the player will actually read keys, since that's the only actor controlled by the keyboard.

If the game is already over, no further processing has to be done (the game can't be won after being lost, or vice versa). Otherwise, the method tests whether the player is touching background lava. If so, the game is lost, and we're done. Finally, if the game really is still going on, it sees whether any other actors overlap the player.

Overlap between actors is detected with the overlap function. It takes two actor objects and returns true when they touch—which is the case when they overlap both along the x-axis and along the y-axis.

```
function overlap(actor1, actor2) {
  return actor1.pos.x + actor1.size.x > actor2.pos.x &&
         actor1.pos.x < actor2.pos.x + actor2.size.x &&
```

```
      actor1.pos.y + actor1.size.y > actor2.pos.y &&
      actor1.pos.y < actor2.pos.y + actor2.size.y;
}
```

If any actor does overlap, its collide method gets a chance to update the state. Touching a lava actor sets the game status to "lost". Coins vanish when you touch them and set the status to "won" when they are the last coin of the level.

```
Lava.prototype.collide = function(state) {
  return new State(state.level, state.actors, "lost");
};

Coin.prototype.collide = function(state) {
  let filtered = state.actors.filter(a => a != this);
  let status = state.status;
  if (!filtered.some(a => a.type == "coin")) status = "won";
  return new State(state.level, filtered, status);
};
```

Actor Updates

Actor objects' update methods take as arguments the time step, the state object, and a keys object. The one for the Lava actor type ignores the keys object.

```
Lava.prototype.update = function(time, state) {
  let newPos = this.pos.plus(this.speed.times(time));
  if (!state.level.touches(newPos, this.size, "wall")) {
    return new Lava(newPos, this.speed, this.reset);
  } else if (this.reset) {
    return new Lava(this.reset, this.speed, this.reset);
  } else {
    return new Lava(this.pos, this.speed.times(-1));
  }
};
```

This update method computes a new position by adding the product of the time step and the current speed to its old position. If no obstacle blocks that new position, it moves there. If there is an obstacle, the behavior depends on the type of the lava block—dripping lava has a reset position, to which it jumps back when it hits something. Bouncing lava inverts its speed by multiplying it by −1 so that it starts moving in the opposite direction.

Coins use their update method to wobble. They ignore collisions with the grid since they are simply wobbling around inside of their own square.

```
const wobbleSpeed = 8, wobbleDist = 0.07;

Coin.prototype.update = function(time) {
  let wobble = this.wobble + time * wobbleSpeed;
  let wobblePos = Math.sin(wobble) * wobbleDist;
  return new Coin(this.basePos.plus(new Vec(0, wobblePos)),
                  this.basePos, wobble);
};
```

The wobble property is incremented to track time and then used as an argument to Math.sin to find the new position on the wave. The coin's current position is then computed from its base position and an offset based on this wave.

That leaves the player itself. Player motion is handled separately per axis because hitting the floor should not prevent horizontal motion, and hitting a wall should not stop falling or jumping motion.

```
const playerXSpeed = 7;
const gravity = 30;
const jumpSpeed = 17;

Player.prototype.update = function(time, state, keys) {
  let xSpeed = 0;
  if (keys.ArrowLeft) xSpeed -= playerXSpeed;
  if (keys.ArrowRight) xSpeed += playerXSpeed;
  let pos = this.pos;
  let movedX = pos.plus(new Vec(xSpeed * time, 0));
  if (!state.level.touches(movedX, this.size, "wall")) {
    pos = movedX;
  }

  let ySpeed = this.speed.y + time * gravity;
  let movedY = pos.plus(new Vec(0, ySpeed * time));
  if (!state.level.touches(movedY, this.size, "wall")) {
    pos = movedY;
  } else if (keys.ArrowUp && ySpeed > 0) {
    ySpeed = -jumpSpeed;
  } else {
    ySpeed = 0;
  }
  return new Player(pos, new Vec(xSpeed, ySpeed));
};
```

The horizontal motion is computed based on the state of the left and right arrow keys. When there's no wall blocking the new position created by this motion, it is used. Otherwise, the old position is kept.

Vertical motion works in a similar way but has to simulate jumping and gravity. The player's vertical speed (ySpeed) is first accelerated to account for gravity.

We check for walls again. If we don't hit any, the new position is used. If there *is* a wall, there are two possible outcomes. When the up arrow is pressed *and* we are moving down (meaning the thing we hit is below us), the speed is set to a relatively large, negative value. This causes the player to jump. If that is not the case, the player simply bumped into something, and the speed is set to zero.

The gravity strength, jumping speed, and pretty much all other constants in this game have been set by trial and error. I tested values until I found a combination I liked.

Tracking Keys

For a game like this, we do not want keys to take effect once per keypress. Rather, we want their effect (moving the player figure) to stay active as long as they are held.

We need to set up a key handler that stores the current state of the left, right, and up arrow keys. We will also want to call preventDefault for those keys so that they don't end up scrolling the page.

The following function, when given an array of key names, will return an object that tracks the current position of those keys. It registers event handlers for "keydown" and "keyup" events and, when the key code in the event is present in the set of codes that it is tracking, updates the object.

```
function trackKeys(keys) {
  let down = Object.create(null);
  function track(event) {
    if (keys.includes(event.key)) {
      down[event.key] = event.type == "keydown";
      event.preventDefault();
    }
  }
  window.addEventListener("keydown", track);
  window.addEventListener("keyup", track);
  return down;
}

const arrowKeys =
  trackKeys(["ArrowLeft", "ArrowRight", "ArrowUp"]);
```

The same handler function is used for both event types. It looks at the event object's type property to determine whether the key state should be updated to true ("keydown") or false ("keyup").

Running the Game

The `requestAnimationFrame` function, which we saw in Chapter 14, provides a good way to animate a game. But its interface is quite primitive—using it requires us to track the time at which our function was called the last time around and call `requestAnimationFrame` again after every frame.

Let's define a helper function that wraps those boring parts in a convenient interface and allows us to simply call `runAnimation`, giving it a function that expects a time difference as an argument and draws a single frame. When the frame function returns the value `false`, the animation stops.

```
function runAnimation(frameFunc) {
  let lastTime = null;
  function frame(time) {
    if (lastTime != null) {
      let timeStep = Math.min(time - lastTime, 100) / 1000;
      if (frameFunc(timeStep) === false) return;
    }
    lastTime = time;
    requestAnimationFrame(frame);
  }
  requestAnimationFrame(frame);
}
```

I have set a maximum frame step of 100 milliseconds (one-tenth of a second). When the browser tab or window with our page is hidden, `requestAnimationFrame` calls will be suspended until the tab or window is shown again. In this case, the difference between `lastTime` and `time` will be the entire time in which the page was hidden. Advancing the game by that much in a single step would look silly and might cause weird side effects, such as the player falling through the floor.

The function also converts the time steps to seconds, which are an easier quantity to think about than milliseconds.

The `runLevel` function takes a `Level` object and a display constructor and returns a promise. It displays the level (in `document.body`) and lets the user play through it. When the level is finished (lost or won), `runLevel` waits one more second (to let the user see what happens) and then clears the display, stops the animation, and resolves the promise to the game's end status.

```
function runLevel(level, Display) {
  let display = new Display(document.body, level);
  let state = State.start(level);
  let ending = 1;
  return new Promise(resolve => {
    runAnimation(time => {
      state = state.update(time, arrowKeys);
      display.syncState(state);
```

```
      if (state.status == "playing") {
        return true;
      } else if (ending > 0) {
        ending -= time;
        return true;
      } else {
        display.clear();
        resolve(state.status);
        return false;
      }
    });
  });
}
```

A game is a sequence of levels. Whenever the player dies, the current level is restarted. When a level is completed, we move on to the next level. This can be expressed by the following function, which takes an array of level plans (strings) and a display constructor:

```
async function runGame(plans, Display) {
  for (let level = 0; level < plans.length;) {
    let status = await runLevel(new Level(plans[level]),
                                Display);
    if (status == "won") level++;
  }
  console.log("You've won!");
}
```

Because we made runLevel return a promise, runGame can be written using an async function, as shown in Chapter 11. It returns another promise, which resolves when the player finishes the game.

There is a set of level plans available in the GAME_LEVELS binding in this chapter's sandbox (*https://eloquentjavascript.net/code#16*). This page feeds them to runGame, starting an actual game.

```
<link rel="stylesheet" href="css/game.css">

<body>
  <script>
    runGame(GAME_LEVELS, DOMDisplay);
  </script>
</body>
```

Exercises

Game Over

It's traditional for platform games to have the player start with a limited number of *lives* and subtract one life each time they die. When the player is out of lives, the game restarts from the beginning.

Adjust `runGame` to implement lives. Have the player start with three. Output the current number of lives (using `console.log`) every time a level starts.

Pausing the Game

Make it possible to pause (suspend) and unpause the game by pressing the ESC key.

This can be done by changing the `runLevel` function to use another keyboard event handler and interrupting or resuming the animation whenever the ESC key is pressed.

The `runAnimation` interface may not look like it is suitable for this at first glance, but it is if you rearrange the way `runLevel` calls it.

When you have that working, there is something else you could try. The way we have been registering keyboard event handlers is somewhat problematic. The `arrowKeys` object is currently a global binding, and its event handlers are kept around even when no game is running. You could say they *leak* out of our system. Extend `trackKeys` to provide a way to unregister its handlers and then change `runLevel` to register its handlers when it starts and unregister them again when it is finished.

A Monster

It is traditional for platform games to have enemies that you can jump on top of to defeat. This exercise asks you to add such an actor type to the game.

We'll call it a monster. Monsters move only horizontally. You can make them move in the direction of the player, bounce back and forth like horizontal lava, or have any movement pattern you want. The class doesn't have to handle falling, but it should make sure the monster doesn't walk through walls.

When a monster touches the player, the effect depends on whether the player is jumping on top of the monster or not. You can approximate this by checking whether the player's bottom is near the monster's top. If this is the case, the monster disappears. If not, the game is lost.

"Drawing is deception."
—M.C. Escher, cited by Bruno Ernst
in *The Magic Mirror of M.C. Escher*

17

DRAWING ON CANVAS

Browsers give us several ways to display graphics. The simplest way is to use styles to position and color regular DOM elements. This can get you quite far, as the game in the previous chapter showed. By adding partially transparent background images to the nodes, we can make them look exactly the way we want. It is even possible to rotate or skew nodes with the transform style.

But we'd be using the DOM for something that it wasn't originally designed for. Some tasks, such as drawing a line between arbitrary points, are extremely awkward to do with regular HTML elements.

There are two alternatives. The first is DOM-based but utilizes *Scalable Vector Graphics* (SVG), rather than HTML. Think of SVG as a document-markup dialect that focuses on shapes rather than text. You can embed an SVG document directly in an HTML document or include it with an `<img>` tag.

The second alternative is called a *canvas*. A canvas is a single DOM element that encapsulates a picture. It provides a programming interface for drawing shapes onto the space taken up by the node. The main difference between a canvas and an SVG picture is that in SVG the original description of the shapes is preserved so that they can be moved or resized at any time.

A canvas, on the other hand, converts the shapes to pixels (colored dots on a raster) as soon as they are drawn and does not remember what these pixels represent. The only way to move a shape on a canvas is to clear the canvas (or the part of the canvas around the shape) and redraw it with the shape in a new position.

SVG

This book will not go into SVG in detail, but I will briefly explain how it works. In "Choosing a Graphics Interface" on page 305, I'll come back to the trade-offs that you must consider when deciding which drawing mechanism is appropriate for a given application.

This is an HTML document with a simple SVG picture in it:

```
<p>Normal HTML here.</p>
<svg xmlns="http://www.w3.org/2000/svg">
  <circle r="50" cx="50" cy="50" fill="red"/>
  <rect x="120" y="5" width="90" height="90"
        stroke="blue" fill="none"/>
</svg>
```

The xmlns attribute changes an element (and its children) to a different *XML namespace*. This namespace, identified by a URL, specifies the dialect that we are currently speaking. The <circle> and <rect> tags, which do not exist in HTML, do have a meaning in SVG—they draw shapes using the style and position specified by their attributes.

The document is displayed like this:

Normal HTML here.

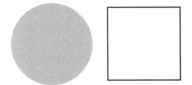

These tags create DOM elements, just like HTML tags, that scripts can interact with. For example, this changes the <circle> element to be colored cyan instead:

```
let circle = document.querySelector("circle");
circle.setAttribute("fill", "cyan");
```

The Canvas Element

Canvas graphics can be drawn onto a <canvas> element. You can give such an element width and height attributes to determine its size in pixels.

A new canvas is empty, meaning it is entirely transparent and thus shows up as empty space in the document.

The <canvas> tag is intended to allow different styles of drawing. To get access to an actual drawing interface, we first need to create a *context*, an object whose methods provide the drawing interface. There are currently two widely supported drawing styles: "2d" for two-dimensional graphics and "webgl" for three-dimensional graphics through the OpenGL interface.

This book won't discuss WebGL—we'll stick to two dimensions. But if you are interested in three-dimensional graphics, I do encourage you to look into WebGL. It provides a direct interface to graphics hardware and allows you to render even complicated scenes efficiently, using JavaScript.

You create a context with the getContext method on the <canvas> DOM element.

```
<p>Before canvas.</p>
<canvas width="120" height="60"></canvas>
<p>After canvas.</p>
<script>
  let canvas = document.querySelector("canvas");
  let context = canvas.getContext("2d");
  context.fillStyle = "red";
  context.fillRect(10, 10, 100, 50);
</script>
```

After creating the context object, the example draws a red rectangle 100 pixels wide and 50 pixels high, with its top-left corner at coordinates (10,10).

Before canvas.

After canvas.

Just like in HTML (and SVG), the coordinate system that the canvas uses puts (0,0) at the top-left corner, and the positive y-axis goes down from there. So (10,10) is 10 pixels below and to the right of the top-left corner.

Lines and Surfaces

In the canvas interface, a shape can be *filled*, meaning its area is given a certain color or pattern, or it can be *stroked*, which means a line is drawn along its edge. The same terminology is used by SVG.

The fillRect method fills a rectangle. It takes first the x- and y-coordinates of the rectangle's top-left corner, then its width, and then its height. A similar method, strokeRect, draws the outline of a rectangle.

Neither method takes any further parameters. The color of the fill, thickness of the stroke, and so on, are not determined by an argument to the method (as you might reasonably expect) but rather by properties of the context object.

The `fillStyle` property controls the way shapes are filled. It can be set to a string that specifies a color, using the color notation used by CSS.

The `strokeStyle` property works similarly but determines the color used for a stroked line. The width of that line is determined by the `lineWidth` property, which may contain any positive number.

```
<canvas></canvas>
<script>
  let cx = document.querySelector("canvas").getContext("2d");
  cx.strokeStyle = "blue";
  cx.strokeRect(5, 5, 50, 50);
  cx.lineWidth = 5;
  cx.strokeRect(135, 5, 50, 50);
</script>
```

This code draws two squares, using a thicker line for the second one.

When no `width` or `height` attribute is specified, as in the example, a canvas element gets a default width of 300 pixels and height of 150 pixels.

Paths

A path is a sequence of lines. The 2D canvas interface takes a peculiar approach to describing such a path. It's done entirely through side effects. Paths are not values that can be stored and passed around. Instead, if you want to do something with a path, you make a sequence of method calls to describe its shape.

```
<canvas></canvas>
<script>
  let cx = document.querySelector("canvas").getContext("2d");
  cx.beginPath();
  for (let y = 10; y < 100; y += 10) {
    cx.moveTo(10, y);
    cx.lineTo(90, y);
  }
  cx.stroke();
</script>
```

This example creates a path with a number of horizontal line segments and then strokes it using the `stroke` method. Each segment created with `lineTo` starts at the path's *current* position. That position is usually the end of the last segment, unless `moveTo` was called. In that case, the next segment would start at the position passed to `moveTo`.

The path described by the previous program looks like this:

When filling a path (using the `fill` method), each shape is filled separately. A path can contain multiple shapes—each `moveTo` motion starts a new one. But the path needs to be *closed* (meaning its start and end are in the same position) before it can be filled. If the path is not already closed, a line is added from its end to its start, and the shape enclosed by the completed path is filled.

```
<canvas></canvas>
<script>
  let cx = document.querySelector("canvas").getContext("2d");
  cx.beginPath();
  cx.moveTo(50, 10);
  cx.lineTo(10, 70);
  cx.lineTo(90, 70);
  cx.fill();
</script>
```

This example draws a filled triangle. Note that only two of the triangle's sides are explicitly drawn. The third, from the bottom-right corner back to the top, is implied and wouldn't be there when you stroke the path.

You could also use the `closePath` method to explicitly close a path by adding an actual line segment back to the path's start. This segment *is* drawn when stroking the path.

Curves

A path may also contain curved lines. These are unfortunately a bit more involved to draw.

The quadraticCurveTo method draws a curve to a given point. To determine the curvature of the line, the method is given a control point as well as a destination point. Imagine this control point as *attracting* the line, giving it its curve. The line won't go through the control point, but its direction at the start and end points will be such that a straight line in that direction would point toward the control point. The following example illustrates this:

```
<canvas></canvas>
<script>
  let cx = document.querySelector("canvas").getContext("2d");
  cx.beginPath();
  cx.moveTo(10, 90);
  // control=(60,10) goal=(90,90)
  cx.quadraticCurveTo(60, 10, 90, 90);
  cx.lineTo(60, 10);
  cx.closePath();
  cx.stroke();
</script>
```

It produces a path that looks like this:

We draw a quadratic curve from the left to the right, with (60,10) as control point, and then draw two line segments going through that control point and back to the start of the line. The result somewhat resembles a *Star Trek* insignia. You can see the effect of the control point: the lines leaving the lower corners start off in the direction of the control point and then curve toward their target.

The bezierCurveTo method draws a similar kind of curve. Instead of a single control point, this one has two—one for each of the line's endpoints. Here is a similar sketch to illustrate the behavior of such a curve:

```
<canvas></canvas>
<script>
  let cx = document.querySelector("canvas").getContext("2d");
  cx.beginPath();
  cx.moveTo(10, 90);
  // control1=(10,10) control2=(90,10) goal=(50,90)
```

```
    cx.bezierCurveTo(10, 10, 90, 10, 50, 90);
    cx.lineTo(90, 10);
    cx.lineTo(10, 10);
    cx.closePath();
    cx.stroke();
</script>
```

The two control points specify the direction at both ends of the curve. The farther away they are from their corresponding point, the more the curve will "bulge" in that direction.

Such curves can be hard to work with—it's not always clear how to find the control points that provide the shape you are looking for. Sometimes you can compute them, and sometimes you'll just have to find a suitable value by trial and error.

The arc method is a way to draw a line that curves along the edge of a circle. It takes a pair of coordinates for the arc's center, a radius, and then a start angle and end angle.

Those last two parameters make it possible to draw only part of the circle. The angles are measured in radians, not degrees. This means a full circle has an angle of 2π, or 2 * Math.PI, which is about 6.28. The angle starts counting at the point to the right of the circle's center and goes clockwise from there. You can use a start of 0 and an end bigger than 2π (say, 7) to draw a full circle.

```
<canvas></canvas>
<script>
  let cx = document.querySelector("canvas").getContext("2d");
  cx.beginPath();
  // center=(50,50) radius=40 angle=0 to 7
  cx.arc(50, 50, 40, 0, 7);
  // center=(150,50) radius=40 angle=0 to 1/2 pi
  cx.arc(150, 50, 40, 0, 0.5 * Math.PI);
  cx.stroke();
</script>
```

The resulting picture contains a line from the right of the full circle (first call to arc) to the right of the quarter-circle (second call). Like other path-drawing methods, a line drawn with arc is connected to the previous path segment. You can call moveTo or start a new path to avoid this.

Drawing a Pie Chart

Imagine you've just taken a job at EconomiCorp, Inc., and your first assignment is to draw a pie chart of its customer satisfaction survey results.

The results binding contains an array of objects that represent the survey responses.

```
const results = [
  {name: "Satisfied", count: 1043, color: "lightblue"},
  {name: "Neutral", count: 563, color: "lightgreen"},
  {name: "Unsatisfied", count: 510, color: "pink"},
  {name: "No comment", count: 175, color: "silver"}
];
```

To draw a pie chart, we draw a number of pie slices, each made up of an arc and a pair of lines to the center of that arc. We can compute the angle taken up by each arc by dividing a full circle (2π) by the total number of responses and then multiplying that number (the angle per response) by the number of people who picked a given choice.

```
<canvas width="200" height="200"></canvas>
<script>
  let cx = document.querySelector("canvas").getContext("2d");
  let total = results
    .reduce((sum, {count}) => sum + count, 0);
  // Start at the top
  let currentAngle = -0.5 * Math.PI;
  for (let result of results) {
    let sliceAngle = (result.count / total) * 2 * Math.PI;
    cx.beginPath();
    // center=100,100, radius=100
    // from current angle, clockwise by slice's angle
    cx.arc(100, 100, 100,
           currentAngle, currentAngle + sliceAngle);
    currentAngle += sliceAngle;
    cx.lineTo(100, 100);
    cx.fillStyle = result.color;
    cx.fill();
  }
</script>
```

This draws the following chart:

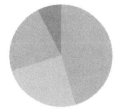

But a chart that doesn't tell us what the slices mean isn't very helpful. We need a way to draw text to the canvas.

Text

A 2D canvas drawing context provides the methods fillText and strokeText. The latter can be useful for outlining letters, but usually fillText is what you need. It will fill the outline of the given text with the current fillStyle.

```
<canvas></canvas>
<script>
  let cx = document.querySelector("canvas").getContext("2d");
  cx.font = "28px Georgia";
  cx.fillStyle = "fuchsia";
  cx.fillText("I can draw text, too!", 10, 50);
</script>
```

You can specify the size, style, and font of the text with the font property. This example just gives a font size and family name. It is also possible to add italic or bold to the start of the string to select a style.

The last two arguments to fillText and strokeText provide the position at which the font is drawn. By default, they indicate the position of the start of the text's alphabetic baseline, which is the line that letters "stand" on, not counting hanging parts in letters such as *j* or *p*. You can change the horizontal position by setting the textAlign property to "end" or "center" and the vertical position by setting textBaseline to "top", "middle", or "bottom".

We'll come back to our pie chart, and the problem of labeling the slices, in the exercises at the end of the chapter.

Images

In computer graphics, a distinction is often made between *vector* graphics and *bitmap* graphics. The first is what we have been doing so far in this chapter—specifying a picture by giving a logical description of shapes. Bitmap graphics, on the other hand, don't specify actual shapes but rather work with pixel data (rasters of colored dots).

The `drawImage` method allows us to draw pixel data onto a canvas. This pixel data can originate from an `<img>` element or from another canvas. The following example creates a detached `<img>` element and loads an image file into it. But it cannot immediately start drawing from this picture because the browser may not have loaded it yet. To deal with this, we register a `"load"` event handler and do the drawing after the image has loaded.

```
<canvas></canvas>
<script>
  let cx = document.querySelector("canvas").getContext("2d");
  let img = document.createElement("img");
  img.src = "img/hat.png";
  img.addEventListener("load", () => {
    for (let x = 10; x < 200; x += 30) {
      cx.drawImage(img, x, 10);
    }
  });
</script>
```

By default, `drawImage` will draw the image at its original size. You can also give it two additional arguments to set a different width and height.

When `drawImage` is given *nine* arguments, it can be used to draw only a fragment of an image. The second through fifth arguments indicate the rectangle (x, y, width, and height) in the source image that should be copied, and the sixth to ninth arguments give the rectangle (on the canvas) into which it should be copied.

This can be used to pack multiple *sprites* (image elements) into a single image file and then draw only the part you need. For example, we have this picture containing a game character in multiple poses:

By alternating which pose we draw, we can show an animation that looks like a walking character.

To animate a picture on a canvas, the `clearRect` method is useful. It resembles `fillRect`, but instead of coloring the rectangle, it makes it transparent, removing the previously drawn pixels.

We know that each *sprite*, each subpicture, is 24 pixels wide and 30 pixels high. The following code loads the image and then sets up an interval (repeated timer) to draw the next frame:

```
<canvas></canvas>
<script>
  let cx = document.querySelector("canvas").getContext("2d");
  let img = document.createElement("img");
  img.src = "img/player.png";
  let spriteW = 24, spriteH = 30;
```

```
    img.addEventListener("load", () => {
      let cycle = 0;
      setInterval(() => {
        cx.clearRect(0, 0, spriteW, spriteH);
        cx.drawImage(img,
                     // source rectangle
                     cycle * spriteW, 0, spriteW, spriteH,
                     // destination rectangle
                     0,              0, spriteW, spriteH);
        cycle = (cycle + 1) % 8;
      }, 120);
    });
</script>
```

The cycle binding tracks our position in the animation. For each frame, it is incremented and then clipped back to the 0 to 7 range by using the remainder operator. This binding is then used to compute the x-coordinate that the sprite for the current pose has in the picture.

Transformation

But what if we want our character to walk to the left instead of to the right? We could draw another set of sprites, of course. But we can also instruct the canvas to draw the picture the other way round.

Calling the scale method will cause anything drawn after it to be scaled. This method takes two parameters, one to set a horizontal scale and one to set a vertical scale.

```
<canvas></canvas>
<script>
  let cx = document.querySelector("canvas").getContext("2d");
  cx.scale(3, .5);
  cx.beginPath();
  cx.arc(50, 50, 40, 0, 7);
  cx.lineWidth = 3;
  cx.stroke();
</script>
```

Because of the call to scale, the circle is drawn three times as wide and half as high.

Scaling will cause everything about the drawn image, including the line width, to be stretched out or squeezed together as specified. Scaling by a negative amount will flip the picture around. The flipping happens around point (0,0), which means it will also flip the direction of the coordinate system. When a horizontal scaling of −1 is applied, a shape drawn at x position 100 will end up at what used to be position −100.

So to turn a picture around, we can't simply add cx.scale(-1, 1) before the call to drawImage because that would move our picture outside of the canvas, where it won't be visible. You could adjust the coordinates given to drawImage to compensate for this by drawing the image at x position −50 instead of 0. Another solution, which doesn't require the code that does the drawing to know about the scale change, is to adjust the axis around which the scaling happens.

There are several other methods besides scale that influence the coordinate system for a canvas. You can rotate subsequently drawn shapes with the rotate method and move them with the translate method. The interesting—and confusing—thing is that these transformations *stack*, meaning that each one happens relative to the previous transformations.

So if we translate by 10 horizontal pixels twice, everything will be drawn 20 pixels to the right. If we first move the center of the coordinate system to (50,50) and then rotate by 20 degrees (about 0.1π radians), that rotation will happen *around* point (50,50).

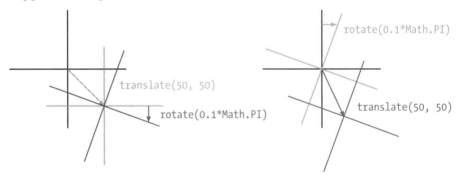

But if we *first* rotate by 20 degrees and *then* translate by (50,50), the translation will happen in the rotated coordinate system and thus produce a different orientation. The order in which transformations are applied matters.

To flip a picture around the vertical line at a given x position, we can do the following:

```
function flipHorizontally(context, around) {
  context.translate(around, 0);
  context.scale(-1, 1);
  context.translate(-around, 0);
}
```

We move the y-axis to where we want our mirror to be, apply the mirroring, and finally move the y-axis back to its proper place in the mirrored universe. The following picture explains why this works.

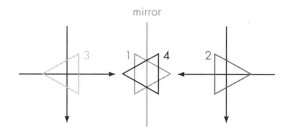

This shows the coordinate systems before and after mirroring across the central line. The triangles are numbered to illustrate each step. If we draw a triangle at a positive x position, it would, by default, be in the place where triangle 1 is. A call to `flipHorizontally` first does a translation to the right, which gets us to triangle 2. It then scales, flipping the triangle over to position 3. This is not where it should be, if it were mirrored in the given line. The second `translate` call fixes this—it "cancels" the initial translation and makes triangle 4 appear exactly where it should.

We can now draw a mirrored character at position (100,0) by flipping the world around the character's vertical center.

```
<canvas></canvas>
<script>
  let cx = document.querySelector("canvas").getContext("2d");
  let img = document.createElement("img");
  img.src = "img/player.png";
  let spriteW = 24, spriteH = 30;
  img.addEventListener("load", () => {
    flipHorizontally(cx, 100 + spriteW / 2);
    cx.drawImage(img, 0, 0, spriteW, spriteH,
                 100, 0, spriteW, spriteH);
  });
</script>
```

Storing and Clearing Transformations

Transformations stick around. Everything else we draw after drawing that mirrored character would also be mirrored. That might be inconvenient.

It is possible to save the current transformation, do some drawing and transforming, and then restore the old transformation. This is usually the proper thing to do for a function that needs to temporarily transform the coordinate system. First, we save whatever transformation the code that called the function was using. Then the function does its thing, adding more transformations on top of the current transformation. Finally, we revert to the transformation we started with.

The save and restore methods on the 2D canvas context do this transformation management. They conceptually keep a stack of transformation states. When you call save, the current state is pushed onto the stack, and when you call restore, the state on top of the stack is taken off and used as the context's current transformation. You can also call `resetTransform` to fully reset the transformation.

The `branch` function in the following example illustrates what you can do with a function that changes the transformation and then calls a function (in this case itself), which continues drawing with the given transformation.

This function draws a treelike shape by drawing a line, then moving the center of the coordinate system to the end of the line, and then calling itself twice—first rotated to the left and then rotated to the right. Every call reduces the length of the branch drawn, and the recursion stops when the length drops below 8.

```
<canvas width="600" height="300"></canvas>
<script>
  let cx = document.querySelector("canvas").getContext("2d");
  function branch(length, angle, scale) {
    cx.fillRect(0, 0, 1, length);
    if (length < 8) return;
    cx.save();
    cx.translate(0, length);
    cx.rotate(-angle);
    branch(length * scale, angle, scale);
    cx.rotate(2 * angle);
    branch(length * scale, angle, scale);
    cx.restore();
  }
  cx.translate(300, 0);
  branch(60, 0.5, 0.8);
</script>
```

The result is a simple fractal.

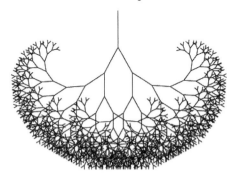

If the calls to save and restore were not there, the second recursive call to branch would end up with the position and rotation created by the first call. It wouldn't be connected to the current branch but rather to the inner-most, rightmost branch drawn by the first call. The resulting shape might also be interesting, but it is definitely not a tree.

Back to the Game

We now know enough about canvas drawing to start working on a canvas-based display system for the game from the previous chapter. The new display will no longer be showing just colored boxes. Instead, we'll use drawImage to draw pictures that represent the game's elements.

We define another display object type called CanvasDisplay, supporting the same interface as DOMDisplay from "Drawing" on page 273, namely, the methods syncState and clear.

This object keeps a little more information than DOMDisplay. Rather than using the scroll position of its DOM element, it tracks its own viewport, which tells us what part of the level we are currently looking at. And finally, it keeps a flipPlayer property so that even when the player is standing still, it keeps facing the direction it last moved in.

```
class CanvasDisplay {
  constructor(parent, level) {
    this.canvas = document.createElement("canvas");
    this.canvas.width = Math.min(600, level.width * scale);
    this.canvas.height = Math.min(450, level.height * scale);
    parent.appendChild(this.canvas);
    this.cx = this.canvas.getContext("2d");

    this.flipPlayer = false;

    this.viewport = {
      left: 0,
      top: 0,
      width: this.canvas.width / scale,
      height: this.canvas.height / scale
    };
  }

  clear() {
    this.canvas.remove();
  }
}
```

The syncState method first computes a new viewport and then draws the game scene at the appropriate position.

```
CanvasDisplay.prototype.syncState = function(state) {
  this.updateViewport(state);
  this.clearDisplay(state.status);
  this.drawBackground(state.level);
  this.drawActors(state.actors);
};
```

Contrary to DOMDisplay, this display style *does* have to redraw the background on every update. Because shapes on a canvas are just pixels, after we draw them there is no good way to move them (or remove them). The only way to update the canvas display is to clear it and redraw the scene. We may also have scrolled, which requires the background to be in a different position.

The updateViewport method is similar to DOMDisplay's scrollPlayerIntoView method. It checks whether the player is too close to the edge of the screen and moves the viewport when this is the case.

```
CanvasDisplay.prototype.updateViewport = function(state) {
  let view = this.viewport, margin = view.width / 3;
  let player = state.player;
  let center = player.pos.plus(player.size.times(0.5));

  if (center.x < view.left + margin) {
    view.left = Math.max(center.x - margin, 0);
  } else if (center.x > view.left + view.width - margin) {
    view.left = Math.min(center.x + margin - view.width,
                         state.level.width - view.width);
  }
  if (center.y < view.top + margin) {
    view.top = Math.max(center.y - margin, 0);
  } else if (center.y > view.top + view.height - margin) {
    view.top = Math.min(center.y + margin - view.height,
                        state.level.height - view.height);
  }
};
```

The calls to Math.max and Math.min ensure that the viewport does not end up showing space outside of the level. Math.max(x, 0) makes sure the resulting number is not less than zero. Math.min similarly guarantees that a value stays below a given bound.

When clearing the display, we'll use a slightly different color depending on whether the game is won (brighter) or lost (darker).

```
CanvasDisplay.prototype.clearDisplay = function(status) {
  if (status == "won") {
    this.cx.fillStyle = "rgb(68, 191, 255)";
  } else if (status == "lost") {
    this.cx.fillStyle = "rgb(44, 136, 214)";
  } else {
    this.cx.fillStyle = "rgb(52, 166, 251)";
  }
  this.cx.fillRect(0, 0,
                   this.canvas.width, this.canvas.height);
};
```

To draw the background, we run through the tiles that are visible in the current viewport, using the same trick used in the touches method from the previous chapter.

```
let otherSprites = document.createElement("img");
otherSprites.src = "img/sprites.png";

CanvasDisplay.prototype.drawBackground = function(level) {
  let {left, top, width, height} = this.viewport;
  let xStart = Math.floor(left);
  let xEnd = Math.ceil(left + width);
  let yStart = Math.floor(top);
  let yEnd = Math.ceil(top + height);

  for (let y = yStart; y < yEnd; y++) {
    for (let x = xStart; x < xEnd; x++) {
      let tile = level.rows[y][x];
      if (tile == "empty") continue;
      let screenX = (x - left) * scale;
      let screenY = (y - top) * scale;
      let tileX = tile == "lava" ? scale : 0;
      this.cx.drawImage(otherSprites,
                        tileX,          0, scale, scale,
                        screenX, screenY, scale, scale);
    }
  }
};
```

Tiles that are not empty are drawn with drawImage. The otherSprites image contains the pictures used for elements other than the player. It contains, from left to right, the wall tile, the lava tile, and the sprite for a coin.

Background tiles are 20 by 20 pixels since we will use the same scale that we used in DOMDisplay. Thus, the offset for lava tiles is 20 (the value of the scale binding), and the offset for walls is 0.

We don't bother waiting for the sprite image to load. Calling drawImage with an image that hasn't been loaded yet will simply do nothing. Thus, we might fail to draw the game properly for the first few frames, while the image is still loading, but that is not a serious problem. Since we keep updating the screen, the correct scene will appear as soon as the loading finishes.

The walking character shown earlier will be used to represent the player. The code that draws it needs to pick the right sprite and direction based on the player's current motion. The first eight sprites contain a walking animation. When the player is moving along a floor, we cycle through them based on the current time. We want to switch frames every 60 milliseconds, so the time is divided by 60 first. When the player is standing still, we draw the ninth sprite. During jumps, which are recognized by the fact that the vertical speed is not zero, we use the tenth, rightmost sprite.

Because the sprites are slightly wider than the player object—24 instead of 16 pixels, to allow some space for feet and arms—the method has to adjust the x-coordinate and width by a given amount (playerXOverlap).

```
let playerSprites = document.createElement("img");
playerSprites.src = "img/player.png";
const playerXOverlap = 4;

CanvasDisplay.prototype.drawPlayer = function(player, x, y,
                                              width, height){
  width += playerXOverlap * 2;
  x -= playerXOverlap;
  if (player.speed.x != 0) {
    this.flipPlayer = player.speed.x < 0;
  }

  let tile = 8;
  if (player.speed.y != 0) {
    tile = 9;
  } else if (player.speed.x != 0) {
    tile = Math.floor(Date.now() / 60) % 8;
  }

  this.cx.save();
  if (this.flipPlayer) {
    flipHorizontally(this.cx, x + width / 2);
  }
  let tileX = tile * width;
  this.cx.drawImage(playerSprites, tileX, 0, width, height,
                                   x,     y, width, height);
  this.cx.restore();
};
```

The drawPlayer method is called by drawActors, which is responsible for drawing all the actors in the game.

```
CanvasDisplay.prototype.drawActors = function(actors) {
  for (let actor of actors) {
    let width = actor.size.x * scale;
    let height = actor.size.y * scale;
    let x = (actor.pos.x - this.viewport.left) * scale;
    let y = (actor.pos.y - this.viewport.top) * scale;
    if (actor.type == "player") {
      this.drawPlayer(actor, x, y, width, height);
```

```
    } else {
      let tileX = (actor.type == "coin" ? 2 : 1) * scale;
      this.cx.drawImage(otherSprites,
                        tileX, 0, width, height,
                        x,     y, width, height);
    }
  }
};
```

When drawing something that is not the player, we look at its type to find the offset of the correct sprite. The lava tile is found at offset 20, and the coin sprite is found at 40 (two times scale).

We have to subtract the viewport's position when computing the actor's position since (0,0) on our canvas corresponds to the top left of the viewport, not the top left of the level. We could also have used translate for this. Either way works.

That concludes the new display system. The resulting game looks something like this:

Choosing a Graphics Interface

So when you need to generate graphics in the browser, you can choose between plain HTML, SVG, and canvas. There is no single *best* approach that works in all situations. Each option has strengths and weaknesses.

Plain HTML has the advantage of being simple. It also integrates well with text. Both SVG and canvas allow you to draw text, but they won't help you position that text or wrap it when it takes up more than one line. In an HTML-based picture, it is much easier to include blocks of text.

SVG can be used to produce crisp graphics that look good at any zoom level. Unlike HTML, it is designed for drawing and is thus more suitable for that purpose.

Both SVG and HTML build up a data structure (the DOM) that represents your picture. This makes it possible to modify elements after they are drawn. If you need to repeatedly change a small part of a big picture in response to what the user is doing or as part of an animation, doing it in a canvas can be needlessly expensive. The DOM also allows us to register mouse event handlers on every element in the picture (even on shapes drawn with SVG). You can't do that with canvas.

But canvas's pixel-oriented approach can be an advantage when drawing a huge number of tiny elements. The fact that it does not build up a data structure but only repeatedly draws onto the same pixel surface gives canvas a lower cost per shape.

There are also effects, such as rendering a scene one pixel at a time (for example, using a ray tracer) or postprocessing an image with JavaScript (blurring or distorting it), that can be realistically handled only by a pixel-based approach.

In some cases, you may want to combine several of these techniques. For example, you might draw a graph with SVG or canvas but show textual information by positioning an HTML element on top of the picture.

For nondemanding applications, it really doesn't matter much which interface you choose. The display we built for our game in this chapter could have been implemented using any of these three graphics technologies since it does not need to draw text, handle mouse interaction, or work with an extraordinarily large number of elements.

Summary

In this chapter we discussed techniques for drawing graphics in the browser, focusing on the `<canvas>` element.

A canvas node represents an area in a document that our program may draw on. This drawing is done through a drawing context object, created with the `getContext` method.

The 2D drawing interface allows us to fill and stroke various shapes. The context's `fillStyle` property determines how shapes are filled. The `strokeStyle` and `lineWidth` properties control the way lines are drawn.

Rectangles and pieces of text can be drawn with a single method call. The `fillRect` and `strokeRect` methods draw rectangles, and the `fillText` and `strokeText` methods draw text. To create custom shapes, we must first build up a path.

Calling `beginPath` starts a new path. A number of other methods add lines and curves to the current path. For example, `lineTo` can add a straight line. When a path is finished, it can be filled with the `fill` method or stroked with the `stroke` method.

Moving pixels from an image or another canvas onto our canvas is done with the `drawImage` method. By default, this method draws the whole source image, but by giving it more parameters, you can copy a specific area of the image. We used this for our game by copying individual poses of the game character out of an image that contained many such poses.

Transformations allow you to draw a shape in multiple orientations. A 2D drawing context has a current transformation that can be changed with the translate, scale, and rotate methods. These will affect all subsequent drawing operations. A transformation state can be saved with the save method and restored with the restore method.

When showing an animation on a canvas, the clearRect method can be used to clear part of the canvas before redrawing it.

Exercises

Shapes

Write a program that draws the following shapes on a canvas:

1. A trapezoid (a rectangle that is wider on one side)

2. A red diamond (a rectangle rotated 45 degrees or ¼π radians)

3. A zigzagging line

4. A spiral made up of 100 straight line segments

5. A yellow star

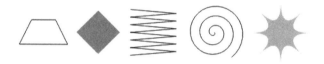

When drawing the last two, you may want to refer to the explanation of Math.cos and Math.sin in "Positioning and Animating" on page 240, which describes how to get coordinates on a circle using these functions.

I recommend creating a function for each shape. Pass the position, and optionally other properties such as the size or the number of points, as parameters. The alternative, which is to hard-code numbers all over your code, tends to make the code needlessly hard to read and modify.

The Pie Chart

In "Drawing a Pie Chart" on page 294, we saw an example program that drew a pie chart. Modify this program so that the name of each category is shown next to the slice that represents it. Try to find a pleasing-looking way to automatically position this text that would work for other data sets as well. You may assume that categories are big enough to leave ample room for their labels.

You might need Math.sin and Math.cos again, which are described in "Positioning and Animating" on page 240.

A Bouncing Ball

Use the requestAnimationFrame technique that we saw in Chapter 14 and Chapter 16 to draw a box with a bouncing ball in it. The ball moves at a constant speed and bounces off the box's sides when it hits them.

Precomputed Mirroring

One unfortunate thing about transformations is that they slow down the drawing of bitmaps. The position and size of each pixel has to be transformed, and though it is possible that browsers will get cleverer about transformation in the future, they currently cause a measurable increase in the time it takes to draw a bitmap.

In a game like ours, where we are drawing only a single transformed sprite, this is a nonissue. But imagine that we need to draw hundreds of characters or thousands of rotating particles from an explosion.

Think of a way to allow us to draw an inverted character without loading additional image files and without having to make transformed drawImage calls every frame.

"Communication must be stateless in nature . . .
such that each request from client to server
must contain all of the information necessary
to understand the request, and cannot take
advantage of any stored context on the server."

—Roy Fielding, *Architectural Styles and the Design
of Network-based Software Architectures*

18

HTTP AND FORMS

The *Hypertext Transfer Protocol,* already mentioned in Chapter 13, is the mechanism through which data is requested and provided on the World Wide Web. This chapter describes the protocol in more detail and explains the way browser JavaScript has access to it.

The Protocol

If you type *eloquentjavascript.net/18_http.html* into your browser's address bar, the browser first looks up the address of the server associated with *eloquentjavascript.net* and tries to open a TCP connection to it on port 80, the default port for HTTP traffic. If the server exists and accepts the connection, the browser might send something like this:

```
GET /18_http.html HTTP/1.1
Host: eloquentjavascript.net
User-Agent: Your browser's name
```

Then the server responds, through that same connection.

```
HTTP/1.1 200 OK
Content-Length: 65585
```

```
Content-Type: text/html
Last-Modified: Mon, 07 Jan 2019 10:29:45 GMT

<!doctype html>
... the rest of the document
```

The browser takes the part of the response after the blank line, its *body* (not to be confused with the HTML <body> tag), and displays it as an HTML document.

The information sent by the client is called the *request*. It starts with this line:

```
GET /18_http.html HTTP/1.1
```

The first word is the *method* of the request. GET means that we want to *get* the specified resource. Other common methods are DELETE to delete a resource, PUT to create or replace it, and POST to send information to it. Note that the server is not obliged to carry out every request it gets. If you walk up to a random website and tell it to DELETE its main page, it'll probably refuse.

The part after the method name is the path of the *resource* the request applies to. In the simplest case, a resource is simply a file on the server, but the protocol doesn't require it to be. A resource may be anything that can be transferred *as if* it is a file. Many servers generate the responses they produce on the fly. For example, if you open *https://github.com/marijnh*, the server looks in its database for a user named *marijnh*, and if it finds one, it will generate a profile page for that user.

After the resource path, the first line of the request mentions HTTP/1.1 to indicate the version of the HTTP protocol it is using.

In practice, many sites use HTTP version 2, which supports the same concepts as version 1.1 but is a lot more complicated so that it can be faster. Browsers will automatically switch to the appropriate protocol version when talking to a given server, and the outcome of a request is the same regardless of which version is used. Because version 1.1 is more straightforward and easier to play around with, we'll focus on that.

The server's response will start with a version as well, followed by the status of the response, first as a three-digit status code and then as a human-readable string.

```
HTTP/1.1 200 OK
```

Status codes starting with a 2 indicate that the request succeeded. Codes starting with 4 mean there was something wrong with the request. 404 is probably the most famous HTTP status code—it means that the resource could not be found. Codes that start with 5 mean an error happened on the server and the request is not to blame.

The first line of a request or response may be followed by any number of *headers*. These are lines in the form `name: value` that specify extra information about the request or response. These headers were part of the example response:

```
Content-Length: 65585
Content-Type: text/html
Last-Modified: Thu, 04 Jan 2018 14:05:30 GMT
```

This tells us the size and type of the response document. In this case, it is an HTML document of 65,585 bytes. It also tells us when that document was last modified.

For most headers, the client and server are free to decide whether to include them in a request or response. But a few are required. For example, the `Host` header, which specifies the hostname, should be included in a request because a server might be serving multiple hostnames on a single IP address, and without that header, the server won't know which hostname the client is trying to talk to.

After the headers, both requests and responses may include a blank line followed by a body, which contains the data being sent. `GET` and `DELETE` requests don't send along any data, but `PUT` and `POST` requests do. Similarly, some response types, such as error responses, do not require a body.

Browsers and HTTP

As we saw in the example, a browser will make a request when we enter a URL in its address bar. When the resulting HTML page references other files, such as images and JavaScript files, those are also retrieved.

A moderately complicated website can easily include anywhere from 10 to 200 resources. To be able to fetch those quickly, browsers will make several `GET` requests simultaneously, rather than waiting for the responses one at a time.

HTML pages may include *forms*, which allow the user to fill out information and send it to the server. This is an example of a form:

```
<form method="GET" action="example/message.html">
  <p>Name: <input type="text" name="name"></p>
  <p>Message:<br><textarea name="message"></textarea></p>
  <p><button type="submit">Send</button></p>
</form>
```

This code describes a form with two fields: a small one asking for a name and a larger one to write a message in. When you click the Send button, the form is *submitted*, meaning that the content of its field is packed into an HTTP request and the browser navigates to the result of that request.

When the `<form>` element's `method` attribute is `GET` (or is omitted), the information in the form is added to the end of the `action` URL as a *query string*. The browser might make a request to this URL:

```
GET /example/message.html?name=Jean&message=Yes%3F HTTP/1.1
```

The question mark indicates the end of the path part of the URL and the start of the query. It is followed by pairs of names and values, corresponding to the `name` attribute on the form field elements and the content of those elements, respectively. An ampersand character (&) is used to separate the pairs.

The actual message encoded in the URL is `Yes?`, but the question mark is replaced by a strange code. Some characters in query strings must be escaped. The question mark, represented as `%3F`, is one of those. There seems to be an unwritten rule that every format needs its own way of escaping characters. This one, called *URL encoding*, uses a percent sign followed by two hexadecimal (base 16) digits that encode the character code. In this case, 3F, which is 63 in decimal notation, is the code of a question mark character. JavaScript provides the `encodeURIComponent` and `decodeURIComponent` functions to encode and decode this format.

```
console.log(encodeURIComponent("Yes?"));
// → Yes%3F
console.log(decodeURIComponent("Yes%3F"));
// → Yes?
```

If we change the `method` attribute of the HTML form in the example we saw earlier to `POST`, the HTTP request made to submit the form will use the `POST` method and put the query string in the body of the request, rather than adding it to the URL.

```
POST /example/message.html HTTP/1.1
Content-length: 24
Content-type: application/x-www-form-urlencoded

name=Jean&message=Yes%3F
```

`GET` requests should be used for requests that do not have side effects but simply ask for information. Requests that change something on the server, for example creating a new account or posting a message, should be expressed with other methods, such as `POST`. Client-side software, such as a browser, knows that it shouldn't blindly make `POST` requests but will often implicitly make `GET` requests—for example to prefetch a resource it believes the user will soon need.

We'll come back to forms and how to interact with them from JavaScript in "Form Fields" on page 317.

Fetch

The interface through which browser JavaScript can make HTTP requests is called fetch. Since it is relatively new, it conveniently uses promises (which is rare for browser interfaces).

```
fetch("example/data.txt").then(response => {
  console.log(response.status);
  // → 200
  console.log(response.headers.get("Content-Type"));
  // → text/plain
});
```

Calling fetch returns a promise that resolves to a Response object holding information about the server's response, such as its status code and its headers. The headers are wrapped in a Map-like object that treats its keys (the header names) as case insensitive because header names are not supposed to be case sensitive. This means headers.get("Content-Type") and headers.get("content-TYPE") will return the same value.

Note that the promise returned by fetch resolves successfully even if the server responded with an error code. It *might* also be rejected if there is a network error or if the server that the request is addressed to can't be found.

The first argument to fetch is the URL that should be requested. When that URL doesn't start with a protocol name (such as *http:*), it is treated as *relative*, which means it is interpreted relative to the current document. When it starts with a slash (/), it replaces the current path, which is the part after the server name. When it does not, the part of the current path up to and including its last slash character is put in front of the relative URL.

To get at the actual content of a response, you can use its text method. Because the initial promise is resolved as soon as the response's headers have been received, and because reading the response body might take a while longer, this again returns a promise.

```
fetch("example/data.txt")
  .then(resp => resp.text())
  .then(text => console.log(text));
// → This is the content of data.txt
```

A similar method, called json, returns a promise that resolves to the value you get when parsing the body as JSON or rejects if it's not valid JSON.

By default, fetch uses the GET method to make its request and does not include a request body. You can configure it differently by passing an object with extra options as a second argument. For example, this request tries to delete example/data.txt:

```
fetch("example/data.txt", {method: "DELETE"}).then(resp => {
  console.log(resp.status);
```

```
// → 405
});
```

The 405 status code means "method not allowed," an HTTP server's way of saying "I can't do that."

To add a request body, you can include a body option. To set headers, there's the headers option. For example, this request includes a Range header, which instructs the server to return only part of a response.

```
fetch("example/data.txt", {headers: {Range: "bytes=8-19"}})
  .then(resp => resp.text())
  .then(console.log);
// → the content
```

The browser will automatically add some request headers, such as Host and those needed for the server to figure out the size of the body. But adding your own headers is often useful to include things such as authentication information or to tell the server which file format you'd like to receive.

HTTP Sandboxing

Making HTTP requests in web page scripts once again raises concerns about security. The person who controls the script might not have the same interests as the person on whose computer it is running. More specifically, if I visit *themafia.org*, I do not want its scripts to be able to make a request to *mybank.com*, using identifying information from my browser, with instructions to transfer all my money to some random account.

For this reason, browsers protect us by disallowing scripts to make HTTP requests to other domains (names such as *themafia.org* and *mybank.com*).

This can be an annoying problem when building systems that want to access several domains for legitimate reasons. Fortunately, servers can include a header like this in their response to explicitly indicate to the browser that it is okay for the request to come from another domain:

```
Access-Control-Allow-Origin: *
```

Appreciating HTTP

When building a system that requires communication between a JavaScript program running in the browser (client-side) and a program on a server (server-side), there are several different ways to model this communication.

A commonly used model is that of *remote procedure calls*. In this model, communication follows the patterns of normal function calls, except that the function is actually running on another machine. Calling it involves making a request to the server that includes the function's name and arguments. The response to that request contains the returned value.

When thinking in terms of remote procedure calls, HTTP is just a vehicle for communication, and you will most likely write an abstraction layer that hides it entirely.

Another approach is to build your communication around the concept of resources and HTTP methods. Instead of a remote procedure called addUser, you use a PUT request to /users/larry. Instead of encoding that user's properties in function arguments, you define a JSON document format (or use an existing format) that represents a user. The body of the PUT request to create a new resource is then such a document. A resource is fetched by making a GET request to the resource's URL (for example, /user/larry), which again returns the document representing the resource.

This second approach makes it easier to use some of the features that HTTP provides, such as support for caching resources (keeping a copy on the client for fast access). The concepts used in HTTP, which are well designed, can provide a helpful set of principles to design your server interface around.

Security and HTTPS

Data traveling over the internet tends to follow a long, dangerous road. To get to its destination, it must hop through anything from coffee shop Wi-Fi hotspots to networks controlled by various companies and states. At any point along its route it may be inspected or even modified.

If it is important that something remain secret, such as the password to your email account, or that it arrive at its destination unmodified, such as the account number you transfer money to via your bank's website, plain HTTP is not good enough.

The secure HTTP protocol, used for URLs starting with *https://*, wraps HTTP traffic in a way that makes it harder to read and tamper with. Before exchanging data, the client verifies that the server is who it claims to be by asking it to prove that it has a cryptographic certificate issued by a certificate authority that the browser recognizes. Next, all data going over the connection is encrypted in a way that should prevent eavesdropping and tampering.

Thus, when it works right, HTTPS prevents other people from impersonating the website you are trying to talk to and from snooping on your communication. It is not perfect, and there have been various incidents where HTTPS failed because of forged or stolen certificates and broken software, but it is a *lot* safer than plain HTTP.

Form Fields

Forms were originally designed for the pre-JavaScript web to allow websites to send user-submitted information in an HTTP request. This design assumes that interaction with the server always happens by navigating to a new page.

But their elements are part of the DOM like the rest of the page, and the DOM elements that represent form fields support a number of properties and events that are not present on other elements. These make it possible to inspect and control such input fields with JavaScript programs and do things such as adding new functionality to a form or using forms and fields as building blocks in a JavaScript application.

A web form consists of any number of input fields grouped in a `<form>` tag. HTML allows several different styles of fields, ranging from simple on/off checkboxes to drop-down menus and fields for text input. This book won't try to comprehensively discuss all field types, but we'll start with a rough overview.

A lot of field types use the `<input>` tag. This tag's type attribute is used to select the field's style. These are some commonly used `<input>` types:

text   A single-line text field
password   Same as text but hides the text that is typed
checkbox   An on/off switch
radio   (Part of) a multiple-choice field
file   Allows the user to choose a file from their computer

Form fields do not necessarily have to appear in a `<form>` tag. You can put them anywhere in a page. Such form-less fields cannot be submitted (only a form as a whole can), but when responding to input with JavaScript, we often don't want to submit our fields normally anyway.

```
<p><input type="text" value="abc"> (text)</p>
<p><input type="password" value="abc"> (password)</p>
<p><input type="checkbox" checked> (checkbox)</p>
<p><input type="radio" value="A" name="choice">
   <input type="radio" value="B" name="choice" checked>
   <input type="radio" value="C" name="choice"> (radio)</p>
<p><input type="file"> (file)</p>
```

The fields created with this HTML code look like this:

abc   (text)

•••   (password)

☑ (checkbox)

○ ○ ◉ (radio)

[Choose File] snippets.txt (file)

The JavaScript interface for such elements differs with the type of the element.

Multiline text fields have their own tag, `<textarea>`, mostly because using an attribute to specify a multiline starting value would be awkward. The `<textarea>` tag requires a matching `</textarea>` closing tag and uses the text between those two, instead of the value attribute, as starting text.

```
<textarea>
one
two
three
</textarea>
```

Finally, the `<select>` tag is used to create a field that allows the user to select from a number of predefined options.

```
<select>
  <option>Pancakes</option>
  <option>Pudding</option>
  <option>Ice cream</option>
</select>
```

Such a field looks like this:

Whenever the value of a form field changes, it will fire a "change" event.

Focus

Unlike most elements in HTML documents, form fields can get *keyboard focus*. When clicked or activated in some other way, they become the currently active element and the recipient of keyboard input.

Thus, you can type into a text field only when it is focused. Other fields respond differently to keyboard events. For example, a `<select>` menu tries to move to the option that contains the text the user typed and responds to the arrow keys by moving its selection up and down.

We can control focus from JavaScript with the focus and blur methods. The first moves focus to the DOM element it is called on, and the second removes focus. The value in `document.activeElement` corresponds to the currently focused element.

```
<input type="text">
<script>
  document.querySelector("input").focus();
  console.log(document.activeElement.tagName);
  // → INPUT
  document.querySelector("input").blur();
  console.log(document.activeElement.tagName);
  // → BODY
</script>
```

For some pages, the user is expected to want to interact with a form field immediately. JavaScript can be used to focus this field when the document is loaded, but HTML also provides the autofocus attribute, which produces the same effect while letting the browser know what we are trying to achieve. This gives the browser the option to disable the behavior when it is not appropriate, such as when the user has put the focus on something else.

Browsers traditionally also allow the user to move the focus through the document by pressing the TAB key. We can influence the order in which elements receive focus with the tabindex attribute. The following example document will let the focus jump from the text input to the OK button, rather than going through the help link first:

```
<input type="text" tabindex=1> <a href=".">(help)</a>
<button onclick="console.log('ok')" tabindex=2>OK</button>
```

By default, most types of HTML elements cannot be focused. But you can add a tabindex attribute to any element that will make it focusable. A tabindex of -1 makes tabbing skip over an element, even if it is normally focusable.

Disabled Fields

All form fields can be *disabled* through their disabled attribute. It is an attribute that can be specified without value—the fact that it is present at all disables the element.

```
<button>I'm all right</button>
<button disabled>I'm out</button>
```

Disabled fields cannot be focused or changed, and browsers make them look gray and faded.

I'm all right   I'm out

When a program is in the process of handling an action caused by some button or other control that might require communication with the server and thus take a while, it can be a good idea to disable the control until the action finishes. That way, when the user gets impatient and clicks it again, they don't accidentally repeat their action.

The Form as a Whole

When a field is contained in a <form> element, its DOM element will have a form property linking back to the form's DOM element. The <form> element, in turn, has a property called elements that contains an array-like collection of the fields inside it.

The name attribute of a form field determines the way its value will be identified when the form is submitted. It can also be used as a property name when accessing the form's `elements` property, which acts both as an array-like object (accessible by number) and a map (accessible by name).

```
<form action="example/submit.html">
  Name: <input type="text" name="name"><br>
  Password: <input type="password" name="password"><br>
  <button type="submit">Log in</button>
</form>
<script>
  let form = document.querySelector("form");
  console.log(form.elements[1].type);
  // → password
  console.log(form.elements.password.type);
  // → password
  console.log(form.elements.name.form == form);
  // → true
</script>
```

A button with a `type` attribute of `submit` will, when pressed, cause the form to be submitted. Pressing ENTER when a form field is focused has the same effect.

Submitting a form normally means that the browser navigates to the page indicated by the form's `action` attribute, using either a GET or a POST request. But before that happens, a `"submit"` event is fired. You can handle this event with JavaScript and prevent this default behavior by calling `preventDefault` on the event object.

```
<form action="example/submit.html">
  Value: <input type="text" name="value">
  <button type="submit">Save</button>
</form>
<script>
  let form = document.querySelector("form");
  form.addEventListener("submit", event => {
    console.log("Saving value", form.elements.value.value);
    event.preventDefault();
  });
</script>
```

Intercepting `"submit"` events in JavaScript has various uses. We can write code to verify that the values the user entered make sense and immediately show an error message instead of submitting the form. Or we can disable the regular way of submitting the form entirely, as in the example, and have our program handle the input, possibly using `fetch` to send it to a server without reloading the page.

Text Fields

Fields created by <textarea> tags or by <input> tags with a type of text or password share a common interface. Their DOM elements have a value property that holds their current content as a string value. Setting this property to another string changes the field's content.

The selectionStart and selectionEnd properties of text fields give us information about the cursor and selection in the text. When nothing is selected, these two properties hold the same number, indicating the position of the cursor. For example, 0 indicates the start of the text, and 10 indicates the cursor is after the 10th character. When part of the field is selected, the two properties will differ, giving us the start and end of the selected text. Like value, these properties may also be written to.

Imagine you are writing an article about Khasekhemwy but have some trouble spelling his name. The following code wires up a <textarea> tag with an event handler that, when you press F2, inserts the string "Khasekhemwy" for you.

```
<textarea></textarea>
<script>
  let textarea = document.querySelector("textarea");
  textarea.addEventListener("keydown", event => {
    // The key code for F2 happens to be 113
    if (event.keyCode == 113) {
      replaceSelection(textarea, "Khasekhemwy");
      event.preventDefault();
    }
  });
  function replaceSelection(field, word) {
    let from = field.selectionStart, to = field.selectionEnd;
    field.value = field.value.slice(0, from) + word +
                  field.value.slice(to);
    // Put the cursor after the word
    field.selectionStart = from + word.length;
    field.selectionEnd = from + word.length;
  }
</script>
```

The replaceSelection function replaces the currently selected part of a text field's content with the given word and then moves the cursor after that word so that the user can continue typing.

The "change" event for a text field does not fire every time something is typed. Rather, it fires when the field loses focus after its content was changed. To respond immediately to changes in a text field, you should register a handler for the "input" event instead, which fires for every time the user types a character, deletes text, or otherwise manipulates the field's content.

The following example shows a text field and a counter displaying the current length of the text in the field:

```
<input type="text"> length: <span id="length">0</span>
<script>
  let text = document.querySelector("input");
  let output = document.querySelector("#length");
  text.addEventListener("input", () => {
    output.textContent = text.value.length;
  });
</script>
```

Checkboxes and Radio Buttons

A checkbox field is a binary toggle. Its value can be extracted or changed through its checked property, which holds a Boolean value.

```
<label>
  <input type="checkbox" id="purple"> Make this page purple
</label>
<script>
  let checkbox = document.querySelector("#purple");
  checkbox.addEventListener("change", () => {
    document.body.style.background =
      checkbox.checked ? "mediumpurple" : "";
  });
</script>
```

The <label> tag associates a piece of document with an input field. Clicking anywhere on the label will activate the field, which focuses it and toggles its value when it is a checkbox or radio button.

A radio button is similar to a checkbox, but it's implicitly linked to other radio buttons with the same name attribute so that only one of them can be active at any time.

```
Color:
<label>
  <input type="radio" name="color" value="orange"> Orange
</label>
<label>
  <input type="radio" name="color" value="lightgreen"> Green
</label>
<label>
  <input type="radio" name="color" value="lightblue"> Blue
</label>
<script>
  let buttons = document.querySelectorAll("[name=color]");
```

```
    for (let button of Array.from(buttons)) {
      button.addEventListener("change", () => {
        document.body.style.background = button.value;
      });
    }
</script>
```

The square brackets in the CSS query given to querySelectorAll are used to match attributes. It selects elements whose name attribute is "color".

Select Fields

Select fields are conceptually similar to radio buttons—they also allow the user to choose from a set of options. But where a radio button puts the layout of the options under our control, the appearance of a <select> tag is determined by the browser.

Select fields also have a variant that is more akin to a list of checkboxes, rather than radio boxes. When given the multiple attribute, a <select> tag will allow the user to select any number of options, rather than just a single option. This will, in most browsers, show up differently than a normal select field, which is typically drawn as a *drop-down* control that shows the options only when you open it.

Each <option> tag has a value. This value can be defined with a value attribute. When that is not given, the text inside the option will count as its value. The value property of a <select> element reflects the currently selected option. For a multiple field, though, this property doesn't mean much since it will give the value of only *one* of the currently selected options.

The <option> tags for a <select> field can be accessed as an array-like object through the field's options property. Each option has a property called selected, which indicates whether that option is currently selected. The property can also be written to select or deselect an option.

This example extracts the selected values from a multiple select field and uses them to compose a binary number from individual bits. Hold CTRL (or COMMAND on a Mac) to select multiple options.

```
<select multiple>
  <option value="1">0001</option>
  <option value="2">0010</option>
  <option value="4">0100</option>
  <option value="8">1000</option>
</select> = <span id="output">0</span>
<script>
  let select = document.querySelector("select");
  let output = document.querySelector("#output");
  select.addEventListener("change", () => {
    let number = 0;
    for (let option of Array.from(select.options)) {
```

```
    if (option.selected) {
      number += Number(option.value);
    }
  }
  output.textContent = number;
});
</script>
```

File Fields

File fields were originally designed as a way to upload files from the user's machine through a form. In modern browsers, they also provide a way to read such files from JavaScript programs. The field acts as a kind of gatekeeper. The script cannot simply start reading private files from the user's computer, but if the user selects a file in such a field, the browser interprets that action to mean that the script may read the file.

A file field usually looks like a button labeled with something like "choose file" or "browse," with information about the chosen file next to it.

```
<input type="file">
<script>
  let input = document.querySelector("input");
  input.addEventListener("change", () => {
    if (input.files.length > 0) {
      let file = input.files[0];
      console.log("You chose", file.name);
      if (file.type) console.log("It has type", file.type);
    }
  });
</script>
```

The files property of a file field element is an array-like object (again, not a real array) containing the files chosen in the field. It is initially empty. The reason there isn't simply a file property is that file fields also support a multiple attribute, which makes it possible to select multiple files at the same time.

Objects in the files object have properties such as name (the filename), size (the file's size in bytes, which are chunks of 8 bits), and type (the media type of the file, such as text/plain or image/jpeg).

What it does not have is a property that contains the content of the file. Getting at that is a little more involved. Since reading a file from disk can take time, the interface must be asynchronous to avoid freezing the document.

```
<input type="file" multiple>
<script>
  let input = document.querySelector("input");
```

```
    input.addEventListener("change", () => {
      for (let file of Array.from(input.files)) {
        let reader = new FileReader();
        reader.addEventListener("load", () => {
          console.log("File", file.name, "starts with",
                      reader.result.slice(0, 20));
        });
        reader.readAsText(file);
      }
    });
  </script>
```

Reading a file is done by creating a `FileReader` object, registering a "load" event handler for it, and calling its `readAsText` method, giving it the file we want to read. Once loading finishes, the reader's `result` property contains the file's content.

FileReaders also fire an "error" event when reading the file fails for any reason. The error object itself will end up in the reader's `error` property. This interface was designed before promises became part of the language. You could wrap it in a promise like this:

```
function readFileText(file) {
  return new Promise((resolve, reject) => {
    let reader = new FileReader();
    reader.addEventListener(
      "load", () => resolve(reader.result));
    reader.addEventListener(
      "error", () => reject(reader.error));
    reader.readAsText(file);
  });
}
```

Storing Data Client-Side

Simple HTML pages with a bit of JavaScript can be a great format for "mini applications"—small helper programs that automate basic tasks. By connecting a few form fields with event handlers, you can do anything from converting between centimeters and inches to computing passwords from a master password and a website name.

When such an application needs to remember something between sessions, you cannot use JavaScript bindings—those are thrown away every time the page is closed. You could set up a server, connect it to the internet, and have your application store something there. We will see how to do that in Chapter 20. But that's a lot of extra work and complexity. Sometimes it is enough to just keep the data in the browser.

The `localStorage` object can be used to store data in a way that survives page reloads. This object allows you to file string values under names.

```
localStorage.setItem("username", "marijn");
console.log(localStorage.getItem("username"));
// → marijn
localStorage.removeItem("username");
```

A value in localStorage sticks around until it is overwritten, it is removed with removeItem, or the user clears their local data.

Sites from different domains get different storage compartments. That means data stored in localStorage by a given website can, in principle, be read (and overwritten) only by scripts on that same site.

Browsers do enforce a limit on the size of the data a site can store in localStorage. That restriction, along with the fact that filling up people's hard drives with junk is not really profitable, prevents the feature from eating up too much space.

The following code implements a crude note-taking application. It keeps a set of named notes and allows the user to edit notes and create new ones.

```
Notes: <select></select> <button>Add</button><br>
<textarea style="width: 100%"></textarea>

<script>
  let list = document.querySelector("select");
  let note = document.querySelector("textarea");

  let state;
  function setState(newState) {
    list.textContent = "";
    for (let name of Object.keys(newState.notes)) {
      let option = document.createElement("option");
      option.textContent = name;
      if (newState.selected == name) option.selected = true;
      list.appendChild(option);
    }
    note.value = newState.notes[newState.selected];

    localStorage.setItem("Notes", JSON.stringify(newState));
    state = newState;
  }
  setState(JSON.parse(localStorage.getItem("Notes")) || {
    notes: {"shopping list": "Carrots\nRaisins"},
    selected: "shopping list"
  });

  list.addEventListener("change", () => {
    setState({notes: state.notes, selected: list.value});
  });
```

```
      note.addEventListener("change", () => {
        setState({
          notes: Object.assign({}, state.notes,
                               {[state.selected]: note.value}),
          selected: state.selected
        });
      });
    document.querySelector("button")
      .addEventListener("click", () => {
        let name = prompt("Note name");
        if (name) setState({
          notes: Object.assign({}, state.notes, {[name]: ""}),
          selected: name
        });
      });
  </script>
```

The script gets its starting state from the "Notes" value stored in localStorage or, if that is missing, creates an example state that has only a shopping list in it. Reading a field that does not exist from localStorage will yield null. Passing null to JSON.parse will make it parse the string "null" and return null. Thus, the || operator can be used to provide a default value in a situation like this.

The setState method makes sure the DOM is showing a given state and stores the new state to localStorage. Event handlers call this function to move to a new state.

The use of Object.assign in the example is intended to create a new object that is a clone of the old state.notes, but with one property added or overwritten. Object.assign takes its first argument and adds all properties from any further arguments to it. Thus, giving it an empty object will cause it to fill a fresh object. The square brackets notation in the third argument is used to create a property whose name is based on some dynamic value.

There is another object, similar to localStorage, called sessionStorage. The difference between the two is that the content of sessionStorage is forgotten at the end of each *session*, which for most browsers means whenever the browser is closed.

Summary

In this chapter, we discussed how the HTTP protocol works. A *client* sends a request, which contains a method (usually GET) and a path that identifies a resource. The *server* then decides what to do with the request and responds with a status code and a response body. Both requests and responses may contain headers that provide additional information.

The interface through which browser JavaScript can make HTTP requests is called fetch. Making a request looks like this:

```
fetch("/18_http.html").then(r => r.text()).then(text => {
  console.log(`The page starts with ${text.slice(0, 15)}`);
});
```

Browsers make GET requests to fetch the resources needed to display a web page. A page may also contain forms, which allow information entered by the user to be sent as a request for a new page when the form is submitted.

HTML can represent various types of form fields, such as text fields, checkboxes, multiple-choice fields, and file pickers.

Such fields can be inspected and manipulated with JavaScript. They fire the "change" event when changed, fire the "input" event when text is typed, and receive keyboard events when they have keyboard focus. Properties like value (for text and select fields) or checked (for checkboxes and radio buttons) are used to read or set the field's content.

When a form is submitted, a "submit" event is fired on it. A JavaScript handler can call preventDefault on that event to disable the browser's default behavior. Form field elements may also occur outside of a form tag.

When the user has selected a file from their local file system in a file picker field, the FileReader interface can be used to access the content of this file from a JavaScript program.

The localStorage and sessionStorage objects can be used to save information in a way that survives page reloads. The first object saves the data forever (or until the user decides to clear it), and the second saves it until the browser is closed.

Exercises

Content Negotiation

One of the things HTTP can do is called *content negotiation*. The Accept request header is used to tell the server what type of document the client would like to get. Many servers ignore this header, but when a server knows of various ways to encode a resource, it can look at this header and send the one that the client prefers.

The URL *https://eloquentjavascript.net/author* is configured to respond with either plaintext, HTML, or JSON, depending on what the client asks for. These formats are identified by the standardized *media types* text/plain, text/html, and application/json.

Send requests to fetch all three formats of this resource. Use the headers property in the options object passed to fetch to set the header named Accept to the desired media type.

Finally, try asking for the media type application/rainbows+unicorns and see which status code that produces.

A JavaScript Workbench

Build an interface that allows people to type and run pieces of JavaScript code.

Put a button next to a `<textarea>` field that, when pressed, uses the Function constructor we saw in "Evaluating Data as Code" on page 170 to wrap the text in a function and call it. Convert the return value of the function, or any error it raises, to a string and display it below the text field.

Conway's Game of Life

Conway's Game of Life is a simple simulation that creates artificial "life" on a grid, each cell of which is either alive or not. Each generation (turn), the following rules are applied:

- Any live cell with fewer than two or more than three live neighbors dies.

- Any live cell with two or three live neighbors lives on to the next generation.

- Any dead cell with exactly three live neighbors becomes a live cell.

A *neighbor* is defined as any adjacent cell, including diagonally adjacent ones.

Note that these rules are applied to the whole grid at once, not one square at a time. That means the counting of neighbors is based on the situation at the start of the generation, and changes happening to neighbor cells during this generation should not influence the new state of a given cell.

Implement this game using whichever data structure you find appropriate. Use Math.random to populate the grid with a random pattern initially. Display it as a grid of checkbox fields, with a button next to it to advance to the next generation. When the user checks or unchecks the checkboxes, their changes should be included when computing the next generation.

"I look at the many colors before me. I look at my blank canvas. Then, I try to apply colors like words that shape poems, like notes that shape music."

—Joan Miró

19

PROJECT: A PIXEL ART EDITOR

The material from the previous chapters gives you all the elements you need to build a basic web application. In this chapter, we will do just that.

Our application will be a pixel-drawing program, where you can modify a picture pixel-by-pixel by manipulating a zoomed-in view of it, shown as a grid of colored squares. You can use the program to open image files, scribble on them with your mouse or other pointer device, and save them. This is what it will look like:

Painting on a computer is great. You don't need to worry about materials, skill, or talent. You just start smearing.

Components

The interface for the application shows a big <canvas> element on top, with a number of form fields below it. The user draws on the picture by selecting a tool from a <select> field and then clicking, touching, or dragging across the canvas. There are tools for drawing single pixels or rectangles, for filling an area, and for picking a color from the picture.

We will structure the editor interface as a number of *components*, objects that are responsible for a piece of the DOM and that may contain other components inside them.

The state of the application consists of the current picture, the selected tool, and the selected color. We'll set things up so that the state lives in a single value, and the interface components always base the way they look on the current state.

To see why this is important, let's consider the alternative—distributing pieces of state throughout the interface. Up to a certain point, this is easier to program. We can just put in a color field and read its value when we need to know the current color.

But then we add the color picker—a tool that lets you click the picture to select the color of a given pixel. To keep the color field showing the correct color, that tool would have to know that the color field exists and update it whenever it picks a new color. If you ever add another place that makes the color visible (maybe the mouse cursor could show it), you have to update your color-changing code to keep that synchronized.

In effect, this creates a problem where each part of the interface needs to know about all other parts, which is not very modular. For small applications like the one in this chapter, that may not be a problem. For bigger projects, it can turn into a real nightmare.

To avoid this nightmare on principle, we're going to be strict about *data flow*. There is a state, and the interface is drawn based on that state. An interface component may respond to user actions by updating the state, at which point the components get a chance to synchronize themselves with this new state.

In practice, each component is set up so that when it is given a new state, it also notifies its child components, insofar as those need to be updated. Setting this up is a bit of a hassle. Making this more convenient is the main selling point of many browser programming libraries. But for a small application like this, we can do it without such infrastructure.

Updates to the state are represented as objects, which we'll call *actions*. Components may create such actions and *dispatch* them—give them to a central state management function. That function computes the next state, after which the interface components update themselves to this new state.

We're taking the messy task of running a user interface and applying some structure to it. Though the DOM-related pieces are still full of side effects, they are held up by a conceptually simple backbone: the state update cycle. The state determines what the DOM looks like, and the only way DOM events can change the state is by dispatching actions to the state.

There are *many* variants of this approach, each with its own benefits and problems, but their central idea is the same: state changes should go through a single well-defined channel, not happen all over the place.

Our components will be classes conforming to an interface. Their constructor is given a state—which may be the whole application state or some smaller value if it doesn't need access to everything—and uses that to build up a dom property. This is the DOM element that represents the component. Most constructors will also take some other values that won't change over time, such as the function they can use to dispatch an action.

Each component has a syncState method that is used to synchronize it to a new state value. The method takes one argument, the state, which is of the same type as the first argument to its constructor.

The State

The application state will be an object with picture, tool, and color properties. The picture is itself an object that stores the width, height, and pixel content of the picture. The pixels are stored in an array, in the same way as the matrix class from Chapter 6—row by row, from top to bottom.

```
class Picture {
  constructor(width, height, pixels) {
    this.width = width;
    this.height = height;
    this.pixels = pixels;
  }
  static empty(width, height, color) {
    let pixels = new Array(width * height).fill(color);
    return new Picture(width, height, pixels);
  }
  pixel(x, y) {
    return this.pixels[x + y * this.width];
  }
  draw(pixels) {
    let copy = this.pixels.slice();
    for (let {x, y, color} of pixels) {
      copy[x + y * this.width] = color;
    }
    return new Picture(this.width, this.height, copy);
  }
}
```

We want to be able to treat a picture as an immutable value, for reasons that we'll get back to later in the chapter. But we also sometimes need to update a whole bunch of pixels at a time. To be able to do that, the class has a draw method that expects an array of updated pixels—objects with x, y, and color properties—and creates a new picture with those pixels overwritten. This method uses `slice` without arguments to copy the entire pixel array—the start of the slice defaults to 0, and the end defaults to the array's length.

The `empty` method uses two pieces of array functionality that we haven't seen before. The `Array` constructor can be called with a number to create an empty array of the given length. The `fill` method can then be used to fill this array with a given value. These are used to create an array in which all pixels have the same color.

Colors are stored as strings containing traditional CSS color codes made up of a hash mark (#) followed by six hexadecimal (base-16) digits—two for the red component, two for the green component, and two for the blue component. This is a somewhat cryptic and inconvenient way to write colors, but it is the format the HTML color input field uses, and it can be used in the `fillStyle` property of a canvas drawing context, so for the ways we'll use colors in this program, it is practical enough.

Black, where all components are zero, is written `"#000000"`, and bright pink looks like `"#ff00ff"`, where the red and blue components have the maximum value of 255, written `ff` in hexadecimal digits (which use *a* to *f* to represent digits 10 to 15).

We'll allow the interface to dispatch actions as objects whose properties overwrite the properties of the previous state. The color field, when the user changes it, could dispatch an object like {color: field.value}, from which this update function can compute a new state.

```
function updateState(state, action) {
  return Object.assign({}, state, action);
}
```

This rather cumbersome pattern, in which `Object.assign` is used to first add the properties of `state` to an empty object and then overwrite some of those with the properties from `action`, is common in JavaScript code that uses immutable objects. A more convenient notation for this, in which the triple-dot operator is used to include all properties from another object in an object expression, is in the final stages of being standardized. With that addition, you could write {...state, ...action} instead. At the time of writing, this doesn't yet work in all browsers.

DOM Building

One of the main things that interface components do is create DOM structure. We again don't want to directly use the verbose DOM methods for that, so here's a slightly expanded version of the `elt` function:

```
function elt(type, props, ...children) {
  let dom = document.createElement(type);
  if (props) Object.assign(dom, props);
```

```
  for (let child of children) {
    if (typeof child != "string") dom.appendChild(child);
    else dom.appendChild(document.createTextNode(child));
  }
  return dom;
}
```

The main difference between this version and the one we used in "Drawing" on page 273 is that this version assigns *properties* to DOM nodes, not *attributes*. This means we can't use it to set arbitrary attributes, but we *can* use it to set properties whose value isn't a string, such as onclick, which can be set to a function to register a click event handler.

This allows the following style of registering event handlers:

```
<body>
  <script>
    document.body.appendChild(elt("button", {
      onclick: () => console.log("click")
    }, "The button"));
  </script>
</body>
```

The Canvas

The first component we'll define is the part of the interface that displays the picture as a grid of colored boxes. This component is responsible for two things: showing a picture and communicating pointer events on that picture to the rest of the application.

As such, we can define it as a component that knows about only the current picture, not the whole application state. Because it doesn't know how the application as a whole works, it cannot directly dispatch actions. Rather, when responding to pointer events, the component calls a callback function provided by the code that created it, which will handle the application-specific parts.

```
const scale = 10;

class PictureCanvas {
  constructor(picture, pointerDown) {
    this.dom = elt("canvas", {
      onmousedown: event => this.mouse(event, pointerDown),
      ontouchstart: event => this.touch(event, pointerDown)
    });
    this.syncState(picture);
  }
  syncState(picture) {
    if (this.picture == picture) return;
```

```
    this.picture = picture;
    drawPicture(this.picture, this.dom, scale);
  }
}
```

We draw each pixel as a 10-by-10 square, as determined by the scale constant. To avoid unnecessary work, the component keeps track of its current picture, and it does a redraw only when syncState is given a new picture.

The actual drawing function sets the size of the canvas based on the scale and picture size and fills it with a series of squares, one for each pixel.

```
function drawPicture(picture, canvas, scale) {
  canvas.width = picture.width * scale;
  canvas.height = picture.height * scale;
  let cx = canvas.getContext("2d");

  for (let y = 0; y < picture.height; y++) {
    for (let x = 0; x < picture.width; x++) {
      cx.fillStyle = picture.pixel(x, y);
      cx.fillRect(x * scale, y * scale, scale, scale);
    }
  }
}
```

When the left mouse button is pressed while the mouse is over the picture canvas, the component calls the pointerDown callback, giving it the position of the pixel that was clicked—in picture coordinates. This will be used to implement mouse interaction with the picture. The callback may return another callback function to be notified when the pointer is moved to a different pixel while the button is held down.

```
PictureCanvas.prototype.mouse = function(downEvent, onDown) {
  if (downEvent.button != 0) return;
  let pos = pointerPosition(downEvent, this.dom);
  let onMove = onDown(pos);
  if (!onMove) return;
  let move = moveEvent => {
    if (moveEvent.buttons == 0) {
      this.dom.removeEventListener("mousemove", move);
    } else {
      let newPos = pointerPosition(moveEvent, this.dom);
      if (newPos.x == pos.x && newPos.y == pos.y) return;
      pos = newPos;
      onMove(newPos);
    }
  };
  this.dom.addEventListener("mousemove", move);
};
```

```
function pointerPosition(pos, domNode) {
  let rect = domNode.getBoundingClientRect();
  return {x: Math.floor((pos.clientX - rect.left) / scale),
          y: Math.floor((pos.clientY - rect.top) / scale)};
}
```

Since we know the size of the pixels and we can use `getBoundingClientRect` to find the position of the canvas on the screen, it is possible to go from mouse event coordinates (`clientX` and `clientY`) to picture coordinates. These are always rounded down so that they refer to a specific pixel.

With touch events, we have to do something similar, but we must use different events and make sure we call `preventDefault` on the "touchstart" event to prevent panning.

```
PictureCanvas.prototype.touch = function(startEvent,
                                         onDown) {
  let pos = pointerPosition(startEvent.touches[0], this.dom);
  let onMove = onDown(pos);
  startEvent.preventDefault();
  if (!onMove) return;
  let move = moveEvent => {
    let newPos = pointerPosition(moveEvent.touches[0],
                                 this.dom);
    if (newPos.x == pos.x && newPos.y == pos.y) return;
    pos = newPos;
    onMove(newPos);
  };
  let end = () => {
    this.dom.removeEventListener("touchmove", move);
    this.dom.removeEventListener("touchend", end);
  };
  this.dom.addEventListener("touchmove", move);
  this.dom.addEventListener("touchend", end);
};
```

For touch events, `clientX` and `clientY` aren't available directly on the event object, but we can use the coordinates of the first touch object in the touches property.

The Application

To make it possible to build the application piece by piece, we'll implement the main component as a shell around a picture canvas and a dynamic set of tools and controls that we pass to its constructor.

The *controls* are the interface elements that appear below the picture. They'll be provided as an array of component constructors.

The *tools* do things like drawing pixels or filling in an area. The application shows the set of available tools as a <select> field. The currently selected tool determines what happens when the user interacts with the picture with a pointer device. The set of available tools is provided as an object that maps the names that appear in the drop-down field to functions that implement the tools. Such functions get a picture position, a current application state, and a dispatch function as arguments. They may return a move handler function that gets called with a new position and a current state when the pointer moves to a different pixel.

```
class PixelEditor {
  constructor(state, config) {
    let {tools, controls, dispatch} = config;
    this.state = state;

    this.canvas = new PictureCanvas(state.picture, pos => {
      let tool = tools[this.state.tool];
      let onMove = tool(pos, this.state, dispatch);
      if (onMove) return pos => onMove(pos, this.state);
    });
    this.controls = controls.map(
      Control => new Control(state, config));
    this.dom = elt("div", {}, this.canvas.dom, elt("br"),
                   ...this.controls.reduce(
                     (a, c) => a.concat(" ", c.dom), []));
  }
  syncState(state) {
    this.state = state;
    this.canvas.syncState(state.picture);
    for (let ctrl of this.controls) ctrl.syncState(state);
  }
}
```

The pointer handler given to PictureCanvas calls the currently selected tool with the appropriate arguments and, if that returns a move handler, adapts it to also receive the state.

All controls are constructed and stored in this.controls so that they can be updated when the application state changes. The call to reduce introduces spaces between the controls' DOM elements. That way they don't look so pressed together.

The first control is the tool selection menu. It creates a <select> element with an option for each tool and sets up a "change" event handler that updates the application state when the user selects a different tool.

```
class ToolSelect {
  constructor(state, {tools, dispatch}) {
    this.select = elt("select", {
      onchange: () => dispatch({tool: this.select.value})
    }, ...Object.keys(tools).map(name => elt("option", {
      selected: name == state.tool
    }, name)));
    this.dom = elt("label", null, "🖊 Tool: ", this.select);
  }
  syncState(state) { this.select.value = state.tool; }
}
```

By wrapping the label text and the field in a <label> element, we tell the browser that the label belongs to that field so that you can, for example, click the label to focus the field.

We also need to be able to change the color, so let's add a control for that. An HTML <input> element with a type attribute of color gives us a form field that is specialized for selecting colors. Such a field's value is always a CSS color code in "#RRGGBB" format (red, green, and blue components, two digits per color). The browser will show a color picker interface when the user interacts with it.

Depending on the browser, the color picker might look like this:

This control creates such a field and wires it up to stay synchronized with the application state's color property.

```
class ColorSelect {
  constructor(state, {dispatch}) {
    this.input = elt("input", {
      type: "color",
      value: state.color,
      onchange: () => dispatch({color: this.input.value})
    });
    this.dom = elt("label", null, "🎨 Color: ", this.input);
  }
  syncState(state) { this.input.value = state.color; }
}
```

Drawing Tools

Before we can draw anything, we need to implement the tools that will control the functionality of mouse or touch events on the canvas.

The most basic tool is the draw tool, which changes any pixel you click or tap to the currently selected color. It dispatches an action that updates the picture to a version in which the pointed-at pixel is given the currently selected color.

```
function draw(pos, state, dispatch) {
  function drawPixel({x, y}, state) {
    let drawn = {x, y, color: state.color};
    dispatch({picture: state.picture.draw([drawn])});
  }
  drawPixel(pos, state);
  return drawPixel;
}
```

The function immediately calls the drawPixel function but then also returns it so that it is called again for newly touched pixels when the user drags or swipes over the picture.

To draw larger shapes, it can be useful to quickly create rectangles. The rectangle tool draws a rectangle between the point where you start dragging and the point that you drag to.

```
function rectangle(start, state, dispatch) {
  function drawRectangle(pos) {
    let xStart = Math.min(start.x, pos.x);
    let yStart = Math.min(start.y, pos.y);
    let xEnd = Math.max(start.x, pos.x);
    let yEnd = Math.max(start.y, pos.y);
    let drawn = [];
    for (let y = yStart; y <= yEnd; y++) {
      for (let x = xStart; x <= xEnd; x++) {
        drawn.push({x, y, color: state.color});
      }
    }
    dispatch({picture: state.picture.draw(drawn)});
  }
  drawRectangle(start);
  return drawRectangle;
}
```

An important detail in this implementation is that when dragging, the rectangle is redrawn on the picture from the *original* state. That way, you can make the rectangle larger and smaller again while creating it, without the intermediate rectangles sticking around in the final picture. This is one of the reasons why immutable picture objects are useful—we'll see another reason later.

Implementing flood fill is somewhat more involved. This tool fills the pixel under the pointer and all adjacent pixels that have the same color. "Adjacent" means horizontally or vertically adjacent, not diagonally. This picture illustrates the set of pixels colored when the flood fill tool is used at the marked pixel:

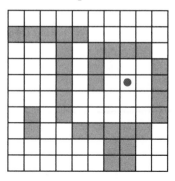 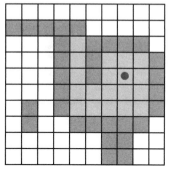

Interestingly, the way we'll do this looks a bit like the pathfinding code from Chapter 7. Whereas that code searched through a graph to find a route, this code searches through a grid to find all "connected" pixels. The problem of keeping track of a branching set of possible routes is similar.

```
const around = [{dx: -1, dy: 0}, {dx: 1, dy: 0},
                {dx: 0, dy: -1}, {dx: 0, dy: 1}];

function fill({x, y}, state, dispatch) {
  let targetColor = state.picture.pixel(x, y);
  let drawn = [{x, y, color: state.color}];
  for (let done = 0; done < drawn.length; done++) {
    for (let {dx, dy} of around) {
      let x = drawn[done].x + dx, y = drawn[done].y + dy;
      if (x >= 0 && x < state.picture.width &&
          y >= 0 && y < state.picture.height &&
          state.picture.pixel(x, y) == targetColor &&
          !drawn.some(p => p.x == x && p.y == y)) {
        drawn.push({x, y, color: state.color});
      }
    }
  }
  dispatch({picture: state.picture.draw(drawn)});
}
```

The array of drawn pixels doubles as the function's work list. For each pixel reached, we have to see whether any adjacent pixels have the same color and haven't already been painted over. The loop counter lags behind the length of the drawn array as new pixels are added. Any pixels ahead of it still need to be explored. When it catches up with the length, no unexplored pixels remain, and the function is done.

The final tool is a color picker, which allows you to point at a color in the picture to use it as the current drawing color.

```
function pick(pos, state, dispatch) {
  dispatch({color: state.picture.pixel(pos.x, pos.y)});
}
```

Saving and Loading

When we've drawn our masterpiece, we'll want to save it for later. We should add a button for downloading the current picture as an image file. This control provides that button:

```
class SaveButton {
  constructor(state) {
    this.picture = state.picture;
    this.dom = elt("button", {
      onclick: () => this.save()
    }, "💾 Save");
  }
  save() {
    let canvas = elt("canvas");
    drawPicture(this.picture, canvas, 1);
    let link = elt("a", {
      href: canvas.toDataURL(),
      download: "pixelart.png"
    });
    document.body.appendChild(link);
    link.click();
    link.remove();
  }
  syncState(state) { this.picture = state.picture; }
}
```

The component keeps track of the current picture so that it can access it when saving. To create the image file, it uses a <canvas> element that it draws the picture on (at a scale of one pixel per pixel).

The toDataURL method on a canvas element creates a URL that starts with *data:*. Unlike *http:* and *https:* URLs, data URLs contain the whole resource in the URL. They are usually very long, but they allow us to create working links to arbitrary pictures right in the browser.

To actually get the browser to download the picture, we then create a link element that points at this URL and has a download attribute. Such links, when clicked, make the browser show a file save dialog. We add that link to the document, simulate a click on it, and remove it again.

You can do a lot with browser technology, but sometimes the way to do it is rather odd.

And it gets worse. We'll also want to be able to load existing image files into our application. To do that, we again define a button component.

```
class LoadButton {
  constructor(_, {dispatch}) {
    this.dom = elt("button", {
      onclick: () => startLoad(dispatch)
    }, "🖼 Load");
  }
  syncState() {}
}

function startLoad(dispatch) {
  let input = elt("input", {
    type: "file",
    onchange: () => finishLoad(input.files[0], dispatch)
  });
  document.body.appendChild(input);
  input.click();
  input.remove();
}
```

To get access to a file on the user's computer, we need the user to select the file through a file input field. But I don't want the load button to look like a file input field, so we create the file input when the button is clicked and then pretend that this file input itself was clicked.

When the user has selected a file, we can use FileReader to get access to its contents, again as a data URL. That URL can be used to create an <img> element, but because we can't get direct access to the pixels in such an image, we can't create a Picture object from that.

```
function finishLoad(file, dispatch) {
  if (file == null) return;
  let reader = new FileReader();
  reader.addEventListener("load", () => {
    let image = elt("img", {
      onload: () => dispatch({
        picture: pictureFromImage(image)
      }),
      src: reader.result
    });
  });
  reader.readAsDataURL(file);
}
```

To get access to the pixels, we must first draw the picture to a <canvas> element. The canvas context has a getImageData method that allows a script to read its pixels. So, once the picture is on the canvas, we can access it and construct a Picture object.

```
function pictureFromImage(image) {
  let width = Math.min(100, image.width);
  let height = Math.min(100, image.height);
```

```
let canvas = elt("canvas", {width, height});
let cx = canvas.getContext("2d");
cx.drawImage(image, 0, 0);
let pixels = [];
let {data} = cx.getImageData(0, 0, width, height);

function hex(n) {
  return n.toString(16).padStart(2, "0");
}
for (let i = 0; i < data.length; i += 4) {
  let [r, g, b] = data.slice(i, i + 3);
  pixels.push("#" + hex(r) + hex(g) + hex(b));
}
return new Picture(width, height, pixels);
}
```

We'll limit the size of images to 100 by 100 pixels since anything bigger will look *huge* on our display and might slow down the interface.

The data property of the object returned by getImageData is an array of color components. For each pixel in the rectangle specified by the arguments, it contains four values, which represent the red, green, blue, and *alpha* components of the pixel's color, as numbers between 0 and 255. The alpha part represents opacity—when it is zero, the pixel is fully transparent, and when it is 255, it is fully opaque. For our purpose, we can ignore it.

The two hexadecimal digits per component, as used in our color notation, correspond precisely to the 0 to 255 range—two base-16 digits can express $16^2 = 256$ numbers. The toString method of numbers can be given a base as argument, so n.toString(16) will produce a string representation in base 16. We have to make sure that each number takes up two digits, so the hex helper function calls padStart to add a leading zero when necessary.

We can load and save now! That leaves one more feature to implement before we're done.

Undo History

Half of the process of editing is making little mistakes and correcting them. So an important feature in a drawing program is an undo history.

To be able to undo changes, we need to store previous versions of the picture. Since it's an immutable value, that is easy. But it does require an additional field in the application state.

We'll add a done array to keep previous versions of the picture. Maintaining this property requires a more complicated state update function that adds pictures to the array.

But we don't want to store *every* change, only changes a certain amount of time apart. To be able to do that, we'll need a second property, doneAt, tracking the time at which we last stored a picture in the history.

```
function historyUpdateState(state, action) {
  if (action.undo == true) {
    if (state.done.length == 0) return state;
    return Object.assign({}, state, {
      picture: state.done[0],
      done: state.done.slice(1),
      doneAt: 0
    });
  } else if (action.picture &&
             state.doneAt < Date.now() - 1000) {
    return Object.assign({}, state, action, {
      done: [state.picture, ...state.done],
      doneAt: Date.now()
    });
  } else {
    return Object.assign({}, state, action);
  }
}
```

When the action is an undo action, the function takes the most recent picture from the history and makes that the current picture. It sets doneAt to zero so that the next change is guaranteed to store the picture back in the history, allowing you to revert back to it another time if you want.

Otherwise, if the action contains a new picture and the last time we stored something is more than a second (1000 milliseconds) ago, the done and doneAt properties are updated to store the previous picture.

The undo button component doesn't do much. It dispatches undo actions when clicked and disables itself when there is nothing to undo.

```
class UndoButton {
  constructor(state, {dispatch}) {
    this.dom = elt("button", {
      onclick: () => dispatch({undo: true}),
      disabled: state.done.length == 0
    }, "⤺ Undo");
  }
  syncState(state) {
    this.dom.disabled = state.done.length == 0;
  }
}
```

Let's Draw

To set up the application, we need to create a state, a set of tools, a set of controls, and a dispatch function. We can pass them to the PixelEditor constructor to create the main component. Since we'll need to create several editors in the exercises, we first define some bindings.

```
const startState = {
  tool: "draw",
  color: "#000000",
  picture: Picture.empty(60, 30, "#f0f0f0"),
  done: [],
  doneAt: 0
};

const baseTools = {draw, fill, rectangle, pick};

const baseControls = [
  ToolSelect, ColorSelect, SaveButton, LoadButton, UndoButton
];

function startPixelEditor({state = startState,
                           tools = baseTools,
                           controls = baseControls}) {
  let app = new PixelEditor(state, {
    tools,
    controls,
    dispatch(action) {
      state = historyUpdateState(state, action);
      app.syncState(state);
    }
  });
  return app.dom;
}
```

When destructuring an object or array, you can use = after a binding name to give the binding a default value, which is used when the property is missing or holds undefined. The startPixelEditor function uses this to accept an object with a number of optional properties as an argument. If you don't provide a tools property, for example, tools will be bound to baseTools.

This is how we get an actual editor on the screen:

```
<div></div>
<script>
  document.querySelector("div")
    .appendChild(startPixelEditor({}));
</script>
```

Why Is This So Hard?

Browser technology is amazing. It provides a powerful set of interface building blocks, ways to style and manipulate them, and tools to inspect and debug your applications. The software you write for the browser can be run on almost every computer and phone on the planet.

At the same time, browser technology is ridiculous. You have to learn a large number of silly tricks and obscure facts to master it, and the default programming model it provides is so problematic that most programmers prefer to cover it in several layers of abstraction rather than deal with it directly.

And though the situation is definitely improving, it mostly does so in the form of more elements being added to address shortcomings—creating even more complexity. A feature used by a million websites can't really be replaced. Even if it could, it would be hard to decide what it should be replaced with.

Technology never exists in a vacuum—we're constrained by our tools and the social, economic, and historical factors that produced them. This can be annoying, but it is generally more productive to try to build a good understanding of how the *existing* technical reality works—and why it is the way it is—than to rage against it or hold out for another reality.

New abstractions *can* be helpful. The component model and data flow convention I used in this chapter is a crude form of that. As mentioned, there are libraries that try to make user interface programming more pleasant. At the time of writing, React and Angular are popular choices, but there's a whole cottage industry of such frameworks. If you're interested in programming web applications, I recommend investigating a few of them to understand how they work and what benefits they provide.

Exercises

There is still room for improvement in our program. Let's add a few more features as exercises.

Keyboard Bindings

Add keyboard shortcuts to the application. The first letter of a tool's name selects the tool, and CTRL-Z or COMMAND-Z activates undo.

Do this by modifying the `PixelEditor` component. Add a `tabIndex` property of 0 to the wrapping `<div>` element so that it can receive keyboard focus. Note that the *property* corresponding to the `tabindex` *attribute* is called `tabIndex`, with a capital I, and our `elt` function expects property names. Register the key event handlers directly on that element. This means you have to click, touch, or tab to the application before you can interact with it with the keyboard.

Remember that keyboard events have `ctrlKey` and `metaKey` (for the COMMAND key on a Mac) properties that you can use to see whether those keys are held down.

Efficient Drawing

During drawing, the majority of work that our application does happens in `drawPicture`. Creating a new state and updating the rest of the DOM isn't very expensive, but repainting all the pixels on the canvas is quite a bit of work.

Find a way to make the syncState method of PictureCanvas faster by re-drawing only the pixels that actually changed.

Remember that drawPicture is also used by the save button, so if you change it, either make sure the changes don't break the old use or create a new version with a different name.

Also note that changing the size of a <canvas> element (by setting its width or height properties) clears it, making it entirely transparent again.

Circles

Define a tool called circle that draws a filled circle when you drag. The center of the circle lies at the point where the drag or touch gesture starts, and its radius is determined by the distance dragged.

Proper Lines

This is a more advanced exercise than the preceding two, and it will require you to design a solution to a nontrivial problem. Make sure you have plenty of time and patience before starting to work on this exercise, and do not get discouraged by initial failures.

On most browsers, when you use the draw tool and quickly drag across the picture, you don't get a closed line. Rather, you get dots with gaps between them because the "mousemove" or "touchmove" events did not fire quickly enough to hit every pixel.

Improve the draw tool to make it draw a full line. This means you have to make the motion handler function remember the previous position and connect that to the current one. To do this, since the pixels can be an arbitrary distance apart, you'll have to write a general line drawing function.

A line between two pixels is a connected chain of pixels that is as straight as possible. Diagonally adjacent pixels count as connected, so a slanted line should look like the picture on the left, not the picture on the right.

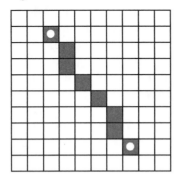 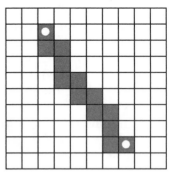

Finally, if we have code that draws a line between two arbitrary points, we might as well use it to also define a line tool, which draws a straight line between the start and end of a drag.

PART III

NODE

"A student asked, 'The programmers of old used only simple machines and no programming languages, yet they made beautiful programs. Why do we use complicated machines and programming languages?'
Fu-Tzu replied, 'The builders of old used only sticks and clay, yet they made beautiful huts.'"

—Master Yuan-Ma, *The Book of Programming*

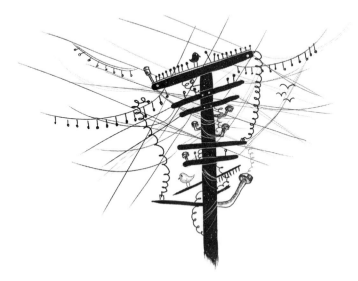

20

NODE.JS

So far, we've used the JavaScript language in a single environment: the browser. This chapter and the next briefly introduce Node.js, a program that allows you to apply your JavaScript skills outside of the browser. With Node.js, you can build anything from small command line tools to HTTP servers that power dynamic websites.

These chapters aim to teach you the main concepts that Node.js uses and to give you enough information to write useful programs for it. They do not try to be a complete, or even a thorough, treatment of the platform.

If you want to follow along and run the code in this chapter, you'll need to install Node.js version 10.1 or higher. To do so, go to *https://nodejs.org* and follow the installation instructions for your operating system. You can also find further documentation for Node.js there.

Background

One of the more difficult problems with writing systems that communicate over the network is managing input and output—that is, the reading and writing of data to and from the network and hard drive. Moving data around takes time, and scheduling it cleverly can make a big difference in how quickly a system responds to the user or to network requests.

In such programs, asynchronous programming is often helpful. It allows the program to send and receive data from and to multiple devices at the same time without complicated thread management and synchronization.

Node was initially conceived for the purpose of making asynchronous programming easy and convenient. JavaScript lends itself well to a system like Node. It is one of the few programming languages that does not have a built-in way to do input and output. Thus, JavaScript could be fit onto Node's rather eccentric approach to in- and output without ending up with two inconsistent interfaces. In 2009, when Node was being designed, people were already doing callback-based programming in the browser, so the community around the language was used to an asynchronous programming style.

The node Command

When Node.js is installed on a system, it provides a program called node, which is used to run JavaScript files. Say you have a file hello.js, containing this code:

```
let message = "Hello world";
console.log(message);
```

You can then run node from the command line like this to execute the program:

```
$ node hello.js
Hello world
```

The console.log method in Node does something similar to what it does in the browser. It prints out a piece of text. But in Node, the text will go to the process's standard output stream, rather than to a browser's JavaScript console. When running node from the command line, that means you see the logged values in your terminal.

If you run node without giving it a file, it provides you with a prompt at which you can type JavaScript code and immediately see the result.

```
$ node
> 1 + 1
2
> [-1, -2, -3].map(Math.abs)
[1, 2, 3]
> process.exit(0)
$
```

The process binding, just like the console binding, is available globally in Node. It provides various ways to inspect and manipulate the current program. The exit method ends the process and can be given an exit status code, which tells the program that started node (in this case, the command line shell) whether the program completed successfully (code zero) or encountered an error (any other code).

To find the command line arguments given to your script, you can read process.argv, which is an array of strings. Note that it also includes the name of the node command and your script name, so the actual arguments start at index 2. If showargv.js contains the statement console.log(process.argv), you could run it like this:

```
$ node showargv.js one --and two
["node", "/tmp/showargv.js", "one", "--and", "two"]
```

All the standard JavaScript global bindings, such as Array, Math, and JSON, are also present in Node's environment. Browser-related functionality, such as document or prompt, is not.

Modules

Beyond the bindings I mentioned, such as console and process, Node puts few additional bindings in the global scope. If you want to access built-in functionality, you have to ask the module system for it.

The CommonJS module system, based on the require function, was described in "CommonJS" on page 171. This system is built into Node and is used to load anything from built-in modules to downloaded packages to files that are part of your own program.

When require is called, Node has to resolve the given string to an actual file that it can load. Pathnames that start with /, ./, or ../ are resolved relative to the current module's path, where ./ stands for the current directory, ../ for one directory up, and / for the root of the file system. So if you ask for "./graph" from the file /tmp/robot/robot.js, Node will try to load the file /tmp/robot/graph.js.

The .js extension may be omitted, and Node will add it if such a file exists. If the required path refers to a directory, Node will try to load the file named index.js in that directory.

When a string that does not look like a relative or absolute path is given to require, it is assumed to refer to either a built-in module or a module installed in a node_modules directory. For example, require("fs") will give you Node's built-in file system module. And require("robot") might try to load the library found in node_modules/robot/. A common way to install such libraries is by using NPM, which we'll come back to in a moment.

Let's set up a small project consisting of two files. The first one, called main.js, defines a script that can be called from the command line to reverse a string.

```
const {reverse} = require("./reverse");

// Index 2 holds the first actual command line argument
let argument = process.argv[2];

console.log(reverse(argument));
```

The file reverse.js defines a library for reversing strings, which can be used both by this command line tool and by other scripts that need direct access to a string-reversing function.

```
exports.reverse = function(string) {
  return Array.from(string).reverse().join("");
};
```

Remember that adding properties to exports adds them to the interface of the module. Since Node.js treats files as CommonJS modules, main.js can take the exported reverse function from reverse.js.

We can now call our tool like this:

```
$ node main.js JavaScript
tpircSavaJ
```

Installing with NPM

NPM, which was introduced in Chapter 10, is an online repository of Java-Script modules, many of which are specifically written for Node. When you install Node on your computer, you also get the npm command, which you can use to interact with this repository.

NPM's main use is downloading packages. We saw the ini package in Chapter 10. We can use NPM to fetch and install that package on our computer.

```
$ npm install ini
npm WARN enoent ENOENT: no such file or directory,
         open '/tmp/package.json'
+ ini@1.3.5
added 1 package in 0.552s

$ node
> const {parse} = require("ini");
> parse("x = 1\ny = 2");
{ x: '1', y: '2' }
```

After running npm install, NPM will have created a directory called node_modules. Inside that directory will be an ini directory that contains the library. You can open it and look at the code. When we call `require("ini")`, this library is loaded, and we can call its `parse` property to parse a configuration file.

By default NPM installs packages under the current directory, rather than in a central place. If you are used to other package managers, this may seem unusual, but it has advantages—it puts each application in full control of the packages it installs and makes it easier to manage versions and clean up when removing an application.

Package Files

In the `npm install` example, you could see a warning about the fact that the `package.json` file did not exist. It is recommended to create such a file for each project, either manually or by running `npm init`. It contains some information about the project, such as its name and version, and lists its dependencies.

The robot simulation from Chapter 7, as modularized in the exercise "A Modular Robot" on page 177, might have a `package.json` file like this:

```
{
  "author": "Marijn Haverbeke",
  "name": "eloquent-javascript-robot",
  "description": "Simulation of a package-delivery robot",
  "version": "1.0.0",
  "main": "run.js",
  "dependencies": {
    "dijkstrajs": "^1.0.1",
    "random-item": "^1.0.0"
  },
  "license": "ISC"
}
```

When you run `npm install` without naming a package to install, NPM will install the dependencies listed in `package.json`. When you install a specific package that is not already listed as a dependency, NPM will add it to `package.json`.

Versions

A `package.json` file lists both the program's own version and versions for its dependencies. Versions are a way to deal with the fact that packages evolve separately, and code written to work with a package as it existed at one point may not work with a later, modified version of the package.

NPM demands that its packages follow a schema called *semantic versioning*, which encodes some information about which versions are *compatible* (don't break the old interface) in the version number. A semantic version consists of three numbers, separated by periods, such as 2.3.0. Every time new functionality is added, the middle number has to be incremented.

Every time compatibility is broken, so that existing code that uses the package might not work with the new version, the first number has to be incremented.

A caret character (^) in front of the version number for a dependency in package.json indicates that any version compatible with the given number may be installed. So, for example, "^2.3.0" would mean that any version greater than or equal to 2.3.0 and less than 3.0.0 is allowed.

The npm command is also used to publish new packages or new versions of packages. If you run npm publish in a directory that has a package.json file, it will publish a package with the name and version listed in the JSON file to the registry. Anyone can publish packages to NPM—though only under a package name that isn't in use yet, since it would be somewhat scary if random people could update existing packages.

Since the npm program is a piece of software that talks to an open system—the package registry—there is nothing unique about what it does. Another program, yarn, which can be installed from the NPM registry, fills the same role as npm using a somewhat different interface and installation strategy.

This book won't delve further into the details of NPM usage. Refer to *https://npmjs.org* for further documentation and a way to search for packages.

The File System Module

One of the most commonly used built-in modules in Node is the fs module, which stands for *file system*. It exports functions for working with files and directories.

For example, the function called readFile reads a file and then calls a callback with the file's contents.

```
let {readFile} = require("fs");
readFile("file.txt", "utf8", (error, text) => {
  if (error) throw error;
  console.log("The file contains:", text);
});
```

The second argument to readFile indicates the *character encoding* used to decode the file into a string. There are several ways in which text can be encoded to binary data, but most modern systems use UTF-8. So unless you have reasons to believe another encoding is used, pass "utf8" when reading a text file. If you do not pass an encoding, Node will assume you are interested in the binary data and will give you a Buffer object instead of a string. This is an array-like object that contains numbers representing the bytes (8-bit chunks of data) in the files.

```
const {readFile} = require("fs");
readFile("file.txt", (error, buffer) => {
  if (error) throw error;
```

```
console.log("The file contained", buffer.length, "bytes.",
            "The first byte is:", buffer[0]);
});
```

A similar function, writeFile, is used to write a file to disk.

```
const {writeFile} = require("fs");
writeFile("graffiti.txt", "Node was here", err => {
  if (err) console.log(`Failed to write file: ${err}`);
  else console.log("File written.");
});
```

Here it was not necessary to specify the encoding—writeFile will assume that when it is given a string to write, rather than a Buffer object, it should write it out as text using its default character encoding, which is UTF-8.

The fs module contains many other useful functions: readdir will return the files in a directory as an array of strings, stat will retrieve information about a file, rename will rename a file, unlink will remove one, and so on. See the documentation at *https://nodejs.org* for specifics.

Most of these take a callback function as the last parameter, which they call either with an error (the first argument) or with a successful result (the second). As we saw in Chapter 11, there are downsides to this style of programming—the biggest one being that error handling becomes verbose and error-prone.

Though promises have been part of JavaScript for a while, at the time of writing their integration into Node.js is still a work in progress. There is an object promises exported from the fs package since version 10.1 that contains most of the same functions as fs but uses promises rather than callback functions.

```
const {readFile} = require("fs").promises;
readFile("file.txt", "utf8")
  .then(text => console.log("The file contains:", text));
```

Sometimes you don't need asynchronicity, and it just gets in the way. Many of the functions in fs also have a synchronous variant, which has the same name with Sync added to the end. For example, the synchronous version of readFile is called readFileSync.

```
const {readFileSync} = require("fs");
console.log("The file contains:",
            readFileSync("file.txt", "utf8"));
```

Do note that while such a synchronous operation is being performed, your program is stopped entirely. If it should be responding to the user or to other machines on the network, being stuck on a synchronous action might produce annoying delays.

The HTTP Module

Another central module is called http. It provides functionality for running HTTP servers and making HTTP requests.

This is all it takes to start an HTTP server:

```
const {createServer} = require("http");
let server = createServer((request, response) => {
  response.writeHead(200, {"Content-Type": "text/html"});
  response.write(`
    <h1>Hello!</h1>
    <p>You asked for <code>${request.url}</code></p>`);
  response.end();
});
server.listen(8000);
console.log("Listening! (port 8000)");
```

If you run this script on your own machine, you can point your web browser at *http://localhost:8000/hello* to make a request to your server. It will respond with a small HTML page.

The function passed as argument to createServer is called every time a client connects to the server. The request and response bindings are objects representing the incoming and outgoing data. The first contains information about the request, such as its url property, which tells us to what URL the request was made.

So, when you open that page in your browser, it sends a request to your own computer. This causes the server function to run and send back a response, which you can then see in the browser.

To send something back, you call methods on the response object. The first, writeHead, will write out the response headers (see Chapter 18). You give it the status code (200 for "OK" in this case) and an object that contains header values. The example sets the Content-Type header to inform the client that we'll be sending back an HTML document.

Next, the actual response body (the document itself) is sent with response.write. You are allowed to call this method multiple times if you want to send the response piece by piece, for example to stream data to the client as it becomes available. Finally, response.end signals the end of the response.

The call to server.listen causes the server to start waiting for connections on port 8000. This is why you have to connect to *localhost:8000* to speak to this server, rather than just *localhost*, which would use the default port 80.

When you run this script, the process just sits there and waits. When a script is listening for events—in this case, network connections—node will not automatically exit when it reaches the end of the script. To close it, press CTRL-C.

A real web server usually does more than the one in the example—it looks at the request's method (the method property) to see what action the client is trying to perform and looks at the request's URL to find out which resource this action is being performed on. We'll see a more advanced server in "A File Server" on page 363.

To act as an HTTP *client*, we can use the request function in the http module.

```
const {request} = require("http");
let requestStream = request({
  hostname: "eloquentjavascript.net",
  path: "/20_node.html",
  method: "GET",
  headers: {Accept: "text/html"}
}, response => {
  console.log("Server responded with status code",
              response.statusCode);
});
requestStream.end();
```

The first argument to request configures the request, telling Node what server to talk to, what path to request from that server, which method to use, and so on. The second argument is the function that should be called when a response comes in. It is given an object that allows us to inspect the response, for example to find out its status code.

Just like the response object we saw in the server, the object returned by request allows us to stream data into the request with the write method and finish the request with the end method. The example does not use write because GET requests should not contain data in their request body.

There's a similar request function in the https module that can be used to make requests to *https:* URLs.

Making requests with Node's raw functionality is rather verbose. There are much more convenient wrapper packages available on NPM. For example, node-fetch provides the promise-based fetch interface that we know from the browser.

Streams

We've seen two instances of writable streams in the HTTP examples—namely, the response object that the server could write to and the request object that was returned from request.

Writable streams are a widely used concept in Node. Such objects have a write method that can be passed a string or a Buffer object to write something to the stream. Their end method closes the stream and optionally takes a value to write to the stream before closing. Both of these methods can also be given a callback as an additional argument, which they will call when the writing or closing has finished.

It is possible to create a writable stream that points at a file with the createWriteStream function from the fs module. Then you can use the write method on the resulting object to write the file one piece at a time, rather than in one shot as with writeFile.

Readable streams are a little more involved. Both the request binding that was passed to the HTTP server's callback and the response binding passed to the HTTP client's callback are readable streams—a server reads requests and then writes responses, whereas a client first writes a request and then reads a response. Reading from a stream is done using event handlers, rather than methods.

Objects that emit events in Node have a method called on that is similar to the addEventListener method in the browser. You give it an event name and then a function, and it will register that function to be called whenever the given event occurs.

Readable streams have "data" and "end" events. The first is fired every time data comes in, and the second is called whenever the stream is at its end. This model is most suited for *streaming* data that can be immediately processed, even when the whole document isn't available yet. A file can be read as a readable stream by using the createReadStream function from fs.

This code creates a server that reads request bodies and streams them back to the client as all-uppercase text:

```
const {createServer} = require("http");
createServer((request, response) => {
  response.writeHead(200, {"Content-Type": "text/plain"});
  request.on("data", chunk =>
    response.write(chunk.toString().toUpperCase()));
  request.on("end", () => response.end());
}).listen(8000);
```

The chunk value passed to the data handler will be a binary Buffer. We can convert this to a string by decoding it as UTF-8 encoded characters with its toString method.

The following piece of code, when run with the uppercasing server active, will send a request to that server and write out the response it gets:

```
const {request} = require("http");
request({
  hostname: "localhost",
  port: 8000,
  method: "POST"
}, response => {
  response.on("data", chunk =>
    process.stdout.write(chunk.toString()));
}).end("Hello server");
// → HELLO SERVER
```

The example writes to `process.stdout` (the process's standard output, which is a writable stream) instead of using `console.log`. We can't use `console.log` because it adds an extra newline character after each piece of text that it writes, which isn't appropriate here since the response may come in as multiple chunks.

A File Server

Let's combine our newfound knowledge about HTTP servers and working with the file system to create a bridge between the two: an HTTP server that allows remote access to a file system. Such a server has all kinds of uses—it allows web applications to store and share data, or it can give a group of people shared access to a bunch of files.

When we treat files as HTTP resources, the HTTP methods GET, PUT, and DELETE can be used to read, write, and delete the files, respectively. We will interpret the path in the request as the path of the file that the request refers to.

We probably don't want to share our whole file system, so we'll interpret these paths as starting in the server's working directory, which is the directory in which it was started. If I ran the server from /tmp/public/ (or C:\tmp\public\ on Windows), then a request for /file.txt should refer to /tmp/public/file.txt (or C:\tmp\public\file.txt).

We'll build the program piece by piece, using an object called methods to store the functions that handle the various HTTP methods. Method handlers are async functions that get the request object as argument and return a promise that resolves to an object that describes the response.

```
const {createServer} = require("http");

const methods = Object.create(null);

createServer((request, response) => {
  let handler = methods[request.method] || notAllowed;
  handler(request)
    .catch(error => {
      if (error.status != null) return error;
      return {body: String(error), status: 500};
    })
    .then(({body, status = 200, type = "text/plain"}) => {
      response.writeHead(status, {"Content-Type": type});
      if (body && body.pipe) body.pipe(response);
      else response.end(body);
    });
}).listen(8000);
```

```
async function notAllowed(request) {
  return {
    status: 405,
    body: `Method ${request.method} not allowed.`
  };
}
```

This starts a server that just returns 405 error responses, which is the code used to indicate that the server refuses to handle a given method.

When a request handler's promise is rejected, the catch call translates the error into a response object, if it isn't one already, so that the server can send back an error response to inform the client that it failed to handle the request.

The status field of the response description may be omitted, in which case it defaults to 200 (OK). The content type, in the type property, can also be left off, in which case the response is assumed to be plain text.

When the value of body is a readable stream, it will have a pipe method that is used to forward all content from a readable stream to a writable stream. If not, it is assumed to be either null (no body), a string, or a buffer, and it is passed directly to the response's end method.

To figure out which file path corresponds to a request URL, the urlPath function uses Node's built-in url module to parse the URL. It takes its pathname, which will be something like "/file.txt", decodes that to get rid of the %20-style escape codes, and resolves it relative to the program's working directory.

```
const {parse} = require("url");
const {resolve, sep} = require("path");

const baseDirectory = process.cwd();

function urlPath(url) {
  let {pathname} = parse(url);
  let path = resolve(decodeURIComponent(pathname).slice(1));
  if (path != baseDirectory &&
      !path.startsWith(baseDirectory + sep)) {
    throw {status: 403, body: "Forbidden"};
  }
  return path;
}
```

As soon as you set up a program to accept network requests, you have to start worrying about security. In this case, if we aren't careful, it is likely that we'll accidentally expose our whole file system to the network.

File paths are strings in Node. To map such a string to an actual file, there is a nontrivial amount of interpretation happening. Paths may, for example, include ../ to refer to a parent directory. So one obvious source of problems would be requests for paths like /../secret_file.

To avoid such problems, urlPath uses the resolve function from the path module, which resolves relative paths. It then verifies that the result is *below* the working directory. The process.cwd function (where cwd stands for *current working directory*) can be used to find this working directory. The sep binding from the path package is the system's path separator—a backslash on Windows and a forward slash on most other systems. When the path doesn't start with the base directory, the function throws an error response object, using the HTTP status code indicating that access to the resource is forbidden.

We'll set up the GET method to return a list of files when reading a directory and to return the file's content when reading a regular file.

One tricky question is what kind of Content-Type header we should set when returning a file's content. Since these files could be anything, our server can't simply return the same content type for all of them. NPM can help us again here. The mime package (content type indicators like text/plain are also called *MIME types*) knows the correct type for a large number of file extensions.

The following npm command, in the directory where the server script lives, installs a specific version of mime:

```
$ npm install mime@2.2.0
```

When a requested file does not exist, the correct HTTP status code to return is 404. We'll use the stat function, which looks up information about a file, to find out both whether the file exists and whether it is a directory.

```
const {createReadStream} = require("fs");
const {stat, readdir} = require("fs").promises;
const mime = require("mime");

methods.GET = async function(request) {
  let path = urlPath(request.url);
  let stats;
  try {
    stats = await stat(path);
  } catch (error) {
    if (error.code != "ENOENT") throw error;
    else return {status: 404, body: "File not found"};
  }
  if (stats.isDirectory()) {
    return {body: (await readdir(path)).join("\n")};
  } else {
    return {body: createReadStream(path),
            type: mime.getType(path)};
  }
};
```

Because it has to touch the disk and thus might take a while, stat is asynchronous. Since we're using promises rather than callback style, it has to be imported from promises instead of directly from fs.

When the file does not exist, stat will throw an error object with a code property of "ENOENT". These somewhat obscure, Unix-inspired codes are how you recognize error types in Node.

The stats object returned by stat tells us a number of things about a file, such as its size (size property) and its modification date (mtime property). Here we are interested in the question of whether it is a directory or a regular file, which the isDirectory method tells us.

We use readdir to read the array of files in a directory and return it to the client. For normal files, we create a readable stream with createReadStream and return that as the body, along with the content type that the mime package gives us for the file's name.

The code to handle DELETE requests is slightly simpler.

```
const {rmdir, unlink} = require("fs").promises;

methods.DELETE = async function(request) {
  let path = urlPath(request.url);
  let stats;
  try {
    stats = await stat(path);
  } catch (error) {
    if (error.code != "ENOENT") throw error;
    else return {status: 204};
  }
  if (stats.isDirectory()) await rmdir(path);
  else await unlink(path);
  return {status: 204};
};
```

When an HTTP response does not contain any data, the status code 204 ("no content") can be used to indicate this. Since the response to deletion doesn't need to transmit any information beyond whether the operation succeeded, that is a sensible thing to return here.

You may be wondering why trying to delete a nonexistent file returns a success status code, rather than an error. When the file that is being deleted is not there, you could say that the request's objective is already fulfilled. The HTTP standard encourages us to make requests *idempotent*, which means that making the same request multiple times produces the same result as making it once. In a way, if you try to delete something that's already gone, the effect you were trying to do has been achieved—the thing is no longer there.

This is the handler for PUT requests:

```
const {createWriteStream} = require("fs");

function pipeStream(from, to) {
  return new Promise((resolve, reject) => {
    from.on("error", reject);
    to.on("error", reject);
    to.on("finish", resolve);
    from.pipe(to);
  });
}

methods.PUT = async function(request) {
  let path = urlPath(request.url);
  await pipeStream(request, createWriteStream(path));
  return {status: 204};
};
```

We don't need to check whether the file exists this time—if it does, we'll just overwrite it. We again use pipe to move data from a readable stream to a writable one, in this case from the request to the file. But since pipe isn't written to return a promise, we have to write a wrapper, pipeStream, that creates a promise around the outcome of calling pipe.

When something goes wrong when opening the file, createWriteStream will still return a stream, but that stream will fire an "error" event. The output stream to the request may also fail, for example if the network goes down. So we wire up both streams' "error" events to reject the promise. When pipe is done, it will close the output stream, which causes it to fire a "finish" event. That's the point where we can successfully resolve the promise (returning nothing).

The full script for the server is available at *https://eloquentjavascript.net/code/file_server.js*. You can download that and, after installing its dependencies, run it with Node to start your own file server. And, of course, you can modify and extend it to solve this chapter's exercises or to experiment.

The command line tool curl, widely available on Unix-like systems (such as macOS and Linux), can be used to make HTTP requests. The following session briefly tests our server. The -X option is used to set the request's method, and -d is used to include a request body.

```
$ curl http://localhost:8000/file.txt
File not found
$ curl -X PUT -d hello http://localhost:8000/file.txt
$ curl http://localhost:8000/file.txt
hello
```

```
$ curl -X DELETE http://localhost:8000/file.txt
$ curl http://localhost:8000/file.txt
File not found
```

The first request for file.txt fails since the file does not exist yet. The PUT request creates the file, and behold, the next request successfully retrieves it. After deleting it with a DELETE request, the file is again missing.

Summary

Node is a nice, small system that lets us run JavaScript in a nonbrowser context. It was originally designed for network tasks to play the role of a *node* in a network. But it lends itself to all kinds of scripting tasks, and if writing JavaScript is something you enjoy, automating tasks with Node works well.

NPM provides packages for everything you can think of (and quite a few things you'd probably never think of), and it allows you to fetch and install those packages with the npm program. Node comes with a number of built-in modules, including the fs module for working with the file system and the http module for running HTTP servers and making HTTP requests.

All input and output in Node is done asynchronously, unless you explicitly use a synchronous variant of a function, such as readFileSync. When calling such asynchronous functions, you provide callback functions, and Node will call them with an error value and (if available) a result when it is ready.

Exercises

Search Tool

On Unix systems, there is a command line tool called grep that can be used to quickly search files for a regular expression.

Write a Node script that can be run from the command line and acts somewhat like grep. It treats its first command line argument as a regular expression and treats any further arguments as files to search. It should output the names of any file whose content matches the regular expression.

When that works, extend it so that when one of the arguments is a directory, it searches through all files in that directory and its subdirectories.

Use asynchronous or synchronous file system functions as you see fit. Setting things up so that multiple asynchronous actions are requested at the same time might speed things up a little, but not a huge amount, since most file systems can read only one thing at a time.

Directory Creation

Though the DELETE method in our file server is able to delete directories (using rmdir), the server currently does not provide any way to *create* a directory.

Add support for the MKCOL method ("make collection"), which should create a directory by calling mkdir from the fs module. MKCOL is not a widely used HTTP method, but it does exist for this same purpose in the *WebDAV* standard, which specifies a set of conventions on top of HTTP that make it suitable for creating documents.

A Public Space on the Web

Since the file server serves up any kind of file and even includes the right Content-Type header, you can use it to serve a website. Since it allows everybody to delete and replace files, it would be an interesting kind of website: one that can be modified, improved, and vandalized by everybody who takes the time to create the right HTTP request.

Write a basic HTML page that includes a simple JavaScript file. Put the files in a directory served by the file server and open them in your browser.

Next, as an advanced exercise or even a weekend project, combine all the knowledge you gained from this book to build a more user-friendly interface for modifying the website—from *inside* the website.

Use an HTML form to edit the content of the files that make up the website, allowing the user to update them on the server by using HTTP requests, as described in Chapter 18.

Start by making only a single file editable. Then make it so that the user can select which file to edit. Use the fact that our file server returns lists of files when reading a directory.

Don't work directly in the code exposed by the file server since if you make a mistake, you are likely to damage the files there. Instead, keep your work outside of the publicly accessible directory and copy it there when testing.

"If you have knowledge, let others light
their candles at it."
—Margaret Fuller

21

PROJECT: SKILL-SHARING WEBSITE

A *skill-sharing* meeting is an event where people with a shared interest come together and give small, informal presentations about things they know. At a gardening skill-sharing meeting, someone might explain how to cultivate celery. Or in a programming skill-sharing group, you could drop by and tell people about Node.js.

Such meetups—also often called *users' groups* when they are about computers—are a great way to broaden your horizons, learn about new developments, or simply meet people with similar interests. Many larger cities have JavaScript meetups. They are typically free to attend, and I've found the ones I've visited to be friendly and welcoming.

In this final project chapter, our goal is to set up a website for managing talks given at a skill-sharing meeting. Imagine a small group of people meeting up regularly in the office of one of the members to talk about unicycling. The previous organizer of the meetings moved to another town, and nobody stepped forward to take over this task. We want a system that will let the participants propose and discuss talks among themselves, without a central organizer.

The full code for the project can be downloaded from the book's website at *https://eloquentjavascript.net/code/skillsharing.zip*.

Design

There is a *server* part to this project, written for Node.js, and a *client* part, written for the browser. The server stores the system's data and provides it to the client. It also serves the files that implement the client-side system.

The server keeps the list of talks proposed for the next meeting, and the client shows this list. Each talk has a presenter name, a title, a summary, and an array of comments associated with it. The client allows users to propose new talks (adding them to the list), delete talks, and comment on existing talks. Whenever the user makes such a change, the client makes an HTTP request to tell the server about it.

Skill Sharing

Your name:

Fatma

Unituning [Delete]
by **Jamal**

Modifying your cycle for extra style

Iman: *Will you talk about raising a cycle?*
Jamal: *Definitely*
Iman: *I'll be there*
[   ] [Add comment]

Submit a talk
Title:
[   ]
Summary:
[   ]
[Submit]

The application will be set up to show a *live* view of the current proposed talks and their comments. Whenever someone, somewhere, submits a new talk or adds a comment, all people who have the page open in their browsers should immediately see the change. This poses a bit of a challenge—there is no way for a web server to open a connection to a client, nor is there a good way to know which clients are currently looking at a given website.

A common solution to this problem is called *long polling*, which happens to be one of the motivations for Node's design.

Long Polling

To be able to immediately notify a client that something changed, we need a connection to that client. Since web browsers do not traditionally accept connections and clients are often behind routers that would block such connections anyway, having the server initiate this connection is not practical.

We can arrange for the client to open the connection and keep it around so that the server can use it to send information when it needs to do so.

But an HTTP request allows only a simple flow of information: the client sends a request, the server comes back with a single response, and that is it. There is a technology called *WebSockets*, supported by modern browsers, that makes it possible to open connections for arbitrary data exchange. But using them properly is somewhat tricky.

In this chapter, we use a simpler technique—long polling—where clients continuously ask the server for new information using regular HTTP requests, and the server stalls its answer when it has nothing new to report.

As long as the client makes sure it constantly has a polling request open, it will receive information from the server quickly after it becomes available. For example, if Fatma has our skill-sharing application open in her browser, that browser will have made a request for updates and will be waiting for a response to that request. When Iman submits a talk on Extreme Downhill Unicycling, the server will notice that Fatma is waiting for updates and send a response containing the new talk to her pending request. Fatma's browser will receive the data and update the screen to show the talk.

To prevent connections from timing out (being aborted because of a lack of activity), long polling techniques usually set a maximum time for each request, after which the server will respond anyway, even though it has nothing to report, after which the client will start a new request. Periodically restarting the request also makes the technique more robust, allowing clients to recover from temporary connection failures or server problems.

A busy server that is using long polling may have thousands of waiting requests, and thus TCP connections, open. Node, which makes it easy to manage many connections without creating a separate thread of control for each one, is a good fit for such a system.

HTTP Interface

Before we start designing either the server or the client, let's think about the point where they touch: the HTTP interface over which they communicate.

We will use JSON as the format of our request and response body. Like in the file server from Chapter 20, we'll try to make good use of HTTP methods and headers. The interface is centered around the /talks path. Paths that do not start with /talks will be used for serving static files—the HTML and JavaScript code for the client-side system.

A GET request to /talks returns a JSON document like this:

```
[{"title": "Unituning",
  "presenter": "Jamal",
  "summary": "Modifying your cycle for extra style",
  "comments": []}]
```

Creating a new talk is done by making a PUT request to a URL like /talks/Unituning, where the part after the second slash is the title of the talk. The PUT request's body should contain a JSON object that has presenter and summary properties.

Since talk titles may contain spaces and other characters that may not appear normally in a URL, title strings must be encoded with the encodeURIComponent function when building up such a URL.

```
console.log("/talks/" + encodeURIComponent("How to Idle"));
// → /talks/How%20to%20Idle
```

A request to create a talk about idling might look something like this:

```
PUT /talks/How%20to%20Idle HTTP/1.1
Content-Type: application/json
Content-Length: 92

{"presenter": "Maureen",
 "summary": "Standing still on a unicycle"}
```

Such URLs also support GET requests to retrieve the JSON representation of a talk and DELETE requests to delete a talk.

Adding a comment to a talk is done with a POST request to a URL like /talks/Unituning/comments, with a JSON body that has author and message properties.

```
POST /talks/Unituning/comments HTTP/1.1
Content-Type: application/json
Content-Length: 72

{"author": "Iman",
 "message": "Will you talk about raising a cycle?"}
```

To support long polling, GET requests to /talks may include extra headers that inform the server to delay the response if no new information is available. We'll use a pair of headers normally intended to manage caching: ETag and If-None-Match.

Servers may include an ETag ("entity tag") header in a response. Its value is a string that identifies the current version of the resource. Clients, when they later request that resource again, may make a *conditional request* by including an If-None-Match header whose value holds that same string. If the resource hasn't changed, the server will respond with status code 304, which means "not modified," telling the client that its cached version is still current. When the tag does not match, the server responds as normal.

We need something like this, where the client can tell the server which version of the list of talks it has, and the server responds only when that list has changed. But instead of immediately returning a 304 response, the server should stall the response and return only when something new is available or a given amount of time has elapsed. To distinguish long polling requests from normal conditional requests, we give them another header, Prefer: wait=90, which tells the server that the client is willing to wait up to 90 seconds for the response.

The server will keep a version number that it updates every time the talks change and will use that as the ETag value. Clients can make requests like this to be notified when the talks change:

```
GET /talks HTTP/1.1
If-None-Match: "4"
Prefer: wait=90

(time passes)

HTTP/1.1 200 OK
Content-Type: application/json
ETag: "5"
Content-Length: 295

[....]
```

The protocol described here does not do any access control. Everybody can comment, modify talks, and even delete them. (Since the internet is full of hooligans, putting such a system online without further protection probably wouldn't end well.)

The Server

Let's start by building the server-side part of the program. The code in this section runs on Node.js.

Routing

Our server will use createServer to start an HTTP server. In the function that handles a new request, we must distinguish between the various kinds of requests (as determined by the method and the path) that we support. This can be done with a long chain of if statements, but there is a nicer way.

A *router* is a component that helps dispatch a request to the function that can handle it. You can tell the router, for example, that PUT requests with a path that matches the regular expression /^\/talks\/([^\/]+)$/ (/talks/ followed by a talk title) can be handled by a given function. In addition, it can help extract the meaningful parts of the path (in this case the talk title), wrapped in parentheses in the regular expression, and pass them to the handler function.

There are a number of good router packages on NPM, but here we'll write one ourselves to illustrate the principle.

This is router.js, which we will later require from our server module:

```
const {parse} = require("url");

module.exports = class Router {
  constructor() {
```

```
    this.routes = [];
  }
  add(method, url, handler) {
    this.routes.push({method, url, handler});
  }
  resolve(context, request) {
    let path = parse(request.url).pathname;

    for (let {method, url, handler} of this.routes) {
      let match = url.exec(path);
      if (!match || request.method != method) continue;
      let urlParts = match.slice(1).map(decodeURIComponent);
      return handler(context, ...urlParts, request);
    }
    return null;
  }
};
```

The module exports the Router class. A router object allows new handlers to be registered with the add method and can resolve requests with its resolve method.

The latter will return a response when a handler was found, and null otherwise. It tries the routes one at a time (in the order in which they were defined) until a matching one is found.

The handler functions are called with the context value (which will be the server instance in our case), match strings for any groups they defined in their regular expression, and the request object. The strings have to be URL-decoded since the raw URL may contain %20-style codes.

Serving Files

When a request matches none of the request types defined in our router, the server must interpret it as a request for a file in the public directory. It would be possible to use the file server defined in Chapter 20 to serve such files, but we neither need nor want to support PUT and DELETE requests on files, and we would like to have advanced features such as support for caching. So let's use a solid, well-tested static file server from NPM instead.

I opted for ecstatic. This isn't the only such server on NPM, but it works well and fits our purposes. The ecstatic package exports a function that can be called with a configuration object to produce a request handler function. We use the root option to tell the server where it should look for files. The handler function accepts request and response parameters and can be passed directly to createServer to create a server that serves *only* files. We want to first check for requests that we should handle specially, though, so we wrap it in another function.

```
const {createServer} = require("http");
const Router = require("./router");
```

```
const ecstatic = require("ecstatic");

const router = new Router();
const defaultHeaders = {"Content-Type": "text/plain"};

class SkillShareServer {
  constructor(talks) {
    this.talks = talks;
    this.version = 0;
    this.waiting = [];

    let fileServer = ecstatic({root: "./public"});
    this.server = createServer((request, response) => {
      let resolved = router.resolve(this, request);
      if (resolved) {
        resolved.catch(error => {
          if (error.status != null) return error;
          return {body: String(error), status: 500};
        }).then(({body,
                  status = 200,
                  headers = defaultHeaders}) => {
          response.writeHead(status, headers);
          response.end(body);
        });
      } else {
        fileServer(request, response);
      }
    });
  }
  start(port) {
    this.server.listen(port);
  }
  stop() {
    this.server.close();
  }
}
```

This uses a similar convention as the file server from the previous chapter for responses—handlers return promises that resolve to objects describing the response. It wraps the server in an object that also holds its state.

Talks as Resources

The talks that have been proposed are stored in the talks property of the server, an object whose property names are the talk titles. These will be exposed as HTTP resources under /talks/[title], so we need to add handlers to our router that implement the various methods that clients can use to work with them.

The handler for requests that GET a single talk must look up the talk and respond either with the talk's JSON data or with a 404 error response.

```
const talkPath = /^\/talks\/([^\/]+)$/;

router.add("GET", talkPath, async (server, title) => {
  if (title in server.talks) {
    return {body: JSON.stringify(server.talks[title]),
            headers: {"Content-Type": "application/json"}};
  } else {
    return {status: 404, body: `No talk '${title}' found`};
  }
});
```

Deleting a talk is done by removing it from the talks object.

```
router.add("DELETE", talkPath, async (server, title) => {
  if (title in server.talks) {
    delete server.talks[title];
    server.updated();
  }
  return {status: 204};
});
```

The updated method, which we will define in the next section, notifies waiting long polling requests about the change.

To retrieve the content of a request body, we define a function called readStream, which reads all content from a readable stream and returns a promise that resolves to a string.

```
function readStream(stream) {
  return new Promise((resolve, reject) => {
    let data = "";
    stream.on("error", reject);
    stream.on("data", chunk => data += chunk.toString());
    stream.on("end", () => resolve(data));
  });
}
```

One handler that needs to read request bodies is the PUT handler, which is used to create new talks. It has to check whether the data it was given has presenter and summary properties, which are strings. Any data coming from outside the system might be nonsense, and we don't want to corrupt our internal data model or crash when bad requests come in.

If the data looks valid, the handler stores an object that represents the new talk in the talks object, possibly overwriting an existing talk with this title, and again calls updated.

```
router.add("PUT", talkPath,
           async (server, title, request) => {
  let requestBody = await readStream(request);
  let talk;
  try { talk = JSON.parse(requestBody); }
  catch (_) { return {status: 400, body: "Invalid JSON"}; }

  if (!talk ||
      typeof talk.presenter != "string" ||
      typeof talk.summary != "string") {
    return {status: 400, body: "Bad talk data"};
  }
  server.talks[title] = {title,
                         presenter: talk.presenter,
                         summary: talk.summary,
                         comments: []};
  server.updated();
  return {status: 204};
});
```

Adding a comment to a talk works similarly. We use readStream to get the content of the request, validate the resulting data, and store it as a comment when it looks valid.

```
router.add("POST", /^\/talks\/([^\/]+)\/comments$/,
           async (server, title, request) => {
  let requestBody = await readStream(request);
  let comment;
  try { comment = JSON.parse(requestBody); }
  catch (_) { return {status: 400, body: "Invalid JSON"}; }

  if (!comment ||
      typeof comment.author != "string" ||
      typeof comment.message != "string") {
    return {status: 400, body: "Bad comment data"};
  } else if (title in server.talks) {
    server.talks[title].comments.push(comment);
    server.updated();
    return {status: 204};
  } else {
    return {status: 404, body: `No talk '${title}' found`};
  }
});
```

Trying to add a comment to a nonexistent talk returns a 404 error.

Long Polling Support

The most interesting aspect of the server is the part that handles long polling. When a GET request comes in for /talks, it may be either a regular request or a long polling request.

There will be multiple places in which we have to send an array of talks to the client, so we first define a helper method that builds up such an array and includes an ETag header in the response.

```
SkillShareServer.prototype.talkResponse = function() {
  let talks = [];
  for (let title of Object.keys(this.talks)) {
    talks.push(this.talks[title]);
  }
  return {
    body: JSON.stringify(talks),
    headers: {"Content-Type": "application/json",
              "ETag": `"${this.version}"`}
  };
};
```

The handler itself needs to look at the request headers to see whether If-None-Match and Prefer headers are present. Node stores headers, whose names are specified to be case insensitive, under their lowercase names.

```
router.add("GET", /^\/talks$/, async (server, request) => {
  let tag = /"(.*)"/.exec(request.headers["if-none-match"]);
  let wait = /\bwait=(\d+)/.exec(request.headers["prefer"]);
  if (!tag || tag[1] != server.version) {
    return server.talkResponse();
  } else if (!wait) {
    return {status: 304};
  } else {
    return server.waitForChanges(Number(wait[1]));
  }
});
```

If no tag was given or a tag was given that doesn't match the server's current version, the handler responds with the list of talks. If the request is conditional and the talks did not change, we consult the Prefer header to see whether we should delay the response or respond right away.

Callback functions for delayed requests are stored in the server's waiting array so that they can be notified when something happens. The waitForChanges method also immediately sets a timer to respond with a 304 status when the request has waited long enough.

```
SkillShareServer.prototype.waitForChanges = function(time) {
  return new Promise(resolve => {
    this.waiting.push(resolve);
    setTimeout(() => {
      if (!this.waiting.includes(resolve)) return;
      this.waiting = this.waiting.filter(r => r != resolve);
      resolve({status: 304});
    }, time * 1000);
  });
};
```

Registering a change with updated increases the version property and wakes up all waiting requests.

```
SkillShareServer.prototype.updated = function() {
  this.version++;
  let response = this.talkResponse();
  this.waiting.forEach(resolve => resolve(response));
  this.waiting = [];
};
```

That concludes the server code. If we create a SkillShareServer instance and start it on port 8000, the resulting HTTP server serves files from the subdirectory public alongside a talk-managing interface under the /talks URL.

```
new SkillShareServer(Object.create(null)).start(8000);
```

The Client

The client-side part of the skill-sharing website consists of three files: a tiny HTML page, a style sheet, and a JavaScript file.

HTML

It is a widely used convention for web servers to try to serve a file named index.html when a request is made directly to a path that corresponds to a directory. The file server module we use, ecstatic, supports this convention. When a request is made to the path /, the server looks for the file ./public/index.html (./public being the root we gave it) and returns that file if found.

Thus, if we want a page to show up when a browser is pointed at our server, we should put it in public/index.html. This is our index file:

```
<!doctype html>
<meta charset="utf-8">
<title>Skill Sharing</title>
<link rel="stylesheet" href="skillsharing.css">
```

```
<h1>Skill Sharing</h1>

<script src="skillsharing_client.js"></script>
```

It defines the document title and includes a style sheet, which defines a few styles to, among other things, make sure there is some space between talks.

At the bottom, it adds a heading at the top of the page and loads the script that contains the client-side application.

Actions

The application state consists of the list of talks and the name of the user, and we'll store it in a {talks, user} object. We don't allow the user interface to directly manipulate the state or send off HTTP requests. Rather, it may emit *actions* that describe what the user is trying to do.

The handleAction function takes such an action and makes it happen. Because our state updates are so simple, state changes are handled in the same function.

```
function handleAction(state, action) {
  if (action.type == "setUser") {
    localStorage.setItem("userName", action.user);
    return Object.assign({}, state, {user: action.user});
  } else if (action.type == "setTalks") {
    return Object.assign({}, state, {talks: action.talks});
  } else if (action.type == "newTalk") {
    fetchOK(talkURL(action.title), {
      method: "PUT",
      headers: {"Content-Type": "application/json"},
      body: JSON.stringify({
        presenter: state.user,
        summary: action.summary
      })
    }).catch(reportError);
  } else if (action.type == "deleteTalk") {
    fetchOK(talkURL(action.talk), {method: "DELETE"})
      .catch(reportError);
  } else if (action.type == "newComment") {
    fetchOK(talkURL(action.talk) + "/comments", {
      method: "POST",
      headers: {"Content-Type": "application/json"},
      body: JSON.stringify({
        author: state.user,
        message: action.message
      })
```

```
    }).catch(reportError);
  }
  return state;
}
```

We'll store the user's name in localStorage so that it can be restored when the page is loaded.

The actions that need to involve the server make network requests, using fetch, to the HTTP interface described earlier. We use a wrapper function, fetchOK, which makes sure the returned promise is rejected when the server returns an error code.

```
function fetchOK(url, options) {
  return fetch(url, options).then(response => {
    if (response.status < 400) return response;
    else throw new Error(response.statusText);
  });
}
```

This helper function is used to build up a URL for a talk with a given title.

```
function talkURL(title) {
  return "talks/" + encodeURIComponent(title);
}
```

When the request fails, we don't want to have our page just sit there, doing nothing without explanation. So we define a function, reportError, which at least shows the user a dialog that tells them something went wrong.

```
function reportError(error) {
  alert(String(error));
}
```

Rendering Components

We'll use an approach similar to the one we saw in Chapter 19, splitting the application into components. But since some of the components either never need to update or are always fully redrawn when updated, we'll define those not as classes but as functions that directly return a DOM node. For example, here is a component that shows the field where the user can enter their name:

```
function renderUserField(name, dispatch) {
  return elt("label", {}, "Your name: ", elt("input", {
    type: "text",
    value: name,
```

```
    onchange(event) {
      dispatch({type: "setUser", user: event.target.value});
    }
  }));
}
```

The elt function used to construct DOM elements is the one we used in Chapter 19.

A similar function is used to render talks, which include a list of comments and a form for adding a new comment.

```
function renderTalk(talk, dispatch) {
  return elt(
    "section", {className: "talk"},
    elt("h2", null, talk.title, " ", elt("button", {
      type: "button",
      onclick() {
        dispatch({type: "deleteTalk", talk: talk.title});
      }
    }, "Delete")),
    elt("div", null, "by ",
        elt("strong", null, talk.presenter)),
    elt("p", null, talk.summary),
    ...talk.comments.map(renderComment),
    elt("form", {
      onsubmit(event) {
        event.preventDefault();
        let form = event.target;
        dispatch({type: "newComment",
                  talk: talk.title,
                  message: form.elements.comment.value});
        form.reset();
      }
    }, elt("input", {type: "text", name: "comment"}), " ",
       elt("button", {type: "submit"}, "Add comment")));
}
```

The "submit" event handler calls form.reset to clear the form's content after creating a "newComment" action.

When creating moderately complex pieces of DOM, this style of programming starts to look rather messy. There's a widely used (non-standard) JavaScript extension called *JSX* that lets you write HTML directly in your scripts, which can make such code prettier (depending on what you consider pretty). Before you can actually run such code, you have to run a program on your script to convert the pseudo-HTML into JavaScript function calls much like the ones we use here.

Comments are simpler to render.

```
function renderComment(comment) {
  return elt("p", {className: "comment"},
             elt("strong", null, comment.author),
             ": ", comment.message);
}
```

Finally, the form that the user can use to create a new talk is rendered like this:

```
function renderTalkForm(dispatch) {
  let title = elt("input", {type: "text"});
  let summary = elt("input", {type: "text"});
  return elt("form", {
    onsubmit(event) {
      event.preventDefault();
      dispatch({type: "newTalk",
                title: title.value,
                summary: summary.value});
      event.target.reset();
    }
  }, elt("h3", null, "Submit a Talk"),
     elt("label", null, "Title: ", title),
     elt("label", null, "Summary: ", summary),
     elt("button", {type: "submit"}, "Submit"));
}
```

Polling

To start the app we need the current list of talks. Since the initial load is closely related to the long polling process—the ETag from the load must be used when polling—we'll write a function that keeps polling the server for /talks and calls a callback function when a new set of talks is available.

```
async function pollTalks(update) {
  let tag = undefined;
  for (;;) {
    let response;

    try {
      response = await fetchOK("/talks", {
        headers: tag && {"If-None-Match": tag,
                         "Prefer": "wait=90"}
      });
    } catch (e) {
      console.log("Request failed: " + e);
```

```
      await new Promise(resolve => setTimeout(resolve, 500));
      continue;
    }
    if (response.status == 304) continue;
    tag = response.headers.get("ETag");
    update(await response.json());
  }
}
```

This is an async function so that looping and waiting for the request is easier. It runs an infinite loop that, on each iteration, retrieves the list of talks—either normally or, if this isn't the first request, with the headers included that make it a long polling request.

When a request fails, the function waits a moment and then tries again. This way, if your network connection goes away for a while and then comes back, the application can recover and continue updating. The promise resolved via setTimeout is a way to force the async function to wait.

When the server gives back a 304 response, that means a long polling request timed out, so the function should just immediately start the next request. If the response is a normal 200 response, its body is read as JSON and passed to the callback, and its ETag header value is stored for the next iteration.

The Application

The following component ties the whole user interface together:

```
class SkillShareApp {
  constructor(state, dispatch) {
    this.dispatch = dispatch;
    this.talkDOM = elt("div", {className: "talks"});
    this.dom = elt("div", null,
                   renderUserField(state.user, dispatch),
                   this.talkDOM,
                   renderTalkForm(dispatch));
    this.syncState(state);
  }

  syncState(state) {
    if (state.talks != this.talks) {
      this.talkDOM.textContent = "";
      for (let talk of state.talks) {
        this.talkDOM.appendChild(
          renderTalk(talk, this.dispatch));
      }
      this.talks = state.talks;
    }
```

```
    }
  }
```

When the talks change, this component redraws all of them. This is simple but also wasteful. We'll get back to that in the exercises.

We can start the application like this:

```
function runApp() {
  let user = localStorage.getItem("userName") || "Anon";
  let state, app;
  function dispatch(action) {
    state = handleAction(state, action);
    app.syncState(state);
  }

  pollTalks(talks => {
    if (!app) {
      state = {user, talks};
      app = new SkillShareApp(state, dispatch);
      document.body.appendChild(app.dom);
    } else {
      dispatch({type: "setTalks", talks});
    }
  }).catch(reportError);
}

runApp();
```

If you run the server and open two browser windows next to each other for *http://localhost:8000*, you can see that the actions you perform in one window are immediately visible in the other.

Exercises

The following exercises will involve modifying the system defined in this chapter. To work on them, make sure you download the code first (*https://eloquentjavascript.net/code/skillsharing.zip*), have Node installed *https://nodejs.org*, and have installed the project's dependency with npm install.

Disk Persistence

The skill-sharing server keeps its data purely in memory. This means that when it crashes or is restarted for any reason, all talks and comments are lost.

Extend the server so that it stores the talk data to disk and automatically reloads the data when it is restarted. Do not worry about efficiency—do the simplest thing that works.

Comment Field Resets

The wholesale redrawing of talks works pretty well because you usually can't tell the difference between a DOM node and its identical replacement. But there are exceptions. If you start typing something in the comment field for a talk in one browser window and then, in another, add a comment to that talk, the field in the first window will be redrawn, removing both its content and its focus.

In a heated discussion, where multiple people are adding comments at the same time, this would be annoying. Can you come up with a way to solve it?

"The big optimizations come from refining the high-level design, not the individual routines."
—Steve McConnell, *Code Complete*

22

JAVASCRIPT AND PERFORMANCE

Running a computer program on a machine requires bridging the gap between the programming language and the machine's own instruction format. This can be done by writing a program that *interprets* other programs, as we did in Chapter 11, but it is usually done by *compiling* (translating) the program to machine code.

Some languages, such as the C and Rust programming languages, are designed to express exactly those things that the machine is known to be good at. This makes them easy to compile efficiently. JavaScript is designed in a very different way, focusing on simplicity and ease of use instead. Almost none of its features correspond directly to features of the machine. That makes JavaScript a lot more difficult to compile.

Yet somehow modern JavaScript *engines* (the programs that compile and run JavaScript) do manage to run scripts at a surprising speed. It is possible to write JavaScript programs that are about 10 percent as fast as an equivalent C or Rust program. That may still sound like a huge gap, but older JavaScript engines (as well as contemporary implementations of languages with a similar design, such as Python and Ruby), tend to be closer to 1 percent the speed of C. Compared to these languages, modern JavaScript is strikingly fast—so fast that you'll rarely be forced to switch to another language because of performance problems.

Still, you may occasionally need to rewrite your code to avoid the slower aspects of JavaScript. As an example of that process, this chapter works through a speed-hungry program and makes it faster. In the process we'll discuss the way JavaScript engines compile your programs.

Staged Compilation

First you must understand that JavaScript compilers do not simply compile a program once, the way classical compilers do. Instead, code is compiled and recompiled as needed, while the program is running.

With most languages, compiling a big program takes a while. That is usually acceptable because programs are compiled ahead of time and distributed in compiled form.

For JavaScript the situation is different. A website might include a large amount of code that is retrieved in text form and must be compiled every time the website is opened. If that took five minutes, the user wouldn't be happy. A JavaScript compiler must be able to start running a program—even a big program—almost instantaneously.

To do this, JavaScript compilers have multiple compilation strategies. When a website is opened, the scripts are first compiled in a cheap, superficial way. This doesn't result in very fast execution, but it allows the script to start quickly. Functions may not be compiled at all until the first time they are called.

In a typical program, most code is run only a handful of times (or not at all). For these parts of the program, the cheap compilation strategy is sufficient—they won't take much time anyway. But functions that are called often or that contain loops that do a lot of work have to be treated differently. While running the program, the JavaScript engine observes how often each piece of code runs. When it looks like some code might consume a serious amount of time (this is often called *hot code*), it is recompiled with a more advanced but slower compiler. This compiler performs more *optimizations* to produce faster code. There may even be more than two compilation strategies, with ever more expensive optimizations being applied to *very* hot code.

Interleaving running and compiling code means that by the time the clever compiler starts working with a piece of code, it has already been run multiple times. This makes it possible to *observe* the running code and gather information about it. Later in the chapter we'll see how that can allow the compiler to create more efficient code.

Graph Layout

Our example problem for this chapter concerns itself with graphs again. Pictures of graphs can be useful to describe road systems, networks, the way control flows through a computer program, and so on. The following picture shows a graph representing some countries in the Middle East, with edges between those that share land borders:

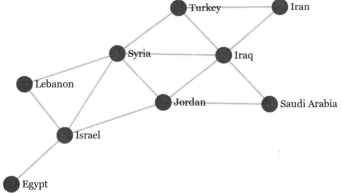

Deriving a picture like this from the definition of a graph is called *graph layout*. It involves assigning a place to each node in such a way that connected nodes are near each other, yet the nodes don't crowd into each other. A random layout of the same graph is a lot harder to interpret.

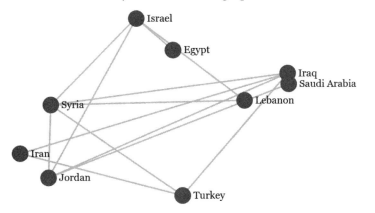

Finding a nice-looking layout for a given graph is a notoriously difficult problem. There is no known solution that reliably does this for arbitrary graphs, and large, densely connected graphs are especially hard. But for some specific types of graphs, for example, *planar* ones (which can be drawn without edges crossing each other), effective approaches exist.

To lay out a small graph (say, up to 200 nodes) that isn't too tangled, we can apply an approach called *force-directed graph layout*. This runs a simplified physics simulation on the nodes of the graph, treating edges as if they are springs and having the nodes themselves repel each other as if electrically charged.

In this chapter we'll implement a force-directed graph layout system and observe its performance. We can run such a simulation by repeatedly computing the forces that act on each node and moving the nodes around in response to those forces. Performance of such a program is important since it might take a lot of iterations to reach a good-looking layout and each iteration computes a lot of forces.

Defining a Graph

We can represent a graph layout as an array of `GraphNode` objects, each of which carries its current position and an array of the nodes to which it has edges. We randomize their starting positions.

```
class GraphNode {
  constructor() {
    this.pos = new Vec(Math.random() * 1000,
                       Math.random() * 1000);
    this.edges = [];
  }
  connect(other) {
    this.edges.push(other);
    other.edges.push(this);
  }
  hasEdge(other) {
    return this.edges.includes(other);
  }
}
```

This uses the familiar `Vec` class from previous chapters to represent positions and forces.

The `connect` method is used to connect a node to another node when building up a graph. To find out whether two nodes are connected, we'll call the `hasEdge` method.

To build up graphs to test our programs, we'll use a function called `treeGraph`. It takes two parameters that specify the depth of the tree and the number of branches to create at each split, and it recursively constructs a tree-shaped graph with the specified shape.

```
function treeGraph(depth, branches) {
  let graph = [new GraphNode()];
  if (depth > 1) {
    for (let i = 0; i < branches; i++) {
      let subGraph = treeGraph(depth - 1, branches);
      graph[0].connect(subGraph[0]);
      graph = graph.concat(subGraph);
    }
  }
  return graph;
}
```

Tree-shaped graphs don't contain cycles, which makes them relatively easy to lay out and allows even the unsophisticated program we build in this chapter to produce good-looking shapes.

The graph created by treeGraph(3, 5) would be a tree of depth 3, with five branches.

To allow us to inspect the layouts produced by our code, I've defined a drawGraph function that draws the graph onto a canvas. This function is defined in the code at *eloquentjavascript.net/code/draw_layout.js* and is available in the online sandbox.

Force-Directed Layout

We'll move nodes one at a time, computing the forces that act on the current node and immediately moving that node in the direction of the sum of these forces.

The force that an (idealized) spring applies can be approximated with Hooke's law, which says that this force is proportional to the difference between the spring's resting length and its current length. The binding springLength defines the resting length of our edge springs. The rigidity of the springs is defined by springStrength, which we'll multiply by the length difference to determine the resulting force.

```
const springLength = 40;
const springStrength = 0.1;
```

To model the repulsion between nodes, we use another physical formula—Coulomb's law—which says that the repulsion between two electrically charged particles is inversely proportional to the square of the distance between them. When two nodes are almost on top of each other, the squared distance is tiny, and the resulting force is gigantic. As the nodes move further apart, the squared distance grows rapidly so that the repelling force quickly weakens.

We'll again multiply by an experimentally determined constant, repulsionStrength, which controls the strength with which nodes repel each other.

```
const repulsionStrength = 1500;
```

The force that acts on a given node is computed by looping over all other nodes and applying the repelling force for each of them. When another node shares an edge with the current node, the force caused by the spring is also applied.

Both of these forces depend on the distance between the two nodes. For each pair of nodes, our function will compute a vector named apart that represents the path from the current node to the other node. The function then takes the length of the vector to find the actual distance. When the distance is less than one, we set it to one to prevent dividing by zero or by very small numbers because that will produce NaN values or forces so gigantic they catapult the node into outer space.

Using this distance, we can compute the magnitude of the force that acts between these two given nodes. To go from a magnitude to a force vector, we must multiply the magnitude by a normalized version of the apart vector. *Normalizing* a vector means creating a vector with the same direction but with a length of one. We can do that by dividing the vector by its own length.

```
function forceDirected_simple(graph) {
  for (let node of graph) {
    for (let other of graph) {
      if (other == node) continue;
      let apart = other.pos.minus(node.pos);
      let distance = Math.max(1, apart.length);
      let forceSize = -repulsionStrength / (distance * distance);
      if (node.hasEdge(other)) {
        forceSize += (distance - springLength) * springStrength;
      }
      let normalized = apart.times(1 / distance);
      node.pos = node.pos.plus(normalized.times(forceSize));
    }
  }
}
```

We will use the following function to test a given implementation of our graph layout system. It runs the model for 4,000 steps and tracks the time this takes. To give us something to look at while the code runs, it draws the current layout of the graph after every 100 steps.

```
function runLayout(implementation, graph) {
  function run(steps, time) {
    let startTime = Date.now();
    for (let i = 0; i < 100; i++) {
      implementation(graph);
    }
    time += Date.now() - startTime;
    drawGraph(graph);
```

```
    if (steps == 0) console.log(time);
    else requestAnimationFrame(() => run(steps - 100, time));
  }
  run(4000, 0);
}
```

We could now run this first implementation and see how much time it takes.

```
<script>
  runLayout(forceDirected_simple, treeGraph(4, 4));
</script>
```

On my machine, using version 58 of the Firefox browser, those 4,000 iterations took a little more than two seconds, so that's two iterations per millisecond. That's a lot. Let's see whether we can do better.

Avoiding Work

The fastest way to do something is to avoid doing it—or at least part of it—at all. By thinking about what the code is doing, you can often spot unnecessary redundancy or things that can be done in a faster way.

In the case of our example project, there is such an opportunity for doing less work. Every pair of nodes has the forces between them computed twice, once when moving the first node and once when moving the second. Since the force that node *X* exerts on node *Y* is exactly the opposite of the force *Y* exerts on *X*, we do not need to compute these forces twice.

The next version of the function changes the inner loop to go over only the nodes that come after the current one so that each pair of nodes is looked at exactly once. After computing a force between a pair of nodes, the function updates the position of both.

```
function forceDirected_noRepeat(graph) {
  for (let i = 0; i < graph.length; i++) {
    let node = graph[i];
    for (let j = i + 1; j < graph.length; j++) {
      let other = graph[j];
      let apart = other.pos.minus(node.pos);
      let distance = Math.max(1, apart.length);
      let forceSize = -repulsionStrength / (distance * distance);
      if (node.hasEdge(other)) {
        forceSize += (distance - springLength) * springStrength;
      }
      let applied = apart.times(forceSize / distance);
      node.pos = node.pos.plus(applied);
      other.pos = other.pos.minus(applied);
    }
```

```
      }
}
```

Measuring this code shows a significant speed boost. It is twice as fast on Firefox 58, about 30 percent faster on Chrome 63, and 75 percent faster on Edge 6.

The big boost on Firefox and Edge is only partially a result of the actual optimization. Because we need the inner loop to go over only part of the array, the new function replaces the for/of loops with regular for loops. On Chrome, this has no measurable effect on the speed of the program, but on Firefox simply not using iterators makes the code 20 percent faster—and on Edge it makes a 50 percent difference.

So, different JavaScript engines work differently and may run programs at different speeds. A change that makes code run faster in one engine may not help (or may even hurt) in another engine—or even a different version of the same engine.

Interestingly, Chrome's engine, which is called V8 and is also the one Node.js uses, is able to optimize for/of loops over arrays to code that's no slower than looping over the index. Remember that the iterator interface involves a method call that returns an object for each element in the iterator. Somehow, V8 manages to optimize most of that away.

Taking another good look at what our program is doing, possibly by calling console.log to output forceSize, it becomes clear that the forces generated between most pairs of nodes are so tiny that they aren't really impacting the layout at all. Specifically, when nodes are not connected and are far away from each other, the forces between them don't amount to much. Yet we still compute vectors for them and move the nodes a tiny bit. What if we just didn't?

This next version defines a distance above which pairs of (unconnected) nodes will no longer compute and apply forces. With that distance set to 175, forces below 0.05 are ignored.

```
const skipDistance = 175;

function forceDirected_skip(graph) {
  for (let i = 0; i < graph.length; i++) {
    let node = graph[i];
    for (let j = i + 1; j < graph.length; j++) {
      let other = graph[j];
      let apart = other.pos.minus(node.pos);
      let distance = Math.max(1, apart.length);
      let hasEdge = node.hasEdge(other);
      if (!hasEdge && distance > skipDistance) continue;
      let forceSize = -repulsionStrength / (distance * distance);
      if (hasEdge) {
        forceSize += (distance - springLength) * springStrength;
      }
      let applied = apart.times(forceSize / distance);
```

```
      node.pos = node.pos.plus(applied);
      other.pos = other.pos.minus(applied);
    }
  }
}
```

This yields another 50 percent improvement in speed, with no discernable degradation of the layout. We cut a corner and got away with it.

Profiling

We were able to speed up the program quite a bit just by reasoning about it. But when it comes *micro-optimization*—the process of doing things slightly differently to make them faster—it is usually hard to predict which changes will help and which won't. There we can no longer rely on reasoning—we have to *observe*.

Our runLayout function measures the time the program currently takes. That's a good start. To improve something, you must measure it. Without measuring, you have no way of knowing whether your changes are having the effect you intended.

The developer tools in modern browsers provide an even better way to measure the speed of your program. This tool is called a *profiler*. It will, while a program is running, gather information about the time used by the various parts of the program.

If your browser has a profiler, it will be available from the developer tool interface, probably on a tab called Performance. The profiler in Chrome spits out the following table when I have it record 4,000 iterations of our current program:

Self time		Total time		Function
816.6 ms	75.4 %	1030.4 ms	95.2 %	forceDirected_skip
194.1 ms	17.9 %	199.8 ms	18.5 %	includes
32.0 ms	3.0 %	32.0 ms	3.0 %	Minor GC
2.1 ms	0.2 %	1043.6 ms	96.4 %	run

This lists the functions (or other tasks) that took a serious amount of time. For each function, it reports the time spent executing the function, both in milliseconds and as a percentage of the total time taken. The first column shows only the time that control was actually in the function, whereas the second column includes time spent in functions called by this function.

As far as profiles go, that's a *very* simple one since the program doesn't *have* a lot of functions. For more complicated programs, the lists will be much, much longer. But because the functions that take the most time are shown at the top, it is still usually easy to find the interesting information.

From this table, we can tell that by far the most time is spent in the physics simulation function. That wasn't unexpected. But on the second row, we see the includes array method, as used in GraphNode.hasEdge, taking up about 18 percent of the program's time.

That *is* a bit more than I expected. We are calling it a lot—in an 85-node graph (which you get with treeGraph(4, 4)), there are 3,570 pairs of nodes. So with 4,000 iterations, that's more than 14 million calls to hasEdge.

Let's see whether we can do better. We add another variant of the hasEdge method to the GraphNode class and create a new variant of our simulation function that calls that instead of hasEdge.

```
GraphNode.prototype.hasEdgeFast = function(other) {
  for (let i = 0; i < this.edges.length; i++) {
    if (this.edges[i] === other) return true;
  }
  return false;
};
```

On Chrome, this shaves about 17 percent off the time it takes to compute the layout, which is most of the time taken by includes in the profile. On Edge, it makes the program 40 percent faster. But on Firefox, it makes it slightly (about 3 percent) slower. So, in this case, Firefox's engine (called SpiderMonkey) did a better job optimizing calls to includes.

The row labeled "Minor GC" in the profile gives us the time spent cleaning up memory that is no longer being used. Given that our program creates a huge number of vector objects, the 3 percent time spent reclaiming memory is strikingly low. JavaScript engines tend to have very effective garbage collectors.

Function Inlining

No vector methods (such as times) show up in the profile we saw, even though they are being used heavily. This is because the compiler *inlined* them. Rather than having the code in the inner function call an actual method to multiply vectors, the vector-multiplication code is put directly inside the function, and no actual method calls happen in the compiled code.

There are various ways in which inlining helps make code fast. Functions and methods are, at the machine level, called using a protocol that requires putting the arguments and the return address (the place where execution must continue when the function returns) somewhere the function can find them. The way a function call gives control to another part of the program also often requires saving some of the processor's state so that the called function can use the processor without interfering with data that the caller still needs. All of this becomes unnecessary when a function is inlined.

Furthermore, a good compiler will do its best to find ways to simplify the code it generates. If functions are treated as black boxes that might do anything, the compiler does not have a lot to work with. On the other hand, if it can see and include the function body in its analysis, it might find additional opportunities to optimize the code.

For example, a JavaScript engine could avoid creating some of the vector objects in our code altogether. In an expression like the following one, if we can see through the methods, it is clear that the resulting vector's coordinates are the result of adding force's coordinates to the product of normalized's coordinates and the forceSize binding. Thus, there is no need to create the intermediate object produced by the times method.

```
pos.plus(normalized.times(forceSize))
```

But JavaScript allows us to replace methods at any time. How does the compiler figure out which function this times method actually is? And what if someone changes the value stored in Vec.prototype.times later? The next time code that has inlined that function runs, it might continue to use the old definition, violating the programmer's assumptions about the way their program behaves.

This is where the interleaving of execution and compilation starts to pay off. When a hot function is compiled, it has already run a number of times. If, during those runs, it always called the same function, it is reasonable to try inlining that function. The code is optimistically compiled with the assumption that, in the future, the same function is going to be called here.

To handle the pessimistic case, where another function ends up being called, the compiler inserts a test that compares the called function to the one that was inlined. If the two do not match, the optimistically compiled code is wrong, and the JavaScript engine must *deoptimize*, meaning it falls back to a less optimized version of the code.

Creating Less Garbage

Though some of the vector objects that we are creating might be optimized away entirely by some engines, there is likely still a cost to creating all those objects. To estimate the size of this cost, let's write a version of the code that does the vector computations "by hand," using local bindings for both dimensions.

```
function forceDirected_noVector(graph) {
  for (let i = 0; i < graph.length; i++) {
    let node = graph[i];
    for (let j = i + 1; j < graph.length; j++) {
      let other = graph[j];
      let apartX = other.pos.x - node.pos.x;
      let apartY = other.pos.y - node.pos.y;
      let distance = Math.max(1, Math.sqrt(apartX * apartX +
                                          apartY * apartY));
      let hasEdge = node.hasEdgeFast(other);
      if (!hasEdge && distance > skipDistance) continue;
      let forceSize = -repulsionStrength / (distance * distance);
      if (hasEdge) {
```

```
        forceSize += (distance - springLength) * springStrength;
      }
      let forceX = apartX * forceSize / distance;
      let forceY = apartY * forceSize / distance;
      node.pos.x += forceX; node.pos.y += forceY;
      other.pos.x -= forceX; other.pos.y -= forceY;
    }
  }
}
```

The new code is wordier and more repetitive, but if I measure it, the improvement is large enough to consider doing this kind of manual object flattening in performance-sensitive code. On both Firefox and Chrome the new version is about 30 percent faster than the previous one. On Edge it's about 60 percent faster.

Taking all these steps together, we've made the program about 5 times faster than the initial version on Chrome and Firefox and more than 20 times faster on Edge. That's quite an improvement. But remember that doing this work is useful only for code that actually takes a lot of time. Trying to optimize everything right away will only slow you down and leave you with a lot of needlessly overcomplicated code.

Garbage Collection

So why is the code that avoids creating objects faster? There are several reasons. The engine has to find a place to store the objects, it has to figure out when they are no longer used and reclaim them, and when you access their properties, it has to figure out where in memory those are stored. JavaScript engines are good at all these things but usually not so good that they become free.

Imagine memory, again, as a long, long row of bits. When the program starts, it might receive an empty piece of memory and just start putting the objects it creates in there, one after the other. But at some point, the space is full, and some of the objects in it are no longer used. The JavaScript engine has to figure out which objects are used, and which are not, so that it can reuse the unused pieces of memory.

Now the program's memory space is a bit of a mess, containing living objects interspersed with free space. Creating a new object involves finding a piece of free space large enough for the object, which might require some searching. Alternatively, the engine could move all live objects to the start of the memory space, which makes creating new objects cheaper (they can just be put one after the other again) but requires more work when moving the old objects.

In principle, figuring out which objects are still used requires tracing through all reachable objects, starting from the global scope and the currently active local scope. Any object referenced from those scopes, directly or indirectly, is still alive. If your program has a lot of data in memory, this is quite a lot of work.

A technique called *generational garbage collection* can help reduce these costs. This approach exploits the fact that most objects have short lives. It splits the memory available to the JavaScript program into two or more *generations*. New objects are created in the space reserved for the young generation. When this space is full, the engine figures out which of the objects in it are still alive and moves those to the next generation. If only a small fraction of the objects in the young generation are still alive when this occurs, only a small amount of work has to be done to move them.

Of course, figuring out which objects are alive does require knowing about all references to objects in the live generation. The garbage collector wants to avoid looking through all the objects in the older generations every time the young generation is collected. So when a reference is created from an old object to a new object, this reference must be recorded so that it can be taken into account during the next collection. This makes writing to old objects slightly more expensive, but that cost is more than compensated for by the time saved during garbage collection.

Dynamic Types

JavaScript expressions like `node.pos`, which fetch a property from an object, are far from trivial to compile. In many languages, *bindings* have a type, and thus, when you perform an operation on the value they hold, the compiler already knows what kind of operation you need. In JavaScript, only *values* have types, and a binding can end up holding values of different types.

This means that initially the compiler knows little about the property the code might be trying to access and has to produce code that handles all possible types. If `node` holds an undefined value, the code must throw an error. If it holds a string, it must look up `pos` in `String.prototype`. If it holds an object, the way the `pos` property is extracted from it depends on the shape of object. And so on.

Fortunately, though JavaScript does not require it, bindings in most programs *do* have a single type. And if the compiler knows this type, it can use that information to produce more efficient code. If `node` has always been an object with `pos` and `edges` properties so far, the optimizing compiler code can create code that fetches the property from its known position in such an object, which is simple and fast.

But events observed in the past do not give any guarantees about events that will occur in the future. Some piece of code that hasn't run yet might still pass another type of value to our function—a different kind of node object, for example, that also has an `id` property.

So the compiled code still has to *check* whether its assumptions hold and take an appropriate action if they don't. An engine could deoptimize entirely, falling back to the unoptimized version of the function. Or it could compile a new version of the function that also handles the newly observed type.

You can observe the slowdown caused by the failure to predict object types by intentionally messing up the uniformity of the input objects for our graph layout function, as in this example:

```
let mangledGraph = treeGraph(4, 4);
for (let node of mangledGraph) {
  node[`p${Math.floor(Math.random() * 999)}`] = true;
}

runLayout(forceDirected_noVector, mangledGraph);
```

Every node gets an extra property with a random name. If we run our fast simulation code on the resulting graph, it becomes 5 times as slow on Chrome 63 and 10 (!) times as slow on Firefox 58. Now that object types vary, the code has to look up the properties without prior knowledge about the shape of the object, which is a lot more expensive to do.

Interestingly, after running this code, forceDirected_noVector has become slow even when run on a regular, non-mangled graph. The messy types have "poisoned" the compiled code, at least for a while—at some point, browsers tend to throw away compiled code and recompile it from scratch, removing this effect.

A similar technique is used for things other than property access. The + operator, for example, means different things depending on what kind of values it is applied to. Instead of always running the full code that handles all these meanings, a smart JavaScript compiler will use previous observations to build up some expectation of the type that the operator is probably being applied to. If it is applied only to numbers, a much simpler piece of machine code can be generated to handle it. But again, such assumptions must be checked every time the function runs.

The moral of this story is that if a piece of code needs to be fast, you can help by feeding it consistent types. JavaScript engines can handle cases where a few different types occur relatively well—they will generate code that handles all these types and deoptimizes only when a new type is seen. But even there, the resulting code is slower than what you would get for a single type.

Summary

Thanks to the enormous amount of money being poured into the web, as well as the rivalry between the different browsers, JavaScript compilers are good at what they do: making code run fast.

But sometimes you have to help them a little and rewrite your inner loops to avoid more expensive JavaScript features. Creating fewer objects (and arrays and strings) often helps.

Before you start mangling your code to be faster, think about ways to make it do less work. The biggest opportunities for optimization are often found in that direction.

JavaScript engines compile hot code multiple times and will use information gathered during previous execution to compile more efficient code. You can help by giving your bindings a consistent type.

Exercises

Pathfinding

Write a function findPath that, like the function you saw in Chapter 7, tries to find the shortest path between two nodes in a graph. It takes two GraphNode objects (as used throughout this chapter) as arguments and returns either null, if no path could be found, or an array of nodes that represents a path through the graph. Nodes that occur next to each other in this array should have an edge between them.

A good approach for finding a path in a graph goes like this:

1. Create a work list that contains a single path that contains only the starting node.

2. Start with the first path in the work list.

3. If the node at the end of the current path is the goal node, return this path.

4. Otherwise, for each neighbor of the node at the end of the path, if that node has not been looked at before (does not occur at the end of any paths in the work list), create a new path by extending the current path with that neighbor and add it to the work list.

5. If there are more paths in the work list, go to the next path and continue at step 3.

6. Otherwise, there is no path.

By "spreading out" paths from the start node, this approach ensures that it always reaches a given other node by the shortest path since longer paths are considered only after all shorter paths have been tried.

Implement this program and test it on some simple tree graphs. Construct a graph with a cycle in it (for example, by adding edges to a tree graph with the connect method) and see whether your function can find the shortest path when there are multiple possibilities.

Timing

Use Date.now() to measure the time it takes your findPath function to find a path in a more complicated graph. Since treeGraph always puts the root at the start of the graph array and a leaf at the end, you can give your function a nontrivial task by doing something like this:

```
let graph = treeGraph(6, 6);
console.log(findPath(graph[0], graph[graph.length - 1]).length);
// → 6
```

Create a test case that has a running time of around half a second. Be careful with passing larger numbers to treeGraph—the size of the graph increases exponentially, so you can easily make your graph so big that it'll take huge amounts of time and memory to find a path through them.

Optimizing

Now that you have a measured test case, find ways to make your findPath function faster.

Think both about macro-optimization (doing less work) and micro-optimization (doing the given work in a cheaper way). Also, consider ways to use less memory and allocate fewer or smaller data structures.

EXERCISE HINTS

The hints below might help when you are stuck with one of the exercises in this book. They don't give away the entire solution, but rather try to help you find it yourself.

Chapter 2: Program Structure

Looping a Triangle

You can start with a program that prints the numbers 1 to 7, which you can derive by making a few modifications to the even number printing example in "while and do Loops" on page 30, where the for loop was introduced.

Now consider the equivalence between numbers and strings of hash characters. You can go from 1 to 2 by adding 1 (+= 1). You can go from "#" to "##" by adding a character (+= "#"). Thus, your solution can closely follow the number-printing program.

FizzBuzz

Going over the numbers is clearly a looping job, and selecting what to print is a matter of conditional execution. Remember the trick of using the remainder (%) operator for checking whether a number is divisible by another number (has a remainder of zero).

In the first version, there are three possible outcomes for every number, so you'll have to create an if/else if/else chain.

The second version of the program has a straightforward solution and a clever one. The simple solution is to add another conditional "branch" to precisely test the given condition. For the clever solution, build up a string containing the word or words to output and print either this word or the number if there is no word, potentially by making good use of the || operator.

Chessboard

You can build the string by starting with an empty one ("") and repeatedly adding characters. A newline character is written "\n".

To work with two dimensions, you will need a loop inside of a loop. Put braces around the bodies of both loops to make it easy to see where they start and end. Try to properly indent these bodies. The order of the loops must follow the order in which we build up the string (line by line, left to right, top to bottom). So the outer loop handles the lines, and the inner loop handles the characters on a line.

You'll need two bindings to track your progress. To know whether to put a space or a hash sign at a given position, you could test whether the sum of the two counters is even (% 2).

Terminating a line by adding a newline character must happen after the line has been built up, so do this after the inner loop but inside the outer loop.

Chapter 3: Functions

Minimum

If you have trouble putting braces and parentheses in the right place to get a valid function definition, start by copying one of the examples in this chapter and modifying it.

A function may contain multiple return statements.

Recursion

Your function will likely look somewhat similar to the inner find function in the recursive findSolution example in Chapter 3, with an if/else if/else chain that tests which of the three cases applies. The final else, corresponding to the third case, makes the recursive call. Each of the branches should contain a return statement or in some other way arrange for a specific value to be returned.

When given a negative number, the function will recurse again and again, passing itself an ever more negative number, thus getting further and further away from returning a result. It will eventually run out of stack space and abort.

Bean Counting

Your function will need a loop that looks at every character in the string. It can run an index from zero to one below its length (< `string.length`). If the character at the current position is the same as the one the function is looking for, it adds 1 to a counter variable. Once the loop has finished, the counter can be returned.

Take care to make all the bindings used in the function *local* to the function by properly declaring them with the `let` or `const` keyword.

Chapter 4: Data Structures: Objects and Arrays

The Sum of a Range

Building up an array is most easily done by first initializing a binding to [] (a fresh, empty array) and repeatedly calling its `push` method to add a value. Don't forget to return the array at the end of the function.

Since the end boundary is inclusive, you'll need to use the `<=` operator rather than `<` to check for the end of your loop.

The step parameter can be an optional parameter that defaults (using the `=` operator) to 1.

Having `range` understand negative step values is probably best done by writing two separate loops—one for counting up and one for counting down—because the comparison that checks whether the loop is finished needs to be `>=` rather than `<=` when counting downward.

It might also be worthwhile to use a different default step, namely, −1, when the end of the range is smaller than the start. That way, `range(5, 2)` returns something meaningful, rather than getting stuck in an infinite loop. It is possible to refer to previous parameters in the default value of a parameter.

Reversing an Array

There are two obvious ways to implement `reverseArray`. The first is to simply go over the input array from front to back and use the `unshift` method on the new array to insert each element at its start. The second is to loop over the input array backward and use the `push` method. Iterating over an array backward requires a (somewhat awkward) `for` specification, like (let i = array.length - 1; i >= 0; i-).

Reversing the array in place is harder. You have to be careful not to overwrite elements that you will later need. Using `reverseArray` or otherwise copying the whole array (`array.slice(0)` is a good way to copy an array) works but is cheating.

The trick is to *swap* the first and last elements, then the second and second-to-last, and so on. You can do this by looping over half the length of the array (use `Math.floor` to round down—you don't need to touch the middle element in an array with an odd number of elements) and swapping the element at position i with the one at position array.length - 1 - i. You can use a local binding to briefly hold on to one of the elements, overwrite that one with its mirror image, and then put the value from the local binding in the place where the mirror image used to be.

A List

Building up a list is easier when done back to front. So arrayToList could iterate over the array backward (see the previous exercise) and, for each element, add an object to the list. You can use a local binding to hold the part of the list that was built so far and use an assignment like list = {value: X, rest: list} to add an element.

To run over a list (in listToArray and nth), a for loop specification like this can be used:

```
for (let node = list; node; node = node.rest) {}
```

Can you see how that works? Every iteration of the loop, node points to the current sublist, and the body can read its value property to get the current element. At the end of an iteration, node moves to the next sublist. When that is null, we have reached the end of the list, and the loop is finished.

The recursive version of nth will, similarly, look at an ever smaller part of the "tail" of the list and at the same time count down the index until it reaches zero, at which point it can return the value property of the node it is looking at. To get the zeroth element of a list, you simply take the value property of its head node. To get element $N + 1$, you take the Nth element of the list that's in this list's rest property.

Deep Comparison

Your test for whether you are dealing with a real object will look something like typeof x == "object" && x != null. Be careful to compare properties only when *both* arguments are objects. In all other cases you can just immediately return the result of applying ===.

Use Object.keys to go over the properties. You need to test whether both objects have the same set of property names and whether those properties have identical values. One way to do that is to ensure that both objects have the same number of properties (the lengths of the property lists are the same). And then, when looping over one of the object's properties to compare them, always first make sure the other actually has a property by that name. If they have the same number of properties and all properties in one also exist in the other, they have the same set of property names.

Returning the correct value from the function is best done by immediately returning false when a mismatch is found and returning true at the end of the function.

Chapter 5: Higher-Order Functions

Everything

Like the && operator, the every method can stop evaluating further elements as soon as it has found one that doesn't match. So the loop-based version can jump out of the loop—with break or return—as soon as it runs into an element for which the predicate function returns false. If the loop runs to its end without finding such an element, we know that all elements matched and we should return true.

To build every on top of some, we can apply *De Morgan's laws*, which state that a && b equals !(!a || !b). This can be generalized to arrays, where all elements in the array match if there is no element in the array that does not match.

Dominant Writing Direction

Your solution might look a lot like the first half of the textScripts example. You again have to count characters by a criterion based on characterScript and then filter out the part of the result that refers to uninteresting (script-less) characters.

Finding the direction with the highest character count can be done with reduce. If it's not clear how, refer to the example earlier in the chapter, where reduce was used to find the script with the most characters.

Chapter 6: The Secret Life of Objects

A Vector Type

Look back to the Rabbit class example if you're unsure how class declarations look.

Adding a getter property to the constructor can be done by putting the word get before the method name. To compute the distance from (0, 0) to (x, y), you can use the Pythagorean theorem, which says that the square of the distance we are looking for is equal to the square of the x-coordinate plus the square of the y-coordinate. Thus, $\sqrt{x^2 + y^2}$ is the number you want, and Math.sqrt is the way you compute a square root in JavaScript.

Groups

The easiest way to do this is to store an array of group members in an instance property. The includes or indexOf methods can be used to check whether a given value is in the array.

Your class's constructor can set the member collection to an empty array. When add is called, it must check whether the given value is in the array or add it, for example with push, otherwise.

Deleting an element from an array, in delete, is less straightforward, but you can use filter to create a new array without the value. Don't forget to overwrite the property holding the members with the newly filtered version of the array.

The from method can use a for/of loop to get the values out of the iterable object and call add to put them into a newly created group.

Iterable Groups

It is probably worthwhile to define a new class GroupIterator. Iterator instances should have a property that tracks the current position in the group. Every time next is called, it checks whether it is done and, if not, moves past the current value and returns it.

The Group class itself gets a method named by Symbol.iterator that, when called, returns a new instance of the iterator class for that group.

Borrowing a Method

Remember that methods that exist on plain objects come from Object .prototype.

Also remember that you can call a function with a specific this binding by using its call method.

Chapter 7: Project: A Robot

Measuring a Robot

You'll have to write a variant of the runRobot function that, instead of logging the events to the console, returns the number of steps the robot took to complete the task.

Your measurement function can then, in a loop, generate new states and count the steps each of the robots takes. When the function has generated enough measurements, it can use console.log to output the average for each robot, which is the total number of steps taken divided by the number of measurements.

Robot Efficiency

The main limitation of goalOrientedRobot is that it considers only one parcel at a time. It will often walk back and forth across the village because the parcel it happens to be looking at happens to be at the other side of the map, even if there are others much closer.

One possible solution would be to compute routes for all packages and then take the shortest one. Even better results can be obtained, if there are multiple shortest routes, by preferring the ones that go to pick up a package instead of delivering a package.

Persistent Group

The most convenient way to represent the set of member values is still as an array since arrays are easy to copy.

When a value is added to the group, you can create a new group with a copy of the original array that has the value added (for example, using concat). When a value is deleted, you filter it from the array.

The class's constructor can take such an array as argument and store it as the instance's (only) property. This array is never updated.

To add a property (empty) to a constructor that is not a method, you have to add it to the constructor after the class definition, as a regular property.

You need only one empty instance because all empty groups are the same and instances of the class don't change. You can create many different groups from that single empty group without affecting it.

Chapter 8: Bugs and Errors

Retry

The call to primitiveMultiply should definitely happen in a try block. The corresponding catch block should rethrow the exception when it is not an instance of MultiplicatorUnitFailure and ensure the call is retried when it is.

To do the retrying, you can either use a loop that stops only when a call succeeds—as in the look example in "Exceptions" on page 135—or use recursion and hope you don't get a string of failures so long that it overflows the stack (which is a pretty safe bet).

The Locked Box

This exercise calls for a finally block. Your function should first unlock the box and then call the argument function from inside a try body. The finally block after it should lock the box again.

To make sure we don't lock the box when it wasn't already locked, check its lock at the start of the function and unlock and lock it only when it started out locked.

Chapter 9: Regular Expressions

Quoting Style

The most obvious solution is to replace only quotes with a nonword character on at least one side—something like /\ W'|'\ W/. But you also have to take the start and end of the line into account.

In addition, you must ensure that the replacement also includes the characters that were matched by the \W pattern so that those are not dropped. This can be done by wrapping them in parentheses and including their groups in the replacement string ($1, $2). Groups that are not matched will be replaced by nothing.

Numbers Again

First, do not forget the backslash in front of the period.

Matching the optional sign in front of the number, as well as in front of the exponent, can be done with [+\-]? or (\+|-|) (plus, minus, or nothing).

The more complicated part of the exercise is the problem of matching both "5." and ".5" without also matching ".". For this, a good solution is to use the | operator to separate the two cases—either one or more digits optionally followed by a dot and zero or more digits *or* a dot followed by one or more digits.

Finally, to make the *e* case insensitive, either add an i option to the regular expression or use [eE].

Chapter 10: Modules

A Modular Robot

I would have taken the following approach (but again, there is no single *right* way to design a given module).

The code used to build the road graph lives in the graph module. I'd rather use dijkstrajs from NPM than our own pathfinding code, so we'll make this build the kind of graph data that dijkstrajs expects. This module exports a single function, buildGraph. I'd have buildGraph accept an array of two-element arrays, rather than strings containing hyphens, to make the module less dependent on the input format.

The roads module contains the raw road data (the roads array) and the roadGraph binding. This module depends on ./graph and exports the road graph.

The VillageState class lives in the state module. It depends on the ./roads module because it needs to be able to verify that a given road exists. It also needs randomPick. Since that is a three-line function, we could just put it into the state module as an internal helper function. But randomRobot needs it too. So we'd have to either duplicate it or put it into its own module. Since this function happens to exist on NPM in the random-item package, a good solution is to just make both modules depend on that. We can add the runRobot function to this module as well, since it's small and closely related to state management. The module exports both the VillageState class and the runRobot function.

Finally, the robots, along with the values that they depend on such as mailRoute, could go into an example-robots module, which depends on ./roads and exports the robot functions. To make it possible for goalOrientedRobot to do route-finding, this module also depends on dijkstrajs.

By offloading some work to NPM modules, the code became a little smaller. Each individual module does something rather simple and can be read on its own. Dividing code into modules also often suggests further improvements to the program's design. In this case, it seems a little odd that the VillageState and the robots depend on a specific road graph. It might be a better idea to make the graph an argument to the state's constructor and make the robots read it from the state object—this reduces dependencies (which is always good) and makes it possible to run simulations on different maps (which is even better).

Is it a good idea to use NPM modules for things that we could have written ourselves? In principle, yes—for nontrivial things like the pathfinding function you are likely to make mistakes and waste time writing them yourself. For tiny functions like random-item, writing them yourself is easy enough. But adding them wherever you need them does tend to clutter your modules.

However, you should also not underestimate the work involved in *finding* an appropriate NPM package. And even if you find one, it might not work well or may be missing some feature you need. On top of that, depending on NPM packages means you have to make sure they are installed, you have to distribute them with your program, and you might have to periodically upgrade them.

So again, this is a trade-off, and you can decide either way depending on how much the packages help you.

Roads Module

Since this is a CommonJS module, you have to use require to import the graph module. That was described as exporting a buildGraph function, which you can pick out of its interface object with a destructuring const declaration.

To export roadGraph, you add a property to the exports object. Because buildGraph takes a data structure that doesn't precisely match roads, the splitting of the road strings must happen in your module.

Circular Dependencies

The trick is that require adds modules to its cache *before* it starts loading the module. That way, if any require call made while it is running tries to load it, it is already known, and the current interface will be returned, rather than starting to load the module once more (which would eventually overflow the stack).

If a module overwrites its module.exports value, any other module that has received its interface value before it finished loading will have gotten hold of the default interface object (which is likely empty), rather than the intended interface value.

Chapter 11: Asynchronous Programming

Tracking the Scalpel

This can be done with a single loop that searches through the nests, moving forward to the next when it finds a value that doesn't match the current nest's name and returning the name when it finds a matching value. In the async function, a regular for or while loop can be used.

To do the same in a plain function, you will have to build your loop using a recursive function. The easiest way to do this is to have that function return a promise by calling then on the promise that retrieves the storage value. Depending on whether that value matches the name of the current nest, the handler returns that value or a further promise created by calling the loop function again.

Don't forget to start the loop by calling the recursive function once from the main function.

In the async function, rejected promises are converted to exceptions by await. When an async function throws an exception, its promise is rejected. So that works.

If you implemented the non-async function as outlined earlier, the way then works also automatically causes a failure to end up in the returned promise. If a request fails, the handler passed to then isn't called, and the promise it returns is rejected with the same reason.

Building Promise.all

The function passed to the Promise constructor will have to call then on each of the promises in the given array. When one of them succeeds, two things need to happen. The resulting value needs to be stored in the correct position of a result array, and we must check whether this was the last pending promise and finish our own promise if it was.

The latter can be done with a counter that is initialized to the length of the input array and from which we subtract 1 every time a promise succeeds. When it reaches 0, we are done. Make sure you take into account the situation where the input array is empty (and thus no promise will ever resolve).

Handling failure requires some thought but turns out to be extremely simple. Just pass the reject function of the wrapping promise to each of the promises in the array as a catch handler or as a second argument to then so that a failure in one of them triggers the rejection of the whole wrapper promise.

Chapter 12: Project: A Programming Language

Arrays

The easiest way to do this is to represent Egg arrays with JavaScript arrays.

The values added to the top scope must be functions. By using a rest argument (with triple-dot notation), the definition of array can be *very* simple.

Closure

Again, we are riding along on a JavaScript mechanism to get the equivalent feature in Egg. Special forms are passed the local scope in which they are evaluated so that they can evaluate their subforms in that scope. The function returned by fun has access to the scope argument given to its enclosing function and uses that to create the function's local scope when it is called.

This means that the prototype of the local scope will be the scope in which the function was created, which makes it possible to access bindings in that scope from the function. This is all there is to implementing closure (though to compile it in a way that is actually efficient, you'd need to do some more work).

Comments

Make sure your solution handles multiple comments in a row, with potential whitespace between or after them.

A regular expression is probably the easiest way to solve this. Write something that matches "whitespace or a comment, zero or more times." Use the exec or match method and look at the length of the first element in the returned array (the whole match) to find out how many characters to slice off.

Fixing Scope

You will have to loop through one scope at a time, using Object.getPrototypeOf to go to the next outer scope. For each scope, use hasOwnProperty to find out whether the binding, indicated by the name property of the first argument to set, exists in that scope. If it does, set it to the result of evaluating the second argument to set and then return that value.

If the outermost scope is reached (Object.getPrototypeOf returns null) and we haven't found the binding yet, it doesn't exist, and an error should be thrown.

Chapter 14: The Document Object Model

Build a Table

You can use document.createElement to create new element nodes, document.createTextNode to create text nodes, and the appendChild method to put nodes into other nodes.

You'll want to loop over the key names once to fill in the top row and then again for each object in the array to construct the data rows. To get an array of key names from the first object, Object.keys will be useful.

To add the table to the correct parent node, you can use document.getElementById or document.querySelector to find the node with the proper id attribute.

Elements by Tag Name

The solution is most easily expressed with a recursive function, similar to the talksAbout function defined earlier in this chapter.

You could call byTagname itself recursively, concatenating the resulting arrays to produce the output. Or you could create an inner function that calls itself recursively and that has access to an array binding defined in the outer function, to which it can add the matching elements it finds. Don't forget to call the inner function once from the outer function to start the process.

The recursive function must check the node type. Here we are interested only in node type 1 (Node.ELEMENT_NODE). For such nodes, we must loop over their children and, for each child, see whether the child matches the query while also doing a recursive call on it to inspect its own children.

The Cat's Hat

Math.cos and Math.sin measure angles in radians, where a full circle is 2π. For a given angle, you can get the opposite angle by adding half of this, which is Math.PI. This can be useful for putting the hat on the opposite side of the orbit.

Chapter 15: Handling Events

Balloon

You'll want to register a handler for the "keydown" event and look at event.key to figure out whether the up or down arrow key was pressed.

The current size can be kept in a binding so that you can base the new size on it. It'll be helpful to define a function that updates the size—both the binding and the style of the balloon in the DOM—so that you can call it from your event handler, and possibly also once when starting, to set the initial size.

You can change the balloon to an explosion by replacing the text node with another one (using replaceChild) or by setting the textContent property of its parent node to a new string.

Mouse Trail

Creating the elements is best done with a loop. Append them to the document to make them show up. To be able to access them later to change their position, you'll want to store the elements in an array.

Cycling through them can be done by keeping a counter variable and adding 1 to it every time the "mousemove" event fires. The remainder operator (% elements.length) can then be used to get a valid array index to pick the element you want to position during a given event.

Another interesting effect can be achieved by modeling a simple physics system. Use the "mousemove" event only to update a pair of bindings that track the mouse position. Then use requestAnimationFrame to simulate the trailing elements being attracted to the position of the mouse pointer. At every animation step, update their position based on their position relative to the pointer (and, optionally, a speed that is stored for each element). Figuring out a good way to do this is up to you.

Tabs

One pitfall you might run into is that you can't directly use the node's childNodes property as a collection of tab nodes. For one thing, when you add the buttons, they will also become child nodes and end up in this object because it is a live data structure. For another, the text nodes created for the whitespace between the nodes are also in childNodes but should not get their own tabs. You can use children instead of childNodes to ignore text nodes.

You could start by building up an array of tabs so that you have easy access to them. To implement the styling of the buttons, you could store objects that contain both the tab panel and its button.

I recommend writing a separate function for changing tabs. You can either store the previously selected tab and change only the styles needed to hide that and show the new one, or you can just update the style of all tabs every time a new tab is selected.

You might want to call this function immediately to make the interface start with the first tab visible.

Chapter 16: Project: A Platform Game

Pausing the Game

An animation can be interrupted by returning false from the function given to runAnimation. It can be continued by calling runAnimation again.

So we need to communicate the fact that we are pausing the game to the function given to runAnimation. For that, you can use a binding that both the event handler and that function have access to.

When unregistering the handlers registered by trackKeys, remember that the *exact* same function value that was passed to addEventListener must be passed to removeEventListener to successfully remove a handler. Thus, the handler function value created in trackKeys must be available to the code that unregisters the handlers.

You can add a property to the object returned by trackKeys, containing either that function value or a method that handles the unregistering directly.

A Monster

If you want to implement a type of motion that is stateful, such as bouncing, make sure you store the necessary state in the actor object—include it as constructor argument and add it as a property.

Remember that update returns a *new* object, rather than changing the old one.

When handling collision, find the player in state.actors and compare its position to the monster's position. To get the *bottom* of the player, you have to add its vertical size to its vertical position. The creation of an updated state will resemble either Coin's collide method (removing the actor) or Lava's (changing the status to "lost"), depending on the player position.

Chapter 17: Drawing on Canvas

Shapes

The trapezoid (1) is easiest to draw using a path. Pick suitable center coordinates and add each of the four corners around the center.

The diamond (2) can be drawn the straightforward way, with a path, or the interesting way, with a rotate transformation. To use rotation, you will have to apply a trick similar to what we did in the flipHorizontally function. Because you want to rotate around the center of your rectangle and not around the point (0,0), you must first translate to there, then rotate, and then translate back.

Make sure you reset the transformation after drawing any shape that creates one.

For the zigzag (3) it becomes impractical to write a new call to lineTo for each line segment. Instead, you should use a loop. You can have each iteration draw either two line segments (right and then left again) or one, in which case you must use the evenness (% 2) of the loop index to determine whether to go left or right.

You'll also need a loop for the spiral (4). If you draw a series of points, with each point moving further along a circle around the spiral's center, you get a circle. If, during the loop, you vary the radius of the circle on which you are putting the current point and go around more than once, the result is a spiral.

The star (5) depicted is built out of quadraticCurveTo lines. You could also draw one with straight lines. Divide a circle into eight pieces for a star with eight points, or however many pieces you want. Draw lines between these points, making them curve toward the center of the star. With quadraticCurveTo, you can use the center as the control point.

The Pie Chart

You will need to call fillText and set the context's textAlign and textBaseline properties in such a way that the text ends up where you want it.

A sensible way to position the labels would be to put the text on the line going from the center of the pie through the middle of the slice. You don't want to put the text directly against the side of the pie but rather move the text out to the side of the pie by a given number of pixels.

The angle of this line is currentAngle + 0.5 * sliceAngle. The following code finds a position on this line 120 pixels from the center:

```
let middleAngle = currentAngle + 0.5 * sliceAngle;
let textX = Math.cos(middleAngle) * 120 + centerX;
let textY = Math.sin(middleAngle) * 120 + centerY;
```

For textBaseline, the value "middle" is probably appropriate when using this approach. What to use for textAlign depends on which side of the circle we are on. On the left, it should be "right", and on the right, it should be "left", so that the text is positioned away from the pie.

If you are not sure how to find out which side of the circle a given angle is on, look to the explanation of Math.cos in "Positioning and Animating" on page 240. The cosine of an angle tells us which x-coordinate it corresponds to, which in turn tells us exactly which side of the circle we are on.

A Bouncing Ball

A box is easy to draw with strokeRect. Define a binding that holds its size or define two bindings if your box's width and height differ. To create a round ball, start a path and call arc(x, y, radius, 0, 7), which creates an arc going from zero to more than a whole circle. Then fill the path.

To model the ball's position and speed, you can use the Vec class from "Actors" on page 269. Give it a starting speed, preferably one that is not purely vertical or horizontal, and for every frame multiply that speed by the amount of time that elapsed. When the ball gets too close to a vertical wall, invert the x component in its speed. Likewise, invert the y component when it hits a horizontal wall.

After finding the ball's new position and speed, use clearRect to delete the scene and redraw it using the new position.

Precomputed Mirroring

The key to the solution is the fact that we can use a canvas element as a source image when using drawImage. It is possible to create an extra <canvas> element, without adding it to the document, and draw our inverted sprites to it, once. When drawing an actual frame, we just copy the already inverted sprites to the main canvas.

Some care would be required because images do not load instantly. We do the inverted drawing only once, and if we do it before the image loads, it won't draw anything. A "load" handler on the image can be used to draw the inverted images to the extra canvas. This canvas can be used as a drawing source immediately (it'll simply be blank until we draw the character onto it).

Chapter 18: HTTP and Forms

Content Negotiation

Base your code on the `fetch` examples in "Fetch" on page 315.

Asking for a bogus media type will return a response with code 406, "Not acceptable," which is the code a server should return when it can't fulfill the `Accept` header.

A JavaScript Workbench

Use `document.querySelector` or `document.getElementById` to get access to the elements defined in your HTML. An event handler for `"click"` or `"mousedown"` events on the button can get the `value` property of the text field and call `Function` on it.

Make sure you wrap both the call to `Function` and the call to its result in a try block so you can catch the exceptions it produces. In this case, we really don't know what type of exception we are looking for, so catch everything.

The `textContent` property of the output element can be used to fill it with a string message. Or, if you want to keep the old content around, create a new text node using `document.createTextNode` and append it to the element. Remember to add a newline character to the end so that not all output appears on a single line.

Conway's Game of Life

To solve the problem of having the changes conceptually happen at the same time, try to see the computation of a generation as a pure function, which takes one grid and produces a new grid that represents the next turn.

Representing the matrix can be done in the way shown in "The Iterator Interface" on page 107. You can count live neighbors with two nested loops, looping over adjacent coordinates in both dimensions. Take care not to count cells outside of the field and to ignore the cell in the center, whose neighbors we are counting.

Ensuring that changes to checkboxes take effect on the next generation can be done in two ways. An event handler could notice these changes and update the current grid to reflect them, or you could generate a fresh grid from the values in the checkboxes before computing the next turn.

If you choose to go with event handlers, you might want to attach attributes that identify the position that each checkbox corresponds to so that it is easy to find out which cell to change.

To draw the grid of checkboxes, you can either use a `<table>` element (see "Build a Table" on page 243) or simply put them all in the same element and put `<br>` (line break) elements between the rows.

Chapter 19: Project: A Pixel Art Editor

Keyboard Bindings

The key property of events for letter keys will be the lowercase letter itself, if SHIFT isn't being held. We're not interested in key events with SHIFT here.

A "keydown" handler can inspect its event object to see whether it matches any of the shortcuts. You can automatically get the list of first letters from the tools object so that you don't have to write them out.

When the key event matches a shortcut, call preventDefault on it and dispatch the appropriate action.

Efficient Drawing

This exercise is a good example of how immutable data structures can make code *faster*. Because we have both the old and the new picture, we can compare them and redraw only the pixels that changed color, saving more than 99 percent of the drawing work in most cases.

You can either write a new function updatePicture or have drawPicture take an extra argument, which may be undefined or the previous picture. For each pixel, the function checks whether a previous picture was passed with the same color at this position and skips the pixel when that is the case.

Because the canvas gets cleared when we change its size, you should also avoid touching its width and height properties when the old picture and the new picture have the same size. If they are different, which will happen when a new picture has been loaded, you can set the binding holding the old picture to null after changing the canvas size because you shouldn't skip any pixels after you've changed the canvas size.

Circles

You can take some inspiration from the rectangle tool. Like that tool, you'll want to keep drawing on the *starting* picture, rather than the current picture, when the pointer moves.

To figure out which pixels to color, you can use the Pythagorean theorem. First figure out the distance between the current pointer position and the start position by taking the square root (Math.sqrt) of the sum of the square (Math.pow(x, 2)) of the difference in x-coordinates and the square of the difference in y-coordinates. Then loop over a square of pixels around the start position, whose sides are at least twice the radius, and color those that are within the circle's radius, again using the Pythagorean formula to figure out their distance from the center.

Make sure you don't try to color pixels that are outside of the picture's boundaries.

Proper Lines

The thing about the problem of drawing a pixelated line is that it is really four similar but slightly different problems. Drawing a horizontal line from the left to the right is easy—you loop over the x-coordinates and color a pixel at every step. If the line has a slight slope (less than 45 degrees or ¼π radians), you can interpolate the y-coordinate along the slope. You still need one pixel per *x* position, with the *y* position of those pixels determined by the slope.

But as soon as your slope goes across 45 degrees, you need to switch the way you treat the coordinates. You now need one pixel per *y* position since the line goes up more than it goes left. And then, when you cross 135 degrees, you have to go back to looping over the x-coordinates, but from right to left.

You don't actually have to write four loops. Since drawing a line from *A* to *B* is the same as drawing a line from *B* to *A*, you can swap the start and end positions for lines going from right to left and treat them as going left to right.

So you need two different loops. The first thing your line drawing function should do is check whether the difference between the x-coordinates is larger than the difference between the y-coordinates. If it is, this is a horizontal-ish line, and if not, a vertical-ish one.

Make sure you compare the *absolute* values of the *x* and *y* difference, which you can get with Math.abs.

Once you know along which axis you will be looping, you can check whether the start point has a higher coordinate along that axis than the endpoint and swap them if necessary. A succinct way to swap the values of two bindings in JavaScript uses destructuring assignment like this:

```
[start, end] = [end, start];
```

Then you can compute the slope of the line, which determines the amount the coordinate on the other axis changes for each step you take along your main axis. With that, you can run a loop along the main axis while also tracking the corresponding position on the other axis, and you can draw pixels on every iteration. Make sure you round the non-main axis coordinates since they are likely to be fractional and the draw method doesn't respond well to fractional coordinates.

Chapter 20: Node.js

Search Tool

Your first command line argument, the regular expression, can be found in process.argv[2]. The input files come after that. You can use the RegExp constructor to go from a string to a regular expression object.

Doing this synchronously, with readFileSync, is more straightforward, but if you use fs.promises again to get promise-returning functions and write an async function, the code looks similar.

To figure out whether something is a directory, you can again use stat (or statSync) and the stats object's isDirectory method.

Exploring a directory is a branching process. You can do it either by using a recursive function or by keeping an array of work (files that still need to be explored). To find the files in a directory, you can call readdir or readdirSync. The strange capitalization—Node's file system function naming is loosely based on standard Unix functions, such as readdir, that are all lowercase, but then it adds Sync with a capital letter.

To go from a filename read with readdir to a full path name, you have to combine it with the name of the directory, putting a slash character (/) between them.

Directory Creation

You can use the function that implements the DELETE method as a blueprint for the MKCOL method. When no file is found, try to create a directory with mkdir. When a directory exists at that path, you can return a 204 response so that directory creation requests are idempotent. If a nondirectory file exists here, return an error code. Code 400 ("bad request") would be appropriate.

A Public Space on the Web

You can create a <textarea> element to hold the content of the file that is being edited. A GET request, using fetch, can retrieve the current content of the file. You can use relative URLs like *index.html*, instead of *http://localhost:8000/index.html*, to refer to files on the same server as the running script.

Then, when the user clicks a button (you can use a <form> element and "submit" event), make a PUT request to the same URL, with the content of the <textarea> as request body, to save the file.

You can then add a <select> element that contains all the files in the server's top directory by adding <option> elements containing the lines returned by a GET request to the URL /. When the user selects another file (a "change" event on the field), the script must fetch and display that file. When saving a file, use the currently selected filename.

Chapter 21: Project: Skill-Sharing Website

Disk Persistence

The simplest solution I can come up with is to encode the whole talks object as JSON and dump it to a file with writeFile. There is already a method that is called every time the server's data changes (updated). It can be extended to write the new data to disk.

Pick a filename, for example `./talks.json`. When the server starts, it can try to read that file with `readFile`, and if that succeeds, the server can use the file's contents as its starting data.

Beware, though. The `talks` object started as a prototype-less object so that the `in` operator could reliably be used. `JSON.parse` will return regular objects with `Object.prototype` as their prototype. If you use JSON as your file format, you'll have to copy the properties of the object returned by `JSON.parse` into a new, prototype-less object.

Comment Field Resets

The best way to do this is probably to make talks component objects, with a `syncState` method, so that they can be updated to show a modified version of the talk. During normal operation, the only way a talk can be changed is by adding more comments, so the `syncState` method can be relatively simple.

The difficult part is that, when a changed list of talks comes in, we have to reconcile the existing list of DOM components with the talks on the new list—deleting components whose talk was deleted and updating components whose talk changed.

To do this, it might be helpful to keep a data structure that stores the talk components under the talk titles so that you can easily figure out whether a component exists for a given talk. You can then loop over the new array of talks, and for each of them, either synchronize an existing component or create a new one. To delete components for deleted talks, you'll have to also loop over the components and check whether the corresponding talks still exist.

Chapter 22: JavaScript and Performance

Pathfinding

The work list can be an array, and you can add paths to it with the `push` method. If you use arrays to represent paths, you can extend them with the `concat` method, as in `path.concat([node])`, so that the old value is left intact.

To find out whether a node has already been seen, you can loop over the existing work list or use the `some` method.

Optimizing

The main opportunity for macro-optimization is to get rid of the inner loop that figures out whether a node has already been looked at. Looking this up in a map is much faster than iterating over the work list to search for the node. Since our keys are node objects, we have to use a `Set` or `Map` instance, rather than a plain object, to store the set of reached nodes.

Another improvement can be made by changing the way paths are stored. Extending an array with a new element without modifying the existing array requires copying the whole array. A data structure like the *list* from

Chapter 4 does not have this problem—it allows multiple extensions of a list to share the data they have in common.

You can make your function internally store paths as objects with at and via properties, where at is the last node in the path and via is either null or another such object holding the rest of the path. This way, extending a path only requires creating an object with two properties, rather than copying a whole array. Make sure you convert the list to an actual array before returning it.

INDEX

then method, 186–188, 191, 416
theory, 133
this binding, 62, 98–99, 101, 130
thread, 182, 183, 198, 259
throw keyword, 135, 136, 139, 141, 413
tile, 303
time, 147, 148, 150, 184, 241, 261, 277, 278, 280, 283, 303, 346
time zone, 150
timeline, 182, 197, 223, 241, 247, 258
timeout, 188, 259, 373, 374, 380
Timeout class, 189
times method, 269
timing, 396
title, 382
title (HTML tag), 222, 223
toDataURL method, 344
toLowerCase method, 62, 243
tool, 145, 164, 175, 334, 339, 340, 342–344, 347, 350, 357
tool property, 335
ToolSelect class, 340
top (CSS), 240–242, 244
top-level scope, *see* global scope
toString method, 99, 100, 103–105, 346, 362
touch, 255, 334
touchend event, 255
touches method, 278
touches property, 255, 339
touchmove event, 255, 339, 350
touchstart event, 255, 337, 339
toUpperCase method, 62, 132, 243, 362
tr (HTML tag), 243, 274
trackKeys function, 282, 285
transform (CSS), 287
transformation, 297–299, 308, 420
translate method, 298, 299
Transmission Control Protocol, 220, 221, 311, 373
transparency, 289, 296, 346
transpilation, 213
trapezoid, 307, 420
traversal, 152
tree, 100, 204, 229
treeGraph function, 394
trial and error, 133, 282, 293
triangle (exercise), 37, 407
trigonometry, 75, 241

trim method, 73, 268
true, 16
trust, 224
try keyword, 136, 137, 190, 413, 422
type, 12, 16, 112
type attribute, 318, 321
type checking, 131, 174
type coercion, 18, 19, 28
type observation, 392, 401, 403
type property, 204, 249
type variable, 131
typeof operator, 16, 80, 410
TypeScript, 131–132
typing, 260
typo, 129

U

Ullman, Ellen, xx
unary operator, 16, 23
uncaught exception, 138, 188
undefined, 18, 19, 25, 42, 47, 61, 63, 77, 129, 130, 134
underline, 237
underscore character, 26, 35, 98, 151, 157
undo history, 346, 347
UndoButton class, 347
Unicode, 15, 17, 87, 92, 147, 162, 163
unicycling, 371
Uniform Resource Locator, *see* URL
uniformity, 204
uniqueness, 239
unit (CSS), 242, 257
Unix, 366–368
Unix time, 150
unlink function, 359, 366
unshift method, 71
unwinding the stack, 135
upcasing server example, 362
updated method, 378, 381, 425
updateState function, 336
upgrading, 169
upload, 325
URL, 221, 224, 288, 313, 315, 317, 360, 373, 383
URL encoding, 314
url package, 364, 380
urlToPath function, 364
usability, 251

Eloquent JavaScript, 3rd Edition is set in New Baskerville, Futura, Dogma, and TheSansMono Condensed. This book was printed and bound by Sheridan Books, Inc. in Chelsea, Michigan.

RESOURCES

Visit *https://nostarch.com/ejs3/* for updates, errata, and other information.

More no-nonsense books from  **NO STARCH PRESS**

JAVASCRIPT FOR KIDS
A Playful Introduction to Programming
by NICK MORGAN
DECEMBER 2014, 336 PP., $34.95
ISBN 978-1-59327-408-5
full color

THE PRINCIPLES OF
OBJECT-ORIENTED JAVASCRIPT
by NICHOLAS C. ZAKAS
FEBRUARY 2014, 120 PP., $24.95
ISBN 978-1-59327-540-2

IF HEMINGWAY
WROTE JAVASCRIPT
by ANGUS CROLL
OCTOBER 2014, 192 PP., $19.95
ISBN 978-1-59327-585-3

PRACTICAL SQL
A Beginner's Guide to
Storytelling with Data
by ANTHONY DEBARROS
MAY 2018, 392 PP., $39.95
ISBN 978-1-59327-827-4

SERIOUS PYTHON
Black-Belt Advice on Deployment,
Scalability, Testing, and More
by JULIEN DANJOU
DECEMBER 2018, 248 PP., $34.95
ISBN 978-1-59327-878-6

THE RUST PROGRAMMING
LANGUAGE (COVERS RUST 2018)
by STEVE KLABNIK *and* CAROL
NICHOLS
AUGUST 2019, 560 PP., $39.95
ISBN 978-1-7185-0044-0

PHONE:
1.800.420.7240 OR
1.415.863.9900

EMAIL:
SALES@NOSTARCH.COM

WEB:
WWW.NOSTARCH.COM